COOKING with CLASS

A SECOND HELPING

D1362246

Published by
The Parents' Council
Charlotte Latin School, Inc.
Charlotte, North Carolina

The recipes in this book were selected by Charlotte Latin School families and friends from their personal collections. The Cookbook Committee cannot attest to the origin or originality of any recipe printed herein.

To order additional copies send
$16.95 plus $2.75 for postage and handling to
CLS Parents' Council
P.O. Box 6143
Charlotte, N.C. 28207-0143
(North Carolina residents add $.96 sales tax)

ISBN: 0-9615616-1-0

Printed in the USA by
WIMMER
The Wimmer Companies
Memphis
1-800-548-2537

FOREWORD

After ten successful years with our first cookbook, **Cooking with Class**, the Charlotte Latin Parents' Council is proud to present a new collection of our favorite recipes, **Cooking with Class - A Second Helping**.

Those who were involved with the first cookbook definitely gave us a tough act to follow. Letters and phone calls from all over the United States singing the praises of **Cooking with Class** were proof enough that if we were to publish a new cookbook it had to be a winner! When the project was presented to the Charlotte Latin family and alumni, they responded with over 1200 mouth-watering recipes. Every recipe submitted was tested. Although we were not able to include all of them, the recipes printed offer delicious variety which we hope will add new selections for your menus.

The Latin family is made up of families from throughout the United States, as well as families representing almost twenty countries. The variety in recipes reflects our diversity. Recipes by the *Hawk*, our school mascot, are favorites from members of the Cookbook Committee.

More men and children are now donning chefs' hats, so there are special sections just for them. The *Light and Luscious* section is provided in response to the demand for lowfat and low-calorie recipes which do not sacrifice taste appeal. The nutritional analysis for recipes in this section was calculated by a professional dietician. As our lives have become busier, meal preparation for many has had to be streamlined. Recipes which are quick and easy are found throughout the book.

Welcome to Charlotte Latin's kitchen. Please sit and dine with us often. Enjoy sharing our favorite dishes with your family and friends. Open the book and have **A Second Helping**.

> Marilyn Thompson
> Dougi O'Bryan
> Irene Kelly

P.S. From our Headmaster:

Eating is the essence of the hearth, the ancient symbol of home. In approaching eating, one must keep in mind that "Home is where the food is." And that "Home is the place where, when you have to go there, they have to feed you." And, again, that "Feeding begins at home." And finally, "If this cookbook be the food of family love, read on."

"We can live without friends, we can live without books, but civilized men and women cannot live without cooks." Or even without cookbooks, especially this one.

> *E. J. Fox, Jr.*
> *Headmaster*

EDITORIAL STAFF

TABLE OF CONTENTS

MENUS

CAROLINA IN THE MORNING BRUNCH

Just Right Bloody Marys
Orange Juice
Fresh Fruit Compote
24-Hour Wine and Cheese Omelet
Cheese Grits
Sausage Muffins
Cheese Blintz
Pineapple Pound Cake

IT'S IN THE CARDS BRIDGE LUNCHEON

Mock Champagne Punch
Steak Salad
Imperial Emerald Rice
Broccoli Salad with Raisins
Crunchy Biscuits
Raspberry-Angel Trifle

TAILGATE TOUCHDOWN

Front Porch Lemonade
Buffalo Wings
Great Biscuits with Ham
Pasta Salad with Fresh Tomatoes
Marinated Beans
Yummy Butterscotch Cookies
Rocky Road Fudge Bars

COOKOUT AT THE HAWKS' NEST

Fruited Mint Tea
Helen's Marinated Flank Steak
Grilled Lemon Chicken
Seven Layer Salad
Dilled Potato Salad
Herb-Cheese Bread
Frozen Strawberry Pie
Amaretto Ice Cream Pie

SUPER BOWL SOUP SUPPER

Apple Knockers
Mini-Reubens
Cripple Creek Chili
Black Bean Soup
Baked Potato Soup
Betty's Corn Muffin Cake
Yogurt Dill Bread
Tunnel of Fudge Cake

―――――――――

SOUTH OF THE BORDER FIESTA

Frozen Margaritas
Designated Driver Sangria
Warm Cheesy Salsa with Corn Chips
Onion Quesadillas
Chicken Enchilada Casserole
Jalapeño Rice
Fiesta Beans
Marie's Cornbread
Pavlova

QUEEN CITY COCKTAIL PARTY

Sliced Marinated Tenderloin
Assorted Rolls
Lemon Horseradish Sauce
Angels on Horseback
Bar-B-Q Shrimp
Mandarin Chicken
Brie with Brown Sugar and Almonds
Assorted Fresh Fruits
Fresh Vegetable Tray with "Dill-icious" Vegetable Dip
Bourbon Brownies
Chocolate-Raspberry Short Bread

DINNER FOR 8 AT 8

Cream of Crab Soup
Fillet Steak and Savory Butter
Marinated Mushrooms
Vermouth Rice
Caesar Salad
Mother's Rolls
Death by Chocolate
Fumé Blanc
Cabernet Sauvignon

A BOUNTIFUL BUFFET

Elegant Turkey or Veal Rolls
Pecan Wild Rice Pilaf
Apricot Salad
Crunchy Pea Salad
Bourbon Carrots
Easy Drop Rolls
Praline Cheesecake
Chocolate Mousse Torte
Chardonnay
Petite Sirah

HOME FOR THE HOLIDAYS DINNER

Roast Turkey
Upstate Cornbread Dressing
Scalloped Oysters
Cranberry Bake
Fresh Spinach Salad with Fruit
Three Vegetable Casserole
Williamsburg Sweet Potatoes
Mother's Rolls
Pumpkin-Pecan Cheesecake
Really Lethal Pecan Pie
Gewürztraminer
Zinfandel (Red)

BEVERAGES

HOT APPLE CIDER
Serve this at your next coffee.

Easy   Yields: 2 quarts

6 cups unsweetened apple juice   1 (3-inch) cinnamon stick
2 cups water   3 whole cloves
1 cup fresh or frozen cranberries, thawed

* Combine all ingredients in a large saucepan.
* Bring to a boil over medium heat, stirring frequently.
* Cover; reduce heat and simmer 15 minutes.
* Strain mixture, discarding cranberries and spices.
* Serve hot.

Irene Kelly

CAPPUCCINO
Share with your friends.

Easy   Yields: 33 servings

1 cup powdered instant non-dairy creamer   1/2 cup sugar
1 cup chocolate milk mix   1/2 teaspoon ground cinnamon
2/3 cup instant coffee   1/2 teaspoon ground nutmeg

* Combine all ingredients. Mix well.
* Store in an airtight container.
* To serve, place 1 tablespoon plus 1 teaspoon mix in a cup. Add boiling water. Stir well.

Carol Lawing

HOT CHOCOLATE MIX

1 (8-quart) box nonfat dry milk
1 (2-pound) box chocolate drink mix
1/2 cup powdered sugar

1 (6-ounce) jar powdered non-dairy
  creamer

* Mix all ingredients in a large bowl. Store in an airtight container.
* For each cup of hot chocolate, pour boiling water over 1/3 to1/2 cup of mix and stir.

Marie Bazemore, Frances Fennebresque

CRANBERRY TEA

Easy

Serves: 8-10

2-1/4 cups pineapple juice
1-3/4 cups water
2 cups cranberry juice
1 tablespoon whole cloves

1-1/2 teaspoons allspice
3 sticks broken cinnamon
1/4 teaspoon salt
1/2 cup brown sugar, firmly packed

* Pour pineapple juice, water and cranberry juice in bottom of an 8 to10 cup percolator.
* Put the remaining ingredients in percolator basket.
* Perk for 10 minutes or until spices have permeated.

Pat Viser, Irene Kelly

FRUITED MINT TEA

Easy

Yields: 2-1/2 quarts

3 cups boiling water
4 regular tea bags
12 sprigs fresh mint
1 cup sugar

1/4 cup fresh lemon juice
1 cup orange juice
5 cups cold water

* Pour boiling water over tea bags and mint. Steep for 5 minutes.
* Add sugar, lemon juice, orange juice and cold water.
* Serve over ice; garnish with mint and orange or lemon slices.

Gail Madara

INSTANT RUSSIAN TEA

Easy

Yields: 4 cups mix

1 (8-ounce) jar instant orange breakfast
  drink
1-1/2 cups instant tea with lemon
1-1/2 cups sugar

1 teaspoon ground cloves
1/2 teaspoon cinnamon
1/2 teaspoon allspice

* Mix all ingredients thoroughly. Store in an airtight container.
* Use 2 or more teaspoons of mix to 1 cup boiling water.

Frances Fennebresque

RUSSIAN TEA

Easy

Serves: 12

1/2 gallon water
3/4 cup sugar
12 whole cloves
3 regular tea bags

juice of 2 lemons
1 cup orange juice
1 cup pineapple juice

* Boil water, sugar, cloves 5 minutes. Remove from heat; add tea bags; steep 5 minutes.
* Add juices and heat to desired temperature for serving.

Melinda Mileham, Julia Todd

FRONT PORCH LEMONADE

Easy

Yields: 2 cups syrup for 2 quarts lemonade

1 tablespoon freshly grated lemon rind
1-1/2 cups granulated sugar

1/2 cup boiling water
1-1/2 cups freshly squeezed lemon juice

* In a jar with a tight fitting lid, combine lemon rind, sugar and boiling water.
* Cover and shake vigorously until sugar dissolves. Add lemon juice.
* Store syrup base in refrigerator. Mix 1 cup base to 3 cups cold water.
* For soda fountain lemonade, add sparkling water instead of tap water.

Heather Long, Pam Richey

MOCK CHAMPAGNE PUNCH

Yields: approximately 1 gallon

1 (12-ounce) can lemonade concentrate, thawed
1 (12-ounce) can frozen pineapple juice, thawed
4 cups cold water

1 (28-ounce) bottle ginger ale, chilled
1 (28-ounce) bottle club soda, chilled
2 bottles sparkling white grape juice, chilled

* Combine juices and water. Chill.
* Make an ice ring with additional ginger ale or pineapple juice, if desired.
* At serving time, combine all ingredients in punch bowl and float ice ring.

Ellen Knott

Variation: Substitute champagne for sparkling grape juice and omit water.

Irene Kelly

CRANBERRY SPARKLE PUNCH
Good for a holiday party - especially for children

Easy

Serves: 25-30

1 small package raspberry-flavored gelatin
3 cups cranberry juice, divided
1 (6-ounce) can frozen lemonade

84 ounces lemon-lime soda or ginger ale, chilled
ice cubes

* Dissolve gelatin in 1 cup of hot cranberry juice.
* Add remaining juice and lemonade. Stir well.
* Just before serving, add soda and stir.
* Serve over ice cubes.

Dougi O'Bryan

SERVICE RECOGNITION PUNCH
Always a hit

Yields: 12-16 cups

1 (2-liter) bottle Cheerwine   *1 (46-ounce) can pineapple juice*

* Chill Cheerwine and pineapple juice thoroughly.
* When ready to serve, mix in large pitcher or punch bowl.
* Add ice or ice ring. Serve immediately.

The Hawk

SUNSHINE PUNCH
Great for afternoon or evening get-togethers

Yields: 18 (4-ounce) servings

1 (6-ounce) can frozen orange juice concentrate, thawed
1 (6-ounce) can frozen lemonade concentrate, thawed
4 cups water

1 (6-ounce) can frozen limeade concentrate, thawed
1 (28-ounce) bottle chilled lemon-lime soda or ginger ale

* Combine concentrated juices and water in punch bowl or large pitcher.
* Add lemon-lime soda just before serving.
* Add an ice ring to the punch bowl.

Susan Grove

DESIGNATED DRIVER SANGRIA
A non-alcoholic fruit punch similar to the wine punch so popular in Spain

Yields: 20 (8-ounce) glasses

1 (48-ounce) can orange juice drink
1 (48-ounce) can pineapple or apple juice
2 (20-ounce) bottles sparkling red grape juice

1 (32-ounce) bottle club soda
2 oranges, thinly sliced
1 lemon, thinly sliced

* Mix all ingredients and chill. Serve over ice.

> *Wendy Perkins*
> *Jean Skidmore*
> *Ann Ayala*

APPLE KNOCKERS
Great aprés ski! Makes the kitchen smell wonderful!

Yields: 3 quarts

3 cinnamon sticks
2 teaspoons whole cloves
1/2 teaspoon ground nutmeg
1/2 gallon apple cider

1/4 to 1/2 cup sugar
2 cups orange juice
1/2 cup lemon juice
1 cup any fruit-flavored brandy (optional)

* Tie cinnamon, cloves and nutmeg in cheese cloth or a tea ball.
* Simmer cider and sugar with spices for about 15 minutes.
* Remove spices.
* Add orange juice, lemon juice and brandy.
* Heat for 10 minutes and serve.

> *Colleen Huber*

JUST RIGHT BLOODY MARY MIX

Easy   Serves: 8

1 teaspoon beef bouillon granules
2 tablespoons very hot water
2 (6-ounce) cans spicy hot cocktail
   vegetable juice

1 (46-ounce) can cocktail vegetable juice
juice of 1 lemon
2 teaspoons Worcestershire sauce
1/2 teaspoon Morton's Nature's Seasons

* Dissolve the beef bouillon in hot water.
* Mix all ingredients thoroughly in a pitcher.
* Serve over cracked ice, garnished with lime wedges and a celery stick. May add a
  jigger of vodka, if desired.

Note: Mixture keeps well in the refrigerator for several days. Good for the whole family
as a breakfast juice without the vodka.

Hilda Rutherford

CHOCOLATE NOG
Yummy enough to be dessert

Easy   Serves: 12-16

2 quarts commercial eggnog, chilled
1 (12-ounce) container frozen whipped
   topping, thawed and divided

1 cup chocolate syrup
1/2 cup brandy (optional)
shaved chocolate bar for garnish

* In large bowl combine eggnog, 3 cups whipped topping, chocolate syrup and brandy.
  Mix with electric mixer at low speed until smooth.
* Pour mixture into punch bowl.
* Serve immediately with a dollop of whipped topping and a sprinkle of chocolate
  shavings.

Dougi O'Bryan

COFFEE FRAPPÉ

Yields: 24 cups

4 quarts strong, hot coffee
1 quart milk
1-1/2 cups sugar

2 teaspoons vanilla
1/2 gallon vanilla or coffee ice cream
1/2 pint whipping cream, whipped

* Mix coffee, milk, sugar and vanilla. Chill.
* Put ice cream in punch bowl. Pour coffee mixture over.
* Break ice cream into chunks as you serve punch.
* Top with whipped cream or put a dollop in each cup as it is served.

Variation: Add 1 cup kahlúa or brandy. May garnish with a cinnamon stick.

Ellen Knott

EASY FROZEN FRUIT DAIQUIRIS
Delicious but potent

Serves: 6-8

1 (6-ounce) can frozen concentrated
   limeade
6 ounces light rum
10 to 15 ice cubes

2 very ripe bananas or
1 pint ripe strawberries or
1-1/2 to 2 cups peeled, sliced ripe
peaches

* In blender, combine limeade and rum. Blend 5 seconds.
* Add fruit slowly; blend until pureed.
* Add ice cubes one at a time until desired slushiness.
* Keep in freezer until ready to serve.

Irene Kelly

HILTON HEAD FREEZE

Yields: 12 ounces

1-1/2 ounces light rum
2-1/2 ounces orange juice
1-1/2 ounces coconut cream

1/2 ounce grenadine
1/2 medium ripe banana

* Put banana in blender.
* Add ice and remaining ingredients.
* Blend until creamy and stiff.

Variation: For **Daufuskie Freeze** (named for island near Hilton Head), use first 3 ingredients, but substitute 3 to 4 fresh strawberries for banana. Omit grenadine. May also use 2 ounces of frozen strawberries. Prepare the same way.

Note: Both versions are also delicious without alcohol.

Ellen Knott

HOLIDAY GLÖGG

Yields: 10 cups

1 cup water
1 cup sugar
2 sticks cinnamon
20 whole cloves
juice of 6 fresh lemons

1 (64-ounce) bottle cranberry juice cocktail
1 (750 ML) bottle Burgundy
1/2 cup brandy
clove-studded lemon slices for garnish

* In a large saucepan, combine water, sugar and spices.
* Bring to a boil, stirring to dissolve sugar. Simmer 5 minutes.
* Add remaining ingredients and heat thoroughly.
* Pour into punch bowl.
* For garnish, float clove-studded lemon slices in punch bowl.

Cynthia Barnes
Ann Hedbacker

FROZEN MARGARITAS

Serves: 6

*1 (6-ounce) can frozen limeade
  concentrate*

*1 limeade can tequila
1/2 limeade can Triple Sec*

* Put ingredients in blender. Blend with ice cubes until smooth and thick.

Len Efird

HOT BUTTERED RUM

*1 pint vanilla ice cream, softened
2 sticks butter, softened
1 cup powdered sugar
1 cup brown sugar*

*2 teaspoons nutmeg or
  1 teaspoon cinnamon and 1 teaspoon
  nutmeg*

* Mix all ingredients well. Store in freezer.
* To serve, put 2 to 3 tablespoons of the mix in a mug; add 1 to 2 shots of light rum and
  boiling water to fill mug.

Judy Beise, Candy Hansberger

ORANGE LIQUEUR
Must begin three and a half weeks before using.

Yields: About 4 cups

*3 medium oranges
3 cups brandy*

1 cup honey

* Carefully peel oranges; remove rind only and leave inner white membrane on fruit.
* Cut orange peel in 2x1/4-inch strips. Reserve oranges for other use.
* Combine brandy and orange peel in a tightly covered jar.
* Let stand 3 weeks at room temperature.
* Remove orange rind and stir in honey. Let stand 3 days.
* Strain off clear liquid; store in airtight container. Reserve cloudy portion for cooking.

Mary Moon Guerrant

ALMOND LIQUEUR
Make your own amaretto.

Yields: 6-1/2 cups

3 cups sugar　　　　　　　　　*1 quart vodka*
2-1/4 cups water　　　　　　　 *3 tablespoons almond extract*
finely grated rind of 3 lemons　*2 tablespoons vanilla*

* Combine sugar, water and lemon rind in Dutch oven or large saucepan.
* Bring to a boil. Reduce heat and simmer for 5 minutes, stirring occasionally.
* Cool completely.
* Stir in remaining ingredients.
* Store in airtight bottles.

Mary Moon Guerrant

KAHLÚA
An old family favorite

Yields: About 3 quarts

1 quart water　　　　　　*1/2 cup instant coffee*
3 cups sugar　　　　　　 *2 ounces vanilla*
5 cups water　　　　　　 *1 fifth of grain alcohol*

* In a heavy saucepan, combine 1 quart water and sugar.
* Boil for 10 to 15 minutes.
* In a separate pot bring 5 cups water to a boil and add instant coffee.
* Combine both of these and cool.
* Once cooled, pour water mixture, vanilla and alcohol into a gallon container and mix.
* Store in airtight containers. Improves with age.

Tom Palmgren

APPETIZERS

BEV'S EASY DIP

Yields: 2 cups

1 (8-ounce) package cream cheese or light cream cheese, at room temperature

1 (8-ounce) bottle Catalina dressing (may use low calorie)

* Mix cream cheese and dressing thoroughly.
* Serve with raw vegetables.

Mary Sue Patten

DELICIOUS BERRY DIP
Excellent with strawberries, raspberries, apple slices or bananas

Easy

Yields: 1-1/4 cups

4 tablespoons sour cream
4 tablespoons whipped topping
2 tablespoons brown sugar

1 tablespoon Grand Marnier
2 tablespoons orange Curacao liqueur
1/2 tablespoon dark rum

* Combine sour cream with whipped topping and brown sugar.
* Add Grand Marnier and whisk. Add Curacao and whisk. Add rum and stir.
* Serve as a dip with berries or top a small dish of fruit with several spoonfuls.

Judi Tingler

"DILL-ICIOUS" DIP

Easy

Yields: 2 cups

1 cup mayonnaise-type salad dressing
1 cup sour cream
1 tablespoon horseradish
1 teaspoon Dijon mustard
dash hot pepper sauce

1 tablespoon fresh dill or 1 teaspoon dried dill
minced onion to taste
garlic salt to taste

* Mix all ingredients. Chill.
* Serve with raw vegetables.

Susan Guarnaccia

DIP DIP DIP

Easy   Yields: 1-1/2 cups

3/4 cup mayonnaise
3/4 cup sour cream
1 tablespoon chopped fresh parsley
1/2 tablespoon chopped fresh dill

1 tablespoon chopped chives, fresh or
  frozen
1 to 2 tablespoons Beau Monde seasoning
freshly ground black pepper

* Mix all ingredients.
* Use as dip for artichokes, raw vegetables, chips or as a baked potato topping.

Francine LaPointe Bray,
Elaine Hoffmann, Terry Casto

AMY'S GREEN CHILI DIP

Easy   Yields: 2 cups

3 (4-ounce) cans chopped green chilies
1 tablespoon minced green onion
1 egg
1/4 cup mayonnaise

2 tablespoons milk
1 tablespoon Worcestershire sauce
1 cup grated Cheddar cheese
tortilla chips

* Press chilies in bottom of ungreased 9-inch pie plate. Sprinkle green onions on top.
* Lightly beat egg, mayonnaise, milk and Worcestershire sauce. Pour over chilies. Cover with cheese. Bake at 375 ° for 20 minutes. Serve with tortilla chips.

Lillian Swindell

NO-BEAN CHILI DIP

Easy   Yields: 2 cups

1 (8-ounce) package cream cheese,
  softened

1 (14-ounce) can chili, without beans
2 cups grated taco cheese

* Layer ingredients in order listed in shallow microwave-safe dish.
* Heat in microwave 2 minutes or until cheese is melted. Serve with tortilla chips.

The Hawk

PICADILLO
Men and teenagers love this!

Serves: 20

2 pounds ground beef
1 onion, chopped
2 teaspoons minced garlic
2/3 cup chopped green pepper
1 (16-ounce) can tomatoes, drained and
  chopped
2-1/4 teaspoons salt
1/4 teaspoon pepper
1/4 teaspoon cayenne pepper
1/2 teaspoon cumin

1/2 teaspoon oregano
1/4 cup Worcestershire sauce
2 (10-ounce) cans beef broth
1 (12-ounce) can tomato paste
1 (6-ounce) can black olives, chopped
1 cup slivered almonds
1 (4-ounce) can chopped green chilies
1 cup raisins
1 (8-ounce) can mushrooms, drained

* Brown beef. Drain and discard fat.
* Add next 10 ingredients. Cook over medium heat until vegetables are soft.
* Add remaining ingredients. Simmer 1 hour.
* Serve in chafing dish or crock pot with tortilla chips.
* Freezes well.

Doris Willson

SPICY SALSA MIX
Great way to spice up regular salsa

Easy
Prepare ahead

Yields: 2-1/2 cups

1 (8-ounce) jar hot salsa
1 (8-ounce) jar mild salsa
1 cup grated Cheddar cheese

1 red onion, chopped
1 (2-1/4 ounce) can sliced black olives

* Combine all ingredients. Refrigerate several hours.
* Serve with nacho chips.
* For thicker sauce, may partially drain salsas.

Robin Lowe

WARM CHEESY SALSA DIP

Easy   Yields: 1-3/4 cups

1 cup salsa (strength to taste)   *2 tablespoons sliced green onions*
4 ounces light cream cheese (Neufchatel)   *tortilla chips*
4 ounces (1 cup) shredded Monterey Jack   *1 (8 to 10-inch) tortilla shell (optional)*
cheese

* In medium microwave-safe bowl, combine salsa and cheeses. Microwave on high 2 to 4 minutes or until cheese is melted, stirring twice during cooking.
* Sprinkle with green onions.
* Serve in tortilla bowl with tortilla chips.
* To make tortilla bowl, grease outside of 10-ounce oven-proof bowl and drape tortilla shell over inverted bowl. Bake 5 to 9 minutes at 350° or until brown.

The Hawk

HOT CRAB DIP
The Cheddar-crab flavor is marvelous.

Easy   Yields: 3 cups

1 (8-ounce) package cream cheese   *dash of pepper*
1 (5-ounce) jar Old English Cheddar   *garlic powder to taste*
cheese   *dash Worcestershire sauce*
1/2 cup half-and-half   *1/2 pound crabmeat*

* Melt cream cheese with half-and-half in double boiler. Stir until smooth.
* Add Cheddar cheese. Blend well.
* Add pepper, garlic powder and Worcestershire sauce.
* Fold in crabmeat. Serve warm with assorted crackers.

Jewel Freeman

MEETING STREET CRABMEAT

Everyone loves it.

Easy   Yields: 24 appetizers

4 tablespoons butter
4 tablespoons flour
1/2 pint cream
1 pound well-picked white crabmeat

4 tablespoons sherry
salt and pepper to taste
bite-sized pastry shells

* Melt butter in small saucepan over medium heat.
* Stir in flour. Cook until bubbly.
* Add cream, stirring until mixture thickens.
* Add salt, pepper and sherry.
* Remove from heat.
* Add crabmeat.
* Serve in a chafing dish with a tray of shells.

Patsy Farmer

LOBSTER DIP

Delicious and easy

Yields: 1-3/4 cups

1 (8-ounce) package light cream cheese
1/4 cup mayonnaise or salad dressing
1 clove garlic, crushed
1 teaspoon grated onion
1 teaspoon prepared mustard

1 teaspoon sugar
dash seasoned salt
1 (6-ounce) can lobster meat, flaked
3 tablespoons Sauterne
assorted crackers

* Melt cream cheese over low heat, stirring constantly.
* Blend in mayonnaise, garlic, onion, mustard, sugar and salt.
* Stir in lobster and Sauterne. Heat through.
* Serve with assorted crackers.

Jane Sanders

DIP FOR PEARS
Wonderful in fall - very different

Yields: 2 cups

8 ounces cream cheese
4 ounces bleu cheese
1/2 cup sour cream
1 (6 to 7-ounce) can crab meat

1 tablespoon minced onion
1 tablespoon minced parsley
sliced pears
lemon juice

* Brush pears with lemon juice to keep them from turning brown.
* Mix all ingredients except pears and lemon juice. Chill.
* Serve pear slices on platter with dip.

Hilda Rutherford

FRUIT DIP

Easy

Yields: 4 cups

2 (7-ounce) jars marshmallow cream
2 tablespoons orange juice

1 (8-ounce) package cream cheese, softened

* Mix all ingredients together until smooth.
* Serve with pieces of fresh fruit for dipping.

Lori Spears

SHRIMP DIP

Easy

Yields: 5 cups

1 (14-ounce) bottle ketchup
4 ounces horseradish
3 (3-ounce) packages cream cheese,
  softened

fresh onion juice (cut onion in half and
  scrape with knife)
3 to 4 dashes Worcestershire sauce
1 pound small shrimp, cooked and cleaned

* Blend first 5 ingredients. Add shrimp.
* Serve with crackers.

Ellen Bickett

SPINACH-ARTICHOKE DIP

Easy   Serves: 6-8

1 (14-ounce) can artichoke hearts   salt and pepper to taste
1 stick butter or margarine, divided   1/4 teaspoon sweet basil
2 (10-ounce) packages frozen chopped   1/4 teaspoon dill weed
   spinach, cooked and drained   chopped parsley (optional)
1 (8-ounce) package cream cheese   1/4 cup bread crumbs
juice of 1 lemon   1/4 cup Parmesan cheese

* Drain and finely chop artichoke hearts. Season with salt, pepper and basil.
* Melt 1/3 stick butter. Pour butter and lemon juice over artichoke hearts.
* Melt remaining 2/3 stick of butter and cream cheese. Blend into spinach.
* Add salt, pepper and dill weed.
* Combine spinach and artichoke hearts with bread crumbs and parsley.
* Place in baking dish and cover with Parmesan cheese.
* Bake for 20 minutes at 325°.
* Serve as dip with assorted crackers.

Carol Lawing

THISTLE DIP

Easy   Yields: 1-1/2 cups

1 (6-ounce) jar marinated artichoke hearts   1/2 teaspoon onion salt
1 cup sour cream   dash cayenne pepper

* Place undrained artichokes in blender. Puree until smooth.
* Transfer to bowl. Stir in remaining ingredients.
* Refrigerate 1 hour.
* Serve with crackers, chips or vegetables.

Candy Hansberger

VIDALIA DIP

A favorite appetizer in Peachtree City, Georgia

Easy   Yields: 5 cups

2 cups Vidalia onions, chopped   2 cups mayonnaise
2 cups Swiss cheese, coarsely grated

* Combine all ingredients.
* Spoon into pie plate which has been sprayed with non-stick spray.
* Bake at 325° for 25 minutes.
* Serve with crackers or crusty bread.

Ruth Anne Easler

BRIE WITH BROWN SUGAR AND ALMONDS

Easy   Serves: 8-10

1 (24-ounce) 8-inch round of Brie, top 1/2 cup butter
   rind removed   1 cup slivered almonds or chopped pecans
2 cups firmly packed brown sugar

* Place Brie in lightly buttered 9 to 10-inch quiche or pie plate.
* Melt butter; stir in brown sugar.
* Pour over Brie.
* Bake at 300° for 10 to 15 minutes or microwave on high for 3 to 5 minutes.
* Sprinkle almonds on top.
* Lightly broil until nuts brown slightly.
* Serve with French bread, crackers or fresh fruit.

Tonia Caligiuri
Brandon Chapman

CHIPPED BEEF SPREAD

Easy   Yields: 2 cups

1 teaspoon minced onion
1 tablespoon dry sherry
1 (8-ounce) package cream cheese,
  softened

2 tablespoons mayonnaise
1/4 cup chopped green olives
1 (3-ounce) package smoked, sliced beef,
  chopped

* Mix all ingredients.
* Serve with assorted crackers.

Julia Todd

CAVIAR SPREAD

Easy   Yields: 3 cups

1 (8-ounce) package cream cheese,
  softened
1 (4-ounce) jar caviar, reserve 1 teaspoon
  for garnish
3 hard-boiled eggs, finely chopped

1 small bunch scallions, sliced
1 medium cucumber, peeled, seeded and
  chopped
1/2 cup mayonnaise

* Layer ingredients in order listed in round 8-inch serving dish or quiche plate.
* Garnish with green onion sprigs and reserved caviar.
* Serve with crackers.

Jean Webb

STELLA'S LAYERED CAVIAR SPREAD

1 (14-ounce) can artichoke hearts,
  drained and chopped
thin layer of mayonnaise

1 small onion, chopped
1 (8-ounce) package cream cheese, softened
1 (4-ounce) jar caviar

* Layer ingredients on serving dish in order given.
* Serve with crackers.

Lee Russo

CHUTNEY GLAZED CHEESE PATÉ
Easy hors d'oeuvre and always popular

Serves: 10-12

6 ounces sharp Cheddar cheese, grated
1 (8-ounce) package cream cheese,
  softened
3/4 teaspoon curry powder

3 tablespoons dry sherry
1/4 teaspoon salt
1 (9-ounce) bottle chutney
1 cup or less finely chopped green onions

* In a bowl, beat together cheeses, curry powder, sherry and salt.
* Spread mixture about 1/2-inch thick on a pretty serving dish.
* Cover and chill until firm.
* At serving time, spread top with chutney and sprinkle with green onions.
* Serve with bland crackers.

Ellen Knott

PINE CONE CHEESE SPREAD
Gorgeous on your hors d'oeuvre table

Serves: 20-25

3 jars Port wine cheese
1 can whole almonds

3 (8-ounce) packages cream cheese,
  softened

* Mix cheeses together.
* Shape into ovals (2 small, 1 large). Cover with almonds to resemble pine cones.
* Put in freezer until cold. Do not freeze.
* Arrange on serving plate with a few clean pine tree branches at top of cones.
* Serve with crackers.

Lee Russo

35

EGGS EVERGLADES
Always a hit

Easy   Serves: 12

1 can chicken broth, divided   *1-1/2 cups mayonnaise*
4 hard-boiled eggs   *2 envelopes unflavored gelatin*
1/2 teaspoon hot pepper sauce   *1-1/2 teaspoons curry powder or to taste*
juice of 1/2 lemon   *1/4 teaspoon salt*

* Soak gelatin in 1/4 cup chicken broth.
* Heat remaining broth with curry and salt.
* Dissolve softened gelatin in hot broth.
* Put eggs, hot pepper sauce, lemon juice and mayonnaise in blender. Pour in broth mixture and blend well.
* Pour into a greased 5-cup mold.
* Chill until firm.
* Serve with club crackers.

Betty Mullen

ENGLISH MUFFIN YUMMIES

Easy   Yields: 24 pieces

1 cup chopped black olives   *1-1/2 cups grated Parmesan cheese*
1/2 cup chopped green onions   *6 English muffins, split*
1/2 cup mayonnaise

* Mix all ingredients except muffins.
* Spread on English muffins. Cut into quarters.
* Broil 10 minutes or until lightly browned.

Teresa Ernsberger
Nancy Gaskin

Variation: Grate 8 ounces mozzarella cheese and top each muffin half before broiling.

Judi Tingler

MUSHROOM PATÉ
Fabulous!

May be prepared ahead   Serves: 8-10

2 tablespoons unsalted butter
8 ounces fresh mushrooms, finely chopped
1-1/2 teaspoons minced garlic
1/4 cup minced green onions, white parts
  only
1/3 cup chicken broth

4 ounces cream cheese, softened (can use
  cream cheese with chives)
2 tablespoons unsalted butter, softened
2 tablespoons minced fresh parsley or green
  onion tops
salt and pepper to taste

* Heat 2 tablespoons butter in large skillet over high heat.
* Add mushrooms and sauté 2 to 3 minutes.
* Add garlic and onions and sauté 1 minute more.
* Add chicken broth and cook until all liquid has evaporated.
* Cool to room temperature.
* Mix cream cheese and softened butter.
* Add all ingredients and mix well. Refrigerate.
* Serve at room temperature with crisp crackers.

Betty Rosbottom

SHRIMP SPREAD

Easy   Serves: 12

1 (8-ounce) package cream cheese,
  softened
1 stick of butter or margarine, softened

pinch of salt
1 tablespoon lemon juice
1 (4-1/2-ounce) can baby shrimp

* Mix together all ingredients. Chill.
* Serve with crackers.

Fran Stroud

Variation: For 1 stick of butter, substitute 4 teaspoons mayonnaise and 1/2 stick butter.
Add 1/2 small onion, minced.

Katrina Hidy

THREE-LAYER APPETIZER PIE

Nice to serve with cocktails or wine

Prepare ahead   Serves: 12-16

1 (8-ounce) package cream cheese   *1 tablespoon pimientos*
1-1/2 ounces bleu cheese, crumbled   *1/4 teaspoon salt*
1 teaspoon Worcestershire sauce   *dash of pepper*
1 to 2 tablespoons minced fresh parsley   *1 tablespoon mayonnaise*
1 (4-ounce) can deviled ham   *1 tablespoon Durkee's Sauce*
2 tablespoons sweet pickle relish   *parsley for garnish*
4 hard-boiled eggs, finely chopped

* Cream cheeses with Worcestershire sauce and parsley.
* Pack into bottom of an 8-inch pie plate, spreading evenly.
* Cover with mixture of deviled ham and relish.
* Mix together eggs, pimientos, mayonnaise, Durkee's Sauce, salt and pepper. Spread on top of ham layer.
* Chill several hours.
* Garnish with parsley and serve with crackers.

Dougi O'Bryan

FRESH VEGETABLE SPREAD

Easy   Yields: 1-1/2 cups

1 small onion, grated   *1 to 2 tablespoons mayonnaise*
1 small carrot, grated   *1 (8-ounce) package cream cheese, softened*
1/2 cucumber, grated

* Drain vegetables. Add to cream cheese and mayonnaise. Beat together well.
* Chill several hours.
* Serve on crackers or toasted bread rounds as an appetizer.

Sharon Edge
Joan Anderson

VIDALIA ONION SPREAD

Easy   Yields: 2 cups

3 Vidalia onions, chopped   1/2 cup water
1/2 cup vinegar   1/2 cup mayonnaise
1/2 cup sugar   celery seed

* Cover chopped onions with vinegar, sugar and water.
* Soak covered in refrigerator for 24 hours.
* Drain well on paper towels.
* Mix with mayonnaise and celery seed.
* Add salt and pepper to taste.
* Serve with crackers.

Joanna Fox

ASPARAGUS ROLL-UPS
These disappear fast!

Easy   Yields: 2 dozen

1 loaf thin-sliced white bread   2 (15-ounce) cans asparagus spears,
1 (8-ounce) carton cream cheese with   drained
  chives   grated Parmesan cheese
1 stick butter, softened

* Trim crust from bread. Roll slices flat with a glass.
* Spread one side of bread with thin layer of butter. Spread other side with cream cheese.
* Place one asparagus spear on cream cheese side of bread; roll up.
* Sprinkle roll-ups with Parmesan cheese.
* Bake at 400° for 5 minutes. Serve hot.

Cindy Rawald

ASPARAGUS TEA SANDWICHES

A delicious spread for party sandwiches

Yields: 2-1/2 cups

*1 (8-ounce) package cream cheese,
softened*
*1 (16-ounce) can green asparagus,
drained and mashed*

3 tablespoons mayonnaise
2 teaspoons grated onion
1/2 cup finely chopped almonds
salt to taste

* Combine all ingredients.
* Spread on thin-sliced bread.

Peggy Buchanan

ARTICHOKES FRITATTA

May be served as an appetizer or main course

Easy

Yields: 4 large or 12 small squares

2 jars marinated artichoke hearts
*1 (8-ounce) package jalapeño Monterey
Jack cheese, grated*

1 medium onion, chopped
2 eggs, lightly beaten
10 saltine crackers, crushed

* Drain artichoke hearts and reserve marinade.
* Sauté onion in marinade until transparent. Drain.
* Chop artichoke hearts. Remove and discard tough leaves.
* Mix all ingredients together in large mixing bowl.
* Press entire mixture into an oiled 8x8-inch pan.
* Bake at 325° for 35 minutes.
* Allow to sit for a few minutes before cutting into squares for serving.

Note: For milder flavor, substitute 4 ounces grated Cheddar cheese for half the jalapeño Monterey Jack cheese.

Terry Casto

ARTICHOKES WITH SPECIAL ARTICHOKE SAUCE

Serves: 4

2 tablespoons lemon juice, for steam
    preparation
Special Artichoke Sauce:
2 tablespoons Dijon mustard
1/2 cup vegetable oil
2 tablespoons olive oil
3 tablespoons cider vinegar

4 whole fresh artichokes

1 to 2 tablespoons honey
1 hard-boiled egg (optional)
2 tablespoons fresh parsley, chopped

* Cut off bottom of each artichoke so it will sit level.
* Cut off the very top of each artichoke and the top point of each leaf.
* Cook artichokes in microwave or steam in saucepan.
* Microwave Preparation: Wrap artichokes individually in plastic wrap. Microwave on high 2 minutes each. Let sit 2 minutes before serving.
* Steaming Preparation: Place artichokes in saucepan in 1 to 2 inches water with lemon juice. Bring water to boil. Steam 45 minutes or until leaves pull off easily.
* Serve hot or cold with Special Artichoke Sauce.
* To prepare sauce, place all ingredients in blender jar. Pulse for a few seconds. Repeat until thickened.
* Do not over blend as the sauce is better when thick.

Helen Kluiters

BAKED ARTICHOKE HEARTS

Yields: 2-1/2 cups

2 (14-ounce) cans artichoke hearts
1/4 pound butter or margarine

4 ounces bleu cheese, crumbled

* Quarter artichoke hearts. Place artichokes in oven-proof dish.
* Melt butter and cheese together. Pour butter-cheese mixture over artichoke hearts.
* Bake at 350° for 15 to 20 minutes.

Sabra Leadbitter

CHEESE BISCUITS

Easy   Serves: 30

1 pound Cheddar cheese, shredded   2 cups chopped pecans (optional) - can
2 sticks butter   also use crispy rice cereal
3 cups flour   dash cayenne pepper

* Let cheese and butter sit 1 hour at room temperature.
* Cream butter and cheese.
* Add pecans, flour and cayenne pepper. Mix well.
* Form dough in two rolls. Chill 1 hour or more.
* Cut dough into 1/4-inch slices.
* Bake at 350° for 15 to 20 minutes. Store in airtight container.

Susan Basini, Crickett Byler-Martyn
Frances Fennebresque, Pam Richey

Variation: Omit pecans. Roll chilled dough 1/4-inch thick. Cut with small biscuit cutter.
Bake at 300° for 30 minutes. While hot, roll in powdered sugar.

Sara Rose

HOT CHEESE CROUSTADES

Easy   Yields: 48 mini croustades

1 pound sharp Cheddar cheese, grated   pinch red pepper
1/2 pound Parmesan cheese, grated   mayonnaise - enough to hold cheeses
1 teaspoon lemon juice   together
2 boxes mini-croustades

* Combine cheeses with lemon juice and red pepper.
* Add mayonnaise.
* Fill each croustade half full with cheese mixture.
* Place on baking sheet and bake at 350° for 5 minutes or until cheese melts.

Suggestion: Cheese mixture may be made in advance and refrigerated.

Carol Lawing

MINIATURE CHEESE QUICHES

Yields: 24 appetizers

1 large egg, slightly beaten
1/2 cup milk
1/4 teaspoon salt
1 (3-ounce) package cream cheese

1/2 cup butter or margarine
1 cup all-purpose flour
1 cup grated Swiss or Cheddar cheese

* Cream together butter and cream cheese; work in flour.
* Chill if very soft.
* Roll into 24 balls and press each ball over bottom and sides of small muffin tins.
* Divide cheese into unbaked shells.
* Mix egg, milk and salt together.
* Slowly drizzle 1 teaspoon of egg mixture into each cheese-filled shell.
* Bake in preheated 350° oven for 30 minutes.
* Serve hot.

Suggestion: This is a great make-ahead appetizer and is also easily doubled to keep a supply on hand in freezer for drop-in guests. Reheat frozen quiches for 20 minutes at 350° or reheat in microwave until hot.

Gail Madara

MEXICAN GREEN CHILI CHEESE BITES

Yields: 24-36 squares

1/2 cup butter or margarine, melted
10 eggs
1/2 cup flour
1 teaspoon baking powder

1 pound Cheddar cheese
1 teaspoon salt
2 (4-ounce) cans sliced green chilies
1 pint cottage cheese

* Beat eggs lightly in large bowl.
* Add butter and remaining ingredients. Mix until well blended.
* Pour into 13x9-inch pan coated with non-stick vegetable spray.
* Bake at 400° for 15 minutes.
* Reduce heat to 350° and bake 25 to 35 minutes, or until middle is firm and set.
* Cut into squares. Serve slightly cooled.

Lynne Frauenheim

MARVELOUS MUSHROOMS

Easy - must prepare ahead

Yields: 1 quart

3 pounds fresh mushrooms (caps or whole)
1/3 cup red wine vinegar
1/3 cup salad oil
1 small onion, sliced in rings
1 teaspoon salt
1 teaspoon dried parsley
1 teaspoon prepared mustard

1 teaspoon brown sugar
1-1/3 cups red wine vinegar
1-1/3 cups salad oil
3 small onions, sliced in rings
3 teaspoons salt
3 teaspoons dried parsley
3 teaspoons prepared mustard
3 teaspoons brown sugar

* Combine mushrooms and next 7 ingredients in large pot.
* Boil 3 minutes. Drain and discard liquid.
* Combine remaining ingredients and pour over mushrooms in bowl.
* Marinate at room temperature until cool.
* Cover and place in refrigerator for at least 24 hours before serving.
* Keeps indefinitely in refrigerator.

Barbara Henson

YUMMY MUSHROOM ROLL-UPS

Easy

Yields: 24 appetizers

1 package refrigerated crescent rolls
1 (8-ounce) package cream cheese
1 (4-ounce) can mushrooms, drained and chopped

1 teaspoon seasoned salt
1 egg white
poppy seed

* Unroll crescent rolls. Make 2 rectangles by pinching seams together. Stretch dough into 8x10-inch shape.
* In blender, mix cream cheese, mushrooms and dash of seasoned salt.
* Spread mixture on each rectangle. Roll up, starting from long side.
* Brush each roll with beaten egg white and sprinkle with poppy seed.
* Cut each roll into 1/2-inch slices.
* Bake on a cookie sheet at 375° for 15 minutes. Serve hot.

Nancy DeBiase, Pat Viser

MUSHROOM "APPE-PIE-ZER"

Serve as a first course.

Easy   Serves: 10-12

pastry for a two-crust, 9-inch pie   *3 eggs, well-beaten*
1/2 pound fresh mushrooms, chopped   *8 ounces mozzarella cheese, shredded*
2 bunches spring onions, chopped   *1/4 cup grated Parmesan cheese*
3 tablespoons margarine   *1 teaspoon Morton's Nature's Seasons*
1/2 cup chopped fresh parsley   *1 teaspoon Italian seasoning or oregano*

* Sauté onions and mushrooms in margarine.
* Remove from heat and stir in remaining ingredients.
* Line 9-inch pie pan with pastry. Add mushroom mixture.
* Top with crust from remaining pastry.
* Bake at 350° for about 45 minutes or until a knife inserted in center of pie comes out clean. Cut into thin wedges. Serve while warm.

Hilda Rutherford

VEGETABLE PIZZA

Easy - may be prepared ahead   Serves: 10-12

2 packages (8-count size) refrigerated   *Suggested fresh vegetables, chopped or*
  crescent rolls   *sliced: mushrooms, broccoli, red onions,*
2 (8-ounce) packages cream cheese with   *green or red peppers, carrots,*
  chives and onion   *cauliflower, zucchini, spring onions*

* Roll and flatten crescent rolls on a jellyroll (17x11-inch) pan and bake according to package directions. Cool.
* Spread cream cheese over pastry.
* Choose 4 to 6 vegetables. Wash and dry. Cut into small pieces and arrange over top.
* Refrigerate several hours or overnight. Cut into small squares.

Andi Brown

Variation: Add 1 cup mayonnaise and 1 package dry ranch dressing to cream cheese and spread over pastry. Grated cheese can be sprinkled on top of vegetables.

Nancy DeBiase, Judy DuBose

CARAMELIZED ONION QUESADILLA

Excellent appetizer for a Mexican meal

Yields: 18 wedges

3 tablespoons vegetable oil
1 pound very thinly sliced onions (3-4)
1 teaspoon dried basil
2 tablespoons honey
1 cup chicken stock

salt to taste
6 flour tortillas
1 to 1-1/2 cups grated Monterey Jack
  cheese
salsa

* In large skillet, over medium heat, sauté onions in oil until they begin to soften.
* Sprinkle in basil and continue stirring over medium to medium-low heat for 15 minutes. Do not brown onions.
* Stir in honey and cook 5 minutes.
* Add chicken stock; increase heat to make stock simmer. Continue cooking and stirring until stock has almost evaporated.
* Remove from heat. Sprinkle cheese onto tortillas, then spoon on onions.
* Fold each tortilla in half.
* Bake at 350° long enough for cheese to melt without drying tortillas.
* Slice each tortilla into thirds. Serve with salsa for dipping.

Frances Brackett

TOASTED PECANS

Great for gifts, or at a party

Easy

Yields: about 4 cups

1 pound pecan halves
1 stick butter

1/2 tablespoon sugar
salt

* Put pecans in jellyroll pan. Cut up butter over top of nuts.
* Sprinkle with sugar and salt.
* Bake at 250° for 10 minutes. Stir and salt again.
* Repeat every 15 minutes until toasted (about 1 hour).
* Drain on newspaper covered with paper towels. Salt again to taste.
* Freezes well.

Betty Mullen

ANGELS ON HORSEBACK
Great for a crowd - men love it!

Serves: 12

5 dozen oysters
1 cup chili sauce
2 tablespoons Worcestershire sauce
2 tablespoons chopped green pepper

12 slices uncooked bacon
1 cup Parmesan cheese
party rye bread

* Cook bacon until transparent and chop into fine pieces.
* Heat oysters in casserole dish and drain.
* Return oysters to casserole dish and cover with sauces and green pepper.
* Sprinkle with bacon and cheese.
* Bake at 350° for 30 minutes.
* Serve with party rye bread.

Karen Peters

CLAM PUFFS
Quick, easy, elegant

Easy

Serves: 12

1 (3-ounce) package cream cheese,
    softened
2 tablespoons heavy cream
1 cup minced clams
1/4 teaspoon dry mustard

1 tablespoon Worcestershire sauce
1/4 teaspoon salt
1/2 teaspoon grated onion or onion juice
melba toast rounds

* Mix all ingredients except toast rounds.
* Heap the mixture on toast.
* Broil 1 to 2 minutes. Serve hot.

Crickett Byler-Martyn

CRAB-SWISS BITES

Yields: 36

1/2 pound crab meat, picked and flaked
1 tablespoon minced spring onion
4 ounces Swiss cheese, shredded
1/2 cup mayonnaise

1 teaspoon lemon juice
1/4 teaspoon curry powder
1 package flaky refrigerator biscuit dough
sliced water chestnuts

* Combine and mix well all ingredients except biscuit dough and water chestnuts.
* Separate each biscuit into three layers.
* Place biscuit dough on an ungreased cookie sheet and top each with crab mixture.
* Place a slice of water chestnut on each piece.
* Bake at 400° for 10 to 12 minutes or until golden brown and puffed.

Peggy Buchanan

SEVICHE

Unusual, pretty, spicy hors d'oeuvre

Yields: 5 cups

2 pounds of any raw white fish, flaked
   (fish can be any fresh, firm-fleshed fish
   that has been skinned with bones
   removed, eg. flounder, lemon sole,
   pompano, orange roughy)
approximately 2 cups bottled lime juice,
   to cover fish
1/4 cup salad oil

1/8 cup vinegar
1/2 cup chopped, seeded fresh tomato
1/2 cup chopped onion (mixture of green,
   red and white onions)
1/4 cup parsley
1/4 cup chives
green chilies to taste
crackers

Step One (night before):
* Pour lime juice over flaked fish.
* Seal container and refrigerate overnight.
Step Two (next day):
* Squeeze fish dry in a paper towel.
* Add fish to all other ingredients.
* Mix and refrigerate until ready to serve.
* Serve with crackers.

Hanna Kane

BAR-B-Q SHRIMP

Easy   Serves: 10

1 cup finely chopped onions
2 tablespoons butter
3/4 cup chili sauce
1/4 cup water
3 tablespoons Worcestershire sauce
3 tablespoons light brown sugar, packed

1 tablespoon distilled white vinegar
1 tablespoon tomato paste
1/4 teaspoon dried mustard
1/8 teaspoon hot pepper sauce
40 medium shrimp, peeled
40 (2-1/2-inch) strips bacon

* Sauté onion in butter until transparent. Add next 8 ingredients.
* Heat to boiling. Reduce heat and simmer 20 minutes until thickened.
* Wrap shrimp with bacon. Secure with toothpick. Dip in sauce.
* Place on broiler tray.
* Broil 4 inches from heat 3 to 4 minutes on each side.

Crickett Byler-Martyn

THAI SHRIMP WITH CASHEWS

Yields: 20 small biscuits

1/2 pound finely chopped, cooked
shrimp or 1 large shredded, cooked
chicken breast
1 cup finely chopped yellow onion
1 cup peeled and shredded carrots
1 cup finely chopped Chinese or
regular cabbage

1/4 cup finely chopped cashews
2 teaspoons corn oil
1 teaspoon Oriental sesame oil
1 teaspoon curry powder
1/2 teaspoon cumin
salt and pepper to taste

* In a medium bowl, combine the shrimp, onion, carrots, cabbage and cashews.
* Combine oils in large saucepan over medium heat.
* Add seasonings. Sauté 1 minute, stirring.
* Add the shrimp mixture.
* Sauté until heated through, about 5 minutes.
* Transfer to a serving platter and serve hot, or refrigerate covered and serve cold.
* Can use as a filling for small biscuits or over rice.

Nancy Langston

ALMOND-HAM ROLL-UPS

Delicious and easy to serve

Easy   Yields: 5 dozen

1 (8-ounce) package cream cheese,
*   softened*
2 tablespoons mayonnaise
1 teaspoon instant minced onion
1 teaspoon Worcestershire sauce
1/4 teaspoon dry mustard
1/4 teaspoon paprika

1/8 teaspoon pepper
1/8 teaspoon hot pepper sauce
1 tablespoon finely chopped, toasted
*   almonds*
1 (12-ounce) package thinly sliced, boiled
*   ham*

* Combine all ingredients except ham. Stir until well blended.
* Spread 1 tablespoon of mixture on each ham slice.
* Roll up jellyroll fashion, starting at short end.
* Wrap in plastic wrap. Refrigerate.
* To serve, cut each roll into 3/4-inch slices.
* May freeze up to 1 month. Thaw at room temperature 1 hour. Slice and serve.

Jean Skidmore

BACON-WRAPPED WATER CHESTNUTS

Easy   Yields: 20-24 appetizers

1 can whole water chestnuts
bacon

1/2 cup ketchup
1/2 cup dark brown sugar

* Wrap water chestnuts with 1/3 slice of bacon.
* Secure with toothpick.
* Bake uncovered at 350°for 30 minutes.
* Pour off grease.
* Mix ketchup and sugar over low heat.
* Pour over chestnuts and bake 10 to 15 minutes more.
* Serve hot.

Leslie Fischer

MICROWAVE BACON STIX

Can be frozen until ready to serve

Easy   Yields: 10

10 crisp bread sticks (any flavor)   *1/2 cup grated Parmesan cheese*
5 slices bacon, halved lengthwise

* Dredge one side of bacon in cheese.
* Spiral wrap bacon around bread stick. Repeat with remaining breadsticks.
* Place on microwave plate lined with paper towels.
* Microwave on high 4-1/2 to 6 minutes. Roll again in cheese.

Fran Stroud

SWEDISH MEATBALLS

Serves: 4-6

1/2 cup plain breadcrumbs   *1 onion, finely chopped*
1 cold baked potato, mashed   *1 egg*
1 teaspoon salt   *1-1/2 pounds lean ground beef (or*
1/2 teaspoon ground white pepper   *combination of lean pork, veal or beef)*
1/2 to 1 cup cold beef broth, milk or   *3 tablespoons margarine for browning*
water (or combination thereof)

* Add 1/2 cup liquid to breadcrumbs and mashed potato. Let stand until liquid is
  absorbed and forms a smooth mixture.
* Add onion, salt, pepper and egg.
* Combine mixture with ground meat in large bowl and stir until well blended (mixture
  should be firm but not dry - add more liquid if needed).
* Shape into 1-inch balls with wet hands.
* Brown meat balls on all sides in margarine in large skillet over medium-high heat.
* Lower heat and stir occasionally until well done.

Ann Hedbacker

MANDARIN CHICKEN

Easy   Serves: 8

4 chicken breasts, boned and cut into   *2 teaspoons corn oil margarine*
  bite-sized pieces   *1 small can mandarin oranges, drained*
3/4 cup flour   *2/3 cup orange marmalade*
salt and pepper to taste

* Mix flour, salt and pepper. Dredge the cut up chicken pieces in the mixture.
* Heat pan sprayed with cooking oil and melt the margarine.
* Brown chicken pieces. Drain on paper towel.
* Heat oranges and marmalade. Add chicken pieces and stir gently until heated.
* Serve in chafing dish.

Joanna Roberts

KIELBASA PALMIERS
Make several rolls, wrap tightly and freeze until needed.

Yields: 40 palmiers

1 pound kielbasa sausage, finely chopped   *1 (17-ounce) package frozen puff pastry*
  or ground   *dough, thawed*
1 cup hot and sweet mustard, divided

* Brown sausage over medium heat. Drain well.
* Unfold 1 sheet of pastry. Spread with 1/2 cup mustard.
* Spread 1/2 sausage over mustard.
* Roll both long ends tightly and evenly to center of pastry.
* Repeat procedure with remaining pastry, sausage and mustard.
* Wrap tightly in foil. Refrigerate 1 hour.
* Preheat oven to 450°.
* Cut palmiers crosswise into 1/2-inch thick slices.
* Place on ungreased baking sheet. Bake 15 to 20 minutes or until golden brown.
* Serve warm or at room temperature.

Carol Lawing

EGG ROLLS

Serves: 16

1/2 cup shredded pork loin or 1 small
   can baby shrimp
1/2 tablespoon soy sauce
1 teaspoon cornstarch
4 cups shredded cabbage
1 cup shredded celery
1/2 cup shredded carrots

16 egg roll skins
6 cups oil
1 teaspoon salt
1 tablespoon cornstarch
1 tablespoon cold water
1 tablespoon flour
2 tablespoons water

* Marinate shredded pork with soy sauce and 1 teaspoon cornstarch for 1 hour.
* Heat 5 tablespoons oil in frying pan. Stir-fry the shredded pork until color changes. Remove and drain. Add the shredded cabbage, celery and carrots to the frying pan.
* Stir-fry a moment. Add salt and pork.
* Mix cornstarch and 1 tablespoon cold water to make a paste. Add to egg roll filling.
* Place 2 tablespoons filling on an egg roll skin about 1 inch from the edge.
* Roll once or twice. Fold right end, then left end, toward center, rolling into a tight roll.
* Mix flour and 2 tablespoons water to make paste. Brush outer edge of skin with paste.
* Deep fry egg rolls over medium heat for 4 minutes or until golden brown.
* Serve with a sweet and sour sauce or a hot mustard sauce.

Yuh Hui Lee

JEAN'S PEPPERONI ROLL
A great snack for teens

Quick and easy - may be prepared ahead   Serves: 8

1 loaf frozen bread dough (or homemade
   if preferred)
1/4 pound grated logatelli cheese

1/4 pound thinly sliced pepperoni
1/4 pound white American cheese

* Thaw dough and roll into rectangle.
* Layer logatelli cheese, then pepperoni, then white American cheese.
* Roll like a jellyroll. Place folded edge down.
* Let rise for 1 hour.
* Bake at 350° until browned, approximately 40 minutes.
* Slice with bread knife. Freezes well.

Jean Bressler

SAUSAGE BREAD APPETIZERS

Serve immediately

Yields: 4 loaves

2 packages puff pastry sheets, defrosted
12 sweet Italian sausages
2 (10-ounce) packages frozen chopped
 spinach

3 cups (or 12 ounces) shredded mozzarella
 cheese
2 (1-ounce) jars pine nuts

* Remove sausage meat from casing. Cook until browned and drain well.
* Place sausage in food processor and chop well. Set aside.
* Cook spinach. Drain well. Place in food processor and chop.
* Mix sausage, spinach, shredded mozzarella cheese and pine nuts together.
* Roll out puff pastry (not too thin). Spread mixture on dough.
* Roll up and crimp edges. Place on baking sheet seam side down.
* Mix egg and water; brush on loaves.
* Bake at 375° for 30 to 40 minutes or until well-browned. Slice and serve immediately.

Karen Jackson

SPICY SAUSAGE TOASTS
Great appetizer to have on hand for guests or a special treat

Yields: about 30 pieces

1 pound hot Italian or hot pork sausage
1 pound ground beef
1 tablespoon Worcestershire sauce
1 teaspoon oregano

4 shakes hot pepper sauce
1 pound pasteurized process cheese spread,
 cubed
1 package party rye bread

* Brown sausage and beef together. If sausage is in casing, remove casing before cooking. Drain.
* Add Worcestershire, oregano and hot pepper sauce, mixing well.
* Add cheese spread to meat mixture, cooking until cheese is melted and combined well.
* Remove from heat and spread on party rye slices.
* Place party ryes on cookie sheet and freeze until ready to serve.
* At least 1 hour before cooking, remove from freezer.
* Place in preheated 450° oven and bake for 5 to 10 minutes.
* Watch carefully to keep from burning.
* Recipe freezes well up to 4 months in a freezer bag.

Meg Clarke

Soups and Sandwiches

ARTICHOKE SOUP

Easy   Serves: 4-6

2 cups chicken broth   1 teaspoon fresh lemon juice
1 (15-ounce) can artichoke hearts   1/2 cup heavy cream
salt and pepper to taste   chives or scallions

* Bring broth to a boil.
* Drain artichoke hearts. Add to boiling broth. Simmer 10 to 15 minutes.
* Remove cooked artichokes from broth, reserving liquid.
* Puree artichoke hearts in blender. Return to broth. Stir well.
* Add lemon juice, salt and pepper. Stir in cream. Reheat on low.
* Garnish with chopped chives or scallions and serve.

Pat Coyle

ASPARAGUS SOUP

Serves: 6-8

2 pounds fresh asparagus   6 tablespoons butter
2 cups milk   6 tablespoons flour
1 teaspoon dried tarragon or leaves from   6 cups chicken stock
   3 large branches of fresh tarragon   2 tablespoons chopped fresh tarragon
1 cup dry white wine   salt and pepper to taste

* Cook asparagus in large quantity of boiling salted water just until tender, about
  10 to 12 minutes.
* Drain. Cut off flower ends and reserve as a garnish.
* Puree remaining asparagus with a little of the milk. Set aside.
* Combine tarragon, wine and pepper in saucepan. Simmer about 20 minutes or until
  reduced to 1 tablespoon. Set aside.
* Melt butter in saucepan. Add flour. Stir until smooth. Add stock and remaining milk.
  Simmer for a few minutes.
* Stir in asparagus puree. Mix well.
* Pour a cup of the soup into tarragon-wine mixture. Stir over medium heat.
* Pour through sieve into remaining soup.
* Heat to almost boiling and adjust seasoning.
* Serve hot. Garnish with reserved asparagus buds and fresh tarragon.

Nancy Austin

AVGOLEMONO SOUP (GREEK EGG-LEMON SOUP)
Great first course statement

Easy   Serves: 6-8

6 cups chicken broth   3 tablespoons fresh lemon juice
1/2 cup uncooked rice or orzo   2 teaspoons salt
3 eggs   pepper to taste

* Bring chicken broth to boil over high heat.
* Pour in rice. Reduce heat to low. Simmer uncovered for about 15 minutes or until rice is done.
* Beat eggs until frothy.
* Stir lemon juice into eggs very slowly. Add 1/4 cup hot broth to the eggs.
* Remove remaining hot broth from heat. Slowly pour egg mixture into broth, being careful that it does not curdle.
* Serve immediately.

Maria Kleto

U. S. SENATE BEAN SOUP

Easy   Serves: 10-12

1 pound dried navy beans   1 cup sliced carrots
2 cans chicken broth   2 ham hocks
1 broth can water   2 tablespoons olive oil
1 medium onion, chopped   salt and pepper to taste
1 cup diced or sliced celery   crisp bacon (optional)

* Bring beans to quick boil in 2 quarts water. Boil 2 minutes.
* Remove from heat. Cover and let stand 1 hour. Drain and put in large pot.
* Cover with broth and water. Bring to a quick boil.
* Add onion, celery, carrots and ham hocks. Cover and simmer 4 hours.
* Remove ham hocks. Separate meat from bone. Return meat to pot.
* Add oil, salt and pepper 10 minutes before serving. Stir well.
* Sprinkle with crisp bacon pieces.

Janet Povall

BEST BROCCOLI SOUP

Easy   Serves: 12

2 tablespoons oil
3/4 cup chopped onion
6 cups water
6 chicken or vegetable bouillon cubes
1 (8-ounce) package fine egg noodles
1 teaspoon salt

3 (10-ounce) packages frozen chopped
   broccoli
6 cups milk
1 pound pasteurized processed cheese,
   cubed
pepper to taste

* Sauté onion in oil until tender.
* Add water and bouillon cubes. Boil until dissolved.
* Add noodles and salt. Boil 3 minutes.
* Stir in broccoli. Cook about 4 minutes.
* Add milk, cheese and pepper. Cook, stirring until cheese melts.
* Serve hot.

Pattie Bethune

CREAM OF BROCCOLI SOUP

Serves: 4-6

1-1/2 pounds broccoli
boiling water
2 tablespoons butter
1 medium onion, chopped
1 tablespoon flour

salt and pepper to taste
1-1/2 cups chicken broth
1 cup milk
grated Cheddar cheese for garnish

* Rinse broccoli, cut off florets, peel and cut stems into chunks.
* Steam florets and stems in boiling water for 15 minutes or until tender.
* Set aside 1 cup florets.
* In large saucepan melt butter. Add onion and sauté about 3 minutes.
* Blend in flour, salt and pepper. Cook 2 minutes, stirring constantly.
* Gradually stir in broth. Add broccoli.
* Transfer mixture to food processor in small batches, pureeing each. Pour through sieve
  and return to saucepan.
* Add milk. Heat thoroughly.
* Ladle into bowls and garnish with reserved florets and cheese.

Donna Mauerhan

CREAM OF CARROT SOUP

Serves: 6

2 pounds carrots	*1/2 teaspoon salt*
4 cups chicken broth	*1/8 teaspoon cayenne pepper*
1/4 cup butter	*2 cups half-and-half*
1/4 cup flour	*croutons (optional)*

* Peel carrots and cut into 1/2-inch slices.
* Combine sliced carrots and chicken broth in 2-quart saucepan.
* Cook over medium heat until broth begins to boil. Reduce heat to medium low. Cook carrots 20 minutes or until very soft.
* Pour broth from carrots into bowl. Set aside.
* Mash carrots in saucepan until smooth.
* Melt butter in a 3-quart saucepan over medium heat. When butter begins to sizzle, add flour. Cook 3 to 4 minutes longer, stirring often.
* Add mashed carrots, salt and cayenne pepper to butter mixture and stir.
* Slowly pour in broth, stirring until the soup is smooth.
* Add half-and-half and stir. Heat slowly but do not boil.
* Add croutons if desired and serve.

Carroll Thompson

CAULIFLOWER SOUP
So easy, so good!

Serves: 6

1 medium cauliflower, washed and cut up	*3 tablespoons butter*
1 cup milk	*2 tablespoons flour*
1/2 cup whipping cream	*1 teaspoon salt*
1 cup chicken broth	*1/4 teaspoon Worcestershire sauce*

* Boil cauliflower until tender.
* Place in blender with all other ingredients. Blend until smooth.
* Heat in a saucepan. Do not boil. Serve hot.

Peggy Dickerson

HOT CHEESE SOUP

Easy   Serves: 8

1/4 cup butter   2 cans chicken broth
3 onions, chopped   8 ounces grated Cheddar cheese
3 celery stalks, chopped   dash hot pepper sauce
2 carrots, grated   8 ounces sour cream
3 cans cream of potato soup

* Sauté onions, celery and carrots in butter.
* Add soup, chicken broth, Cheddar cheese and hot pepper sauce. Simmer 30 minutes.
* Add sour cream. Simmer 10 more minutes.
* Serve immediately.

Patsy Burns

ESCAROLE SOUP
A tasty main dish soup

Serves: 10-12

3 (14-ounce) cans chicken broth   1/4 teaspoon parsley
2 bunches escarole, washed   1/4 teaspoon basil
2 bunches carrots, cleaned and diced   salt and pepper to taste
3 to 4 pounds ground sirloin   2 cloves garlic, minced
6 eggs   1 cup grated Parmesan cheese

* Steam escarole. Chop into bite-sized pieces.
* Mix sirloin with eggs, parsley, basil, salt, pepper, garlic and cheese. Roll into small meatballs.
* Bring broth to boil. Add meatballs.
* Add escarole and carrots. Simmer 1 hour. Serve hot.
* If desired, chill and skim fat off top of soup. Reheat and serve.
* Can be made ahead and frozen.

Karen Barry

COUNTRY FRENCH ONION SOUP

Elegant first course for a dinner party

Serves: 6

3 teaspoons bacon drippings
3 large onions, finely chopped
2 tablespoons flour
1/2 teaspoon salt
1/8 teaspoon pepper
1 garlic clove, minced
parsley to taste

pinch of thyme
1 quart chicken stock
1 cup dry white wine
1 teaspoon cognac
6 slices toasted French bread
grated Parmesan cheese

* In deep saucepan, heat bacon drippings.
* Sauté onions over medium heat until soft. Add flour, salt, pepper and garlic. Cook until brown.
* Add parsley, thyme, chicken stock and wine. Simmer about 45 minutes.
* Add cognac. Put a slice of toasted bread in each bowl. Sprinkle with Parmesan cheese.
* Pour in soup; top with more Parmesan cheese.

Crickett Byler-Martyn

FRENCH ONION MUSHROOM SOUP

The best ever eaten!

Serves: 6

1 stick butter or margarine
4 large sweet white onions, sliced
3 cups fresh mushrooms, sliced 1/4-inch thick
6 cups beef broth

3 tablespoons dry sherry
6 slices French bread, toasted on both sides
4 ounces shredded Gruyère or Swiss cheese
1/3 cup fresh, grated Parmesan cheese

* Heat butter in a large, heavy saucepan. Add onions. Sauté 5 minutes.
* Add mushrooms and cook 3 minutes, stirring constantly.
* Add beef broth and sherry. Simmer covered 10 minutes.
* Puree half of the soup in blender or food processor. Return to pot. Stir well.
* Pour soup into 6 ovenproof bowls.
* Top each bowl with 1 slice toast, 2 tablespoons Gruyère and 1 tablespoon Parmesan cheese. Broil until cheese is golden brown.

Marilyn Thompson

MARGARET'S SPLIT PEA SOUP
Thick and hearty

Easy   Serves: 8-10

1 ham shank   1 cup dried yellow split peas, washed
3 carrots, peeled and diced   4 quarts water
1 medium onion, diced   salt and pepper to taste
2 large potatoes, peeled and diced

* Simmer ham shank and water in large, covered pot 1 hour or until tender.
* Add potatoes, onions, carrots and peas. Cook until vegetables are tender.
* Cool. Remove ham shank. Force soup through strainer.
* Remove ham from bone. Return meat and soup to pot. Reheat soup; season to taste.

Peg Kempert

SPLIT PEA SOUP WITH KIELBASA
A wonderful cold weather soup

Serves: 8-10

1 pound dried green split peas, rinsed and   4 green onions, chopped
   drained   2 sprigs parsley, chopped
3 fresh ham hocks   2 teaspoons salt
2-1/2 quarts water   1/8 teaspoon dried rosemary
1/4 pound bacon, chopped   1 bay leaf
2 stalks celery, sliced   1-1/2 pounds Kielbasa sausage, sliced
2 medium onions, thinly sliced   croutons

* Bring peas, ham and water to a boil in a large Dutch oven. Cover; simmer 45 minutes.
* Fry bacon until crisp. Add celery, onion and green onion. Sauté about 5 minutes.
* Add bacon, onion mixture, parsley, salt, rosemary and bay leaf to ham and peas.
* Simmer covered 2 hours. Remove from heat.
* Remove ham hocks from Dutch oven and separate meat from bone. Set aside.
* Remove bay leaf and discard.
* Put remaining mixture through food processor or blender.
* Return mixture and ham to Dutch oven.
* Add keilbasa to soup. Add more water if too thick. Simmer covered 30 minutes.
* Serve garnished with croutons.

Karen Barry

POLISH SOUP

Easy   Serves: 6-8

4 cups chicken broth
1 can cream of mushroom soup
1 (16-ounce) can sauerkraut, drained and
    rinsed
8 ounces sliced mushrooms
1 medium potato, cubed
2 carrots, chopped

1 onion, chopped
3/4 pound Kielbasa smoked sausage, sliced
1/2 cup cooked chicken, cubed
2 tablespoons vinegar
2 teaspoons dried dill weed
1/2 teaspoon pepper

* Combine all ingredients in a crock pot.
* Cook 10 to 12 hours on low.
* Skim fat from surface. Serve hot.

Helen Kluiters

HEARTY POTATO SOUP
A meal in a bowl that kids will love

Easy   Serves: 4

4 to 6 medium potatoes, peeled and cubed
1 onion, chopped
1 stalk celery, chopped
2-3 tablespoons margarine

3 tablespoons flour
3/4 cup water
1-1/2 cups milk
salt and pepper to taste

* Cook potatoes, onion, celery, salt and pepper in water until tender.
* Pour off excess water, reserving enough to just cover potatoes.
* Mix flour and 3/4 cup water to form thin paste.
* Add flour paste, margarine and milk to soup mixture.
* Cook 15 to 20 minutes longer.

Jane Tilley

BAKED POTATO SOUP
Better made a day ahead

Serves: 12

1 pound bacon
2 cups chopped celery
2 cups chopped onion
1/2 cup flour
1/4 teaspoon minced garlic
3 pounds baking potatoes
2 quarts chicken stock
Potato Skin Croutons:
potato skins
salt

2 teaspoons basil
1/4 teaspoon pepper
3 cups heavy cream
scant 1/4 cup parsley flakes
1/2 cup sour cream
Cheddar cheese and green onions for
*   garnish*

oil

* Pierce potatoes several times with a fork and bake at 400° for 50 minutes or until tender.
* Chop bacon and fry until crisp. Remove from pan; drain and reserve bacon for garnish.
* Add celery, onions and garlic to bacon drippings. Sauté until soft but not brown, about 10 minutes.
* Stir in flour. Add chicken stock and simmer 5 minutes.
* Cut potatoes in half and scoop out pulp.
* Add potato pulp, basil and pepper to stock. Simmer 5 minutes.
* Mix heavy cream, sour cream and parsley. Add to soup. Stir well.
* Use reserved bacon, Cheddar cheese and green onions for garnish.
* May also use Potato Skin Croutons for garnish.
* To prepare croutons, brush potato skins liberally with butter or oil on both sides.
* Bake at 400° about 15 minutes, turning once, until brown and crisp.
* Remove from oven and sprinkle with 1/2 teaspoon salt and chop into bite-sized pieces.

Karen Barry

PUMPKIN SOUP

Serves: 6-8

1/4 cup butter	2-1/2 cups half-and-half
1/2 cup chopped green peppers	1 teaspoon salt
1/4 cup chopped onion	1 teaspoon brown sugar
2 tablespoons chopped fresh parsley	1/4 teaspoon nutmeg
3 cups chicken stock	1/4 teaspoon chopped dried dill weed
1 cup tomatoes with juice	1/2 teaspoon chopped dried thyme
2-1/2 cups canned pumpkin	1/4 teaspoon freshly ground black pepper
3 tablespoons butter	2 bay leaves
3 tablespoons flour	sour cream

* In a large saucepan, melt butter over low heat. Add peppers, onion and parsley. Sauté until just tender.
* Add chicken stock, tomatoes and pumpkin. Heat thoroughly.
* Puree the mixture in small batches using blender or food processor.
* Return the pureed mixture to saucepan. Heat over medium heat.
* Add the butter and flour. Cook and stir 5 minutes.
* Slowly whisk in half-and-half, stirring until thickened.
* Add brown sugar and seasonings. Simmer for 30 minutes.
* Serve steaming hot, garnished with a dollop of sour cream.

Steve Horsley

QUICK WILD RICE SOUP

Easy   Serves: 6-8

1 cup cooked chicken, cubed	salt and pepper to taste
3 tablespoons margarine	1 (14-1/2-ounce) can chicken broth
3 tablespoons flour	2 cups milk
1/2 cup chopped celery	1 cup cooked wild rice (do not use long
1/2 medium onion, diced	grain-wild rice mixture)

* Melt margarine in saucepan. Sauté onions and celery until tender crisp.
* Stir in flour, salt and pepper.
* Add chicken broth and milk. Stir until thickened.
* Add wild rice and chicken. Simmer 10 to 15 minutes.

Judy Fahl

STEAK SOUP

So hearty it's almost a stew!

Serves: 10-12

1 pound round steak, cut in small pieces
2 tablespoons butter, melted
1/2 pound butter or margarine
1 cup flour
3 cups water
1 cup onions, diced
1 cup carrots, diced
1 cup celery, diced
1 (16-ounce) package frozen corn

1 (20-ounce) package frozen mixed
 vegetables
2 (8-ounce) cans tomato sauce
1 tablespoon Accent
2 tablespoons Bovril
1-1/2 teaspoons Kitchen Bouquet
1-1/2 teaspoons salt
1 teaspoon pepper

* Brown steak in 2 tablespoons butter.
* Melt 1/2 pound butter in large soup pot.
* Stir in flour to make smooth paste.
* Gradually stir in warm water.
* Add all other ingredients.
* Simmer 3 to 4 hours.

Karen Barry

TOMATO SOUP

Serves: 6

1 (28-ounce) can crushed tomatoes
1 teaspoon salt
1 teaspoon sugar
1/2 teaspoon pepper

2 tablespoons margarine
2 tablespoons flour
1-1/2 cups milk

* Combine tomatoes, salt, sugar, and pepper in a heavy saucepan. Simmer 15 minutes.
* Make a white sauce with margarine, flour and milk.
* Gradually add tomato mixture to white sauce, stirring constantly.
* Serve with miniature French toast rounds.

Sharon Edge

10/28/07
oK. Would not make again. Must
find a better recipe.

TORTELLINI SOUP

Great with a green salad and crusty garlic bread

Easy   Serves: 4

1 tablespoon butter or margarine
4 garlic cloves, minced
2 (14-1/2-ounce) cans chicken broth
1 package refrigerated tortellini
1/4 cup grated Parmesan cheese
1 (14-1/2-ounce) can Italian style stewed
* tomatoes*

1/2 bunch fresh spinach, stems removed or
* 1/2 (10-ounce) package frozen spinach,*
* thawed*
6 fresh basil leaves or1 teaspoon dried
* basil*
additional grated Parmesan cheese

* Melt butter in a heavy saucepan over medium heat. Add garlic. Sauté 1 minute.
* Stir in broth and tortellini. Bring to a boil.
* Reduce heat. Add 1/4 cup Parmesan cheese. Simmer until tortellini is just tender, about 5 minutes.
* Stir tomatoes, spinach and basil into soup. Simmer 2 minutes.
* Serve with extra Parmesan cheese.

Kim Martin

TORTILLA SOUP

Easy   Serves: 4

2 (10-1/2-ounce) cans reduced sodium
* chicken soup with rice*
1 (10-ounce) can tomatoes with green
* chilies*

tortilla chips, broken
shredded Cheddar and Monterey Jack
* cheese*

* Combine undiluted soup and tomatoes in blender. Pulse until blended.
* Place in saucepan. Cook until thoroughly heated, stirring occasionally.
* Ladle into bowls. Sprinkle with broken tortilla chips and cheeses.

Mary Moon Guerrant

TURKEY VEGETABLE SOUP
Wonderful use for leftover turkey

Serves: 6-8

1/2 stick butter or margarine
2 medium onions, chopped
2 tablespoons flour
1/2 teaspoon curry powder
3 cups chicken broth
1 cup chopped potatoes
1/2 cup thinly sliced carrots
1/2 cup sliced celery

2 tablespoons chopped fresh parsley
1/2 teaspoon sage
2 cups cubed cooked turkey
1-1/2 cups half-and-half
1 (10-ounce) package frozen chopped
  spinach
salt and pepper to taste

* Melt butter in a large saucepan over medium-high heat. Add onions and sauté until transparent, about 10 minutes.
* Stir in flour and curry powder. Cook 2 to 3 minutes.
* Add broth, potatoes, carrots, celery, parsley and sage. Bring to a boil. Reduce heat. Cover and simmer for 20 minutes.
* Add turkey, half-and-half and spinach. Cover and continue to simmer until heated through, about 30 minutes.
* Season with salt and pepper. Serve hot.
* Very good reheated the next day. If too thick, add a small amount of milk.

Pat Kelly

HIGH HAMPTON VEGETABLE SOUP

Freezes well

Serves: 12

1-1/4 quarts water
1-1/4 quarts chicken broth
1 soup bone
2 pounds cubed beef chuck
1 beef bouillon cube
1 chicken bouillon cube

1 to 2 teaspoons coarse ground pepper
2 (16-ounce) cans tomatoes
2 to 3 stalks celery, coarsely chopped
1 (10-ounce) package frozen cut okra
1 to 2 onions, chopped
2 (16-ounce) packages frozen vegetables

* Combine first 7 ingredients. Boil gently for 1 hour.
* Add remaining ingredients. Simmer for 1 to 1-1/2 hours.
* Remove meat from soup bone; return meat to soup. Simmer until ready to serve.

Sara Rose, Gail Faulkner

CATHERINE'S VEGETABLE SOUP
Well worth the effort - makes enough for several meals

Serves: 12-16

8 pounds beef shanks
soup bones, if desired
1 large rutabaga, cut into pieces
1 large sweet potato, cut into pieces
3 medium potatoes, cut into pieces
1 medium cabbage, shredded
1/2 bunch celery, sliced
2 large onions, chopped
1/2 to 3/4 cup barley
1 (10-ounce) package frozen string beans
1 (10-ounce) package frozen corn

1 (10-ounce) package frozen lima beans
1 (16-ounce) package frozen mixed
  vegetables
1 tablespoon Accent
1 tablespoon basil
1/2 teaspoon thyme
1/2 teaspoon marjoram
1 tablespoon parsley
1 teaspoon salt
1 teaspoon pepper
1 (28-ounce) can tomatoes, cut into pieces

* Cover beef and bones with water in large stock pot. Bring to boil. Simmer 1 hour or until tender.
* Cut beef into pieces. Remove bones and fat.
* Add fresh vegetables and barley to soup. Cook about 45 minutes.
* Add frozen vegetables. Continue to cook about 30 minutes.
* Add spices and canned tomatoes. Simmer 15 more minutes.

Mary Lou Stafford

EASY CHILI
Great with hot dogs

1-1/2 pounds ground chuck
1 package dry onion soup mix
1 (28-ounce) can crushed tomatoes,
  undrained

2 tablespoons chili powder
2 (16-ounce) cans kidney beans (optional)
grated cheese

* Sauté meat. Drain fat.
* Add remaining ingredients. Cook, covered, over low heat for 30 minutes.
* Garnish with grated cheese.

Jane Chanon

CHILI WHEN IT'S CHILLY

Easy   Serves: 10-12

2 pounds lean ground beef
1 cup chopped onion
1 green pepper, chopped
2 cloves garlic, finely chopped
2 (28-ounce) cans whole tomatoes,
  undrained and cut up
2 (28-ounce) cans tomato sauce
3 (16-ounce) cans kidney beans

2 teaspoons salt
1 teaspoon black pepper
3 tablespoons chili powder
1-1/2 teaspoons cumin
1-1/2 teaspoons crushed red pepper (add
  more or less to taste)
shredded Cheddar cheese for garnish

* Brown ground beef in Dutch oven. Drain fat.
* Add remaining ingredients except cheese.
* Bring to a boil. Reduce heat and simmer on low for 1 to 2 hours, stirring often.
* Serve topped with shredded Cheddar cheese.

Patty Szabo

Variation: For spicier chili, add 1 can beer. Use hot chili beans, instead of kidney beans.
Add hot pepper sauce to taste.

Karen Peters

VEGETARIAN CHILI

Easy   Serves: 6

1 medium onion, chopped
1/2 green pepper, chopped
2 tablespoons margarine
1 clove garlic, minced
2 tablespoons chili powder
1 (28-ounce) can crushed tomatoes

3 cups cooked kidney beans or 2 (16-ounce)
  cans
3 cups hot cooked brown rice
salt and pepper to taste
1-1/2 cups shredded Cheddar cheese
1/2 cup chopped green onions (optional)

* Sauté onion and green pepper in margarine until tender.
* Stir in garlic, chili powder, tomatoes and beans. Season to taste with salt and pepper.
* Bring to boil. Simmer 15 minutes. Add cheese. Cook, stirring until melted.
* Spoon over individual mounds of rice. Garnish with green onion.

Nancy Gaskin

DORIS'S CHILI

Bacon gives this a different flavor.

6 slices bacon
2 pounds ground beef
2 (16-ounce) cans tomatoes
2 medium onions, chopped
2 cloves garlic, minced

2 teaspoons salt
2 teaspoons sugar
2 tablespoons chili powder
2 (16-ounce) cans red kidney beans

* Cook bacon until crisp. Crumble. Set aside.
* Cook ground beef, onion and garlic in skillet until meat is brown. Drain excess fat.
* In Dutch oven combine meat with all other ingredients except beans. Bring to a boil. Simmer several hours.
* One hour before serving, skim fat from top. Add kidney beans. Continue to simmer until serving time.

Tonia Fuller, Pam Richey

Variation: Omit bacon and sugar. Add 1 teaspoon black pepper. Place all ingredients in crock pot. Stir. Cover and cook on low for 10 to 12 hours, stirring occasionally. Top with grated cheese, sour cream, chopped green onions or diced green pepper.

Becky Tomsyck

MURRELL'S INLET CLAM CHOWDER

Serves: 6-8

1/4 pound salt pork, finely chopped
1 cup finely chopped onion
1 cup finely chopped celery
2 cups chopped clams
1 cup clam juice

2 cups finely diced potatoes
2 to 3 cups water
salt and pepper to taste
1 cup half-and-half

* In Dutch oven, brown salt pork and remove from drippings.
* Add onion and celery to drippings. Sauté until transparent.
* Add clams. Cook 10 minutes. Add salt pork and clam juice. Simmer 1 hour.
* Add potatoes and water. Simmer 45 minutes. Season with salt and pepper.
* Add half-and-half. Heat thoroughly, being careful not to boil.

Karen Peters

HAM CHOWDER

Serves: 6

1 ham hock
3 potatoes, diced
1 large onion, chopped and sautéed
salt and pepper to taste
2 teaspoons instant chicken broth
1 teaspoon dried parsley flakes

1 (8-ounce) box pasteurized process cheese
  spread, cubed
2 cups cooked cubed ham
1 pint half-and-half
1/2 (10-ounce) package frozen peas

* Cover ham hock with water in Dutch oven. Cover and cook until tender.
* Add potatoes, onion and seasonings. Simmer 15 minutes. Remove ham hock.
* Puree soup mixture.
* Return soup to Dutch oven. Add cheese. Heat until cheese melts and soup thickens.
* Add ham, half-and-half and peas. Simmer about 15 minutes.

Jan Swetenburg

CREAM OF CRAB SOUP

A very nice, mellow flavor

Easy

Serves: 8-10

1/4 cup butter
1/4 cup flour
1 cup chicken broth
1 pound backfin crabmeat

1 quart plus 1 cup half-and-half
1/2 cup dry sherry
1 teaspoon salt
1/4 teaspoon white pepper

* Melt butter in Dutch oven over low heat.
* Add flour, stirring until smooth. Cook 1 minute, stirring constantly.
* Gradually add broth. Cook over medium heat stirring constantly until thick and bubbly.
* Add crabmeat and remaining ingredients.
* Cook over low heat 10 to 15 minutes. Do not boil.
* Serve at once.

Pam McLean
Pat Coyle

SHRIMP AND CRAB SOUP WITH MUSHROOMS
Tastes like you've spent hours!

Serves: 4-6

2 (10-3/4-ounce) cans shrimp soup
1-1/2 soup cans half-and-half
Sautéed Mushrooms:
1 clove garlic, minced
1 tablespoon oil
2 tablespoons butter
1/4 pound fresh mushrooms, sliced
juice of 1/2 lemon

1/2 soup can dry sherry
1/2 pound fresh or frozen crabmeat

2 tablespoons breadcrumbs
2 tablespoons grated Parmesan cheese
1 tablespoon chopped parsley
salt and pepper to taste

* Heat soup with cream and wine until hot but not boiling.
* Add crabmeat.
* Garnish with Sautéed Mushrooms.
* To prepare mushrooms, sauté garlic in oil and butter for 1 minute. Remove garlic.
* Add mushrooms. Cook over medium heat 6 to 7 minutes.
* Add lemon juice. Cook 1 minute.
* Add breadcrumbs, cheese, parsley, salt and pepper.
* Spoon on hot soup.

Camilla Turner

SHARON SANDERS'S CRAB BISQUE

This South Carolina low country cook is famous for her incredibly rich seafood soups.

Serves: 8-10

1/4 cup chopped onion
1/4 cup plus 2 tablespoons butter or
   margarine
2 tablespoons flour
24 ounces fresh backfin crab, well
   cleaned

1 teaspoon salt
dash of white pepper
1 quart plus 2 cups whole milk
1 cup whipping cream
1/4 cup Scotch
chopped fresh parsley

* In large Dutch oven, melt butter. Sauté onion until tender.
* Add flour. Cook 1 minute, stirring constantly.
* Add crab, salt and pepper. Cook on low heat 10 minutes.
* Gradually add milk. Cook over low heat 15 minutes.
* Add cream and Scotch. Stir well and remove from heat.
* Serve with fresh parsley garnish.

Stephanie Fletcher

SHRIMP BISQUE

An elegant first course

Easy   Serves: 6

3/4 pound shrimp, cooked and peeled
2 tablespoons chopped onion
2 tablespoons chopped celery
1/4 cup butter or margarine, melted
2 tablespoons flour

1 teaspoon salt
1/4 teaspoon paprika
dash pepper
4 cups milk
parsley

* Finely chop shrimp in food processor. Set aside.
* Sauté onion and celery in butter until tender.
* Blend in flour and seasonings. Add milk gradually. Cook until thick, stirring constantly.
* Stir in shrimp. Heat thoroughly.
* Garnish with chopped parsley.

Pam McLean

THE ORIGINAL NEW ORLEANS SEAFOOD GUMBO
This is the real thing - best if made a day ahead.

Serves: 10-15

1 cup bacon drippings
1 cup flour
2 tablespoons oil
8 stalks celery, chopped
3 yellow onions, chopped
1 bunch green onions, chopped
1 green pepper, diced
2 cloves garlic, minced
1/2 cup chopped fresh parsley
2 quarts water
2 quarts chicken stock
1/2 cup Worcestershire sauce
hot pepper sauce to taste
1/2 cup ketchup

1 (16-ounce) can tomatoes, undrained and
 chopped
1-1/2 tablespoons salt
large slice of ham, chopped
3 to 4 bay leaves
1/4 teaspoon thyme
1/4 teaspoon rosemary
1 pound mild smoked sausage
2 pounds peeled shrimp
1 pound crabmeat
1 teaspoon brown sugar
1 teaspoon lemon juice
hot cooked white rice
gumbo filé

* Make a roux with flour and bacon drippings by heating on low heat and stirring until dark brown, about 1-1/2 hours. (The roux is the most important ingredient in this gumbo.)
* In skillet heat oil on low, adding celery, onions, green peppers, garlic and parsley.
* Cook this 1 hour, stirring often.
* In large kettle add cooked vegetables, chicken stock, 1-1/2 quarts water, Worcestershire sauce, hot pepper sauce, ketchup, tomatoes, salt, ham, bay leaves, thyme, rosemary and sausage. Cook 2-1/2 hours. Add extra water as needed.
* Add shrimp and crab. Cook 20 minutes.
* Add brown sugar and lemon juice just before serving.
* Serve in deep bowls over white rice.
* Pass gumbo filé separately and sprinkle on top if desired.
* Gumbo filé can be found in grocery spice section.

Leslie Gebert

BAKED CHICKEN SANDWICHES
Pretty for a luncheon

Must make ahead   Yields: 15 sandwich rounds

Filling:
2 (5-ounce) cans chicken or 2 cups   2/3 cup mayonnaise
  finely chopped chicken   1/4 cup finely chopped onion
4 hard-boiled eggs, diced   salt and pepper to taste
1/2 cup chopped ripe or green olives
Icing:
2 (5-ounce) jars Old English Cheese   1 egg, beaten
  Spread   1/2 cup butter
30 thin slices bread

* Mix all filling ingredients.
* Spread on 15 slices of bread. Top with remaining slices.
* Using empty chicken can or similar size cutter, cut sandwiches into rounds.
* Mix ingredients for icing. Spread on top and sides of sandwiches.
* Must refrigerate 24 hours (or may be frozen).
* If frozen, thaw 3 to 4 hours before baking.
* Bake at 350° for 15 to 20 minutes. Serve hot.

Becky Pickens

CHICKEN CRESCENTS

Easy   Serves: 4

2 cups diced cooked chicken   1 teaspoon salt
3 ounces cream cheese, softened   1/8 teaspoon pepper
2 tablespoons melted butter   1 package refrigerated crescent rolls
2 tablespoons milk   breadcrumbs

* Mix chicken, cream cheese, milk, melted butter, salt and pepper.
* Unroll crescent dough on flat surface to make 4 rectangles. Press seams together.
* Put 1/4 of the chicken mixture in center of each dough rectangle.
* Gather up and seal dough edges to form ball shape.
* Place on cookie sheet; brush tops with melted butter and sprinkle with breadcrumbs.
* Bake at 425° for 20 minutes or until brown.

Julia Todd

MONTE CRISTOS
Serve with soup for a great family meal.

Yields: 2 sandwiches

1-1/2 tablespoons unsalted butter, divided
1 whole chicken breast, skinned, boned
    and halved
3 tablespoons mayonnaise
1 tablespoon ketchup
salt and pepper to taste

4 thick slices rye bread
4 slices Swiss cheese
2 whole small sweet pickles, thinly sliced
2 slices red onion
1 large egg
2 tablespoons milk

* In a heavy skillet, heat 1/2 tablespoon butter. Sauté chicken for 15 to 20 minutes, turning once. Remove chicken from skillet and shred.
* Mix mayonnaise, ketchup, salt and pepper. Spread evenly on 2 bread slices.
* Place a cheese slice, half the pickles and an onion slice on both bread slices.
* Place half the chicken on each onion slice. Cover with second slice of bread.
* In shallow dish, whisk egg, milk and a dash of pepper.
* Press each sandwich together firmly. Dip in egg mixture to coat thoroughly on both sides.
* In skillet, heat 1/2 tablespoon butter over medium heat until foam subsides. Cook sandwiches covered 4 minutes.
* Add remaining 1/2 tablespoon butter. Turn sandwiches. Cook 4 more minutes.
* Cut sandwiches in half. Serve immediately.

Linda Battle

MINI-REUBENS
Great with soup or as an appetizer

Easy

Yields: 2 dozen

1/2 cup Thousand Island dressing
24 slices party rye bread
1-1/2 cups chopped sauerkraut, well drained

1/2 pound thinly sliced corned beef
1/4 pound sliced Swiss cheese

* Spread 1/2 teaspoon dressing on each slice of bread.
* Place 1 tablespoon sauerkraut on each slice.
* Place a piece of corned beef and a piece of cheese, cut to fit, on each slice of bread.
* Place sandwiches on cookie sheet. Bake at 400° for 10 minutes or until cheese melts.

Sara Buckles

QUICK FRENCH DIP SANDWICH
Delicious, filling and impressive

Easy   Serves: 4-6

1 pound roast beef, sliced   1/2 pound Provolone or Swiss cheese,
1 loaf French bread   sliced
1 jar Durkee's sauce   1 package of "Au Jus" mix

* Cut French bread in half lengthwise.
* Spread Durkee's sauce on both cut sides.
* Layer roast beef and cheese on bottom slice.
* Top with the other slice of bread.
* Wrap in foil.
* Bake at 350° for about 15 to 20 minutes or until warm.
* While baking, prepare the "Au Jus" according to package directions.
* Cut warm sandwich into serving sized pieces.
* Serve immediately with individual ramekins of "Au Jus".

Len Efird

TASTY TURKEY AND HAM BISCUITS

Easy   Yields: 30 rolls

3 packages party rolls   1 tablespoon grated onion
2 sticks butter or margarine   1/2 pound shaved ham
1 tablespoon poppy seeds   1/2 pound shaved smoked turkey
1 teaspoon spicy mustard   1 pound thinly sliced Provolone cheese
1 teaspoon Worcestershire sauce

* Split rolls in half lengthwise.
* Thoroughly mix butter, poppy seeds, mustard, Worcestershire sauce and grated onion.
* Spread mixture on all halves of rolls.
* On bottom halves layer ham, smoked turkey and cheese.
* Cover with top halves of rolls.
* May be frozen at this point for later use.
* Place rolls on baking sheet. Bake at 325° for 20 minutes.

Dottie Kirkland

BREADS

BITS OF SUNSHINE

Easy to make cheese biscuits - very rich in taste

Easy   Yields: 48 miniature muffins

1 cup margarine   *1 cup sour cream*
8 ounces sharp Cheddar cheese, grated   *2 cups self-rising flour*

* Melt margarine and add grated cheese. Stir.
* Cool 2 minutes.
* Add sour cream and mix well. Stir in flour.
* Fill greased miniature muffin pans 2/3 full.
* Bake at 350° for 20 to 25 minutes.
* Serve immediately.

Carol Lawing

CRUNCHY BISCUITS

Easy   Yields: 40

1 tablespoon seasoned salt   *2 cups finely crushed crispy rice cereal*
1 tablespoon sesame seeds   *2 large cans refrigerated buttermilk biscuits*
1 tablespoon caraway seeds   *1 stick margarine, melted*

* Mix seasoned salt, sesame seeds, caraway seeds and rice cereal to form a dry mixture.
* Cut biscuits in half.
* Dip in melted margarine and then in dry mixture.
* Bake at 400° for 6 to 8 minutes.

Note: Dry mixture can be doubled and kept in a jar for later use.

Ellen Knott

GREAT BISCUITS
Almost Bojangles

Yields: 2 dozen

3 cups self-rising flour
3 teaspoons baking powder
2 teaspoons powdered sugar

1/2 cup vegetable shortening
1-1/4 cups buttermilk
butter

* Mix dry ingredients. Cut in shortening.
* Stir in buttermilk. Knead a few times.
* Roll out on a floured board or counter top.
* Cut with biscuit cutter or floured glass.
* Bake in a preheated 450° oven for 12 minutes.
* Brush with butter.

Ellen Knott

DILLED ROLLS

Easy

Serves: 6

1/4 cup butter or margarine
1-1/2 teaspoons parsley flakes
1 teaspoon dill weed

1/4 teaspoon onion flakes
1 (10-ounce) can refrigerated buttermilk
 biscuits

* Put first 4 ingredients in a 9-inch pie pan. Heat in oven until butter is melted. Blend well.
* Cut biscuits in quarters.
* Swish each piece in melted mixture.
* Arrange pieces touching in pie pan.
* Bake at 425° for 12 minutes or until golden brown.
* Let stand for a few moments to absorb butter and herbs.

Diane Totherow

MONKEY BREAD

Easy   Serves: 12-15

1 stick margarine   *1/2 cup green onion (tops only)*
4 ounces grated Cheddar cheese   *2 (10-ounce) cans extra light biscuits*

* Quarter biscuits and put in large mixing bowl.
* Mix in onion tops and cheese.
* Pour melted margarine over all.
* Mix everything together and put in Bundt pan.
* Bake at 350° for 30 minutes.

Penny Pezdirtz

HERB-CHEESE BREAD

Easy - make ahead   Serves: 10-15

6 ounces Swiss cheese, shredded   *2 tablespoons parsley*
6 ounces Cheddar cheese, shredded   *1/2 teaspoon rosemary*
1 pound bacon, cooked and crumbled   *1/2 teaspoon salt*
1 (4-1/2 -ounce) can chopped mushrooms *1/2 teaspoon pepper*
2/3 cup mayonnaise   *2 loaves French bread, halved lengthwise*
1 tablespoon oregano   *4 tablespoons butter or margarine*

* Combine all ingredients except bread and butter in large mixing bowl.
* Mix until well blended. Cover and refrigerate overnight.
* Lightly butter bread halves.
* Spread the cheese mixture on bread halves.
* Bake at 350° for 10 minutes.
* Remove from oven and allow to stand 5 minutes before slicing and serving.

The Hawk

CHEDDAR BREAD

Yields: 1 loaf

1/4 cup cornmeal	2-1/2 to 3 cups all-purpose flour
1/2 cup boiling water	1 package active dry yeast
1/2 cup cold water	3/4 teaspoon salt
1/4 cup molasses	1 cup shredded Cheddar cheese
2 tablespoons butter or margarine	butter or margarine

* Stir cornmeal into boiling water. Add cold water, molasses and 2 tablespoons of the butter. Cool until 120° to 130°. Reserve.
* Fit processor with steel blade. Measure 1-1/2 cups of the flour, yeast and salt in work bowl. Process on/off to mix.
* Add cooled cornmeal mixture to flour mixture. Process until smooth (20 seconds).
* Turn on processor; add enough remaining flour through feed tube so dough forms ball that cleans the sides of the bowl. Process until ball turns around bowl (about 25 times).
* Turn dough onto lightly floured surface. Knead cheese into dough (cheese should be evenly dispersed throughout dough, not lumped together).
* Shape into ball and place in well-greased 8 or 9-inch pie pan. Flatten dough to fill pan. Cover loosely with plastic wrap; let stand in warm place until doubled (about 1 hour).
* Heat oven to 375°. Bake until golden and loaf sounds hollow when tapped (30 to 35 minutes). Remove immediately from pan. Brush butter over crust. Cool on wire rack.

Elaine Hoffmann

EASY DROP ROLLS

The dough can be kept up to one week.

Yields: 3 dozen large/6 dozen small

3/4 cup margarine	1 package dry yeast
1/4 cup sugar	2 cups warm water
1 egg, slightly beaten	4 cups self-rising flour

* Melt margarine and cool.
* Add all other ingredients and stir until blended. Dough will be soft and sticky.
* Store in airtight covered container in refrigerator several hours or overnight before using.
* To bake, spoon into greased muffin tins. Bake at 400° for 20 minutes.

Lori Spears

MOTHER'S BREAD OR ROLLS

Easy - Prepare ahead

Yields: 3 loaves

6 cups flour
1 teaspoon salt
1/2 cup sugar
3 eggs (at room temperature)

1/2 cup oil
1 package dry yeast
2 cups lukewarm water

* Sift and measure flour, salt and sugar in large bowl.
* Make a hole in flour mixture and add eggs and oil. Blend together.
* Dissolve 1 package yeast in 2 cups warm water. Add to flour mixture.
* Place dough in greased bowl. Cover with greased plate turned face down and refrigerate overnight.
* Grease 3 loaf pans. Divide dough into pans. Cover lightly with cloth or towel.
* In warm place, let dough rise 3 hours at room temperature.
* Bake 325° for 30 to 35 minutes. (Bake rolls at 425° for 10 to 15 minutes.)

Happy Rogers

ANGEL CORN STICKS

This is a yeast cornbread - very light.

Yields: 3 dozen corn sticks

1-1/2 cups white stone-ground cornmeal
 (no substitute)
1 cup all-purpose flour
1 package dry yeast
1 tablespoon sugar
1 teaspoon salt

1-1/2 teaspoons baking powder
1/2 teaspoon soda
2 eggs, beaten
2 cups buttermilk
1/4 cup corn oil

* Combine cornmeal, flour, yeast, sugar, salt, baking powder and soda in large bowl.
* Combine eggs, milk and oil. Add to dry ingredients and stir until smooth.
* Spoon into greased cast iron cornbread stick pans, filling halfway.
* Bake at 450° for 12 to 15 minutes.

Betsey Arnett

BETTY'S CORN MUFFIN CAKE

Easy   Serves: 12

1 box corn muffin mix   2 eggs
1 (8-ounce) can creamed corn   1 stick butter, melted
1 (8-ounce) can whole kernel corn,   8 ounces sour cream
    drained

* Mix all ingredients and pour into 13x9-inch pan. Bake at 350° for approximately
  50 to 60 minutes.

Nola Livingston

BROCCOLI CORNBREAD
This is wonderful for cocktail parties or tailgating.

Easy   Serves: 12

1 (10-ounce) package frozen chopped   4 eggs, beaten
    broccoli   1 cup cottage cheese
1 large onion, chopped   1 teaspoon salt
1/2 cup butter   1 (8-1/2-ounce) package cornbread mix

* Cook and drain broccoli.
* Sauté onion in butter until transparent.
* Combine broccoli, onion, butter, eggs, cottage cheese, salt and cornbread mix.
* Pour into lightly greased 13x9-inch pan.
* Bake at 375° for 50 minutes or until golden.
* Cut into small squares.

Variation: Also can be prepared with egg substitute with no noticeable difference.

Jean Bestall
Diane Thomas
John Leistler
Karen Peters

MARIE'S CORNBREAD
A hard to find old-fashioned recipe

Easy   Serves: 6-8

1 cup cornmeal   *1 egg*
1/2 cup flour   *2 tablespoons butter, melted*
1 teaspoon baking powder   *1 tablespoon sugar*
1/4 teaspoon salt   *3/4 to 1 cup buttermilk*

* Mix all ingredients and pour into greased muffin tins.
* Bake at 450° for approximately 20 minutes.

Sally Gabosch

UPSTATE CORNBREAD DRESSING

Easy   Serves: 12

1 cup onion, finely chopped   *1 quart turkey or chicken broth*
1/4 cup green pepper, finely chopped   *salt to taste*
2 stalks celery with leaves, finely chopped   *1/4 teaspoon black pepper*
1 (9-inch) skillet cornbread, crumbled   *3 to 4 teaspoons ground sage (or to taste)*
4 slices fresh white bread, crumbled   *4 tablespoons margarine*

* Boil vegetables for 10 minutes in enough water to cover.
* Pour over crumbled bread.
* Add salt, pepper, sage, margarine and enough broth to make a very moist (almost wet) mixture.
* Spoon dressing into a greased 13x9-inch pan.
* Bake at 400° for 30 to 40 minutes or until brown on top.

Vernie Pickens

INDIAN HILL BREAD STUFFING

Serves: 10-12

3/4 cup lightly salted butter or margarine
2 cups chopped onions
1/2 pound fresh mushrooms, sliced
  (about 3 cups)
1 pound French or Italian bread,
  crumbled
1 cup chopped fresh parsley

4 large eggs, slightly beaten
1-1/2 cups chicken broth
1/2 teaspoon ground pepper
1/2 pound zucchini, coarsely grated
  (about 2 cups)
1/2 pound carrots, peeled and coarsely
  grated (about 2 cups)

* In a 14-inch skillet, melt butter over moderate heat.
* Add onions and mushrooms. Cook about 5 minutes, stirring occasionally until onions are soft.
* Remove from heat. Add bread and parsley; toss to mix.
* Beat eggs with broth and pepper. Pour over bread mixture and toss to mix.
* Press zucchini and carrots in a dish towel to remove excess moisture.
* Mix with stuffing in skillet.
* Use about half the stuffing to stuff turkey.
* Spoon remainder into a well-buttered 1-1/2-quart baking dish.
* Cover and bake during the last 45 minutes the turkey roasts, uncovering after 30 minutes to brown.

Rhonda Job

STUFFING PATTIES
A change from regular stuffing or dressing

Easy

Serves: 8

1 small bag stuffing
1-1/4 cups chicken broth
1/4 cup chopped onion
1/4 cup chopped celery
1/4 cup chopped green pepper

4 to 6 tablespoons butter
1 egg, beaten
1/4 teaspoon sage
salt and pepper to taste

* Sauté onion, celery and green pepper in butter until soft.
* Add remaining ingredients and mix well.
* Shape into patties. Bake at 350° for 25 to 30 minutes.

Erma Rodgers

QUICK CHOCOLATE-BANANA LOAF

Easy   Yields: 1 loaf

3 cups buttermilk baking mix   1 (6-ounce) bag semi-sweet chocolate
3/4 cup sugar   morsels
1 egg   1 cup mashed ripe bananas (2-3 medium
3/4 cup water   bananas)

* In large bowl combine buttermilk baking mix and sugar; mix thoroughly.
* In small bowl combine egg and water; beat well.
* Stir into flour mixture until moistened. Add semi-sweet chocolate morsels and
  bananas. Spread into well-greased 9x5x3-inch loaf pan.
* Bake at 350° for 60 to 65 minutes. Cool and remove from pan.

Note: Does not freeze well, but slices can be reheated in microwave.

Pat Kelly

VERY LEMON BREAD

Make 24 hours ahead   Yields: 1 loaf

1/3 cup butter, melted   1 teaspoon baking powder
1 cup sugar   1 teaspoon salt
3 tablespoons lemon extract   1/2 cup milk
2 eggs   1-1/2 tablespoons grated lemon rind
1-1/2 cups sifted flour   1/2 cup chopped pecans
Lemon Glaze:
1/4 cup lemon juice   1/2 cup sugar

* In a large bowl mix the melted butter, sugar and lemon extract. Beat in eggs.
* In another bowl sift together flour, baking powder and salt.
* To the butter mixture, add the flour mixture alternately with the milk, beating just
  enough to blend.
* Fold in grated rind and nuts. Pour batter into greased and floured loaf pan.
* Bake at 350° for 45 minutes. Cool 10 minutes.
* Prepare Lemon Glaze while bread cools.
* Remove bread from pan and while warm drizzle lemon glaze over top.
* Wrap in foil and refrigerate for 24 hours before serving.

Laura Welton, Margaret Akers-Hardage

STRAWBERRY BREAD

Easy   Yields: 2 loaves

3 cups flour   *1 cup oil*
2 cups sugar   *1-1/4 cups walnuts or pecans, chopped*
1 teaspoon baking soda   *2 cups sliced fresh strawberries*
3 teaspoons cinnamon   *3 eggs*
1/2 teaspoon salt

* Combine dry ingredients; stir to mix.
* Combine oil and eggs; add dry ingredients.
* Fold in nuts and berries.
* Divide into 2 (9x5-inch) greased loaf pans.
* Bake at 350° for 1 hour.
* Cool in pan for 5 minutes. Remove bread from pans and cool on wire rack.

Lea Tsahakis
Irene Kelly

SPICED ZUCCHINI BREAD

Easy   Yields: 2 loaves

3 cups flour   *1 cup oil*
2 teaspoons soda   *1 teaspoon vanilla*
1 teaspoon salt   *2 cups sugar*
1/2 teaspoon baking powder   *2 cups zucchini, coarsely chopped*
1-1/2 teaspoons ground cinnamon   *1 (8-ounce) can crushed pineapple,*
3/4 cup walnuts, finely chopped   *well-drained*
3 eggs

* Combine flour, soda, salt, baking powder, cinnamon and nuts; set aside.
* Beat eggs lightly in large bowl. Add sugar, oil and vanilla. Beat until creamy.
* Stir in zucchini and pineapple. Add dry ingredients, stirring only until moistened.
* Spoon batter into 2 well-greased and floured 9x5x3-inch loaf pans.
* Bake at 300° for 1 hour.
* Cool 10 minutes before removing from pans. Turn out on rack and cool completely.

Phyllis Herring, Brandon Chapman
Rhonda Job, Fran Stroud

APRICOT-BANANA BUTTERMILK MUFFINS

Easy   Yields: 24 muffins

3 cups flour   1-1/2 cups pureed bananas
2 cups sugar   1-1/2 cups dried apricots, chopped
1/2 cup vegetable oil   1-1/2 cups raisins
3 egg whites   1 cup walnuts
1-1/2 cups buttermilk   1 teaspoon vanilla
2 teaspoons baking soda   oat bran
1 teaspoon salt

* Mix all ingredients except oat bran and pour into 24 greased muffin cups.
* Sprinkle with oat bran and bake at 400° for about 20 minutes.

Woody Clark

GOLDEN HARVEST MUFFINS
Very hearty

Yields: 36 muffins

2 cups all-purpose flour   4 cups peeled and shredded apples (about
2 cups whole wheat flour   5 medium apples)
1-1/2 cups sugar   1 cup shredded carrots
4 teaspoons baking soda   1 cup walnuts or pecans, chopped
4 teaspoons cinnamon   1-1/2 cups oil
1 teaspoon salt   1/2 cup milk
1/2 teaspoon cloves   4 teaspoons vanilla
1 cup raisins   3 eggs, beaten

* In large bowl combine flours, sugar, baking soda, cinnamon, salt and cloves.
* Add raisins, apples, carrots and nuts; mix well.
* Add oil, milk, vanilla and eggs; stir until moistened. Fill greased muffin cups 3/4 full.
* Bake at 350° for 20 to 25 minutes or until toothpick inserted comes out clean.
* Immediately remove from pans.

Bobbie Stelluto

Variation: Add 1 cup sweetened coconut. Can interchange amount of apples and carrots.

Betsy Mitchell

MARTHA'S BRAN MUFFINS
This mixture keeps weeks in the refrigerator.

Prepare ahead   Yields: 4-5 dozen

1 (15-ounce) box raisin bran cereal   2 teaspoons salt
2-1/2 cups sugar   4 eggs, beaten
5 cups flour   1 cup oil
5 teaspoons soda   1 quart buttermilk

* Mix sugar, flour, soda, salt and raisin bran in large bowl.
* In separate bowl, combine eggs, oil and buttermilk.
* Add to dry mixture. Stir until all the cereal is moist.
* Store in refrigerator overnight.
* Fill greased muffin tins 3/4 full.
* Bake at 400° for 18 to 20 minutes.

Judy DuBose

Variation: Add 1/3 cup molasses, 1 teaspoon cinnamon, 1 teaspoon allspice and 1 teaspoon ground cloves (for a more moist and spicy muffin).

Beth Love

RASPBERRY-LEMON MUFFINS

Easy   Yields: 12 large muffins

2 eggs   1/4 teaspoon baking soda
1/2 cup butter or margarine, melted   1/2 teaspoon salt
1 cup sugar   rind of 1 lemon, finely grated
1 cup vanilla yogurt   1-1/2 cups dry frozen raspberries (not
2 cups flour   packed in juice)
1 teaspoon baking powder

* Mix eggs, butter, sugar and yogurt.
* Sift together dry ingredients.
* Stir into egg mixture until well blended.
* Gently fold in raspberries and lemon rind. Spoon into greased muffin tins.
* Bake at 375° for 25 minutes.

Hilda Rutherford

SAUSAGE MUFFINS

From my mountain recipe collection

Easy   Yields: 12 muffins

1 pound sausage, cooked and drained   *1 cup self-rising cornmeal*
1 (8-ounce) container French onion dip   *1 cup plain flour*
1 (2-ounce) jar pimientos   *1/2 cup milk*

* Mix all ingredients in bowl.
* Pour into 12 greased muffin cups.
* Bake at 375° for 30 minutes.

Kathy Tuten

TENNIS TOURNAMENT MUFFINS

Wonderful take-along for an early morning sports event

Easy   Yields: 1 dozen muffins

1 stick butter   *1/2 teaspoon salt*
3/4 cup sugar   *1 cup whole wheat flour*
2 eggs   *3 ripe bananas, mashed*
1 cup flour   *1 teaspoon vanilla*
1 teaspoon baking soda   *3/4 cup chopped walnuts*

* Line muffin tins with paper liners.
* Cream butter and sugar until fluffy. Add eggs one at a time. Beat thoroughly.
* Sift flour, salt and soda. Mix with whole wheat flour.
* Stir flour mixture into creamed mixture only until fully moistened.
* Fold in mashed bananas, nuts and vanilla. Do not over mix.
* Bake at 400° for 25 to 30 minutes until golden.
* Cool completely.

Note: Whole wheat makes these muffins hearty and nutritious.

Brenda Ivanoff

CINNAMON-PECAN CRESCENT ROLLS

Easy   Yields: 8 rolls

1 (8-ounce) package refrigerated   *1/3 cup chopped pecans*
* crescent rolls*   *2 tablespoons butter, melted*
1/3 cup packed light brown sugar   *1/2 cup powdered sugar*
1/4 teaspoon cinnamon (or more)   *1 tablespoon milk*

* Combine sugar, cinnamon and nuts.
* Separate crescent rolls into individual triangles and brush with melted butter.
* Sprinkle with sugar mixture.
* Roll up as you would for crescent rolls. Place on lightly greased baking sheet.
* Bake at 400° for 10 to 12 minutes.
* Mix powdered sugar and milk until smooth. Drizzle over rolls.

Christine Schaeffer

CREAM CHEESE DANISH
Fun to make and serve

Easy   Serves: 12

2 packages refrigerated crescent rolls   *1 teaspoon vanilla*
16 ounces cream cheese, softened   *2 tablespoons lemon juice*
3/4 cup sugar   *1 teaspoon water*
1 egg, separated   *sliced almonds*

* Spray 13x9-inch baking dish with non-stick spray.
* Pat out 1 package crescent rolls in bottom of pan. Seal by pinching seams together.
* Blend cream cheese with sugar.
* Add vanilla, lemon juice and egg yolk. Spread over first layer.
* Pat out other package of rolls on counter.
* Place on top of cream cheese mixture.
* Paint with combined egg white and water.
* Sprinkle almonds on top.
* Bake at 350° for 30 minutes.
* Let sit for 20 minutes before serving.
* Sprinkle with granulated sugar.

Nancy Gaskin

NEW ORLEANS FLOATERS
Taste like the famous French Market beignets

Serve immediately   Serves: 4

1 cup flour   1 egg, well beaten
3 tablespoons sugar   1/3 cup milk
1-1/2 teaspoons baking powder   powdered sugar
1/4 teaspoon salt

* Sift dry ingredients.
* Combine milk and egg in large bowl.
* Again sift dry ingredients into milk and egg. Beat well.
* Drop by teaspoonfuls (a few at a time) into hot deep fat and fry until golden brown.
* Drain on crumpled paper.
* Sprinkle with powdered sugar.

Note: Not nutritious at all, but they surely are good!

Hilda Rutherford

RAISIN-WALNUT PINWHEELS

Yields: 12 pinwheels

1 sheet frozen pastry dough, thawed   1/2 cup raisins
1/3 cup sugar   1/2 cup finely chopped walnuts
1 tablespoon cinnamon   1 egg yolk, beaten
1/4 cup butter or margarine

* On a lightly floured surface, roll out pastry to an 12x8-inch rectangle.
* In a small bowl, combine sugar and cinnamon and set aside.
* In a small saucepan, melt butter. Add raisins and walnuts, stirring well.
* Spread raisin mixture evenly over pastry.
* Sprinkle sugar mixture evenly over raisin mixture.
* Beginning at long edge, roll up pastry.
* Brush pastry seam with egg yolk to seal.
* Place seam side down on a greased baking sheet.
* Bake at 350° for 20 to 25 minutes. Cool completely and cut into 1-inch slices.

Carol Lawing

YUMMY SWEET ROLLS
All my friends' favorite Christmas gift

Complicated - must be prepared ahead   Yields: 2-1/2 dozen

Dough:
1 cup sour cream, scalded
1/2 cup butter or margarine, melted
1/2 cup sugar
1 teaspoon salt

2 eggs, beaten
4 cups flour (all-purpose or bread)
2 packages dry yeast
1/2 cup warm water (105-115°)

Filling:
2 (8-ounce) packages cream cheese,
   softened
3/4 cup sugar

1 egg, beaten
2 teaspoons vanilla
1/2 teaspoon salt

Glaze:
2 cups powdered sugar
1/4 cup milk

2 teaspoons vanilla

* Combine sour cream, eggs, butter, sugar and salt. Mix well.
* Let cool to lukewarm.
* Dissolve yeast in warm water in large mixing bowl to which you have added a dash of salt and 1 teaspoon of sugar. Allow yeast to bubble.
* Add sour cream mixture to yeast.
* Gradually stir in flour. Dough will be soft.
* Cover dough tightly and chill overnight. (Dough should double in bulk.)
* Divide dough into 4 equal portions with knife.
* Turn each portion out on a lightly floured surface and knead 4 or 5 times.
* Roll each portion into a 12x8-inch rectangle.
* To make filling, beat cream cheese, sugar, egg, vanilla and salt until well blended.
* Spread 1/4 of filling over each rectangle, leaving a 1/2-inch margin around edges.
* Roll up jellyroll fashion beginning at long side.
* Firmly pinch edges of dough to seal.
* Cut each roll into 1-1/2-inch slices.
* Place cut side down 2 inches apart on greased baking sheets.
* Cover and let rise in warm place (free from drafts) until doubled in bulk (about 1-1/2 hours).
* Bake at 375° until lightly browned (approximately 15 minutes).
* Mix glaze ingredients and drizzle over warm rolls.

Melinda Mileham

APPLE COFFEE CAKE

Easy   Serves: 8-10

2 eggs
1/2 cup butter, softened
3/4 cup sour cream
1-1/2 cups sugar
3 tablespoons grated orange
   (fruit/juice/peel)
Vanilla Cream Glaze:
2 to 3 tablespoons cream
1/2 teaspoon vanilla

1-1/2 cups flour
2 teaspoons baking powder
1 cup chopped walnuts
2 medium apples, peeled, cored and
   thinly sliced
2 teaspoons cinnamon

3/4 cup sifted powdered sugar

* Beat together first 5 ingredients until blended.
* Add flour, baking powder and walnuts; beat until blended.
* In bowl, toss apples with cinnamon.
* Spread half of batter in greased 10-inch springform pan and place apples evenly over batter. Top with remaining batter and spread evenly.
* Bake at 350° for 45 minutes or until tests done.
* Cool in pan for 20 minutes. Remove sides and cool completely.
* Mix Vanilla Cream Glaze ingredients until well blended.
* When cool, drizzle top of cake with glaze and allow to drip down sides.

Kathy Gately

OVERNIGHT COFFEE CAKE

Easy - Pre-preparation required   Serves: 12-15

1 (25-ounce) package frozen dinner rolls
1/2 small package butterscotch
   pudding (not instant)
1 cup nuts, chopped

3/4 cup brown sugar
1/2 cup butter
3/4 teaspoon cinnamon

* Grease tube or Bundt pan. Arrange rolls in pan.
* Sprinkle with pudding and nuts.
* Bring remaining ingredients to boil and pour over rolls.
* Cover and set aside overnight. Bake at 350° for 30 minutes.

Mary Lee, Joan Anderson,
Mary Moon Guerrant

CRANBERRY COFFEE CAKE

Easy   Serves: 12-15

1 stick margarine   1/2 teaspoon salt
1 cup sugar   1/2 pint sour cream
2 eggs   1 teaspoon almond flavoring
1 teaspoon baking powder   1 (16-ounce) can whole cranberry sauce
1 teaspoon baking soda   1/2 cup chopped walnuts
2 cups flour

* Grease and flour a 10-inch tube pan.
* Cream margarine and sugar; add eggs one at a time.
* Add dry ingredients alternately with sour cream and stir in flavoring.
* Pour one half of the batter into the tube pan.
* Spread half of the cranberry sauce evenly over batter.
* Add remaining batter. Spread with remaining cranberry sauce.
* Sprinkle walnuts on top.
* Bake at 350° for 55 minutes.
* Cool 5 minutes before removing from pan.

Alice Nance

TOFFEE COFFEE CAKE

Easy   Serves: 8

1/4 cup butter, softened   1 teaspoon baking soda
2 cups flour   1 egg
1 cup brown sugar   1 teaspoon vanilla
1/2 cup sugar   5 chocolate-covered toffee candy bars
1 cup buttermilk

* Mix butter, flour, brown sugar and sugar together. Reserve 1/2 cup of mixture.
* Add buttermilk, soda, egg and vanilla to larger portion of original mixture.
* Pour into greased 13x9-inch pan.
* Grind candy bars in food processor.
* Add candy to reserved 1/2 cup mixture and place on top of batter.
* Bake at 350° for 30 minutes.

Sue Docherty

SOUR CREAM COFFEE CAKE

Serves: 12-15

2 sticks butter
2 cups sugar
2 eggs
2 cups flour
1/2 teaspoon salt
Filling:
1 cup chopped pecans
2 teaspoons sugar
Glaze:
1 cup powdered sugar
3/4 teaspoon almond flavoring

1 teaspoon baking powder
1 cup sour cream
1/2 teaspoon vanilla
1 teaspoon almond flavoring

2 teaspoons cinnamon

1/3 cup evaporated milk

* Cream butter and sugar; add 1 egg at a time.
* Sift together flour, salt and baking powder.
* Add dry ingredients and sour cream alternately to creamed mixture.
* Add flavorings.
* Grease and flour tube cake pan.
* Pour half of batter into pan; add filling and cover with remaining batter.
* Bake at 350° for 60 to 70 minutes. Cool cake for 10 minutes before removing from pan.
* Combine glaze ingredients.
* Drizzle glaze over cake and sprinkle with a few chopped nuts.

Jeanie Riggs

BUTTERMILK PANCAKES

Easy   Serves: 4-6

1 cup flour   *1/2 teaspoon salt*
1-1/2 teaspoons baking powder   *1 egg, lightly beaten*
1/2 teaspoon baking soda   *1-1/4 cups buttermilk*

* Sift dry ingredients together.
* Add egg and buttermilk, mixing well.
* Drop batter by 1/4 cup on hot griddle.
* Top with blueberries, sliced bananas or chopped nuts.

Pattie Bethune, Mary Edwards

Suggestion: Leftovers may be frozen by stacking them with wax paper between each pancake. Wrap each stack and freeze. To reheat, microwave frozen pancake 1 minute on 50% power and 10 to 20 seconds on high.

Marge Aultman

OLD-FASHIONED SWEDISH WAFFLES

Can be prepared ahead   Serves: 4-6

2 egg whites   *1/2 cup margarine, melted*
2 cups wheat flour   *1 tablespoon vanilla*
1 teaspoon baking powder   *2 cups milk*
2 egg yolks   *whipped cream, fresh berries or preserves*

* Heat waffle iron.
* Beat egg whites until firm. Let stand.
* Mix flour and baking powder.
* Add egg yolks, melted butter, vanilla and 2/3 of the milk.
* Beat just until smooth.
* Add remaining milk.
* Carefully add beaten egg whites to mixture just before baking.
* Bake to golden brown and cool waffles on rack for crispness.
* Serve with fresh whipped cream, fresh berries or preserves.

Ann Hedbacker

GREAT GOODNESS BARS

Easy   Yields: 24 bars

2/3 cup whole wheat flour   1/2 teaspoon baking powder
2/3 cup oil   1/2 teaspoon or less salt
1 egg or 1/4 cup egg substitute   1-1/2 cups rolled oats
1/3 cup packed brown sugar   1 cup lowfat grated Cheddar cheese
1 teaspoon vanilla   3/4 cup raisins
1/2 teaspoon cinnamon   1 cup apples, peeled and chopped

* Mix flour, oil, egg, sugar, vanilla, cinnamon, baking powder and salt with a wooden spoon.
* Stir in oats, cheese and raisins. Add apples. Stir.
* Drop by spoonfuls onto non-stick baking sheets. Bake at 375° for 20 minutes.
* Store in tightly covered container. (These keep longer if stored in the refrigerator.)

The Hawk

GRANOLA TOPPING

Yields: approximately 12 cups

8 cups oats   1 cup pumpkin seeds
1 cup sliced almonds   1 cup raw sunflower seeds
1 cup coconut chips (optional)   1 cup honey
1 teaspoon salt   2/3 cup salad oil
2 teaspoons cinnamon   2 teaspoons vanilla

* Mix first 7 ingredients.
* Combine liquid ingredients and toss with dry ingredients.
* Divide mixture into 2 large pans. Toast at 350° for 25 to 30 minutes until toasty brown.
* Set timer for every 6 minutes and stir each time it rings. Watch carefully.
* Cool and store in airtight container and refrigerate.

Note: Put 2 tablespoons of mixture plus 1/4 cup raisins on your favorite flake cereal for a healthy treat.

Frances Fennebresque

SALADS AND DRESSINGS

APPLE SALAD
The sauce makes the salad!

Easy - Can prepare ahead

Serves: 8

3 Red Delicious apples, unpeeled, cored and chopped
1 cup grated Cheddar cheese
Sauce:
1/2 cup sugar
2 tablespoons flour
1 egg, beaten

1 cup pineapple chunks, drain and reserve juice
1 cup pecans, chopped

1 cup reserved pineapple juice (add water to make 1 cup, if necessary)

* Mix sauce ingredients in small saucepan.
* Cook over medium heat until thickened, stirring constantly with whisk. Cool.
* Layer fruit, cheese and nuts in bowl.
* Pour cooled sauce over layers and refrigerate.

Nancy Wohlbruck

CANE RIVER APPLE SALAD

Easy

Serves: 4

2 medium apples, diced
3/4 cup Cheddar cheese, diced
Honey Dijon Dressing:
1 tablespoon Dijon mustard
2 tablespoons honey
1/4 cup red wine vinegar

1/2 cup walnut pieces
Bibb or green leaf lettuce

1/3 cup olive oil
salt and pepper to taste

* Place 3 to 4 lettuce leaves on each plate.
* Combine apples, cheese and walnuts and place on lettuce leaves.
* To prepare dressing, mix together mustard, honey and red wine vinegar.
* Slowly whisk in olive oil. Add salt and pepper to taste.
* Pour over salad.

Mary Edwards

CANTALOUPE SALAD

Easy   Serves: 6

2 small cantaloupes   1/2 cup sour cream
1 cup sliced strawberries   1/4 cup mayonnaise
1 cup seedless green grapes   2 tablespoons packed brown sugar
lettuce leaves   1/4 cup chopped nuts

* Pare each cantaloupe, leaving each whole.
* Cut off about 1 inch from each end of the cantaloupes.
* Cut up end pieces and mix with strawberries and grapes.
* Cut each cantaloupe into 3 even rings, removing seeds.
* Place rings on lettuce leaves. Cut each ring into 1-inch pieces, retaining the shape of a
  ring. Spoon mixed fruit into each ring like spokes of a wheel.
* Mix sour cream, mayonnaise and brown sugar until mixture is smooth. Stir in nuts.
* Spoon mixture on each salad.

Barbara Kane

FRESH CRANBERRY-ORANGE SALAD

Easy   Serves: 12

1 (6-ounce) package cherry or black   1 (12-ounce) package fresh cranberries
  cherry gelatin   2 whole oranges, or 1 whole orange and 1
1 cup boiling water   tart apple, cored
juice of 1/2 lemon   1/2 to 1 cup chopped pecans
1/4 cup water   1 cup chopped celery (optional)
1 (15-ounce) can crushed pineapple

* Dissolve gelatin in 1 cup boiling water.
* Add lemon juice, 1/4 cup water and crushed pineapple to gelatin.
* Cut oranges into sections, removing seeds and membrane.
* In food processor or blender, grind together one half of the cranberries and 1 orange.
  Set aside.
* Repeat process with remaining cranberries and remaining orange or apple.
* Add cranberry mixture to gelatin. Stir in nuts and celery.
* Pour into 13x9-inch pan. Chill until firm.

Vernie Pickens, Pam Richey

HEAVENLY APRICOT SALAD
Always a luncheon hit - great as dessert with shortbread or lemon cookie

Serves: 20

2 (3-ounce) packages apricot-flavored
  gelatin
1/3 cup sugar
2/3 cup water
2 (4-3/4-ounce) jars apricot baby food
1-1/2 cups chopped pecans

1 (20-ounce) can crushed pineapple,
  undrained
1 (14-ounce) can sweetened condensed
  milk, chilled
1 (8-ounce) package cream cheese, softened

* Bring gelatin, sugar and water to a boil in small saucepan, stirring to dissolve sugar
  and gelatin.
* Remove from heat and stir in fruit; set aside to cool.
* Beat together condensed milk and cream cheese until smooth.
* Blend in gelatin mixture. Add nuts.
* Pour into a 9-cup mold. Chill until firm.

Sally Gaddy

WILD BLUEBERRY SALAD OR DESSERT
Children love this one!

Serves: 12

1 (6-ounce) package raspberry or grape
  gelatin
1-3/4 cups hot water
1 can blueberries, well drained
1 large can crushed pineapple, drained
  and juice reserved
1 cup chopped nuts (optional)

1 cup pineapple juice (may add water to
  bring to 1 cup)
1 (8-ounce) package cream cheese
1/2 cup granulated sugar
1/2 pint sour cream
1/2 teaspoon vanilla

* Dissolve gelatin in hot water. Add pineapple juice, berries and pineapple. Mix well.
* Pour into 13x9-inch pan. Chill until firm.
* Whip cream cheese, sugar, sour cream and vanilla until smooth and fluffy. Add nuts.
* Spread cream cheese mixture over salad. Chill.

Mildred Thompson
Judy DuBose

GRAPEFRUIT PARTY SALAD

Serves: 8-12

1 cup water, divided
1/2 cup sugar
2 envelopes plain gelatin
2 to 3 grapefruits, halved
Dressing:
1 teaspoon grated onion
1 teaspoon dry mustard
1 teaspoon celery seeds

1 (8-1/4-ounce) can crushed pineapple,
 undrained
1/2 cup chopped pecans

1/4 cup sugar (scant)
1 cup salad oil
1 tablespoon vinegar

* Bring 1/2 cup water and sugar to boil.
* Dissolve gelatin in 1/2 cup cold water. Add to sugar water. Set aside.
* Remove all grapefruit sections and membrane from halves. Reserve grapefruit sections and halves.
* Add pineapple, grapefruit sections and pecans to gelatin mixture. Pour mixture into grapefruit halves. Refrigerate until congealed.
* Mix dressing ingredients together until well blended.
* Slice grapefruit cups in half. Serve topped with dressing.

Lee Russo

LEMON FRUIT MOLD

Delicious complement to brunch or dinner

Serves: 6

1 (6-ounce) package lemon gelatin
3 cups boiling water
1/3 cup mayonnaise
1 (3-ounce) package cream cheese, cubed

1/3 cup frozen lemonade concentrate
fresh fruit for garnish, such as kiwi,
 strawberries or seedless grape halves

* Dissolve gelatin in boiling water. Reserve 3/4 cup. Let stand at room temperature.
* Pour remaining gelatin into blender. Add mayonnaise, cream cheese and lemonade. Blend until smooth. Pour into 9-inch pie plate. Refrigerate until firm.
* Arrange fruit over top of mold and refrigerate.
* Refrigerate reserved gelatin until thick enough to coat a spoon.
* Carefully spoon over fruit to glaze. Refrigerate until firm.

Judi Tingler

ORANGE SALAD

Cool and refreshing - great summer salad!

Easy   Serves: 12

2 (3-ounce) packages orange gelatin   2 (11-ounce) cans mandarin oranges,
2 cups boiling water   reserving juice
1 pint orange sherbet   1 teaspoon lemon juice
1 (8-ounce) container frozen whipped   2 bananas, sliced (optional)
   topping

* Dissolve gelatin in water. Add reserved orange juice.
* Add orange sherbet; stir until dissolved. Chill until mixture thickens slightly.
* Add whipped topping, oranges, lemon juice and bananas. Chill in 13x9-inch pan until firm.

Pam Funderburk

SEAFOAM SALAD

Serves: 6-8

1 (16-ounce) can pears   1 (3-ounce) package cream cheese, softened
1 (3-ounce) package lime-flavored   1 (2-ounce) package whipped topping mix
   gelatin

* Drain pears, reserving juice. Mash pears. Set aside.
* Add enough water to pear juice to make 1 cup of liquid.
* Heat liquid. Add gelatin, stirring until dissolved. Chill until slightly set.
* Beat cream cheese until smooth; add pears.
* Prepare whipped topping mix according to package directions.
* Fold cream cheese mixture and whipped topping into gelatin.
* Pour into a 4-cup mold. Chill until firm.

Maria Kleto

PINK CHRISTMAS FROZEN FRUIT SALAD
Blue Ribbon Winner

Easy   Serves: 8

1 (8-ounce) package cream cheese,   1 (8-ounce) can whole cranberry sauce
  softened   1 cup crushed pineapple, drained
2 tablespoons mayonnaise or salad   1/2 cup chopped pecans
  dressing   1 cup frozen whipped topping
2 tablespoons sugar

* Blend cream cheese, mayonnaise, sugar, cranberry sauce, crushed pineapple and nuts.
* Fold in whipped topping.
* Place paper muffin cups in muffin tins. Fill with salad mixture. Cover with plastic wrap. Freeze.
* After frozen, cups may be placed in a plastic bag and kept in freezer until ready to use.

Pat Kelly

CONGEALED ASPARAGUS SALAD
A colorful sweet-sour salad

Easy - Prepare ahead   Serves: 8

2 envelopes unflavored gelatin   1/2 cup diced celery
1/2 cup cold water   1/2 cup chopped pecans
1 cup water   1 (2-ounce) jar chopped pimientos
1 cup sugar   1 (15-ounce) can cut asparagus, drained
1/2 cup vinegar   juice of 1 lemon
1/2 teaspoon salt   1 teaspoon grated onion

* Dissolve gelatin in 1/2 cup cold water.
* Boil water, sugar, vinegar and salt. Combine with softened gelatin.
* Place in refrigerator until slightly thickened.
* Add remaining ingredients. Pour into 9-inch square pan. Refrigerate until congealed.

Ruth Fitzpatrick

107

MOLDED BROCCOLI SALAD

Prepare ahead   Serves: 8

1 can beef consommé
1 envelope plus 1 teaspoon plain gelatin,
   softened in 1/4 cup water
3/4 cup mayonnaise
1 (10-ounce) package chopped broccoli,
   cooked and drained

3 hard-boiled eggs, chopped
1 small jar green olives, sliced
1 (2-ounce) jar chopped pimientos
1 tablespoon onion juice
1 tablespoon Worcestershire sauce
salt and pepper to taste

* Heat consommé. Stir in softened gelatin until dissolved.
* Whisk mayonnaise with gelatin mixture until completely blended.
* Stir in broccoli, eggs, olives, pimientos and seasonings.
* Pour into 1-1/2-quart mold. Chill until firm.

Joanna Fox

CONGEALED GAZPACHO
Wonderfully cool in the summer

Serves: 8-10

2 packages plain gelatin
3 cups tomato juice
1/4 cup wine vinegar
1 clove garlic, crushed
2 teaspoons salt
1/4 teaspoon pepper
dash of cayenne pepper
2 tomatoes, chopped and drained
1/2 cup finely chopped onion

3/4 cup finely chopped green pepper
3/4 cup chopped cucumber, drained
greens
1/2 cup sour cream
1/2 teaspoon salt
1/3 cup mayonnaise
hot pepper pickles
pickled okra

* Soften gelatin in 1 cup tomato juice. Heat to simmer.
* Pour into bowl and add rest of tomato juice, vinegar, garlic, salt, pepper and dash of cayenne pepper.
* Chill until mixture begins to set. Fold in chopped vegetables.
* Pour into oiled 6-cup mold. Chill until set. Unmold on a bed of greens.
* Mix sour cream, salt and mayonnaise; spread on top.
* Surround with pickled peppers and okra.

Hilda Rutherford

ARTICHOKES ON THE SIDE
A delicious salad or side dish

Easy   Serves: 4

3 tablespoons olive oil or salad oil   3 tablespoons minced parsley
1 small onion, chopped   3 tablespoons red wine vinegar
3 cloves garlic, mashed   salt and pepper to taste
6 to 7 artichoke hearts, drained   lettuce leaves
1 (16-ounce) can tomatoes, chopped

* Heat oil. Sauté onion and garlic until soft.
* Add artichokes. Sauté 6 to 8 minutes or until artichokes are slightly tender.
* Add tomatoes, parsley, red wine vinegar, salt and pepper. Simmer 10 minutes.
* Serve on lettuce leaves.

Lee Russo

MARINATED BEANS
Always a hit at parties!

Serves: 15-20

1 (15-ounce) can of each of the following: 1 cup chopped celery
   shoe peg corn, green lima beans, cut   1-1/2 cups vinegar
   string beans, wax beans, red kidney   1-1/2 cups oil
   beans, green peas   1 tablespoon basil
1 (2-1/2-ounce) jar pimientos   1-1/2 tablespoons dry mustard
large jar button mushrooms   1 cup sugar
1 small onion, chopped   1-1/2 teaspoons salt
1 green pepper, chopped

* Drain cans and jars of vegetables.
* Toss vegetables with onion, green pepper and celery.
* Mix vinegar, oil, basil, mustard, sugar and salt, stirring until sugar is dissolved.
* Pour over vegetable mixture. Marinate for several hours or overnight.

Louise Lucas

BROCCOLI SALAD

Serves: 6-8

1 bunch broccoli	*1/2 cup sugar*
1 small red onion, chopped	*1 cup mayonnaise*
1/2 pound of bacon	*3 tablespoons red wine vinegar*

* Cut broccoli into bite-sized pieces. Blanch broccoli for 3 minutes; drain and cool.
* Fry bacon until crispy (do not use microwave). Crumble bacon. Add to broccoli.
* Add onion to broccoli mixture. Refrigerate.
* Mix together sugar, mayonnaise and vinegar. Refrigerate.
* Just before serving, combine dressing and broccoli. Stir well.
* May need to adjust amount of dressing according to size of broccoli bunch.

Noreen Moody

BROCCOLI-RAISIN SALAD

Good at a picnic instead of potato salad

Easy - Prepare ahead   Serves: 6-8

1 large bunch broccoli, cut into small florets, or 1/2 bunch broccoli and 1/2 head cauliflower florets	*1/2 cup raisins*
	1/2 cup finely chopped red onion
1/2 cup sunflower seeds	*1/2 pound bacon, fried crisp, drained and crumbled*
Dressing:	
1 cup light mayonnaise	*1/2 cup sugar*
2 tablespoons vinegar	

* Mix broccoli, sunflower seeds, raisins and onion.
* Blend dressing ingredients with wire whisk. Add to broccoli mixture. Chill overnight.
* Before serving add bacon and toss well.

Becky Pickens, John Leistler
Noreen Moody, Karen Rottinghaus

Variation: Omit sunflower seeds. Add 1 cup grated Cheddar cheese with the bacon before serving.

Peg Kempert

DUTCH CUCUMBERS IN SOUR CREAM

Easy - Prepare ahead

Yields: 2-3 cups

*1 medium cucumber, peeled and thinly
    sliced*
*1 medium cucumber, unpeeled and thinly
    sliced*
1-1/2 teaspoons salt
Sauce:
2/3 cup mayonnaise
2/3 cup sour cream
1 tablespoon dill weed

*1 large onion, thinly sliced and separated
    into rings*
3/4 cup water
1/4 cup vinegar
1 teaspoon sugar

1 teaspoon Beau Monde seasoning
1 tablespoon dry parsley flakes
1 tablespoon onion flakes

* Place cucumbers and onion in bowl. Sprinkle with salt. Toss.
* Combine water, vinegar and sugar. Pour over cucumber and onion.
* Let stand at room temperature for 1 hour. Drain well.
* Combine ingredients for sauce. Pour over cucumber mixture. Mix well.
* Chill before serving.

Gail Bell

MANDY'S CRUNCHY PEA SALAD

Easy - Prepare ahead

Serves: 8-10

2 (10-ounce) packages frozen green peas
1/4 cup chopped green onions
1 cup chopped celery
1/8 teaspoon pepper
1/2 teaspoon salt

1/2 teaspoon basil
1 pint sour cream
1 cup chopped crisp bacon
1 cup cashew pieces

* Thaw green peas under warm water. Dry on towel. Mix peas with next 6 ingredients.
* Refrigerate 4 hours or overnight. Add bacon and cashews prior to serving.

Nancy Wohlbruck

Variation: Add 1 cup finely chopped cauliflower or broccoli. Substitute 1 cup ranch
dressing for half of the sour cream. Omit the basil.

Hilda Rutherford

111

DILLED POTATO SALAD

Easy - Prepare ahead   Serves: 6-8

4 medium red potatoes
1/2 cup sour cream
1/2 cup mayonnaise
2 green onions, minced, tops included
1 tablespoon fresh dill or 1-1/2 teaspoons
   dried dillweed

2 teaspoons Dijon mustard
1-1/2 teaspoons lemon juice
1/2 teaspoon salt
freshly ground pepper to taste
1/2 pound bacon, fried and crumbled

* Boil potatoes 30 minutes, or until tender. Rinse in cold water. Cut in 1/2-inch cubes. Set aside.
* In large bowl, combine sour cream, mayonnaise, onions, dill, mustard, lemon juice, salt and pepper.
* Add potatoes and toss well. Chill overnight.
* Garnish with crumbled bacon just before serving.

Crickett Byler-Martyn

PERUVIAN POTATO SALAD

This salad is one chili fans will love.

Serves: 6-8

6 medium potatoes, pared and cubed
2 hard-boiled eggs, mashed
1 small onion, finely chopped
1 cup shredded Cheddar cheese
1 teaspoon salt

1 jalapeño or green chili pepper, finely
   chopped
2 tablespoons olive oil or vegetable oil
1/2 cup light cream
iceberg lettuce

* In a saucepan, cook potatoes in boiling, salted water for 15 minutes, or until tender. Drain.
* Return potatoes to saucepan and shake over low heat until dry. Place in a large bowl.
* Mix eggs, onion, cheese, pepper and salt together in small bowl.
* Slowly stir olive oil into egg mixture, blending well. Add cream. Stir until smooth.
* Pour egg mixture over potatoes. Toss until evenly coated.
* Chill about an hour.
* Serve in a large lettuce-lined salad bowl.

Cecilia Briceno

SOUR CREAM POTATO SALAD

Easy - Prepare ahead

Serves: 10-12

8 to 12 medium red potatoes
1-1/2 cups mayonnaise
1 cup sour cream
1-1/2 teaspoons horseradish
1 teaspoon celery seeds

1/2 teaspoon salt
1 cup chopped fresh parsley or 1/2 cup
dried parsley
2 medium onions, finely chopped

* Boil potatoes in skins until cooked. Cut into 1/8-inch slices.
* Combine mayonnaise, sour cream, horseradish, celery seeds and salt.
* Combine parsley and onions.
* In large serving bowl, layer potatoes, dressing, then parsley and onions. Do not stir.
* Refrigerate at least 8 hours.

Karen Pritchett

ZUCCHINI SALAD

Easy

Serves: 4

2 small zucchini, julienne sliced
1 small green pepper, julienne sliced
1 small tomato, chopped
Dressing:
2 tablespoons lemon juice
3 tablespoons olive oil
1-1/2 teaspoons white wine vinegar

1/4 cup chopped parsley
4 olives, chopped
2 large green onions, thinly sliced

1/2 teaspoon dillweed
salt and pepper to taste

* Combine all salad ingredients.
* Mix dressing ingredients together. Pour over salad and toss.
* Refrigerate until chilled.
* Drain salad. Serve on lettuce leaves.

Variation: This salad may also be tossed undrained with cooked fettuccine or any other pasta.

Nola Linker

CRUNCHY SLAW
This unique recipe adds delicious crunch to meals.

Serves: 8-10

*1 head cabbage, shredded or 1/2 red
    and 1/2 green cabbage
1/4 cup slivered almonds, toasted*
Dressing:
*1 chicken bouillon cube
2 tablespoons hot water
1/2 teaspoon garlic powder*

*1/4 cup sesame seeds, toasted
1 (3-ounce) package Ramen noodles (or
    oriental noodle soup mix), crumbled*

*1 tablespoon fresh parsley
1/2 cup olive oil
1/4 cup vinegar*

* Toss cabbage, almonds, sesame seeds and crumbled, uncooked noodles.
* Just before serving add dressing and mix well.
* To prepare dressing, dissolve bouillon cube in 2 tablespoons very hot water. Add remaining ingredients and mix well.

Pat Ford

Dressing Variation: Mix seasoning package from noodle soup mix, 1/2 teaspoon pepper, 1/3 cup oil, 2 tablespoons red wine vinegar and 2 tablespoons sugar. Add dressing just before serving.

Laura Courter, Debbie Ferguson

FAVORITE SLAW
A picnic tradition

Easy

Serves: 4-6

*1/2 head cabbage, grated
2 tablespoons sugar
juice of 1 lemon*

*4 tablespoons mayonnaise
salt and pepper to taste
1 carrot, grated (optional)*

* Grate cabbage. Sprinkle cabbage with sugar. Toss.
* Squeeze lemon juice over cabbage. Mix in mayonnaise. Add salt and pepper to taste.
* Refrigerate 30 minutes prior to serving for flavors to blend.
* May add grated carrot for color.

Christy Spencer

TRUE CAESAR SALAD

1 head romaine lettuce	1/2 small red onion, thinly sliced into rings
2 hard French rolls	3/4 cup Parmesan or Romano cheese
2 garlic cloves, divided	1 egg
2 tablespoons olive oil	1 anchovy
2 slices bacon	freshly ground salt and pepper
juice of 1 large lemon	1 teaspoon Dijon mustard

Several hours ahead of time:
* Wash romaine, drain and refrigerate.
* Put 1 clove garlic in 2 tablespoons olive oil; set aside.
* Cut French rolls into 1/2-inch to 3/4-inch cubes. Bake at 200° for 2 hours, until crisp.

Thirty minutes ahead of time:
* Cook bacon. Reserve grease in pan. Bring egg to room temperature.

When ready to serve:
* Heat and stir croutons in bacon grease.
* Rub anchovy in bottom of wooden bowl. Rub 1 clove garlic in bottom of the bowl.
* Break up romaine into bowl. Add onion rings.
* Grind fresh pepper and salt over all. Add cheese and toss.
* Remove garlic from oil. Pour oil over all. Pour lemon juice over all.
* Add Dijon mustard. Break raw egg over salad. Toss well.

Rizzie Baldwin, Carol Leavelle, Susan Hill

JANE'S INDIAN SPINACH SALAD WITH DRESSING

8 cups spinach, washed and torn into pieces	1/2 cup golden raisins
	1/2 cup peanuts or broken walnuts
1-1/2 cups pared and thinly sliced red apples	2 to 3 green onions, sliced

Dressing:

1/4 cup vinegar	1/2 teaspoon salt
1/4 cup canola oil	1-1/2 teaspoons curry powder
2 tablespoons chutney	1 teaspoon dry mustard
2 teaspoons sugar	

* Combine salad ingredients. Chill until ready to serve.
* Mix all dressing ingredients together. Toss with salad just before serving.

Ellen Knott

FRESH SPINACH SALAD WITH FRUIT
Very colorful and festive

Serves: 6

1 pound fresh spinach, washed and torn
2 kiwis, sliced
Honey Mustard Dressing:
1/2 cup honey
1/4 cup cider or white wine vinegar
1 tablespoon lemon juice
2 tablespoons Dijon mustard

1 pint fresh strawberries, sliced

1 (1-inch) slice of onion
1 teaspoon poppy seeds
1/4 teaspoon salt
1 cup vegetable oil

* In food processor make Honey Mustard Dressing. Combine honey, vinegar, lemon juice, mustard, onion, poppy seeds, salt and 1/4 cup oil. Process until smooth.
* Slowly pour in remaining 3/4 cup oil. Process until well blended.
* Combine spinach, strawberries and kiwis in salad bowl.
* Pour about 1 cup dressing over salad. Toss well.

Gina Clegg
Diane Thomas

WARM SPINACH SALAD

Easy

Serves: 8

2 (8-ounce) cans sliced water chestnuts,
  drained
1 pound fresh spinach
Warm Dressing:
1 cup oil
1/4 cup wine vinegar
1 medium onion, chopped
1/2 cup sugar

4 hard-boiled eggs, sliced
1 pound fresh bean sprouts
1/2 pound bacon, fried and crumbled

1 teaspoon Worcestershire sauce
1/3 cup ketchup
2 teaspoons salt

* Wash and dry spinach.
* Combine with other ingredients in salad bowl. Toss.
* Mix dressing ingredients together. Heat but do not boil.
* Pour warm dressing over salad. Toss well. Serve immediately.

Pat Coyle

ITALIAN SALAD

Great with lasagna or spaghetti

Easy   Serves: 6-8

1/3 pound fresh green beans   *1 ounce chopped pimientos*
1 head iceberg lettuce, shredded   *3/4 cup olive oil*
1/2 head romaine lettuce, shredded   *1/4 cup vinegar*
1 (6-ounce) jar marinated artichoke *1/4 cup Parmesan cheese*
* hearts, drained and quartered* *salt and pepper to taste*

* Cook green beans until crisp-tender. Chill. Cut into 1 to 2-inch lengths.
* Combine lettuce, pimientos, artichoke hearts and beans. Toss well.
* Combine oil, vinegar and Parmesan in a shaker; mix well.
* Coat salad greens generously with dressing. Add salt and pepper.

Pat Kelly

MANDARIN ORANGE SALAD

Easy   Serves: 4-6

1 head iceberg lettuce   *1 (11-ounce) can mandarin oranges,*
romaine lettuce   * drained*
celery, chopped   *1/4 cup slivered almonds*
2 green onions, chopped   *1 tablespoon sugar*
Dressing:
1/4 cup vegetable oil   *1/2 teaspoon salt*
2 tablespoons sugar   *1/4 teaspoon pepper*
2 tablespoons cider vinegar   *dash soy sauce*
1 tablespoon parsley

* Combine all ingredients for dressing. Shake well.
* Combine almonds and sugar. Brown carefully under broiler.
* Combine remaining salad ingredients. Pour dressing over salad.
* Add almonds and toss.

Mary Edwards

HAMMED-UP 7-LAYER SALAD
Looks great in a glass bowl!

Easy - Prepare ahead

Serves: 12

1/2 bag spinach, washed and torn into
  bite-size pieces
1/2 teaspoon sugar
6 to 8 hard-boiled eggs, sliced
1/2 to 3/4 pound ham, diced
1/2 head iceburg lettuce
1 (16-ounce) bag frozen peas, defrosted
  and towel-dried

1 red onion, diced
3/4 to 1 cup sour cream
3/4 to 1 cup mayonnaise
3/4 pound Swiss cheese, cut into small
  strips
optional toppings: bacon bits, crabmeat,
  shrimp

* Sprinkle spinach pieces with 1/2 teaspoon of sugar and place in serving bowl.
* Layer in order: eggs, ham, lettuce, peas, onions.
* Mix sour cream and mayonnaise together. Spread over layered salad. Top with Swiss cheese.
* Cover and refrigerate several hours or overnight.
* Garnish with bacon bits, crabmeat or shrimp.

Maureen Conway

SEVEN-LAYER SALAD

Easy - Prepare ahead

Serves: 12-15

1 head lettuce, chopped
1 cup chopped celery hearts
1 cup chopped bell pepper
1-1/2 cups chopped onion
1 (10-ounce) package frozen peas

1 pint mayonnaise
3 tablespoons sugar
1/4 cup grated Parmesan cheese
1 small jar bacon bits

* Layer, in order, first 5 ingredients.
* Spread mayonnaise on top. Sprinkle with sugar.
* Cover and refrigerate overnight.
* Just before serving add Parmesan cheese and bacon bits. Toss lightly, mixing well.

Mary Wallace
Crickett Byler-Martyn
Pattie Bethune

DAVID'S SPECIAL SALAD
Your food processor is a big help with this one!

Serves: 6-8

1 small onion, chopped
6 slices Genoa salami, chopped
6 strips bacon, cooked and crumbled
12 stuffed green olives, sliced
1 small summer squash, chopped
4 to 6 mushrooms, sliced

1 cup grated Cheddar cheese
3 hard-boiled eggs, grated
salt and pepper, to taste
1 head iceberg lettuce
1 (8-ounce) bottle Italian dressing

* Mix all ingredients except lettuce and dressing.
* Tear lettuce into bite-sized pieces. Add to salad.
* Pour dressing over salad. Toss well.

Pat Kelly

ANTIPASTO SALAD
Great for cookouts - serves a large group

Easy - Prepare ahead

Serves: 8-10

Part 1:
1/2 pound seashell macaroni
1/2 pound rotini twists, colored variety
1/4 pound Genoa salami, cubed
1/4 pound pepperoni, cubed
1 green pepper, chopped
3 stalks celery, diced
Part 2:
1/2 teaspoon salt
1 teaspoon oregano
1/2 teaspoon basil

1 small onion, chopped
1 small jar green olives, drained
1 small can black olives, drained
3 tomatoes, diced
1/2 pound Provolone cheese, cubed

1/2 teaspoon pepper
3/4 cup olive oil
1/2 cup apple cider vinegar

* Cook macaroni and rotini twists according to package directions. Drain well.
* In large bowl combine all ingredients in Part 1. Toss well.
* Combine ingredients in Part 2. Pour over salad; toss well.
* Cover with plastic wrap. Refrigerate at least 8 hours.

Margo Colasanti

FUSILLI SALAD
Hearty and colorful entree salad

Easy   Serves: 6

16 ounces white or green fusilli, cooked
   and drained (linguine or fettuccine may
   be substituted)
1 (7-ounce) jar roasted red peppers,
   drained, rinsed and cut into 1-inch pieces

1 (6-ounce) jar marinated artichoke hearts,
   drained, rinsed and halved
1 (6-ounce) can pitted large black olives,
   drained, rinsed and halved

Dressing:

3 tablespoons corn oil
3 tablespoon rice vinegar
1 tablespoon freshly grated Parmesan
   cheese

1 teaspoon dried oregano
4 teaspoons fresh basil or 1 teaspoon dried
   basil

* In a large serving bowl, gently combine the pasta with the vegetables and olives.
* Whisk together the dressing ingredients.
* Pour dressing over salad. Toss well.
* Serve immediately or cover and refrigerate until ready to serve.

Nancy Langston

PASTA SALAD
Great for informal gatherings

Serves: 15-20

2 (8-ounce) boxes spiral pasta
1 envelope dry zesty Italian dressing
1 cup chopped parsley
1/2 (10-ounce) jar sliced green olives
2 bunches green onions, sliced

1-1/2 cups chopped celery
4 tablespoons vinegar
2 tablespoons Dijon mustard
salt, pepper and mayonnaise to taste

* Cook pasta according to box directions. Rinse with cool water.
* Place in a large bowl. Sprinkle with envelope of dressing while still warm.
* Allow pasta to cool. Add all other ingredients. Toss well. Chill until ready to serve.
* For main dish, add 2 pounds cooked and peeled shrimp or chopped ham.

Terry Klapthor
Shirley Griffin

PASTA SALAD WITH FRESH TOMATOES

Easy   Serves: 4

8 ounces pasta
3 large tomatoes, peeled, seeded and cut
   into pieces
1 clove garlic, peeled and finely chopped
1 small onion, peeled and finely chopped
1 teaspoon basil

1/2 teaspoon oregano
1/2 teaspoon rosemary
dash black pepper
1/2 cup olive oil
juice of 1 lemon

* Cook pasta according to package directions. Toss pasta with remaining ingredients.
* Can be held at room temperature for half a day.

Donna Mauerhan

TORTELLINI SALAD

Serves: 10-12

2 cups fresh snow peas
boiling water
2 cups broccoli florets
2-1/2 cups cherry tomatoes, halved
2 cups fresh mushrooms, sliced
Dressing:
1/2 cup sliced green onions
1/3 cup red wine vinegar
1/3 cup vegetable oil
1/3 cup olive oil
2 tablespoons fresh parsley, chopped
2 cloves garlic, minced

1 (7-3/4-ounce) can whole pitted ripe olives
1 (8-ounce) package cheese-stuffed
   tortellini, cooked and cooled
3 ounces fettuccine, cooked and cooled
1 tablespoon grated Parmesan cheese

2 teaspoons dried basil
1 teaspoon dried dillweed
1 teaspoon salt and 1/2 teaspoon pepper
1/2 teaspoon sugar
1/2 teaspoon dried oregano
1-1/2 teaspoons Dijon mustard

* Drop snow peas into boiling water. Boil 1 minute and remove with slotted spoon.
* Place broccoli in boiling water. Boil 1 minute. Drain.
* Combine peas, broccoli, tomatoes, mushrooms and olives.
* Combine vegetables, pasta and Parmesan cheese in a very large bowl.
* Combine salad dressing ingredients in a jar and cover tightly. Shake vigorously to mix.
* Pour dressing over pasta mixture. Toss well.
* Chill several hours before serving. Can garnish with additional Parmesan cheese.

Mary Lou Stafford

CREAMY TUNA TWIST
Great luncheon salad

Serves: 6-8

4 ounces twist macaroni, cooked and
    drained
1 cup mayonnaise
2 tablespoons cider vinegar
1 tablespoon dried dill weed (or 3
    tablespoons fresh dill weed)

dash of pepper
1 (7-ounce) can tuna, drained and flaked
1 cup frozen peas, thawed
1 cup sliced celery
1/2 cup chopped red onion
fresh lemon to taste (optional)

* In a large bowl, stir together mayonnaise, vinegar, dill and pepper until smooth.
* Add remaining ingredients. Toss well. Cover and chill.

Sue Kaliski

CURRY RICE SALAD
Everyone asks for this recipe.

Serves: 8-10

1 cup mayonnaise
1 cup chopped celery
1/2 cup Major Grey's chutney
4 green onions, chopped
1/2 to 1 teaspoon curry powder

1 cup uncooked rice, cooked according to
    package directions and cooled
1 (10-ounce) package frozen green peas,
    thawed and drained

* Combine first 5 ingredients.
* Toss with peas and rice.
* Cover and refrigerate several hours or overnight.
* Serve on lettuce leaf or stuff in tomatoes.

Variation: Add 1/2 cup cooked shrimp or crabmeat.

Nancy Wohlbruck

IMPERIAL EMERALD RICE

So good that you will be asked to make this over and over

Make ahead

Serves: 6

*1 box curried rice, cooked as directed
  and cooled
1/2 cup chopped onion
1/2 cup sliced celery
1-1/2 cups green grape halves*

*1/2 cup sliced water chestnuts, rinsed
1 cup cashews
1/2 cup mayonnaise
spinach leaves*

* Combine first 6 ingredients in large bowl.
* Add mayonnaise. Mix well.
* Refrigerate until time to serve. Best if made a day ahead.
* Line salad bowl with spinach leaves. Mound rice in center and serve.

Robin Lowe

SALEM CHICKEN-RICE SALAD

Easy - Prepare ahead

Serves: 8-10

*4 chicken breast halves
2 cups uncooked rice
2 to 3 tablespoons vegetable oil
2 to 3 tablespoons dried tarragon
2 to 3 tablespoons fresh lemon juice*

*salt and pepper to taste
1 green pepper, chopped
1 (8-ounce) package mushrooms, sliced
  (optional)*

* Steam chicken. Cool and shred.
* Cook rice and cool.
* Combine all ingredients and toss. Cover and refrigerate overnight.
* Add more seasonings if desired.

Jennie Sheppard

TROPICAL CRAB SALAD
Also delicious with chicken or tuna

Easy   Serves: 6-8

1 cup uncooked rice
1-1/4 cups pineapple juice
2 cups mayonnaise
1/3 cup chopped green onions
2 teaspoons curry powder
2 (6-ounce) packages frozen crab,
* thawed and drained*

1 (16-ounce) can mixed Chinese vegetables
* drained*
1 can water chestnuts, sliced and drained
1 cup sliced celery
1 (11-ounce) can pineapple chunks
* (optional)*

* Cook rice according to package directions, substituting 1 cup pineapple juice for 1 cup of the required liquid. Cool.
* Blend 1/4 cup pineapple juice with mayonnaise, onions and curry. Toss with rice mixture. Chill.
* Mix rice, crab, vegetables and pineapple.

The Hawk

SHRIMP REMOULADE

Easy - Prepare ahead   Serves: 8

6 tablespoons oil
2 tablespoons vinegar
1 tablespoon paprika
1/2 teaspoon salt

4 tablespoons Creole mustard
2 tablespoons finely chopped onion
3 pounds shrimp, cooked and cleaned

* Mix first 6 ingredients.
* Toss with shrimp and chill.
* Serve cold on a bed of lettuce.

Billie Nichols

SHRIMP AND RICE SALAD

Great flavor combination for luncheon, picnic or summer supper

Serves: 6

2 cups cooked rice
2 cups cooked shrimp
1-1/2 cups chopped raw cauliflower or
  broccoli florets
1/2 cup chopped green pepper
2 tablespoons lemon juice

2 tablespoons chopped green olives
2 tablespoons chopped green onions
1 cup mayonnaise
1/4 cup French dressing
1 teaspoon salt
pepper to taste

* Combine lemon juice, olives, onions, mayonnaise, French dressing, salt and pepper. Mix well.
* Toss the remaining ingredients with the dressing.
* Chill.

Ellen Knott

ALMOND-ORIENTAL CHICKEN SALAD

Easy

Serves: 4

1/4 cup soy sauce or teriyaki sauce
3 tablespoons lemon juice
1/4 teaspoon hot red pepper flakes
  (optional)
1/3 cup vegetable oil

1 cup slivered almonds, toasted
3 cups cooked, cubed chicken
1/2 to 1 cup thinly sliced green onions
1 (7-ounce) package frozen snow peas,
  thawed

* Combine soy sauce with lemon juice and pepper flakes.
* Beat in oil, using wire whisk.
* Combine remaining ingredients in large bowl. Pour dressing over; toss and chill.

Pamela Cooke

CARMEN'S BLT CHICKEN SALAD

Serves: 6-8

4 large boneless chicken breasts,
   cooked and cut in bite-sized pieces
mixed salad greens, torn in pieces
3 tomatoes, chopped
bacon bits

1 cup mayonnaise
1 cup barbecue sauce
2 tablespoons lemon juice
1 tablespoon grated onion

* Place chicken, lettuce, tomatoes and bacon bits in separate bowls.
* Mix together mayonnaise, barbecue sauce, lemon juice and grated onion. Place in bowl. Have each guest create his own salad.

Martha Schmitt

CHICKEN SALAD WITH SNOW PEAS

Serves: 6

4 chicken breast halves, skinned and
   boned
2 tablespoons butter, melted
1 (10-ounce) package frozen snow peas
Dressing:
2 tablespoons light soy sauce
1 tablespoon rice vinegar
zest and juice of 1 lemon
2 tablespoons honey

1 cup sliced water chestnuts, drained
juice of 1 lemon
zest of 1 orange and 1 lime
salt and pepper to taste

1/2 cup light vegetable oil (safflower is
   best)
1/4 teaspoon Szechuan pepper (found in
   oriental food stores)

* Put chicken in baking dish sprayed with non-stick spray.
* Pour butter evenly over chicken. Salt and pepper to taste. Add lemon juice.
* Cover tightly with aluminum foil. Bake at 350° for 35 to 45 minutes (the meat should be done and tender but still moist).
* Blanch snow peas 30 to 45 seconds. Drain. Cool in ice water; drain again. Chill overnight.
* Cool chicken. Shred meat. Mix ingredients for dressing. Toss with meat.
* Add water chestnuts. Toss again. Mix in zest of orange and lime. (Zest can be made by peeling rind very thinly, then slicing in tiny strips.)
* To serve, fan snow peas on edge of platter. Spoon salad in center.

Beth Auch

HOT CHINESE CHICKEN SALAD

Easy   Serves: 4

8 chicken thighs, boned and cubed   1 (4-ounce) can sliced mushrooms, drained
1/4 cup corn starch   1 cup slant-sliced celery
1/4 cup oil   1 cup chopped onion
1/8 teaspoon garlic powder   1/4 cup soy sauce
1 large tomato, cubed   1 teaspoon Accent
1/3 cup sliced water chestnuts   2 cups shredded lettuce

* Roll chicken cubes in corn starch.
* In wok, brown in oil over high heat.
* Sprinkle with garlic.
* Add rest of ingredients, except lettuce, and stir.
* Cover, reduce heat and simmer 5 minutes.
* Remove from heat.
* Serve over lettuce or rice if desired.

Lynne Greenoe

JAN'S CHICKEN SALAD

Easy   Serves: 6

4 cups diced, cooked chicken   1/3 cup sour cream
3/4 cup diced celery   1/4 cup slivered almonds
1/4 cup French dressing   1-1/2 cups crushed potato chips
salt and pepper to taste   1 cup grated sharp Cheddar cheese
1/3 cup mayonnaise

* Combine chicken, celery, French dressing, salt and pepper. Cover and chill overnight.
* Combine mayonnaise and sour cream. Add to chicken. Chill.
* Add almonds. Place in shallow ovenproof dish.
* Mix together potato chips and cheese. Sprinkle on chicken.
* Melt cheese under broiler. Watch carefully to keep from burning. Chicken will not be hot.

Joan Erwin

LOW-CAL HIGH-CRUNCH CHICKEN SALAD
Crunchiness makes up for the missing calories.

Easy - Must be prepared ahead

Serves: 4-6

1/2 cup apple juice
1 tablespoon lemon juice
1/2 teaspoon tarragon leaves, crushed
3/4 teaspoon salt
pepper to taste

2 cups cooked, cubed chicken breast
1 cup diced celery
1 cup diced apple (about 1 medium)
2 tablespoons chopped walnuts
2 tablespoons lowfat plain yogurt

* In small saucepan, combine apple juice, lemon juice, tarragon, salt and pepper. Bring to a boil. Reduce heat and simmer covered about 5 minutes.
* Put chicken in bowl and pour apple juice mixture over chicken. Toss thoroughly.
* Cover chicken and refrigerate overnight.
* Stir in yogurt, celery and apples. Add walnuts just before serving.
* Serve on lettuce leaf.

Dougi O'Bryan

ORIENTAL CHICKEN SALAD
Unusual and delicious

Serves: 6-8

4 tablespoons sesame seeds
4 tablespoons slivered almonds
1 cup light sunflower oil
6 tablespoons rice wine vinegar
3 tablespoons lemon juice
2 tablespoons sesame seed oil
4 tablespoons white sugar
1 teaspoon salt

1/2 teaspoon pepper
1 head cabbage, coarsely cut
4 to 6 green onions, chopped
3 (3-ounce) packages Ramen noodles,
*   broken and cooked according to package*
*   directions*
4 chicken breasts, cooked and shredded

* Toast sesame seeds and almonds until golden. Set aside.
* Combine salad oil, rice wine vinegar, lemon juice, sesame seed oil, sugar, salt and pepper.
* In a large bowl combine cabbage, onions, noodles and chicken. Toss well.
* Add dressing. Toss again. Marinate overnight for best flavor.

Pat Kelly

SUGAR-TREE CHICKEN SALAD
Fabulously different - always a success!

Easy   Serves: 4

3 cups thinly sliced chicken   2 tablespoons snipped chives
10 slices bacon, cooked and crumbled   1 cup croutons
2 small tomatoes, peeled, seeded and   1/2 teaspoon garlic salt
   diced   1/2 teaspoon lemon pepper
Dressing:
2 tablespoons red wine vinegar   1 teaspoon sugar
1 tablespoon fresh lemon juice   1/2 teaspoon salt
1 tablespoon Dijon mustard   3/4 cup vegetable oil

* Season chicken slivers with garlic salt and lemon pepper.
* Marinate chicken in dressing overnight.
* Serve tossed with remaining ingredients. Crumble bacon on top.

Lynn Wheeler

STEAK SALAD

Must prepare ahead   Serves: 8-10

2 pounds boneless sirloin, 2 inches thick   1 (14-ounce) can hearts of palm, drained
salt and freshly ground pepper to taste   and sliced
1/2 pound mushrooms, sliced   2 tablespoons each chopped chives,
6 scallions, sliced   parsley and fresh dill
Mustard Vinaigrette:
1 egg, beaten   1 teaspoon Worcestershire sauce
1/3 cup olive oil   1 teaspoon salt
2 teaspoons Dijon mustard   freshly ground pepper
1-1/2 teaspoons lemon juice   dash of hot pepper sauce
3 tablespoons tarragon vinegar

* Combine vinaigrette ingredients and blend well.
* Season steak with salt and pepper. Broil to medium rare.
* Cool steak. Slice thinly into bite-sized pieces. Combine with next 4 ingredients.
* Pour Mustard Vinaigrette over salad and refrigerate overnight.

Robin Lowe

BLEU CHEESE DRESSING

Easy

1 tablespoon salt	1-1/2 cups vinegar
1 clove garlic	2 ounces bleu cheese
1/2 to 2/3 cup sugar	

* Mix all ingredients in a blender until smooth.
* Delicious with salad of tossed greens, toasted sesame seeds, crumbled bacon and sliced Bermuda onion.

Hanna Kane

BLEU CHEESE WALNUT DRESSING

3/4 cup sour cream	1 teaspoon Worcestershire sauce
1/2 teaspoon dry mustard	1 teaspoon dill weed (optional)
1/2 teaspoon black pepper	4 ounces bleu cheese
1/2 teaspoon salt	1 (2-1/2 ounce) package walnuts
1/2 teaspoon garlic powder	1-1/3 cups mayonnaise

* Blend sour cream, mustard, pepper, salt, garlic powder, Worcestershire sauce and dill weed in mixing bowl at low speed for 2 minutes.
* Add mayonnaise. Blend 1/2 minute at low speed, then 2 minutes at medium speed.
* Crumble bleu cheese by hand into mixture. Blend at low speed for 4 minutes or less.
* Fold in walnuts. Refrigerate for 24 hours before using.

Diane Totherow

BLEU CHEESE VINAIGRETTE

3/4 cup olive oil	2 medium cloves garlic, chopped
1/4 cup red wine vinegar	1 (4-ounce) package bleu cheese, crumbled

* Mix all ingredients. Allow time for flavors to blend in refrigerator.
* Bring to room temperature before serving.
* Serve over salad of mixed greens, sliced red onion, tomatoes, cucumbers, croutons and more crumbled bleu cheese.

Mary Edwards

CHEDDAR CHEESE SALAD DRESSING
From the Blue Boar Inn in San Francisco

Yields: 2-1/2 cups

1-1/2 cups mayonnaise
1/2 cup buttermilk
1/2 cup finely shredded Cheddar cheese
dash of Worcestershire sauce

dash of red wine vinegar or to taste
pinch of salt
pinch of freshly ground black pepper
pinch of freshly ground red pepper

* Combine all ingredients in medium bowl. Blend thoroughly.
* Store in tightly covered container in refrigerator. Use within 2 days.

Terry Casto

DIJON DRESSING
Versatile and delicious!

Easy

Yields: 3/4 cup

1 clove garlic, crushed
1 teaspoon Dijon mustard
1 to 2 tablespoons wine vinegar

1 egg or 1/4 cup egg substitute
1/3 cup olive oil

* Place garlic, mustard, vinegar and egg in jar. Beat with fork.
* Add oil slowly. Continue beating with a fork until egg absorbs all of the oil.
* Place top on jar. Shake vigorously just before serving.
* Can be prepared in food processor.
* Toss with romaine lettuce and 1/4 cup dry breadcrumbs.
* May also use as a dip for vegetables or a topping for baked potatoes.

Nola Linker

HONEY DIJON DRESSING

Yields: 1-1/4 cups

1 cup mayonnaise
1 ounce Dijon mustard

1-1/2 to 2 ounces honey

* Mix well. Store in refrigerator.
* For lower fat, may substitute 1 cup plain nonfat yogurt for mayonnaise.

Ellen Knott

FRENCH DRESSING
Wonderful on fruit and vegetable salads

Easy

Yields: 2 cups

1/2 cup honey or 1/2 cup sugar
2 tablespoons ketchup
1 teaspoon prepared mustard
1 tablespoon horseradish
1/2 teaspoon salt
1/2 teaspoon celery seeds

1 tablespoon chopped parsley
1 clove garlic, minced
1/4 cup vinegar
1/4 cup lemon juice
1 cup salad oil

* Combine all ingredients and shake well before serving.

Anne Rutherford

FRUIT SALAD DRESSING

Easy

Yields: 1-1/2 cups

1/2 cup sugar
1 teaspoon salt
1 teaspoon dry mustard
1 teaspoon celery seeds

1 teaspoon paprika
1 teaspoon grated onion
1 cup vegetable oil
1/2 cup vinegar

* Mix dry ingredients. Add onion.
* In blender, mix oil and vinegar alternately, ending with vinegar.

Ellen Bickett

GREEN GODDESS DRESSING
No one would ever guess anchovies are in it!

Easy   Yields: 1-1/2 cups

1 (2-ounce) can anchovy fillets   1 cup mayonnaise
1 clove garlic   2 scant tablespoons wine or tarragon
1 cup (packed) parsley   vinegar
2 spring onions or 1 small white onion

* In blender or food processor puree all ingredients except mayonnaise.
* Add mayonnaise. Blend.
* Pour over salad greens. Toss well and serve.

Lillian Worthy

HEALTHY RANCH DRESSING

Easy   Yields: 1-1/4 cups

3/4 cup nonfat yogurt   2 tablespoons fresh parsley (or 1
1/2 cup light mayonnaise   tablespoon dried parsley)
2 tablespoons tarragon vinegar   1/4 teaspoon Dijon mustard
1 tablespoon minced onion   1/8 teaspoon garlic powder
1/4 teaspoon celery seeds

* Whisk together all ingredients. Chill. Toss with salad greens.
* May also be used for a raw vegetable dip or as a topping for baked potatoes.

Betsy Mitchell

LAST-MINUTE SALAD DRESSING

Easy

Durkee's Sauce   *red wine vinegar*

* Mix equal amounts of Durkee's Sauce and vinegar. Adjust consistency to suit taste.
* Flavors improve overnight. Leftovers keep well.

Ruth Fitzpatrick

LAURIE'S LOW COUNTRY MUSTARD
Great for gifts

Easy - Prepare ahead   Yields: 1-1/2 quarts

1 quart mayonnaise-type salad dressing   *salt and pepper to taste*
1 cup prepared mustard   *1 small onion, finely grated*
1 cup sugar

* Mix all ingredients. Spoon into small sterilized jars. Keep refrigerated.

Karen Peters

LEMON-MUSTARD DRESSING

Easy   Yields: 3/4 cup

1/2 cup olive or vegetable oil   *1 tablespoon Dijon mustard*
1/4 cup lemon juice   *1/2 teaspoon salt*
2 tablespoons snipped chives   *1/2 teaspoon grated lemon peel*

* Shake all ingredients in a tightly covered jar. Serve on mixed green salad.

Barbara Kane

ROQUEFORT DRESSING SUPREME

Yields: 3 cups

1-1/2 cups buttermilk   *1 tablespoon grated onion*
1 teaspoon lemon juice   *2 cups mayonnaise*
1/2 teaspoon dry mustard   *1/2 pound Roquefort cheese, crumbled*
1/2 teaspoon salt   *(do not use domestic bleu cheese)*
1/2 teaspoon white pepper

* Mix buttermilk, lemon juice, seasonings and onion in a large bowl. Stir until smooth.
* Blend in mayonnaise and Roquefort cheese. Mix thoroughly, leaving a few lumps.
* Store in refrigerator.

Todd Chapman

EGGS AND CHEESE

EGGS BERMICELLI

Easy   Serves: 4

6 eggs   2 tablespoons flour
2 jars button mushrooms   salt and pepper to taste
4 English muffins   2 cups milk
2 tablespoons butter   dash of paprika per serving

* Hard boil 6 eggs. Cool and separate yolks from whites.
* Drain liquid from mushrooms.
* Split and butter English muffins. Toast in 350° oven for 15 minutes.
* To prepare a simple white sauce, melt 2 tablespoons butter; add 2 tablespoons flour to
  form a paste; season with salt and pepper. Add milk gradually and stir until smooth
  and beginning to thicken.
* Stir in mushrooms and chopped egg whites.
* Pour over muffin halves and top with grated egg yolks.
* Garnish each with a dash of paprika.

Kathy Booe

ZIPPY CHEESE OMELET

Easy   Serves: 6

1/2 cup picante sauce   6 eggs
1 cup shredded Monterey Jack   1 (8-ounce) container sour cream
  cheese   picante sauce and tomato wedges for
1 cup shredded Cheddar cheese   garnish

* Pour 1/2 cup picante sauce into lightly greased quiche dish.
* Sprinkle cheeses over sauce.
* Place eggs in food processor and beat thoroughly.
* Add sour cream and process until well blended.
* Pour egg mixture over cheeses.
* Bake uncovered at 350° for 30 to 35 minutes or until set.
* Serve with additional picante sauce and garnish with tomatoes.

Kathy Tuten

24-HOUR WINE AND CHEESE OMELET

Prepare ahead   Serves: 12-16

*1 large loaf day-old French or Italian
  bread, broken into pieces*
6 tablespoons unsalted butter, melted
*3/4 pound domestic Swiss cheese,
  shredded*
*1/2 pound Monterey Jack cheese,
  shredded*
*9 thin slices Genoa salami or ham,
  coarsely chopped*

16 eggs
3-1/4 cups milk
1/2 cup dry white wine
4 large green onions, minced
1 tablespoon Dijon mustard
1/4 teaspoon freshly ground pepper
1/8 teaspoon ground red pepper
1-1/2 cups sour cream
2/3 to 1 cup Parmesan cheese

* Butter 2 (13x9-inch) baking dishes. Spread bread over bottoms and drizzle with butter.
* Sprinkle cheeses and meat over bread.
* Beat together eggs, milk, wine, onion, mustard and peppers until foamy.
* Pour over cheese and meat.
* Cover with foil. Refrigerate overnight or up to 24 hours.
* Remove from refrigerator 30 minutes prior to baking.
* Bake covered at 325° for 1 hour or until set.
* Uncover. Spread top with sour cream. Sprinkle with Parmesan cheese. Bake uncovered until crusty, about 10 minutes.

Rose Hegele

CHEESE GRITS SOUFFLÉ

Easy   Serves: 8-12

4 cups water
1 teaspoon salt
*1 cup white hominy grits (quick grits,
  not instant)*
1 (6-ounce) tube garlic cheese, cubed

1 stick margarine or butter, sliced
3 eggs
1/4 cup milk
*4 ounces extra sharp Cheddar cheese,
  grated*

* Cook grits in boiling salted water 5 minutes. Add garlic cheese, margarine or butter.
* Beat eggs and milk together; fold into grits. Pour into 2-quart baking dish.
* Bake at 350° for 45 minutes. Remove from oven and top with grated Cheddar cheese.

Sallye Wentz

RYE-CHEESE CASSEROLE

Easy - Prepare ahead   Serves: 6-8

10 slices rye bread
butter
prepared mustard
3/4 pound sharp Cheddar cheese, grated
3 eggs

3 cups milk
1/2 teaspoon salt
1/2 teaspoon Worcestershire sauce
dash red pepper
1 to 2 teaspoons caraway seeds

* Lightly butter rye bread on one side.
* Spread very lightly with prepared mustard on other side.
* Cut into 2-inch cubes and put into a 3-quart round baking dish.
* Sprinkle with cheese, reserving a little for top.
* In another bowl beat together eggs, milk and seasonings.
* Pour over casserole and top with extra cheese. Refrigerate for 3 hours to 3 days.
* Set casserole dish into a larger pan with 1 inch of water.
* Bake at 350° for 1 hour and 15 minutes.

Lillian Worthy

SAUSAGE AND GRITS CASSEROLE
I won a cooking contest with this recipe!

Prepare ahead   Serves: 8-10

2 cups water
1/2 teaspoon salt
1/2 cup quick grits
4 cups shredded Cheddar cheese
4 beaten eggs

1 cup milk
1/2 teaspoon dried, whole thyme
1/8 teaspoon garlic salt
2 pounds cooked mild sausage

* Bring water and salt to a boil. Stir in grits.
* Return to a boil and reduce heat. Cook 4 minutes.
* Combine grits and cheese in large mixing bowl; stir until cheese is melted.
* Combine eggs, milk, thyme and garlic salt; mix well.
* Add a small amount of grits mixture to egg mixture; stir well.
* Stir egg mixture into grits mixture. Add sausage and stir.
* Put in a 13x9-inch baking dish. Cover and refrigerate overnight.
* Remove from refrigerator and let stand 15 minutes. Bake at 350° for 50 to 55 minutes.

Martha Schmitt

OVERNIGHT FRENCH TOAST

Serves: 10-12

1/2 cup butter, melted
1 cup brown sugar
1 large loaf French bread, cut into
    1-inch slices
6 eggs

1-1/2 cups milk
1 teaspoon vanilla
dash of cinnamon
powdered sugar

* Mix butter and brown sugar. Spread in bottom of 13x9-inch baking dish.
* Place bread slices on top of sugar mixture.
* Combine eggs, milk, vanilla and cinnamon. Pour over bread slices.
* Cover and refrigerate overnight.
* Bake at 350° for 45 minutes. Sprinkle with powdered sugar.

Linda Battle
Susan Guarnaccia

HONEY-ORANGE FRENCH TOAST
Serve with Canadian bacon and fruit.

Serves: 4-6

1/4 cup margarine, melted
2 tablespoons honey
1/2 teaspoon cinnamon
3 eggs

1/2 cup orange juice
1/8 teaspoon salt
6 thick slices bread

* Combine butter and honey in a 13x9-inch pan coated with non-stick spray.
* Spread mixture to cover the bottom of pan and sprinkle with cinnamon.
* Combine eggs and juice with salt and mix well.
* Dip bread in egg mixture, drain and place in pan.
* Bake at 400° for 15 minutes.
* Invert to serve.

Ellen Knott

TOWNHOUSE BAKED CHEESE AND GARLIC GRITS

Serves: 8-10

1/2 cup milk
3 eggs
1/2 pound grated Swiss cheese
2 tablespoons grated Parmesan cheese
1 stick unsalted butter
2 cloves of garlic, minced
1/3 teaspoon black pepper

1 tablespoon minced green onion tops or
   fresh chives
2 tablespoons sun-dried tomatoes or
   crisp, crumbled bacon
4 cups water
1 tablespoon salt
1 cup grits

* In large bowl beat together milk and eggs. Add cheese, butter, garlic and pepper.
* Steam sun-dried tomatoes 5 minutes. Dry and finely chop. (If tomatoes are packed in oil, omit this step.)
* Add sun-dried tomatoes or bacon and green onions. Set mixture aside.
* Bring the water and salt to a boil. Add grits, stirring until they return to a boil. Lower heat to medium and continue cooking, stirring constantly until grits are thickened, approximately 5 minutes.
* Remove grits from heat. Pour into cheese mixture and stir until all butter is melted.
* Pour mixture into a buttered 13x9-inch baking dish. Bake at 350° for 1 hour until set and lightly browned. Cut in squares and serve.

Jack Fulk,
owner of The Townhouse Restaurant

CHEESE GRITS

Easy

Serves: 8

1 quart milk
1/2 cup butter or margarine
1 cup grits
1 teaspoon salt

1/2 teaspoon pepper
2 egg yolks
2 egg whites, stiffly beaten
1 cup grated Cheddar cheese

* Bring milk to a boil. Add butter and then grits, cooking until slightly thickened.
* Remove from heat and add salt and pepper.
* Beat with electric mixer on medium speed for 5 minutes.
* Add egg yolks, then cheese, stirring until cheese melts. Fold in beaten egg whites.
* Pour into shallow greased 2-quart casserole. Bake at 350° for 1 hour.

Judy DuBose

CRUSTLESS MEXICAN QUICHE
Leave your diet behind!

Easy

Serves: 8-10

2 (4-ounce) cans chopped green chilies,
    drained
6 eggs

1 pound Cheddar cheese, shredded
1 pound Monterey Jack cheese, shredded
1 (5-ounce) can evaporated milk

* Spread chilies on bottom of 13x9-inch pan.
* Mix together eggs, cheeses and milk and pour over chilies.
* Bake at 350° for 40 minutes or until top is golden.
* Let stand 10 minutes before cutting.

Meg Clarke

OLIVE-TOMATO QUICHE
A favorite quiche from the old Stonehenge Restaurant

Easy

Serves: 8

1 unbaked (9-inch) deep-dish pie shell
1 small onion, chopped
2 tablespoons corn oil
1 pound tomatoes, peeled and thinly
    sliced
1/2 teaspoon oregano

1/2 teaspoon basil
3 eggs, beaten
1/3 cup stuffed green olives, sliced
1 cup Monterey Jack cheese, shredded
salt and pepper to taste

* Prick slightly and bake pie shell at 425° for 5 minutes. Set aside to cool.
* In large skillet, sauté onion in oil until lightly brown, stirring often.
* Add tomatoes, salt and herbs, cooking over low heat for 5 minutes. Cool slightly.
* Add eggs, olives, one half of the cheese, salt and pepper.
* Pour mixture into pie crust. Sprinkle with remaining cheese.
* Bake at 375° for 45 minutes or until center tests done.
* Let stand 5 minutes before serving.

The Hawk

QUESADILLA QUICHE

Easy   Serves: 6

pastry for 2 pie crusts
1 cup chopped onion
1 tablespoon margarine
1 medium tomato, chopped   .
1 (4-ounce) can sliced black olives,
   drained
1/4 teaspoon garlic salt

1/4 teaspoon cumin
1/8 teaspoon pepper
1 (4-ounce) can chopped green chilies
2 eggs, beaten
1 cup shredded Cheddar cheese
1 cup shredded Monterey Jack cheese
sour cream and salsa

* Prepare 1 pie crust and place in pie pan.
* Sauté onion in margarine until clear. Stir in tomatoes, olives, chilies, garlic and cumin.
* In separate bowl mix eggs and 1/2 cup of each kind of cheese.
* Spread the remaining cheese evenly in pie crust. Add onion mixture to pie crust.
* Pour in the egg mixture. Top with the second pie crust and seal the edges.
* Bake at 375° for 45 to 55 minutes until a knife inserted in center comes out clean.
* Serve with salsa and sour cream as accompaniments.

Mary Gregory

TURKEY QUICHE
Great for leftover Thanksgiving turkey

1 (9-inch) frozen deep-dish pie shell
1 tablespoon butter or margarine
1 cup diced celery
1 cup cooked, diced turkey
1/2 cup frozen peas or 2 tablespoons
   chopped pimiento
3 eggs

1 cup milk
1/4 cup mayonnaise
2 tablespoons prepared mustard
1/2 teaspoon salt
1 cup grated sharp Cheddar cheese or
   Monterey Jack or combination of the two
paprika

* Place pie shell on cookie sheet. Bake at 375° for 10 minutes.
* Cook celery in butter until tender.
* Stir in turkey and peas or pimiento. Spoon into partially cooked pie shell.
* Beat eggs, milk, mayonnaise, mustard and salt together. Pour over turkey mixture.
* Sprinkle with grated cheese and paprika.
* Bake at 350° for 30 to 40 minutes or until knife inserted near center comes out clean.
* Freezes well. Can use egg substitute and fat-free mayonnaise to reduce fat content.

Karen Nagle

SEAFOOD QUICHE

Easy   Serve: 6

1/2 cup chopped onion
2 tablespoons butter
3 eggs, beaten
3/4 cup light cream
3/4 cup milk
1/2 teaspoon salt
1/2 teaspoon finely grated lemon zest

dash ground nutmeg
1 (7-ounce) can crabmeat, drained and
    flaked or 1 (4-1/2-ounce) can shrimp,
    drained and chopped
1-1/2 cups shredded Swiss cheese
1 tablespoon flour
1 unbaked pie shell

* Cook onion in butter until tender.
* Stir together eggs, light cream, milk, salt, lemon zest, nutmeg and onion. Add crab or shrimp.
* Combine shredded cheese and flour; add to egg mixture.
* Line unpricked pastry shell with double thickness of heavy-duty foil.
* Bake at 450° for 5 minutes. Remove foil; bake 5 to 7 minutes more until pastry is nearly done. Remove from oven.
* Reduce oven temperature to 325°. Pour seafood mixture into hot pastry shell.
* Cover edge of crust with foil to prevent over-browning.
* Bake for 35 to 40 minutes or until a knife inserted in center comes out clean.
* Allow to sit for 10 minutes before serving.

Elaine Hoffmann

CRAB QUICHE

Easy   Serves: 6

2 eggs, beaten
1/2 cup milk
1/2 cup mayonnaise
2 level teaspoons flour
8 ounces Swiss cheese, shredded

2 (6-1/4-ounce) cans crabmeat, drained and
    rinsed
1 small onion, chopped
1 frozen deep-dish pie shell
dash of salt and pepper

* Beat eggs and milk. Add the mayonnaise which has been mixed with the flour.
* Add the cheese, crabmeat and onion. Stir in the salt and pepper.
* Bake at 350° for 45 minutes or until center is set. Cool 10 minutes before cutting.

Jean Webb

ITALIAN SPINACH-CHEESE QUICHE

Nice with fruit for a meatless meal

Easy   Serves: 6-8

1 (10-ounce) package frozen, chopped   *1/2 teaspoon salt*
  spinach   *1/4 cup chopped green onion*
1 (3-ounce) package cream cheese,   *2 tablespoons chopped fresh parsley*
  softened   *1 unbaked deep-dish pie shell*
1-1/2 cups shredded sharp Cheddar cheese   *1 tomato, thinly sliced*
5 eggs, slightly beaten   *1/4 cup grated Parmesan cheese*

* Cook spinach according to package directions. Drain well; squeeze to remove excess water. Set aside.
* Combine cream cheese, Cheddar cheese, eggs, salt, onion and parsley; beat lightly with a fork. Stir in spinach.
* Pour into pastry shell. Arrange tomato slices on top; sprinkle with Parmesan cheese.
* Bake at 375° for 35 minutes or until set. May be baked ahead and reheated.

Dougi O'Bryan

ZUCCHINI QUICHE

$40,000 prize-winning recipe

Easy   Serves: 6

4 cups thinly sliced unpeeled zucchini   *1/4 teaspoon oregano*
1 cup chopped onion   *1/4 teaspoon sweet dried basil*
1/2 cup margarine   *2 eggs*
2 tablespoons parsley flakes   *8 ounces shredded mozzarella cheese*
1/2 teaspoon salt   *1 (8-ounce) can refrigerated crescent rolls*
1/2 teaspoon pepper   *2 teaspoons prepared mustard*
1/4 teaspoon garlic powder

* Sauté onion and zucchini in margarine until tender. Stir in all seasonings.
* In large bowl, blend eggs and cheese. Stir in vegetable mixture.
* Separate dough into 8 triangles. Press into ungreased 10-inch pie plate or quiche pan.
* Spread mustard over crust. Pour quiche mixture into pan.
* Bake at 375° for 18 to 20 minutes until knife inserted in center comes out clean.
* Let cool 10 minutes before serving.

Julia Todd

Vegetables
and
Side Dishes

ASPARAGUS-CHEDDAR CHEESE PIE

A nice luncheon dish served with fresh fruit

Easy   Serves: 6

1 (8-ounce) package cream cheese   2 cans asparagus tips, drained
1 can Cheddar cheese soup   2 deep-dish pie shells

* Mix cream cheese and soup in blender or with mixer.
* Stir in asparagus. Pour into pie shell.
* Cover filling with second pie shell. Seal edges.
* Bake at 350° for about 30 minutes or until crust is brown.
* Let sit for 30 minutes before serving.

Phyllis Herring

ASPARAGUS WITH SOUR CREAM SAUCE

Can be served as an hors d'oeuvre

Serves: 6

2 pounds fresh asparagus   1/2 teaspoon salt
1 cup sour cream   2 tablespoons toasted sesame seeds
1/4 cup Parmesan cheese   (optional)
1 teaspoon lemon juice

* Snap off ends of asparagus and discard. Cook asparagus in a steamer or in lightly
  salted simmering water until crunchy (about 5 minutes).
* Let cool and refrigerate.
* Mix remaining ingredients except sesame seeds.
* If serving as a vegetable, put a heaping spoonful or two of sauce on each serving of
  asparagus, sprinkle top with sesame seeds.
* Try this as an hors d'oeuvre by hollowing out a green, red or yellow pepper and filling
  with the sauce. Serve on a tray surrounded by the asparagus on lettuce leaves.

Ellen Knott

ASPARAGUS VINAIGRETTE

Serves: 3-4

1/2 teaspoon Dijon mustard
1/2 teaspoon salt
dash of pepper
2 tablespoons red wine vinegar

6 tablespoons oil
1/4 teaspoon grated onion
1 can asparagus, drained
1 hard-boiled egg

* Combine all ingredients except asparagus and heat thoroughly over low heat, but do not boil.
* Pour over the asparagus and refrigerate.
* Grate a hard-boiled egg over the top before serving.
* Serve cold.

Linda McAlexander

COLD ASPARAGUS WITH PECANS
May be marinated up to 36 hours ahead

Easy

Serves: 6-8

1-1/2 pounds fresh asparagus or
  2 (10-ounce) packages frozen
  asparagus
3/4 cup finely chopped pecans
2 tablespoons vegetable oil

1/4 cup cider vinegar
1/4 cup soy sauce
1/4 cup sugar
pepper to taste

* Cook fresh asparagus in boiling water 6 to 7 minutes or until tender and still bright green. Drain and rinse under cold water. Drain again.
* Arrange in 1 or 2 layers in oblong serving dish.
* Mix remaining ingredients and pour over asparagus, lifting asparagus so mixture penetrates to bottom of dish.
* Sprinkle with pepper.
* Serve chilled.

Nancy Austin

GRANZIE'S SHRIMP AND ASPARAGUS
Different, colorful, delicious!

Easy   Serves: 8

2 (15-ounce) cans asparagus spears   1 can cream of shrimp soup
8 slices sharp Cheddar cheese,   20 fresh boiled shrimp, cleaned and peeled
   sandwich size

* Drain asparagus and place 1 can in baking dish.
* Top with 4 cheese slices and several shrimp.
* Repeat layers of asparagus, cheese and shrimp.
* Pour shrimp soup on top and sprinkle a few remaining shrimp to garnish.
* Bake at 350° about 20 minutes or until bubbly.

Karen Peters

BAKED BEANS
Not your standard baked beans

Easy   Serves: 12

4 slices chopped bacon   1/3 cup ketchup
1 onion, chopped   2 tablespoons Worcestershire sauce
1 (16-ounce) can kidney beans, drained   1/4 pound pasteurized process cheese
1 (16-ounce) can big white limas, drained   spread or sharp Cheddar cheese, cubed
1 (16-ounce) can pork & beans   Parmesan cheese

* Brown bacon and onion in large skillet.
* Add remaining ingredients.
* Heat on top of stove to melt cheese.
* Put in greased 13x9-inch baking dish.
* Sprinkle with Parmesan cheese.
* Bake at 350° for 30 minutes.

Rose Hegele
Kathryn Smith

FIESTA BEANS
Just add cornbread for a meal!

Can prepare ahead   Serves: 16-20

3/4 pound bacon, chopped
3 large onions, chopped
6 (15-ounce) cans pinto beans, drained
3 (12-ounce) bottles of dark beer
3 cups of beef broth (canned)
3 large tomatoes, chopped or
   1 (16-ounce) can

1 teaspoon cilantro seasoning
3 jalapeño chili peppers, seeded and finely
   chopped (use fresh if possible, be sure
   to wash hands thoroughly after
   preparing)
1 tablespoon sugar
freshly ground pepper to taste

* Cook bacon in large, heavy pot over medium-high heat until crisp. Remove from pot with slotted spoon.
* Add onions to pot and cook until tender, stirring frequently.
* Add bacon, beans, beer, stock, tomatoes, cilantro, jalapeño peppers and sugar. Season to taste with freshly ground pepper and bring to a boil.
* Reduce heat and simmer until somewhat thickened, about 1-1/2 hours, stirring occasionally. Ladle beans into a bowl and serve.

Pat Waldron

OLD-FASHIONED BAKED BEANS WITH SPICES

Easy   Serves: 6

1 (31-ounce) can baked beans
1 teaspoon dry mustard
1/8 teaspoon pepper
2 teaspoons salt
1/4 cup brown sugar or 2 tablespoons
   molasses
1 green pepper, chopped

1 large onion, peeled and thinly sliced
1 tablespoon sweet pickle juice or vinegar
1/8 teaspoon ground cinnamon
1/8 teaspoon ground cloves
1/4 cup ketchup or chili sauce
1/2 lemon, quartered
3 slices bacon

* Combine all ingredients except bacon (including lemon quarters which have been squeezed, then added to mixture).
* Pour beans into a greased casserole.
* Lay slices of bacon on top and bake covered at 300° for at least 2 hours.

Camilla Turner

GREEN BEANS IN OIL (LOOB' YEH B'ZAIT)
A wonderful Lebanese dish

Serves: 4-6

1 pound fresh green beans
3/4 cup olive oil
2 medium onions, finely chopped
6 to 8 whole garlic cloves, peeled
1 teaspoon salt

1/2 teaspoon black pepper
oregano to taste (optional)
2 large tomatoes, peeled, seeded and
  chopped
1 to 2 cups water

* Wash and slice beans lengthwise.
* Heat oil in a saucepan. Sauté onions and garlic until slightly browned.
* Add beans, salt, pepper and oregano. Sauté 10 minutes.
* Add tomatoes and 1 cup water. Stir to mix.
* Cover and simmer very slowly, approximately 20 minutes or until beans are tender, adding more water if necessary.
* Remove lid and simmer uncovered to absorb excess juice (approximately 10 minutes).
* Adjust salt and pepper to taste.

Edouard Rassie

SAVORY GREEN BEANS
These beans are also good cold.

Easy

Serves: 6

1-1/2 pounds fresh green beans
1/4 teaspoon garlic powder
2 tablespoons minced onion
2 tablespoons oil (canola or vegetable)

1-1/2 teaspoons dried basil
salt and pepper to taste
1/4 cup water

* Wash beans, trim ends and cut in half.
* In large saucepan, sauté beans in oil and add other ingredients.
* Cover and cook over medium heat 20 minutes or until beans are tender.
* Add additional water if necessary.
* Serve immediately.

Betsy Mitchell

TANGY GREEN BEANS
Worth the effort

Serves: 8

2 (15-ounce) cans whole string beans
Vinaigrette Sauce:
3 tablespoons butter
2 tablespoons vinegar
1 tablespoon tarragon vinegar
1 teaspoon salt

bacon strips cut in half

1 teaspoon paprika
1 tablespoon chopped parsley
1 teaspoon grated onion

* Wrap 6 to 7 string beans in half piece of bacon. Secure with toothpick.
* Repeat with remaining string beans.
* Put bean bundles on broiler pan and broil until bacon is done.
* To prepare Vinaigrette Sauce, combine all ingredients.
* Bring to a boil.
* Put bean bundles on serving dish and pour hot vinaigrette sauce over beans. Serve hot.

Camilla Turner

GREEK-STYLE LIMA BEANS
Dill makes the difference!

Easy

Serves: 6

2 (16-ounce) packages frozen Fordhook
  limas
1 cup finely chopped onions
1/2 cup chopped fresh parsley
1/2 cup chopped fresh dill (or 1
  tablespoon dried)

1/4 cup olive oil
1/4 cup vegetable oil
6 ounces tomato sauce
1-1/2 teaspoons salt
1/2 teaspoon pepper
2 cups water

* Combine all ingredients in 2-quart casserole.
* Bake covered at 350° for 45 minutes. Uncover and bake 15 minutes longer.

Lea Tsahakis

BROCCOLI IN AMBUSH

Serves: 6

6 fresh broccoli spears
Mornay Sauce:
2 tablespoons butter
2 tablespoons flour
1 cup milk
1/2 teaspoon salt

6 fresh medium tomatoes

1/4 teaspoon freshly ground white pepper
1 egg yolk
3 tablespoons grated Swiss cheese or
   1-1/2 tablespoons grated Parmesan

* Cut broccoli into florets. Blanch in boiling water. Remove and cool.
* Cut bottom of tomatoes, so that they sit flat but do not cut into seeds.
* Cut off tops of tomatoes and remove seeds.
* To prepare Mornay Sauce, heat butter in heavy saucepan.
* Stir flour till smooth and cook, stirring constantly, until mixture froths (about 2 minutes) without browning.
* Add the milk, whipping constantly with a wire whisk. Cook until it boils, whipping constantly.
* Add seasonings, cooking on low heat 2 to 3 minutes, stirring constantly with whisk.
* Cool slightly, 6 to 8 minutes. Add egg yolk, beating very fast and hard.
* Fold in cheese with a rubber spatula (do not use a whisk).
* Fill tomatoes 3/4 full with Mornay sauce. Bake at 350° for 15 minutes.
* Top with florets of broccoli to cover all sauce.

Scott Spaulding
Chef, Raintree Country Club

"DOUBLE D" BROCCOLI CASSEROLE

Easy

Serves: 6

2 (10-ounce) packages frozen broccoli
   spears
1 can cream of mushroom soup
1 stick butter, cut into pieces

1 (4-ounce) can mushrooms, drained
1 (10-ounce) tube garlic cheese, cut into
   pieces

* Cook broccoli and cut into bite-sized pieces. Place in 2-quart casserole.
* Mix soup, butter, mushrooms and cheese. Pour soup mixture over broccoli.
* Bake at 350° for 10 minutes. Stir. Continue baking 15 to 20 minutes.

Jane Tilley

BROCCOLI SOUFFLÉ

Easy   Serves: 6-8

4 tablespoons butter   2 packages chopped broccoli, well drained
1 medium onion, chopped   3 eggs, beaten
6 tablespoons flour   2 tablespoons butter
1/2 cup water   breadcrumbs
1 (8-ounce) jar processed cheese spread

* Sauté onion in 4 tablespoons butter in saucepan.
* Add flour and water, cooking over low heat until thickened.
* Add cheese and broccoli.
* Fold in eggs.
* Pour into greased 1-1/2-quart casserole.
* Sprinkle breadcrumbs on top and dot with 2 tablespoons butter.
* Bake at 325° for 30 minutes.

Sue Docherty

CRUNCHY BROCCOLI CASSEROLE
Great fresh taste

Easy   Serves: 6

2 (10-ounce) packages broccoli spears   1 (8-ounce) can sliced water chestnuts,
   or 1 bunch fresh broccoli   drained
1/2 to 1 stick butter   1 cup crispy rice cereal
1 package dry onion soup mix

* Reserving 2 tablespoons of butter, put the remainder in bottom of a 13x9-inch baking
  dish and melt in oven.
* Meanwhile, cook broccoli according to package instructions and drain. Cut up and put
  in casserole.
* Sprinkle dry onion soup mix on top of broccoli. Add water chestnuts and mix well.
* Sprinkle the cereal on top.
* Melt remaining butter and drizzle over cereal.
* Bake at 350° for 20 minutes.

Meg Clarke

MONROE'S FAVORITE BROCCOLI
Great for a buffet

Easy   Serves: 6-8

2 (10-ounce) packages chopped broccoli   2 cups crumbled round buttery crackers
2 eggs, well beaten   1/4 cup butter, melted
2 cups grated sharp Cheddar cheese   salt and pepper to taste

* Cook broccoli in small amount of water until just tender.
* Drain and put in a 13x9-inch pan that has been sprayed with non-stick vegetable spray.
* Salt and pepper eggs to taste. Pour eggs over broccoli.
* Sprinkle with Cheddar cheese.
* Toss cracker crumbs with butter. Crisp crumbs in oven at 325° until just beginning to brown (about 5 minutes).
* Sprinkle on top of cheese.
* Bake at 325° for 30 minutes or until bubbly.

Julia George

CABBAGE CASSEROLE
A little different and very good

Easy   Serves: 8-10

2 cups corn flakes, crushed   1 can cream of celery soup
4 to 5 cups cabbage, shredded   1 cup milk
2 cans sliced water chestnuts, drained   1/2 cup mayonnaise
1 medium onion, chopped   4 to 6 ounces Cheddar cheese, shredded
1 stick margarine, melted

* Spray a 13x9-inch pan with non-stick vegetable spray.
* Layer 1 cup corn flakes, cabbage, water chestnuts and onion.
* Mix margarine, soup, milk and mayonnaise. Pour over casserole.
* Cover with Cheddar cheese and remaining cup of corn flakes.
* Bake at 350° for 1 hour.

Lynda Dobbins

SWEET AND SOUR RED CABBAGE

Serves: 6-8

1 large red cabbage, finely chopped
1/4 cup butter
1 tablespoon sugar
2 apples, peeled, cored and chopped
1 onion, chopped

1/4 cup red wine vinegar
salt to taste
2 tablespoons caraway seeds
1 to 2 cups bouillon
1 to 2 tablespoons flour, optional

* Finely chop red cabbage.
* Brown sugar lightly in butter. Add onions and apples; add cabbage and sauté 10 minutes more stirring constantly. Add vinegar; stir well.
* Add salt and caraway seeds; sauté 10 minutes more. Add bouillon and cook covered until tender.
* May be thickened with flour. Season to taste.

Gabriele Kellmann
Pattie Bethune

BOURBON CARROTS

Serves: 6

1-1/2 pounds peeled carrots
1 tablespoon granulated sugar
3-1/2 tablespoons butter, divided
1-1/2 cups water
salt and pepper to taste

2 tablespoons dark brown sugar
2 tablespoons bourbon
1-1/2 tablespoons chopped parsley
(optional)

* Cut carrots into 1/4-inch slices.
* Combine carrots, granulated sugar, 1-1/2 tablespoons butter in heavy saucepan.
* Add 1-1/2 cups water and bring to a boil.
* Reduce to a simmer; cover and cook 10 to 15 minutes.
* Drain the carrots. Salt and pepper to taste.
* Melt the remaining 2 tablespoons butter with the brown sugar over medium high heat.
* When sugar is dissolved, add carrots and sauté until coated.
* Add bourbon and cook several minutes.
* Garnish with parsley.

Betty Mullen

COMPANY CARROT CASSEROLE

Easy   Serves: 8

4 cups sliced carrots   *salt and pepper to taste*
1 large onion, thinly sliced   *1 cup grated medium Cheddar cheese*
4 tablespoons margarine   *1 stick margarine*
1 can cream of celery soup   *1 cup herb stuffing mix*
1/4 cup water   *paprika*

* Cook carrots in salted water until barely tender. Drain.
* Sauté onion in 4 tablespoons margarine until limp.
* Mix with drained carrots and put in 11x8-inch casserole.
* Mix soup and water and pour over carrots and onions.
* Sprinkle with cheese.
* Melt stick of margarine and lightly sauté stuffing mix. Sprinkle over top of casserole.
* Sprinkle with paprika.
* Bake uncovered at 350° for 30 minutes.

Janet Povall

DAVID HAIN'S GINGERED CARROTS

Easy   Serves: 4-6

24 ounces frozen baby carrots, thawed   *6 tablespoons powdered sugar*
  and drained   *1/2 teaspoon salt*
1 stick butter   *1/4 teaspoon grated ginger*
2/3 cup minced onion   *4 tablespoons minced parsley*

* Place carrots in an oven-proof baking dish.
* Melt butter in a small saucepan over low heat.
* Add onion and powdered sugar. Stir until sugar is dissolved. Add salt and ginger.
* Pour mixture over carrots and sprinkle with parsley.
* Bake covered at 350° for 20 minutes.

Laura Courter

MARINATED CARROT PENNIES
Delicious with baked ham

Make ahead   Serves: 8

2 *pounds sliced carrots*   *1 tablespoon prepared mustard*
1 can tomato soup, undiluted`   *1 tablespoon Worcestershire sauce*
1 cup sugar   *1 large onion, sliced*
1/2 cup cooking oil   *1 green pepper, sliced*
1/4 cup vinegar

* Boil carrots until tender.
* Combine soup, sugar, oil, vinegar, mustard and Worcestershire sauce.
* Simmer sauce uncovered for 20 minutes.
* In medium-size casserole layer the following: carrots, onions, pepper, sauce.
* Repeat layers once more, ending with the sauce. Refrigerate overnight.
* May reheat to serve or may be served chilled.

Note: May substitute 1 (8-ounce) can of tomato sauce for the tomato soup.

Sharon Edge, Leslie Stacks
Carol Landers, Barbara Nesbitt

CAULIFLOWER WITH CREAMY SHRIMP SAUCE
No left-overs - guaranteed

Serves: 8

4 tablespoons butter   *1 cup shredded Cheddar cheese*
3 to 4 tablespoons flour   *2 cups shrimp, cooked and peeled*
2 cups milk   *1 head cauliflower*
salt to taste   *paprika*

* Melt butter over low heat. Add flour and stir 3 to 5 minutes. Slowly stir in milk.
* Add cheese and stir until melted.
* Add shrimp. Set aside and keep warm.
* Trim bottom of cauliflower stem so that head sits flat. Soak 5 minutes in cold water.
* Place in steamer or saucepan with enough water to barely cover.
* Cook 10 to 15 minutes. Drain.
* Place in serving bowl and pour shrimp sauce over cauliflower. Sprinkle with paprika.

Marie Higgins Mullen

CREOLE CORN AND OKRA
Great summer recipe

Serves: 4

1/2 stick butter or margarine	*3 tomatoes, peeled and chopped, or*
1 cup minced green pepper	*1 (10-ounce) can tomatoes*
1 cup minced scallions	*1 tablespoon thyme*
1 cup corn (white preferred)	*salt and pepper to taste*
1 cup sliced okra	

* Melt butter in a skillet.
* Sauté green pepper and scallions over medium-high heat until soft.
* Add corn and okra, reducing heat to medium or medium low.
* Cook and stir the mixture 5 to 10 minutes.
* Add tomatoes, thyme, salt and pepper.
* Reduce heat and simmer covered (or uncovered if the mixture has too much liquid from tomatoes) until the corn and okra reach desired consistency, or about 30 minutes.

Pam Richey

LEEK AND MUSHROOM BAKE

Easy   Serves: 4

2 leeks	*3 eggs*
8 ounces fresh mushrooms	*salt to taste*
1 tablespoon margarine	*white pepper to taste*
1 to 1-1/2 cups half-and-half	

* Wash leeks and cut in slices. Cook in lightly salted water for 5 minutes.
* Cut mushrooms into 4 pieces each and stir-fry in margarine for 5 minutes.
* Drain leeks and place with mushrooms in ovenproof dish.
* Mix eggs, half-and-half, salt and pepper and beat lightly. Pour mixture over vegetables until just covered.
* Bake at 400° for 20 to 25 minutes until golden brown.

Ann Hedbacker

MARINATED MUSHROOMS

Can be served hot or cold as an appetizer or as a side dish with meats

6 (4-1/2-ounce) jars whole mushrooms
1 stick butter or margarine
1/2 to 1 teaspoon hot pepper sauce
1 (10-1/2-ounce) can beef broth or
  consommé
1 tablespoon Worcestershire sauce

2 tablespoons dried minced onions
2 tablespoons dried parsley flakes
1 to 2 teaspoons Italian seasoning
1 cup chili sauce
few drops bottled brown bouquet sauce
  (optional)

* Drain mushrooms; reserve juice.
* In large skillet, sauté mushrooms in butter.
* Add mushroom juice and remaining ingredients.
* Bring to a boil. Turn down heat and simmer 20 to 30 minutes.
* To thicken, add 1 tablespoon flour to 1 cup of the liquid. Blend well and mix back into mushrooms.
* Store covered in the refrigerator. Can be made up to 2 days in advance. Freezes well.

Pamela Cooke

MUSHROOM POLONAISE

Great with tenderloin or roast

Serves: 6

1-1/2 pounds fresh mushrooms, sliced
1/2 cup butter
1 medium onion, minced
2 tablespoons flour
1/4 cup sherry
1 cup sour cream

1/4 cup heavy cream
1/4 teaspoon nutmeg
2 tablespoons chopped parsley
salt and pepper to taste
1/4 cup breadcrumbs
1/4 cup butter, melted

* Sauté mushrooms in butter until slightly brown and liquid has evaporated.
* Add onion and sauté until soft. Stir in flour.
* Cook 5 minutes over low heat, stirring constantly.
* Blend in sherry, sour cream and heavy cream.
* Add seasonings and cook until thick. Stir in parsley.
* Pour into buttered casserole and sprinkle with breadcrumbs which have been tossed with melted butter.
* Bake at 325° for 35 minutes.

Linda Hewitt

OVEN-FRIED OKRA

Calories slashed in a favorite Southern dish

Easy   Serves: 4

1/2 cup cornmeal   6 cups sliced okra
1 teaspoon salt   4 tablespoons oil
1/4 teaspoon pepper

* Combine cornmeal, salt and pepper.
* Dredge okra in corn meal mixture.
* Spread oil in large, shallow baking pan.
* Spread okra evenly in pan.
* Bake at 425° for 40 minutes, stirring every 10 minutes.

Hilda Rutherford

GOLDEN BAKED VIDALIAS

The best onion recipe ever

Easy   Serves: 8

1 stick butter   salt and pepper to taste
6 medium sweet onions, peeled and   3/4 pound Gruyère cheese, grated
  sliced   French bread slices
1 can cream of chicken soup   melted butter
1 cup milk

* Melt stick of butter in large skillet over medium heat. Add onions and cook until
  tender, stirring frequently. Put onions in a greased 2-quart shallow baking dish.
* Combine soup, milk, salt and pepper; pour over onions.
* Sprinkle with cheese. May substitute Swiss if Gruyère cheese is unavailable.
* Dip one side of bread slices in melted butter and arrange buttered side up over onion
  mixture to cover completely.
* Bake at 350° for 30 minutes.

Marilyn Thompson

HONEY BAKED ONIONS
Perfect accompaniment for pork

Easy   Serves: 6-8

4 tablespoons butter   6 large onions, sliced
1/3 cup honey   1 tablespoon lemon juice
1/2 teaspoon salt   4 drops hot pepper sauce

* Heat butter in small saucepan. Add honey and salt.
* Layer onions in baking dish and sprinkle with lemon juice.
* Shake on hot pepper sauce.
* Pour honey mixture over the onions.
* Bake at 425° for 25 to 30 minutes.

Linda McAlexander

ONION PIE

Serves: 6-8

1 cup saltine cracker crumbs   3/4 cup milk
1/2 cup butter, melted   3 eggs, slightly beaten
2-1/2 cups sliced sweet onions   1/2 pound grated sharp Cheddar cheese
2 tablespoons butter

* Mix cracker crumbs with 1/2 cup melted butter and press into a 10-inch pie pan.
* Sauté onions in 2 tablespoons butter and pour into crust.
* Scald milk and add slowly to eggs.
* Add grated cheese to milk and egg mixture and stir until cheese melts. Pour over onions in crust.
* Bake at 350° for 45 minutes.

Marwen McDowell

BLACK-EYED PEAS WITH RICE
Great for New Year's Day

Easy   Serves: 6

2 slices bacon
1 medium onion, chopped
1 (15-ounce) can black-eyed peas, drained
1 (14-1/2-ounce) can stewed tomatoes,
   undrained

1 cup rice, cooked according to package
   directions
1/4 teaspoon salt
1/4 teaspoon pepper

* Cook bacon in large skillet until crisp.
* Remove bacon. Crumble and set aside.
* Sauté onion in bacon drippings.
* Add peas, tomatoes and rice.
* Spoon into 1-1/2 quart casserole.
* Bake at 350° for 30 minutes.
* After baking, garnish with crumbled bacon.

Nancy Wohlbruck

CHEESY POTATO AND PEA CASSEROLE
A meal in itself with a green salad

Serves: 8-10

8 slices bacon
2 cups grated sharp Cheddar cheese,
   divided
1/2 cup milk
1/2 to 3/4 cup mayonnaise
1/2 teaspoon salt

1/2 teaspoon pepper
1 large onion, chopped
5 large potatoes, sliced and cooked
1 (10-ounce) package frozen peas, thawed
   and drained

* Fry bacon. Remove and crumble.
* Cook onion briefly in bacon drippings. Drain.
* Mix milk, mayonnaise, 1 cup cheese, salt and pepper.
* Layer 1/2 potatoes, 1/2 peas, 1/2 bacon and 1/2 onion in a 13x9-inch baking dish.
* Repeat layers.
* Spread mayonnaise mixture over all and sprinkle on remaining cheese.
* Bake at 350° for 25 minutes.

Ellen Knott

CHEESY POTATOES

Prepare ahead   Serves: 10

5 to 6 pounds of boiling potatoes   1 pound sharp Cheddar cheese, coarsely
2 pounds tiny white onions   grated
1/2 cup flour   1/2 teaspoon pepper
2-1/2 cups milk   3/4 teaspoon salt
3 cups light cream   1 teaspoon seasoned salt
1 cup chicken broth   1 clove garlic, crushed
1 cup grated Parmesan cheese

* Cook potatoes in their jackets the day before serving.
* Next day, peel and dice potatoes into 1/2-inch cubes (9 cups).
* Peel onions and cook in salted water or steam until tender. Drain.
* To make sauce, melt 1/2 cup butter in a large skillet. Blend flour until smooth. Add
  milk, cream and chicken broth. Cook until thick, stirring constantly. Add Cheddar
  cheese and Parmesan cheese. Stir and cook gently until cheese melts. (If too thick, add
  1/2 cup milk.) Season with salt, pepper, seasoned salt and garlic.
* Mix with cubed potatoes. Add onions and pour into casserole.
* Bake at 350° for 25 to 30 minutes or until bubbly.

Leslie Gebert

COTTAGE POTATOES

Prepare ahead   Serves: 12

10 medium baking potatoes   chopped parsley to taste
salt and pepper to taste   1 slice bread, cubed
1 onion, chopped   1/2 cup melted margarine
1/2 green or red pepper, chopped   1/2 cup milk
1 small jar pimientos   1 cup crushed cornflakes
1/2 pound American cheese, cubed

* Boil potatoes in jackets until tender. Skin and dice. Add salt and pepper to taste.
* Add all other ingredients except margarine, milk and corn flakes. Toss lightly.
* When well blended, add margarine and milk. Pour into 3-quart casserole.
* Sprinkle with crushed corn flakes. Refrigerate 24 to 48 hours.
* Bring to room temperature. Bake at 350° for 1 hour.

Shirley Acks

HOT GERMAN POTATO SALAD
(Kartoffelsalat)

Serves: 6

12 slices bacon, diced and fried until crisp
  (reserve 6 tablespoons drippings)
3 medium onions, chopped
2 cups less 2 tablespoons cider vinegar
1-1/2 tablespoons sugar
1-1/2 teaspoons salt

1/4 teaspoon pepper
2 to 3 pounds potatoes cooked, peeled and
  cut into 1/4-inch slices
fresh parsley, snipped
paprika

* Heat bacon drippings in skillet.
* Add onion and cook until tender, stirring occasionally.
* Stir in vinegar, sugar, salt and pepper. Heat to boiling.
* Mix in bacon.
* Pour over potato slices in serving dish and toss lightly to coat evenly.
* Garnish with snipped parsley and paprika.
* Serve hot.

Rosi Weber

SHEET POTATOES
These go fast - be sure to make enough!

Serves: 8

7 to 8 baking potatoes, peeled and
  thinly sliced
2 sticks unsalted butter, melted

freshly ground pepper and salt to taste
sprigs of fresh thyme or 1 tablespoon dried

* Soak potato slices in ice water. Drain on paper towels.
* Brush jellyroll pan with some of the butter.
* Arrange potato slices in overlapping rows on pan. Season with salt, pepper and thyme.
* Drizzle remaining butter over potatoes. Bake at 400° for 45 minutes or until potatoes
  are crisp and golden brown.
* Garnish with additional sprigs of thyme.

Marge Aultman

SHRIMP-STUFFED POTATOES
A favorite for dinner parties

Serves: 8

4 baking potatoes
vegetable shortening
1 can cream of shrimp soup
1 cup grated Cheddar cheese

1/4 cup chives
1/4 cup butter, softened
salt and pepper to taste

* Wash, dry and coat potatoes with shortening. Place on foil-covered cookie sheet and bake at 400° until done and skins are hard.
* Cut potatoes in half and scoop out centers into a large mixing bowl.
* Add rest of ingredients, reserving 1/2 cup of cheese; mix with electric mixer on high until smooth. (May need to add milk if too thick.)
* Return potato mixture to shells and top with reserved cheese.
* Bake at 350° for 10 to 15 minutes until cheese is melted and hot.
* Sprinkle with parsley and/or paprika.
* Pretty with several fresh boiled shrimp on top.

Karen Peters

POTATO TOPPER

Easy

1 stick butter or margarine, softened
1/2 cup Parmesan cheese

1 cup mayonnaise
1/2 teaspoon Worcestershire sauce

* Mix all ingredients.
* Refrigerate.
* Use as a topping for baked potatoes.

Nancy Wohlbruck

WILLIAMSBURG SWEET POTATOES

Freezes well   Serves: 8-10

3 pounds sweet potatoes   1/2 teaspoon cinnamon
3/4 cup packed light brown sugar, divided   1/4 teaspoon salt
3 tablespoons butter or margarine   1/2 teaspoon nutmeg

* Cook potatoes in boiling water. Drain, peel and mash potatoes.
* Stir in all remaining ingredients except 2 tablespoons of the sugar.
* Turn mixture into greased 1-1/2-quart casserole and sprinkle with the remaining 2 tablespoons sugar.
* Bake at 400° for 30 minutes.

Dottie Kirkland

CHEESE RATATOUILLE
A winner!

Serves: 6-8

1 large eggplant, cubed   8 ounces Monterey Jack Cheese, cubed
3 to 4 medium tomatoes, cubed   ground pepper to taste
1 large onion, diced   hot cooked rice

* If desired, lightly sauté eggplant in olive oil.
* Combine all ingredients, except rice in large covered casserole.
* Bake at 350° for 30 minutes.
* Remove from oven and stir to blend ingredients.
* Return to oven for 10 minutes or until bubbly.
* Serve over hot rice.

Leslie Stacks

CARIBBEAN RICE
Great with fish

Easy   Serves: 4

3 tablespoons butter, divided   4 drops hot pepper sauce
4 tablespoons chopped onions   1 cup frozen peas or frozen pea and carrot
1 cup converted rice   mixture (do not thaw)
1-1/2 cups water   4 tablespoons chopped fresh parsley
1 bay leaf   1/2 cup shredded coconut (or more to taste)
salt and freshly ground pepper to taste

* Heat 2 tablespoons butter in saucepan.
* Add onion and cook until tender.
* Add rice and stir briefly.
* Add water, bay leaf, salt, pepper and hot pepper sauce.
* Bring to boil. Cover and simmer about 17 minutes.
* Meanwhile, combine frozen peas and remaining tablespoon butter with salt and pepper in a saucepan.
* Cook on medium heat about 1 minute, stirring constantly.
* Add coconut and peas to rice.
* Add parsley to rice and remove bay leaf.

Lynda Dobbins

CLAM RICE
Beautiful and delicious

Serves: 4

1 cup uncooked rice   1 cup clam juice
1/2 stick butter, melted   1/3 cup chopped green pepper
1 teaspoon salt   1/3 cup chopped celery
1 cup chicken broth   1/3 cup chopped carrots

* Stir rice in butter in saucepan over medium heat until translucent. Add salt.
* Mix with broth and juice and put in greased casserole.
* Bake at 350° for 1 hour.
* Stir in vegetables and salt. Cook 5 more minutes.

Lillian Worthy

EASY RICE CASSEROLE

Serves: 6

1-1/2 cups rice
1/4 stick butter
1 can or large jar of mushrooms
2 cans beef consommé

1 large chopped onion (or about 3/4 cup
    chopped scallions)
1 can sliced water chestnuts, drained
salt and pepper to taste

* Combine all ingredients in greased casserole and bake at 350° for 1 hour.

*Pam Richey, Pattie Bethune
Joan Anderson, Judy Thomas*

GREEN RICE

Easy

Serves: 6-8

2 cups steamed rice
2 cups grated cheese
1 cup chopped parsley
2 onions, chopped

2 eggs, beaten
2 cups milk
1/3 cup vegetable oil
1 teaspoon salt

* Combine all ingredients and pour into a 2-quart greased casserole.
* Bake at 350° for 50 minutes.

Judy DuBose

JALAPEÑO RICE

Serves: 8

4-1/2 cups cooked rice, seasoned with
    salt and pepper
4 ounces green chilies

4 ounces pimientos
2 cups sour cream
1 (8-ounce) package casino cheese, grated

* Mix chilies, pimientos and sour cream. Mix together all ingredients except the cheese.
* Put 1/2 of mixture into a buttered 2-quart casserole. Top with 1/2 cheese.
* Repeat layers, ending with cheese. Bake at 350° for 25 minutes.

Lillian Worthy

MUSHROOM RISOTTO

Serves: 4-6

1 cup uncooked rice (preferably Arborio, can use Italian)
1/4 cup chopped onion
8 to 10 small mushrooms, sliced
4 tablespoons butter, divided
2 tomatoes, peeled and chopped

1 pint chicken broth
1 cup dry white wine
salt and pepper to taste
pinch savory (optional)
3 tablespoons grated Parmesan cheese
1/2 cup whipping cream, warmed

* Sauté rice, onion and mushrooms in 3 tablespoons butter until rice just begins to brown. Transfer mixture to pot. (Soak clay pot in water for 15 minutes or use a regular oven baking dish.)
* Add tomatoes, broth, wine, salt, pepper and savory.
* Cover pot and place in a cold oven. Set temperature at 425°. Bake about 40 to 50 minutes or until rice is tender.
* Before serving, stir in grated cheese, remaining tablespoon of butter and warm cream.
* Can serve with additional Parmesan cheese.

Karen Barry

RISOTTO ALLA MILANESE
A good accompaniment to veal

Serves: 6

1/4 cup butter or margarine
1/3 cup minced onion
1-1/2 cups risotto or regular rice
3/4 teaspoon salt

1/8 teaspoon pepper
2 (13-3/4-ounce) cans chicken broth, heated
1/3 cup grated Parmesan cheese

* In a 3-quart oven-safe saucepan, cook onion in butter.
* Add rice and stir.
* Stir in broth, salt and pepper.
* Heat to boiling, stirring constantly.
* Bake at 350° for 30 minutes or until liquid is absorbed.
* Stir in cheese.

Sandy Hibberd

PECAN-WILD RICE PILAF

Serves: 8

4 cups chicken broth
1 cup wild rice, well rinsed
2-1/4 cups water
1-3/4 cups wheat pilaf
1 cup pecan halves, chopped
1 cup dried currants
1 bunch scallions, thinly sliced

1/2 cup chopped parsley
1/2 cup chopped fresh mint leaves
grated zest of 2 oranges
2 tablespoons olive oil
1 tablespoon orange juice
freshly ground black pepper

* In a medium saucepan, bring broth to a boil and add wild rice.
* Cover and reduce heat to medium-low. Cook for 50 minutes or until rice is tender.
* Remove to a large bowl.
* Bring 2-1/4 cups of water to boil. Stir in pilaf. Cover and reduce heat to low.
* Simmer for 15 minutes. Remove from heat. Let rest for 15 minutes; add to wild rice.
* Add remaining ingredients and toss well. Serve at room temperature.

Camilla Turner

SAFFRON RICE

Easy

Serves: 4-6

1/8 teaspoon crushed saffron thread
1-1/2 cups hot water
2 tablespoons butter
1/4 teaspoon salt
1-1/2 cups Basmati rice (available in
    gourmet sections)
1 package frozen peas and carrots

1 teaspoon curry powder
1/4 cup almond slivers
1/4 cup golden raisins
1/4 cup shredded coconut
1/4 cup chopped onion
2 tablespoons butter

* In a 2-quart casserole, mix saffron, water, 2 tablespoons butter and salt.
* Microwave covered on high until boiling (2-1/2 to 3 minutes).
* Stir in rice, peas and carrots, and curry powder. Microwave covered for 15 minutes.
* Fluff with a fork and let rice stand covered while preparing Chicken Curry (see Index).
* In a skillet, brown almonds, raisins, coconut and onion in 2 tablespoons butter. Use to garnish top of rice. Serve with Chicken Curry (see Index).

Shoba Rao

STIR-FRIED RICE

Easy - Prepare ahead   Serves: 6

2 eggs, beaten   *2 tablespoons chopped onions*
1/2 cup cooked, cubed ham   *6 cups cooked rice*
1/2 cup small shrimp, cooked or fresh *2 teaspoons salt*
2 tablespoons green peas   *8 tablespoons oil*

* Heat 2 tablespoons of oil in pan.
* Pour in the beaten eggs and scramble over medium heat until the eggs are in tiny pieces. Remove from pan.
* Heat another 3 tablespoons of oil in the same frying pan.
* Stir-fry shrimp and ham. Add green peas. Stir-fry for about 1 minute and remove from pan.
* Heat another 3 tablespoons of oil in the same frying pan. Stir-fry the onion and cooked rice. Add salt.
* Reduce heat and stir until the rice is thoroughly mixed.
* Add the egg, ham, shrimp and green peas.
* Combine well and serve.

Yuh Hui Lee

VERMOUTH RICE

Goes nicely with beef entree

Easy   Serves: 6

1/4 cup butter or margarine   *1/4 teaspoon pepper*
1 medium onion, chopped   *1 tablespoon Worcestershire sauce*
1 clove garlic, minced   *1 (4-ounce) can mushrooms, drained*
1 cup long grain rice, uncooked   *1/2 to 3/4 cup dry vermouth*
1/2 teaspoon salt   *1 can beef consommé*

* Melt butter; add onion and garlic. Cook, until onion is tender.
* Add rice and stir. Add remaining ingredients.
* Bake in covered casserole at 325° for 45 minutes or until all liquid is absorbed.

Judi Tingler

CHOUCROUTE GARNIE
(Sauerkraut garnished with meat)

Easy   Serves: 4

2 tablespoons oil
2 medium onions, sliced
1 clove garlic, minced
1 tart apple, pared and diced
1 carrot, grated
1 cup dry white wine or beer
1 bay leaf

10 peppercorns
2 cloves
parsley
2 (16-ounce) cans sauerkraut
1 pound Canadian bacon or ham, cut into
    1/4-inch chunks
4 knockwurst, sliced

* In a heavy covered pot, heat oil and cook onions, garlic, apple and carrots until onions brown. Add wine and seasonings. Let simmer.
* Rinse sauerkraut and press dry.
* Stir sauerkraut into liquid mixture. Add meats and cook 20 to 25 minutes.

Irene Kelly

CREAMED SPINACH
From Five Crowns Restaurant, Laguna Beach, California

Serves: 4-6

2 (10-ounce) packages frozen chopped
    spinach
4 slices bacon, finely chopped
1 cup finely chopped onion
4 tablespoons flour

2 teaspoons seasoned salt
1/2 teaspoon seasoned pepper
2 cloves garlic, minced
2 cups milk

* Cook spinach. Drain well.
* Fry bacon and onion together until onion is tender. Remove from heat and stir in flour, salt, pepper and garlic. Blend thoroughly.
* Slowly add milk, returning to medium heat. Stir and cook until smooth and thickened.
* Add spinach and mix thoroughly.

Susan Guarnaccia

Variation: Add 1 tablespoon Dijon mustard and 1/3 cup Parmesan cheese.

Betsy Mitchell

SHERRY'S SPINACH CASSEROLE

Serves: 8

1 (10-ounce) package frozen chopped
   spinach (may substitute chopped
   broccoli)
2 (16-ounce) cartons large-curd cottage
   cheese
6 eggs, beaten
1 small onion, chopped

1/2 pound pasteurized processed cheese,
   diced
1 teaspoon Worcestershire sauce
several dashes hot pepper sauce
additional processed cheese or Parmesan
   cheese for topping

* Defrost and thoroughly drain spinach.
* Mix all ingredients well. Place in greased 13x9-inch casserole.
* Top with additional processed cheese or Parmesan cheese.
* Bake at 350° for 30 to 40 minutes or until set.
* May be baked a day ahead and reheated, well covered.

Ellen Knott

SIMPLE SPINACH CASSEROLE
Simply delicious

Easy

Serves: 4-6

3 (10-ounce) packages frozen chopped
   spinach
1 cup sour cream
1 package dry onion soup mix

4 tablespoons butter
1/2 cup breadcrumbs
1/4 cup grated Parmesan cheese

* Cook and drain spinach.
* Mix sour cream and onion soup mix and stir into spinach. Put into casserole.
* Melt butter. Add crumbs and cheese to butter and put on top of spinach mixture.
* Bake at 325° for 30 to 40 minutes.

Nancy Young

SPINACH CASSEROLE

Easy   Serves: 8

2 (10-ounce) packages frozen, chopped   1 can cream of mushroom soup
  spinach   1 can fried onion rings
1 (8-ounce) package cream cheese

* Follow package instructions to thaw spinach in the microwave. Drain well.
* Mix cream cheese, soup and spinach in casserole. Stir in onion rings.
* Bake at 350° for approximately 20 minutes.

Martha Owen

GREEN AND GOLD SQUASH PIE
A gourmet meatless meal

Serves: 6-8

1 unbaked 10-inch pastry shell   3/4 teaspoon salt
2 medium zucchini, thinly sliced   1/4 teaspoon pepper
2 medium yellow squash, thinly sliced   1/2 teaspoon basil
1/2 medium onion, chopped   2 tablespoons melted butter or margarine
2 green onions, sliced   3 eggs, beaten
1 large clove of garlic, minced (optional) 1/2 cup whipping cream
1 medium tomato, peeled and chopped   1/4 cup grated Parmesan cheese
1 medium green pepper, finely chopped

* Prick bottom and sides of pastry shell. Bake at 450° for 8 minutes or until lightly
  browned. Cool.
* Combine vegetables, salt, pepper, basil and butter in large skillet. Sauté until
  vegetables are tender.
* Spoon into pastry shell, spreading evenly.
* Combine eggs and cream. Mix well. Pour over vegetables.
* Sprinkle with cheese and bake at 350° for 30 minutes or until set.

Sandy Pettyjohn

SOUTH-OF-THE-BORDER SQUASH

Serves: 8

1-1/2 pounds summer squash, diced
1 medium onion, chopped
2 tablespoons butter
1 (4-ounce) can diced green chilies
2 tablespoons flour
1 teaspoon salt

1/2 teaspoon black pepper
1-1/2 cups grated Monterey Jack cheese
1 egg
1 cup cottage cheese
2 teaspoons chopped parsley
1/2 cup Parmesan cheese

* Sauté squash with onion and butter until tender but still crisp.
* Fold in chilies, flour, salt and pepper.
* Place in greased 2-quart baking dish and sprinkle with Monterey Jack cheese.
* Combine egg, cottage cheese and parsley. Pour over squash. Sprinkle with Parmesan cheese.
* Bake uncovered at 400° for 25 to 30 minutes.
* Option: chopped pimiento may be added for color.

Karen Peters

SQUASH CASSEROLE
Even squash-haters ask for this recipe.

Serves: 6-8

2 pounds yellow squash, sliced
2 small zucchini squash, sliced
1 large sweet onion, chopped
1 carrot, grated
2 beaten eggs or 1/2 cup egg substitute

1 cup light mayonnaise
1 cup grated Parmesan cheese
salt and pepper to taste
Italian seasoned breadcrumbs
butter-flavored non-stick vegetable spray

* Cook squash and onion 10 to 15 minutes or until tender. Drain and cool slightly.
* Add carrot, eggs, mayonnaise, Parmesan cheese, salt and pepper.
* Pour into 2-1/2-quart casserole. Sprinkle top with breadcrumbs.
* Spray crumbs lightly with cooking spray.
* Bake at 350° for 45 to 50 minutes or until lightly browned around the edges.

Peggy Buchanan

STIR-FRIED SQUASH WITH SUN-DRIED TOMATOES

Serves: 6

3 to 4 tablespoons olive oil
2 pounds yellow squash, sliced into
   1/4-inch rounds
3 tablespoons chopped fresh rosemary

6 to 8 sun-dried tomatoes, sliced into thin
   strips
salt and freshly ground black pepper

* In a large skillet or wok, heat oil over high heat.
* Add squash and sauté until lightly browned.
* Add remaining ingredients and toss well.
* Serve immediately.

Steve Horsley

A VERY DIFFERENT SQUASH CASSEROLE
A colorful casserole with crunch

Serves: 12-15

1 tablespoon margarine
1 cup chopped pecans
1-2 medium onions, chopped
1/3 cup chopped green pepper
1/3 cup chopped red bell pepper
2 cloves garlic, minced (optional)
2 cups shredded sharp Cheddar cheese

2 pounds yellow squash, sliced,
   blanched and drained
4 eggs
1/4 cup mayonnaise
1/4 cup milk
hot pepper sauce
1 cup breadcrumbs

* Melt margarine and lightly sauté pecans, stirring constantly. Set aside.
* In mixing bowl, stir together onions, peppers, garlic, cheese and squash.
* In another bowl, whisk eggs, mayonnaise, milk and hot pepper sauce.
* Add mixture to vegetables.
* Stir in pecans and breadcrumbs.
* Pour into lightly greased 13x9-inch casserole.
* Bake uncovered at 350° for 35 to 40 minutes.

Kathy Tuten

OVEN-FRIED GREEN TOMATOES

Easy

green tomatoes cut in 1/2-inch slices
  (as many as you wish)
fine dry breadcrumbs

Parmesan cheese
salt and pepper to taste
butter or margarine

* Combine breadcrumbs, Parmesan cheese, salt and pepper.
* Dredge tomato slices in breadcrumb mixture, reserving some for topping.
* Place in pan coated with non-stick cooking spray.
* Sprinkle with reserved mixture and dot with butter.
* Bake at 350° for 45 minutes.

Hilda Rutherford

DELIGHTFUL STUFFED TOMATOES

Serves: 6

6 firm, ripe tomatoes
salt to taste
1 medium green pepper, chopped
1 small onion, chopped
1/4 cup butter or margarine, melted
1 cup (4 ounces) shredded Cheddar
  cheese

1 cup cooked rice
1 well-beaten egg
1/4 teaspoon dried whole oregano
1/4 teaspoon dried whole basil
1/2 teaspoon salt
4 slices bacon, cooked and crumbled
parsley

* Cut a slice from top of each tomato.
* Scoop out pulp, leaving shells intact and reserving pulp.
* Sprinkle inside of tomato shells lightly with salt. Invert to drain.
* Chop tomato pulp.
* Sauté green pepper and onion in butter. Add tomato pulp and all remaining ingredients except parsley. Stir well.
* Spoon mixture into tomato shells. Place in a shallow baking dish.
* Bake at 350° for 25 to 30 minutes.
* Garnish with parsley.

Pam McLean

FRESH TOMATO PIE

Great with seafood

Serves: 6

1 9-inch pie shell, baked and cooled
2 to 3 large tomatoes, peeled and sliced
2 to 3 large green onions, chopped
salt and pepper to taste

1 tablespoon fresh basil, chopped
1 tablespoon fresh chives, chopped
1 cup mayonnaise
1 cup sharp Cheddar cheese, grated

* Sprinkle tomatoes with salt and drain on a cake rack for 15 to 20 minutes.
* Layer tomatoes, onions, salt, pepper, basil and chives in a pie shell.
* Blend mayonnaise and cheese in a mixing bowl and spread over top of pie.
* Bake at 350° for 30 minutes until top is lightly browned.

Teresa Ernsberger

TOMATO DELIGHT

Serve for breakfast or as a vegetable with a meal.

Easy

Serves: 4-6

2 medium-sized ripe tomatoes, unpeeled
oregano
mayonnaise (not salad dressing)

real bacon bits
4 ounces sliced Muenster cheese

* Layer ingredients on top of sliced tomatoes in order listed, using a dash of oregano and a generous dab of mayonnaise.
* Broil until cheese melts.
* Serve immediately.

Janet Povall

TOMATO-ZUCCHINI CHEESE CASSEROLE
A favorite recipe from Eli's

Serves: 8-10

8 small zucchini, unpeeled and sliced
   crosswise
8 small tomatoes, unpeeled and sliced
2 to 3 medium onions, thinly sliced
8 ounces sharp Cheddar cheese

2 cups cracker crumbs, made from
   Bremmer Wafers
1/4 cup butter
brown sugar
salt and pepper to taste

* Spray 13x9-inch pan with non-stick vegetable spray.
* Make a single layer of zucchini, then tomatoes. Sprinkle tomatoes lightly with brown sugar.
* Add a single layer of onion slices. Sprinkle with salt and pepper.
* Top with 1/3 cracker crumbs and 1/3 cheese. Repeat layers two more times.
* Dot top layer of cracker crumbs with butter before adding the last 1/3 cheese.
* Bake at 300° for 1 hour 15 minutes.

Laura Courter

ITALIAN ZUCCHINI PIE
Serve with fruit for brunch or light meal.

Serves: 6

1 large onion, chopped
4 cups thinly sliced zucchini
1/2 cup butter
1 tablespoon parsley
1/4 teaspoon basil
1/4 teaspoon oregano
1/2 teaspoon salt

1/2 teaspoon pepper
pinch of garlic powder
2 teaspoons Dijon mustard
1 cup grated Monterey Jack or
   mozzarella cheese
2 eggs
1 package crescent rolls

* Sauté onion and zucchini in butter until soft. Add herbs, salt and pepper.
* Mix eggs, cheese and zucchini.
* Flatten crescent rolls in pie pan. Spread with mustard.
* Add squash mixture.
* Bake at 350° for 20 minutes or until firm. Let sit 10 minutes before cutting.

Aggie Niess

ZAN'S ZUCCHINI

A favorite use for zucchini and Vidalias

Easy   Serves: 4-6

5 tablespoons butter melted   salt and pepper to taste
3 to 4 medium zucchini, sliced   3 eggs
1 large sweet onion, sliced   1/2 cup mayonnaise
1/2 cup sliced celery   2 teaspoons sugar
1 (8-ounce) can sliced water chestnuts,   Parmesan cheese
    drained

* Melt butter in 2-quart casserole and layer vegetables in order listed.
* Mix eggs, mayonnaise and sugar. Pour over vegetables.
* Top with grated cheese.
* Bake at 350° for 30 minutes.

Zan Gammage

ZUCCHINI CASSEROLE

Easy   Serves: 6-8

2 cups sliced zucchini   1 (8-ounce) package cream cheese, softened
4 sliced carrots   1 can cream of chicken soup, undiluted
1 onion, sliced or chopped   dried herb stuffing mix
1/2 cup butter   Parmesan cheese

* Cook vegetables until fork tender and drain.
* Heat butter, cream cheese and soup together until well blended.
* Add the vegetables to sauce. Pour into buttered casserole.
* Top with stuffing mix and Parmesan cheese.
* Bake at 350° for 30 to 40 minutes.

Note: May mix yellow squash with zucchini. Also, if the mixture appears too saucy, add squash until desired consistency.

Aggie Niess

THREE-VEGETABLE CASSEROLE
A very colorful, delicious company casserole

Easy

Serves: 8

1 (10-ounce) package frozen chopped broccoli
1 (10-ounce) package frozen cauliflower
1 (10-ounce) package frozen brussel sprouts

1 can cream of celery soup
1/2 to 1 can tomatoes with green chilies
1 (4-ounce) jar Old English Cheese Spread
paprika

* Boil all 3 packages of vegetables together in salted water for 5 minutes, drain and put in casserole.
* Mix soup, tomatoes and cheese in saucepan until blended. Heat over low heat.
* Pour soup mixture over vegetables and top with paprika.
* Can be frozen at this point for later use.
* Bake at 350° until bubbly, about 20 to 30 minutes.

Janet Povall

VEGETABLE BAKE
Very easy, nutritious and colorful

Serves: 6

2 medium summer squash, sliced
2 medium zucchini, sliced
1 medium onion, sliced into rings (Vidalia preferred)
1 firm, unpeeled tomato, sliced

10 sliced fresh mushrooms (optional)
2 tablespoons olive oil
1/3 to 1/2 cup grated Parmesan cheese
1 tablespoon Italian seasoning
salt and pepper to taste

* Combine vegetables and toss with olive oil, Italian seasoning, salt and pepper.
* Layer 1/3 mixture in a greased flat casserole and sprinkle liberally with Parmesan cheese.
* Layer second and third parts the same way, topping with Parmesan cheese.
* Cover with aluminum foil and bake at 375° for 30 to 45 minutes.

Parkie Thomas

181

VEGETABLE CASSEROLE

Serves: 6

*1 (10-ounce) package frozen baby lima
  beans
1 (10-ounce) package frozen broccoli
  florets
1 (8-ounce) can sliced water chestnuts
1 (8-ounce) carton sour cream*

*1 can cream of mushroom soup
1 package dry onion soup mix
1 small jar mushroom pieces
1 stick butter
1 cup grated sharp Cheddar cheese
3 cups crispy rice cereal*

* Cook limas following package directions until barely tender.
* Cook broccoli until barely tender.
* Mix with remaining ingredients except for butter, cheese and rice cereal. Put in a greased casserole.
* Melt butter; add cheese and cereal. Spread on top of casserole.
* Cook at 325° for 25 to 30 minutes or until bubbly.

Ellen Knott

BAKED APPLES IN A DISH

Serves: 8

*2 cans sliced apples or 6 apples (Winesap
  or Golden Delicious) peeled, cored and
  quartered
1-1/4 to 1-1/2 cups sugar
juice and grated rind of 1/2 lemon*

*1/3 stick butter
8 slices white bread
1 stick butter, melted
1/4 to 1/2 cup sugar*

* Place apples in 13x9-inch baking dish.
* Add sugar, lemon juice, grated rind and dot with 1/3 stick butter.
* Cover and bake at 350° for 30 minutes.
* Trim crusts from bread slices and cube.
* Spoon melted butter over cubed bread, tossing to coat pieces.
* Add sugar and gently toss with buttered bread cubes until pieces are covered.
* Place bread cubes on top of apples and spread evenly.
* Bake uncovered in 350° oven several minutes until lightly brown.
* Watch closely.

Mary Ann Little

CRANAPPLE BAKE

Can be prepared 24 hours in advance and refrigerated until ready to bake

Serves: 8-12

12 ounces fresh cranberries
1-1/2 cups sugar
5 tablespoons cornstarch
Topping:
1 cup oatmeal
1 cup sugar
1 cup chopped walnuts or pecans

6 to 8 Golden Delicious apples, peeled,
  cored and sliced
1/2 cup cognac or bourbon

1/4 cup flour
1 stick butter, melted
1 tablespoon vanilla

* Spray 13x9-inch glass baking dish with non-stick spray.
* Spread cranberries in pan. Mix cornstarch and sugar; pour over cranberries and stir.
* Place peeled and sliced apples on top of cranberries. Pour the cognac or bourbon on top of the apples.
* Mix all topping ingredients until the butter is well blended with the dry ingredients.
* Spoon topping over apples.
* Bake uncovered at 350° for 1 hour and 20 to 30 minutes, or until bubbly.

Brandon Chapman

CRANBERRY CRUNCH

A side dish that compliments a holiday dinner

Serves: 6-8

4 apples, diced
1 tablespoon lemon juice
1 cup crushed pineapple, drained
1 can whole cranberry sauce or 1 cup
  fresh cranberries

1 cup oatmeal
3/4 cup brown sugar
1/2 cup flour
1/3 cup melted butter
1 teaspoon cinnamon

* Layer apples, lemon juice, pineapple and cranberries in a 2-quart casserole.
* Mix remaining ingredients and sprinkle on top.
* Bake at 350° for 30 minutes or until bubbly.

Susan Hurleigh, Karen Wilson
Carol Lawing, Phyllis Sills

PINEAPPLE AU GRATIN

Easy   Serves: 6

3 tablespoons flour   *1 cup grated sharp Cheddar cheese*
1/2 cup sugar   *12 round buttery crackers*
1 (20-ounce) can pineapple chunks   *4 tablespoons butter, melted*
  (in its own juice)

* Mix flour and sugar.
* Drain and reserve pineapple juice.
* Toss pineapple with flour-sugar mixture. Stir in cheese.
* Place in 11x7-inch casserole dish sprayed with non-stick vegetable spray.
* Drizzle small amount of pineapple juice over top of casserole.
* Crumble crackers over top of casserole and drizzle with butter.
* Bake at 350° for 30 minutes.

Phyllis Herring
Aggie Niess
Kim Martin

HOME-SPICED PEACHES

Easy   Serves: 4

2 (16-ounce) cans peach halves   *1 teaspoon whole cloves*
3/4 cup brown sugar, firmly packed   *1 teaspoon whole allspice*
2 (3-inch) sticks cinnamon   *1/2 cup vinegar*

* Drain peaches, reserving syrup.
* Add sugar, vinegar and spices to syrup in saucepan.
* Boil 5 minutes and pour over peaches.
* Put in tightly sealed jar and refrigerate.
* Serve chilled.

Marie Higgins Mullen

PASTA

CANNELLONI

Serves: 6-8

Meat Filling:

1 package manicotti shells, cooked and
 drained
4 cloves garlic
1 medium onion
2 tablespoons butter
2 tablespoons olive oil
1 pound ground round steak

1 (10-ounce) package frozen chopped
 spinach, thawed and well drained
5 tablespoons grated Parmesan cheese
1/2 teaspoon oregano
salt and pepper to taste
2 tablespoons cream
2 eggs, beaten

Cream Sauce:

4 tablespoons butter
4 tablespoons flour
1 cup milk

1 cup heavy cream
1 teaspoon salt
white pepper to taste

Tomato Sauce:

2 tablespoons olive oil
1 small onion
2 (1-pound) cans tomatoes
3 tablespoons tomato paste
1 teaspoon basil

1 teaspoon sugar
1/2 teaspoon salt
black pepper to taste
3 tablespoons grated Parmesan cheese
butter

* To prepare Meat Filling, blend garlic and onion in processor or blender.
* Add onions and garlic to heated butter and olive oil and cook for 5 minutes.
* Add meat and brown well.
* Add spinach and cook until almost all moisture is out of spinach-meat mixture.
* Add seasonings. Cool.
* Beat eggs. Mix with cream. Add to meat mixture. Stuff shells with mixture.
* To make Cream Sauce, melt butter and add flour.
* Cook for 2 minutes. Add milk and cream, stirring constantly until thickened.
* Add seasonings.
* Prepare Tomato Sauce by blending onion in processor or blender and adding to heated
  olive oil.
* Lightly process tomatoes and add to onion mixture.
* Add tomato paste and seasonings. Simmer partially covered for 30 minutes.
* To assemble casserole, glaze bottom of 13x9-inch baking dish with tomato sauce.
* Arrange stuffed shells in baking dish. Cover with cream sauce and top with tomato
  sauce. Sprinkle with Parmesan cheese and dot with butter.
* Bake at 350° for 30 minutes until bubbly. Brown the top under broiler.

Jan Swetenburg

SAVORY CANNELLONI

Serves: 4

Sauce:

1/4 cup margarine or butter
1 clove garlic, crushed
1/4 cup flour
1-1/2 teaspoons instant chicken bouillon

2 cups half-and-half
1/2 cup combined grated Parmesan and
    Romano cheese

Cannelloni Filling:

6 cannelloni shells (or manicotti shells),
    cooked al dente
2 tablespoons butter
3 tablespoons sliced green onion
1 (10-ounce) package frozen chopped
    spinach, thawed and well drained

1 cup finely chopped cooked chicken
1 cup finely chopped cooked ham
1 cup combined grated Parmesan and
    Romano cheese
2 eggs, beaten
3/4 teaspoon Italian seasoning

* To prepare sauce, sauté garlic in butter. Stir in flour and seasonings. Remove from heat.
* Gradually stir in half-and-half. Bring to boiling over medium heat, stirring constantly.
* Boil and stir 1 minute. Reduce heat to low.
* Stir in cheese until melted. Set aside.
* To make Cannelloni Filling, sauté onion in butter until tender. Remove from heat and stir in remaining ingredients.
* Fill cannelloni shells. Place in buttered 2-quart rectangular baking dish.
* Spoon sauce over filled shells. Bake at 350° for 20 minutes. Broil for last few minutes until sauce becomes golden and bubbly.
* Freezes well.

Susan Brigham

PASTA PRIMAVERA

Serves: 4

1 stick plus 3 tablespoons butter
2 tablespoons chopped onion
1 medium carrot, julienned
1 medium zucchini, julienned
1 cup broccoli florets, finely chopped
  or 3/4 cup frozen tiny green peas

1/2 pound fresh mushrooms, sliced
1/2 cup fresh asparagus tips
1 (16-ounce) package fettuccine, cooked,
  drained and kept warm
1 cup heavy cream
3/4 cup Parmesan cheese

* In 3 tablespoons butter, sauté onion, carrot, zucchini and broccoli or peas for 2 to 4 minutes. Add mushrooms and asparagus. Sauté 1 to 2 minutes or until tender.
* Heat remaining butter and cream together. Stir to blend.
* Toss fettuccine and vegetables together. Add butter-cream mixture. Toss again.
* Sprinkle with cheese. Quickly toss again. Serve immediately with Parmesan cheese.

Mary Edwards, Shirley Griffin

BAKED LASAGNA

Serves: 12

2 pounds ground chuck
1 clove garlic, minced
1 tablespoon parsley flakes
1 tablespoon basil
1-1/2 teaspoons salt
1/2 pound mozzarella cheese, sliced
1/2 pound Cheddar cheese, sliced
1 (16-ounce) can whole tomatoes

2 (6-ounce) cans tomato paste
10 ounces lasagna noodles
3 cups cottage cheese
2 eggs, beaten
2 teaspoons salt
1/2 teaspoon pepper
2 tablespoons parsley flakes
1/2 cup Parmesan cheese

* Cook noodles according to package directions. Drain. Rinse in cold water; set aside.
* Brown meat. Add garlic, parsley, basil, salt, tomatoes and tomato paste. Simmer 30 minutes.
* Mix together cottage cheese, eggs, salt, pepper, parsley flakes and Parmesan cheese.
* In a 13x9-inch baking dish, layer 1/2 noodles, 1/2 cottage cheese mixture, 1/2 mozzarella and Cheddar cheeses, 3/4 of meat sauce.
* Repeat layers, saving sliced cheese for the top.
* Bake covered at 375° for 30 to 45 minutes. Uncover and bake 5 more minutes.

Brandon Chapman, Frances Fennebresque

SAUSAGE-LASAGNA ROLL-UPS

Serves: 8

1 pound (hot or mild) Italian link sausage, cut into 1/2-inch pieces
3/4 cup chopped onion
1 clove garlic, minced
1 (24-ounce) can tomato juice
1 (6-ounce) can tomato paste
1/2 cup water
2 teaspoons sugar
1/2 teaspoon salt

1 bay leaf
2 cups cream-style cottage cheese
1 egg, slightly beaten
1/2 cup grated Parmesan cheese, divided
2 cups shredded mozzarella cheese, divided
1/4 teaspoon salt
1/4 teaspoon pepper
8 lasagna noodles

* Cook sausage in a large, heavy skillet until browned.
* Remove sausage, reserving 1/4 cup drippings in skillet.
* Sauté onion and garlic in drippings until onion is crisp-tender.
* Add sausage, tomato juice, tomato paste, water, sugar, 1/2 teaspoon salt and bay leaf.
* Simmer uncovered 1 hour, stirring occasionally.
* Remove bay leaf.
* Combine cottage cheese, egg, 1/4 cup Parmesan cheese, 1 cup mozzarella cheese, 1/4 teaspoon salt and pepper. Chill thoroughly.
* Cook lasagna noodles according to package directions. Drain, rinse and cool.
* Spread about 1 cup meat sauce in a lightly greased 13x9-inch baking dish.
* Spread 1/4 cup cheese mixture on each lasagna noodle and roll up jellyroll fashion.
* Arrange lasagna rolls, seam side down, in pan. Pour remaining meat sauce over rolls. Top with remaining Parmesan and mozzarella cheeses.
* Bake at 350° for 30 to 40 minutes or until bubbly.

Tonia Caligiuri

BROCCOLI LASAGNA
Won kudos at the 1990 Library Volunteers Luncheon

Serves: 10

*2 (10-3/4-ounce) cans condensed cream
of broccoli soup
1 (10-ounce) package frozen chopped
broccoli
vegetable oil
3 carrots, thinly sliced
1 large onion, diced*

*3/4 pound mushrooms, sliced
12 lasagna noodles
2 (8-ounce) packages shredded mozzarella
cheese
1 (15-ounce) container ricotta cheese
2 large eggs*

* In 2-quart saucepan, heat undiluted broccoli soup and frozen broccoli over medium-low heat until broccoli is thawed.
* In 10-inch skillet, heat 1 tablespoon salad oil over medium-high heat and cook carrots and onion until lightly brown.
* Reduce heat to low and stir in 1/4 cup water. Cover and simmer 15 minutes or until vegetables are very tender. Remove to bowl.
* In same skillet, heat 3 tablespoons salad oil over high heat. Cook mushrooms until lightly browned and all liquid has evaporated. Stir in carrot mixture.
* While vegetables are cooking, prepare noodles according to label directions. Drain.
* In bowl, mix mozzarella, ricotta and eggs.
* In a 13x9-inch baking dish, spread 1 cup broccoli sauce. Arrange half of noodles over sauce, top with half of cheese mixture, and then add all the carrot mixture and half of the remaining sauce.
* Top with the remaining noodles, cheese mixture, then sauce.
* Bake at 375° for 45 minutes or until hot. Remove from oven and let stand 10 minutes for easier serving.

Pat Kelly

MEATLESS LASAGNA

Serves: 6

1 (8-ounce) package lasagna noodles
6 green onions
2 (8-ounce) packages light cream cheese, softened

1 (16-ounce) carton sour cream substitute
1 (16-ounce) carton 1% cottage cheese
1 cup grated Cheddar cheese
1 (14-ounce) jar spaghetti sauce

* Cook noodles according to package instructions.
* Chop onions (green tops included). Mix cream cheese, sour cream, cottage cheese and onions.
* Alternate layers of noodles and cheese mixture. Cover with spaghetti sauce and top with Cheddar cheese.
* Bake at 350° for 30 to 40 minutes or until bubbly.

Billie Nichols

VEGETABLE LASAGNA

Serves: 6-8

1 cup chopped onion
3/4 cup chopped celery
1/3 cup chopped green pepper
3 tablespoons olive oil
1 (28-ounce) can crushed tomatoes
1 cup water
1-1/2 teaspoons crushed oregano

1/2 teaspoon salt
1/2 teaspoon garlic powder
1/2 teaspoon Worcestershire sauce
1/8 teaspoon pepper
1/2 cup shredded mozzarella cheese
9 lasagna noodles, uncooked
2 cups thinly sliced zucchini

* In 2-quart saucepan, cook onion, celery and green pepper in olive oil until tender.
* Add tomatoes, water and seasonings. Bring to boil. Reduce heat and simmer over low heat, uncovered, for 30 minutes.
* To assemble, spread 1 cup sauce in a 12x8-inch baking dish. Top with 3 noodles, 1 cup zucchini and 1 cup sauce.
* Repeat layer of noodles, zucchini and sauce, then noodles and sauce. Sprinkle with cheese. Cover tightly with aluminum foil.
* Bake at 350° for 45 minutes. Remove foil and cook 15 minutes longer.
* Remove from oven and let stand for 15 minutes before serving.

Laurie Guy

HOGWILD NOODLES
Men are crazy about this!

Serves: 6-8

1 (8-ounce) pack medium egg noodles
2 tablespoons butter
1 medium onion, finely chopped
1 tablespoon flour
1 teaspoon Dijon mustard
1/4 teaspoon freshly ground black pepper
1 teaspoon fresh basil or 1/2 teaspoon
  dried
1 teaspoon fresh thyme or 1/2 teaspoon
  dried

1 teaspoon fresh oregano or 1/2 teaspoon
  dried
1 clove fresh garlic, minced, or 1/2
  teaspoon garlic powder
2 cups milk
2 cups sharp Cheddar, or combination of
  1 cup shredded white Cheddar
  1/2 cup shredded Swiss
  1/2 cup shredded Monterey Jack

Topping:
1/2 cup butter

1 cup breadcrumbs

* Cook noodles according to package directions. Do not over cook. Drain, rinse and keep warm.
* Spray a 2-quart casserole with cooking spray.
* In a heavy, medium-sized saucepan melt butter and sauté onion until transparent.
* Stir in flour, mustard, herbs, garlic and pepper.
* Add milk and heat until thick, stirring constantly. Do not let boil.
* Remove from heat and stir in 3/4 of the cheese.
* Put noodles in casserole. Pour on the cheese sauce and mix well. Top with the rest of the cheese.
* In a small pan, melt 1/2 cup butter; add crumbs and stir until crumbs are coated. Sprinkle over casserole.
* Bake uncovered at 400° for 20 minutes until bubbly and brown.

The Hawk

MACARONI MOUSSE

Serves: 8-10

1 cup macaroni, uncooked
1-1/2 cups grated sharp Cheddar cheese
3 or 4 slices white bread, trimmed
2 tablespoons chopped pimientos
2 tablespoons chopped green pepper
2 teaspoons parsley flakes
1/2 cup chopped almonds

1 small onion, finely chopped
3 tablespoons butter or margarine
1-1/2 cups scalded milk
salt and pepper to taste
1 egg, beaten
1 can cream of mushroom soup, optional
1 (15-ounce)can asparagus spears, optional

* Cook macaroni according to package directions. Drain. Place in well-buttered 2-quart casserole.
* Place all other ingredients in large bowl except for milk, egg, soup and asparagus.
* Pour hot milk over all and mix well. Bread should dissolve.
* Add beaten egg, mixed with a little milk, to bread mixture and stir well. Pour this over macaroni in casserole.
* May prepare a day ahead to this point and refrigerate overnight. If it looks too thick the next day, stir in a little milk.
* Bake at 350° for 45 to 50 minutes. Remove from oven; top with undiluted mushroom soup and drained asparagus spears, if desired. Return to oven for 5 minutes.

Hilda Rutherford

SWEET CREAMED NOODLES

Serves: 12

1 pound egg noodles
1 (16-ounce) carton cottage cheese
1 stick margarine or butter, melted
6 eggs

16 ounces sour cream
1-1/2 cups sugar
2 teaspoons vanilla
1 teaspoon cinnamon

* Cook noodles 9 minutes and drain, but do not rinse.
* Microwave cottage cheese for 45 seconds for ease in blending.
* Return noodles to pot with 1 stick of melted margarine or butter.
* Blend remaining ingredients with a spoon; combine with noodles.
* Put in 13x9-inch pyrex dish. Bake at 350° for 1 hour.

Sydney Sass

THREE-CHEESE MACARONI

Easy   Serves: 8

1 (8-ounce) package macaroni   1 teaspoon grated onion
4 tablespoons butter   1 tablespoon A-1 sauce
2 tablespoons flour   1 teaspoon salt
3 cups milk   1 teaspoon pepper
1 cup grated mozzarella cheese   1 teaspoon garlic powder
1/2 cup grated Parmesan cheese   dash of dill weed
1/2 cup grated Cheddar cheese

* Cook macaroni according to package directions. Rinse and drain.
* Melt butter in saucepan. Stir in flour. Add milk and cook, stirring constantly until thickened.
* Blend in remaining ingredients, stirring until cheese melts.
* Remove from heat and stir in macaroni. Pour into buttered 2-quart casserole.
* Bake at 350° for 30 minutes.

Nancy Higgins

CHICKEN OR BEEF AND PASTA CASSEROLE

Freezes well   Yields: 2 casseroles (8 servings each)

3 pounds chicken or 2 pounds ground   8 ounces pasta
  beef   1 (15-ounce) can stewed tomatoes or
3 tablespoons margarine   1 (4-ounce) jar pimientos
1 pound mushrooms   1 can cream of mushroom soup
2 cups chopped celery   1 (8-ounce) can sliced water chestnuts
2 medium onions, chopped   1 cup grated sharp Cheddar cheese
1 green pepper, chopped

* Boil chicken (or sauté beef). Save stock. Chop chicken into bite-sized pieces.
* Sauté mushrooms, celery, onions and green pepper in margarine until tender.
* Cook pasta in stock saved from cooking meat. Drain.
* Mix sautéed vegetables, stewed tomatoes (or pimientos) and soup together.
* Layer pasta, meat and vegetable mixture in two casserole dishes. Top with grated Cheddar cheese. Bake at 350° for 20 minutes.

Anne Rutherford

DIJON CHICKEN WITH PASTA

Serves: 6

6 chicken breast halves
3/4 cup butter or margarine, softened
1/3 cup sliced green onions

1/4 cup chopped fresh parsley
3-1/2 tablespoons Dijon mustard
12 ounces fettuccine, cooked and drained

* Loosen skin from breast halves, forming pocket without detaching skin.
* Combine butter and next 3 ingredients, mixing well.
* Place 1-1/2 tablespoons butter mixture under skin of each chicken breast. Reserve remaining mixture.
* Place chicken, skin side up, in a lightly greased 13x9-inch baking dish.
* Bake at 350° for 1 hour, basting with drippings.
* Toss fettuccine with remaining butter mixture. Return to pot to keep warm.
* Serve chicken on fettuccine.

Pam McLean

PASTA PRIMA CHICKEN

Easy

Serves: 6

1/4 cup butter
1/4 cup olive oil
6 boneless, skinless chicken breasts,
* cut into bite-sized pieces*
1/2 cup sliced green onions, include
* green tops*
1 package Pasta Prima Alfredo Sauce
* Blend*

1 cup whipping cream
1 (15-ounce) can tomatoes, chopped
1/2 teaspoon salt
1/2 teaspoon pepper
1 (8-ounce package) tri-colored rotini,
* prepared according to package*
* directions*

* Sauté chicken in butter and olive oil in a large skillet until done.
* Add green onions, package of Alfredo sauce, whipping cream, tomatoes, salt and pepper. Stir until well blended.
* Heat on low temperature until hot.
* Serve chicken on top of pasta.

Phyllis Herring

SPAGHETTI SAUCE
Carrots make the difference.

Serves: 8

1 to 2 tablespoons vegetable oil
1 onion, chopped
2 cloves garlic, minced
1 green pepper, chopped
1 pound ground beef or turkey (optional)

1/2 to 1 pound hot sausage (optional)
2 (6-ounce) cans tomato paste
2 (28-ounce) cans whole tomatoes, chopped
2 carrots, grated
salt and pepper to taste

* Sauté onion, garlic and green pepper in oil.
* If using meats, brown in separate skillet, pouring off fat.
* Add meat to vegetables, along with tomato paste and tomatoes. Stir well.
* Add grated carrots and pepper. Simmer for at least 45 minutes. Can let sauce cook for 1-1/2 to 2 hours if desired.
* Add salt and pepper to taste after removing from heat.

Marilyn Frucella

SPAGHETTI SAUCE (THE REAL THING)
Old family recipe

Serves: 15-20

1 (28-ounce) can peeled tomatoes
2 (15-ounce) cans tomato sauce
2 (18-ounce) cans tomato paste
3 to 4 chicken breasts, skinned and boned
1-1/2 pounds chopped Italian sausage or ground pork
1-1/2 pounds ground beef
1 cup fresh parsley (whole leaves, loosely packed)

salt to taste
3 tablespoons olive oil
1 whole clove garlic, pressed
1 large onion, chopped
4 tablespoons pesto sauce
5 tablespoons grated Romano cheese
1 tomato paste can of water
1 tablespoon pepper

* In a 10-quart pot sauté onion in oil. Add chicken and meat. Brown. Drain excess oil.
* Force tomatoes through a sieve. Discard pulp and seeds.
* Add tomatoes and remaining ingredients to meat. Cover with a vented lid.
* Simmer 2 to 3 hours, stirring every 15 to 20 minutes. Add more water if sauce gets too thick. Serve over favorite pasta.

Joanne Sutcliffe

MAMIE'S BAKED SPAGHETTI CASSEROLE

Easy   Serves: 6-8

1 pound ground chuck
1/2 teaspoon salt
dash pepper
1 onion, chopped
1 green pepper, chopped (optional)
1 (15-ounce) can tomato sauce
1 (6-ounce) can tomato paste
1 tomato paste can of water

1/4 teaspoon garlic salt
1/2 teaspoon dried basil leaves
1/2 teaspoon dried oregano leaves
1 (1-pound) package spaghetti, cooked and
  drained
1 cup grated Monterey Jack cheese
1 cup grated mozzarella cheese
1/4 cup grated Parmesan cheese

* Brown ground chuck, adding salt and pepper.
* Add onion and green pepper. Cook until tender.
* Add tomato sauce, paste and water. Stir well.
* Add garlic salt, basil leaves and oregano leaves. Simmer 20 minutes.
* Layer spaghetti and sauce twice in a greased 13x9-inch casserole dish.
* Cover the top with grated cheeses.
* Bake at 350° for approximately 25 to 30 minutes. Freezes well.

Mary Sue Patten

STRAW AND HAY

Serves: 4-6

4 ounces linguine
4 ounces spinach linguine
1/2 cup butter
8 ounces (1-1/2 cups) ham strips
3/4 cup peas, cooked but still crunchy

1 (2-1/2-ounce) jar sliced mushrooms
2 egg yolks, well beaten
1 cup heavy cream
1 cup (4-ounces) grated Parmesan cheese

* Cook linguine al dente and drain.
* Add butter, ham, peas and mushrooms.
* Beat egg yolks and cream until foamy. Add to linguine.
* Stir in 1/2 cup Parmesan cheese. Stir gently over medium heat until thickened.
* Sprinkle with Parmesan cheese. Serve immediately.

The Hawk

PATTY'S SAUSAGE-LINGUINE TORTE

A very elegant, do-ahead company meal

Serves: 10

1 pound linguine
2 tablespoons butter or margarine
1 tablespoon olive oil
1 pound Italian sausage, (half sweet,
  half hot)
1 medium onion, finely chopped
1 green pepper, coarsely chopped
3 teaspoons oregano
1 (3-1/2-ounce) can sliced black olives
1/4 cup finely chopped parsley

Cream Sauce:

1/4 cup margarine
1/4 cup flour
1 cup milk
1 cup heavy cream

1/2 teaspoon salt
1/2 teaspoon pepper
3 eggs, slightly beaten
1 (15-ounce) container ricotta cheese
1/4 cup grated Romano cheese
3 tomatoes, thinly sliced
1 cup shredded mozzarella cheese
1 cup shredded Swiss cheese
1 tablespoon grated Parmesan cheese

pinch nutmeg
1 teaspoon salt
1/8 teaspoon white pepper
1/2 cup Parmesan cheese

* Cook linguine in salted, boiling water until almost tender. Drain, toss with margarine and cover.
* Remove and discard sausage casings.
* Finely chop sausage and brown in olive oil. Pour off excess fat.
* Add onion, green pepper and 1 teaspoon oregano. Sauté 5 minutes.
* Combine sausage mixture with olives, parsley, salt and pepper.
* Toss with linguine. Set aside.
* Whisk together eggs, ricotta, 2 teaspoons oregano and Romano until light and fluffy.
* Stir into linguine mixture, toss gently.
* Press half into bottom of lightly greased and floured springform pan.
* Put half of tomatoes on top. Sprinkle with half the mozzarella and Swiss. Repeat layers. Sprinkle with Parmesan.
* Cover tightly with foil and bake at 375° for 50 minutes or until set.
* Remove foil and bake 5 more minutes. Let stand 10 minutes; cut in wedges to serve.
* If frozen, bake 1 hour and 45 minutes covered and 15 minutes uncovered.
* Serve wedges of torte with cream sauce and commercial marinara sauce.
* To prepare Cream Sauce, melt margarine and whisk in flour.
* Gradually add liquids. Stir constantly over medium heat until mixture boils and thickens. Lower heat and simmer 2 to 3 minutes. Remove from heat.
* Stir in remaining ingredients until smooth.

Jean Webb

ANGEL HAIR PASTA WITH CRAB AND PESTO

Serves: 2

1/4 stick unsalted butter
2 ounces fresh mushrooms, sliced
1/2 cup pesto sauce
1 large tomato, seeded and chopped
1 teaspoon grated lemon peel

8 ounces angel hair pasta, cooked and
    drained
2 tablespoons olive oil
1/2 pound crabmeat
freshly grated Parmesan cheese

* Melt butter in a large skillet over medium heat.
* Sauté mushrooms until tender.
* Mix in pesto, tomato and lemon peel.
* Remove from heat.
* Toss pasta with oil.
* Add crab to sauce and stir over medium heat until hot.
* Spoon over pasta and top with Parmesan.

The Hawk

CRABMEAT AND PASTA WITH CHEESE SAUCE

Serves: 4

2 cups sliced and quartered fresh
    zucchini
1/4 cup sliced scallions or minced onions
1/2 cup Chardonnay, divided
2 teaspoons margarine
2 tablespoons flour
2 cups imitation crabmeat, chopped

salt and pepper to taste
pinch of ground nutmeg
2 cups skim milk
1/2 cup grated Parmesan cheese
2 tablespoons minced fresh parsley
4 cups pasta shells, cooked and drained

* Combine zucchini, onion, 1/4 cup wine and margarine in non-stick skillet. Cook and
  stir over moderate heat until wine evaporates.
* Stir flour, salt, pepper and nutmeg into milk. Add to skillet and stir. Cook over low
  heat until thickened.
* Stir in cheese. Add crabmeat and heat through. Remove from heat. Stir in parsley.
* Spoon over hot drained pasta.

Nancy Gaskin

SHRIMP ALDO

Serves: 4-6

1 pound raw shrimp, peeled and deveined
2 sticks butter
2 teaspoons minced garlic
juice of 2 lemons

1 (8-ounce) can mushrooms, drained
1/2 cup white wine
1 pound spaghetti, cooked and drained
1/2 cup grated Romano cheese

* Sauté shrimp, 1 stick of butter and garlic for 3 minutes. Remove shrimp; set aside.
* Add other stick of butter, lemon juice, mushrooms and white wine to pan drippings. Heat thoroughly.
* Add shrimp to sauce and heat 1 minute. Pour over hot spaghetti and toss well. Top with Romano cheese.

Margo Colasanti

ROSBOTTOM'S SHRIMP FETTUCCINE
Fabulous! Worth the calories!

1/2 stick unsalted butter
2 tablespoons olive oil
1 pound large raw shrimp, peeled and deveined
1/2 cup dry white wine
Garlic Butter:
3/4 cup unsalted butter, at room temperature
2 teaspoons very finely chopped garlic
3 tablespoons finely chopped shallots

1 pound fettuccine, cooked and drained
1/4 cup whipping cream
2/3 cup freshly grated Parmesan cheese
2/3 cup chopped fresh parsley
salt and pepper to taste

1/2 cup chopped fresh parsley
1/8 teaspoon salt
freshly ground pepper, to taste

* To make Garlic Butter, mix all ingredients. Cover and refrigerate.
* Bring Garlic Butter to room temperature (if prepared ahead).
* Heat unsalted butter and olive oil over medium heat. Add shrimp. Stir until shrimp turn pink (2 to 3 minutes).
* Add wine and cook 2 minutes. Remove from heat.
* Add shrimp to pasta and toss. Stir in garlic butter until melted.
* Stir in cream, cheese and half the parsley. Mix well.
* Add salt and pepper. Top with remaining parsley.

Marilyn Thompson

SHRIMP SPAGHETTI WITH BLACK OLIVES

Serves: 6

8 ounces vermicelli, cooked and drained
1/3 cup olive oil
1-1/2 pounds medium shrimp, peeled and
 deveined
1 cup chopped onion
2 (16-ounce) cans tomatoes, undrained,
 chopped

1 to 2 teaspoons dried basil
1/2 teaspoon salt
1/4 teaspoon pepper
1/2 cup chopped fresh parsley
3/4 cup sliced ripe olives
3 tablespoons Parmesan cheese

* Heat oil in large Dutch oven on medium-high heat.
* Add onion and shrimp. Cook, stirring constantly for 5 minutes or until shrimp are
 pink.
* Remove shrimp and set aside.
* Add tomatoes and seasonings and bring to a boil. Cook uncovered for 5 to 7 minutes.
* Add vermicelli, shrimp and parsley. Toss until mixture is well coated.
* Transfer to a serving dish. Sprinkle with ripe olives and Parmesan cheese.

Nancy Wohlbruck

SPAGHETTI WITH GARLIC SAUCE

Serves: 4-6

1 pound spaghetti or vermicelli
1 pound mushrooms, sliced
4 tablespoons olive oil
2 tablespoons safflower oil

4 large cloves garlic, finely chopped
hot pepper flakes to taste (optional)
3 tablespoons minced Italian parsley

* Cook pasta in a large pot of boiling water.
* While pasta is cooking, sauté mushrooms in 2 tablespoons of olive oil and 1
 tablespoon of safflower oil until all moisture cooks out.
* When the pasta is cooked, drain, reserving about 1/2 cup cooking water.
* Heat remaining oil and add garlic. Add pepper flakes as garlic begins to color.
* Add pasta and the reserved pasta water and toss for 30 seconds.
* Add parsley and mix well.
* Serve pasta with a mound of cooked mushrooms on top.

Catherine Whittington

CONFETTI SPAGHETTI

Serves: 6-8

1 tablespoon butter or margarine
3 tablespoons olive oil
1 cup diced onions
3 to 4 cloves garlic, minced
1 teaspoon salt
1 teaspoon dried basil
1 teaspoon freshly ground black pepper
2 spears broccoli, chopped
2 cups cauliflower, chopped

1/4 pound mushrooms, chopped
2 cups frozen peas
1 medium red pepper, diced
3 tablespoons tamari sauce
4 to 6 green onions, finely sliced
1 cup (packed) minced parsley
2 cups grated Cheddar cheese
1 pound spaghetti

* Cook spaghetti according to package directions.
* Meanwhile, in a large heavy skillet, combine butter and olive oil.
* Add onions, garlic, salt, pepper and basil; cook 5 minutes until onions are soft.
* Stir in broccoli, cauliflower and mushrooms.
* Cover and cook on medium-low heat until vegetables are just tender.
* Add peas and red pepper and continue to cook until mixture is heated through.
* Remove from heat and add tamari sauce. Pour vegetable mixture over spaghetti.
* Sprinkle with green onions, parsley and cheese. Toss lightly. Serve immediately.

Sherry Thacker

PASTA WITH ARTICHOKE SAUCE

2 tablespoons vegetable oil
1 small onion, finely chopped
1 clove garlic, minced
1 package frozen artichoke hearts,
  thawed and chopped
3 medium tomatoes, peeled and chopped

1 tablespoon fresh parsley
1 teaspoon sweet basil
salt and pepper to taste
1-1/4 cups freshly grated Parmesan cheese
8 ounces spaghetti or fettuccine noodles,
  cooked

* Heat oil in a heavy skillet; cook onion and garlic until transparent.
* Add artichoke hearts, tomatoes, parsley, basil, salt and pepper. Cook slowly over low heat, stirring occasionally, for 1 hour or until thickened.
* Stir in cheese until melted. Serve over spaghetti or fettuccine.
* Can put sauce in blender and puree for variation.

Nancy Gaskin

LIGHT AND
LUSCIOUS

COOKING LIGHT AND LUSCIOUS

Each recipe included in *Light and Luscious* is not just delicious, it has been analyzed by computer for calories, carbohydrate, protein, dietary fiber, sodium, fat (saturated, polyunsaturated, total) and cholesterol. All recipes meet the American Heart Association guidelines for a heart-healthy diet.

If you wish to lose weight, a drastic cut in calories is not necessary. In most cases, merely trimming the fat in your diet will result in weight loss. Fat contains 9 calories per gram, while carbohydrates contain only 4 calories per gram. More calories are burned in the digestion of carbohydrates (vegetables, fruits and starchy foods). Replacing fats in your diet with carbohydrates will decrease your calorie intake while increasing your energy expenditure.

COTTAGE SPINACH DIP

Serves: 12; Calories per serving: 81 (Protein 45%, Carbohydrate 31%, Fat 24%)

1 (10-ounce) bag fresh spinach, chopped
1/2 cup chopped onion
1 (8-ounce) package light Neufchatel
  cream cheese, softened
3/4 cup lowfat cottage cheese
1/2 teaspoon dried basil

1/2 teaspoon dried oregano
1/4 teaspoon salt
1/8 teaspoon garlic powder
1/8 teaspoon pepper
3/4 cup chopped tomatoes
2 tablespoons grated Parmesan cheese

* Place spinach and onions in small saucepan. Cover and cook 5 minutes or until tender.
* Beat cheeses in small bowl with electric mixer until smooth. Add seasonings and blend well.
* Stir in spinach mixture; spread into 9-inch pie plate.
* Bake at 350° for 15 to 20 minutes or until thoroughly heated.
* Top with tomato and Parmesan cheese before serving.
* Serve with rye crisps.

Sodium - 226 Mg
Fiber-Dietary - 0.753 Gm
Cholesterol - 1.448 Mg

Fat - 1.223 Gm
Poly Fat - 0.052 Gm
Saturated Fat - 0.306 Gm

The Hawk

PICANTE BLACK-EYED PEA CAKES

Serves: 8; Calories per serving: 91 (Protein 20%, Carbohydrate 68%, Fat 13%)

*3/4 cup uncooked oats (quick or old
   fashioned)
2 (15-ounce) cans black-eyed peas,
   rinsed and drained
1/3 cup sliced green onions
2 egg whites, slightly beaten*

*1 to 2 tablespoons chili powder
1 teaspoon ground cumin
1/8 teaspoon cayenne pepper
torn lettuce
picante sauce
plain lowfat or nonfat yogurt*

* Place oats in food processor; cover and process about 1 minute. Reserve 1/4 cup oats.
* Add black-eyed peas, green onions, egg whites, chili powder, cumin and cayenne to remaining oats. Process on and off just until blended but still chunky.
* Shape into 8 patties. Coat patties with reserved oats.
* Spray both sides of patties and a large skillet evenly with non-stick cooking spray.
* Brown patties over medium-high heat about 4 to 5 minutes per side or until brown.
* Serve immediately on a bed of lettuce with a dollop of yogurt and picante sauce.

Sodium - 148 Mg
Fiber-Dietary - 3.357 Gm
Cholesterol - 0.250 Mg

Fat - 1.349 Gm
Poly Fat - 0.260 Gm
Saturated Fat - 0.142 Gm

Francie López

MARINATED CUCUMBERS

Serves: 20; Calories per serving: 48 (Protein 3%, Carbohydrate 95%, Fat 2%)

*1 cup sugar
3 tablespoons salt
2 cups apple cider vinegar
2 cups water*

*4 to 5 large cucumbers
1 onion, sliced
1 clove garlic, minced*

* Score cucumbers down side with fork. Cut into thick slices. Soak in ice water 1 hour.
* Bring sugar, salt, vinegar and water to a boil. Let cool.
* Drain cucumbers; mix with garlic and onion.
* Pour liquid over cucumbers. Cover and refrigerate overnight.

Sodium - 962 Mg
Fiber-Dietary - 0.783 Gm
Cholesterol - 0.000 Mg

Fat - 0.103 Gm
Poly Fat - 0.039 Gm
Saturated Fat - 0.025 Gm

Virginia Owen

CHILLED BLUEBERRY SOUP

Serves: 8; Calories per serving: 124 (Protein 4%, Carbohydrate 94%, Fat 2%)

3 cups water
1 quart fresh blueberries
3/4 cup granulated sugar
cinnamon to taste

2 tablespoons cornstarch
1-1/2 tablespoons cold water
lowfat sour cream or yogurt for garnish

* Rinse, stem and drain blueberries.
* Bring water to a boil. Add berries, sugar and cinnamon.
* Cook, stirring until sugar is dissolved. Set aside.
* Mix cornstarch with cold water to make paste. Stir into warm soup and bring to a boil again. Cool. Cover and refrigerate.
* Serve chilled with tablespoon of yogurt or sour cream. Sprinkle with cinnamon.

Sodium - 15.651 Mg
Fiber-Dietary - 1.688 Gm
Cholesterol - 0.250 Mg

Fat - 0.311 Gm
Poly Fat - 0.149 Gm
Saturated Fat - 0.053 Gm

The Hawk

SWIRLED MELON SOUP

Serves: 9; Calories per serving: 116 (Protein 5%, Carbohydrate 86%, Fat 3%)

6-1/2 cups coarsely chopped cantaloupe
  (about 1 large cantaloupe)
6-1/2 cups coarsely chopped honeydew
  (about 1 medium honeydew)

1/4 cup sugar, divided
1/4 cup dry sherry, divided
1/4 cup orange juice, divided
fresh mint sprigs

* Place cantaloupe in blender or food processor.
* Add half the sugar, sherry and orange juice. Process until very smooth.
* Spoon mixture into airtight container. Chill at least 3 hours.
* Repeat with honeydew and remaining sugar, sherry and orange juice.
* For each serving, pour equal amounts of both mixtures into individual bowls, pouring both at the same time. Swirl soup gently with a spoon and garnish with a mint sprig.

Sodium - 23.019 Mg
Fiber-Dietary - 2.043 Gm
Cholesterol - 0.000 Mg

Fat - 0.450 Gm
Poly Fat - 0.001 Gm
Saturated Fat - 0.000 Gm

Betsy Chapman

CHILLED TOMATO SOUP

Serves: 6; Calories per serving: 66 (Protein 25%, Carbohydrate 71%, Fat 3%)

1 (46-ounce) can cocktail vegetable juice
1 pint nonfat yogurt or light sour cream
1/2 tablespoon fresh dill

1 teaspoon dried tarragon
1 clove fresh garlic, minced
salt and pepper to taste

* Blend all ingredients in blender or food processor.
* Chill at least 2 hours.
* May garnish with sprig of fresh parsley.

Sodium - 678 Mg
Fiber-Dietary - 1.941 Gm
Cholesterol - 1.000 Mg

Fat - 0.269 Gm
Poly Fat - 0.070 Gm
Saturated Fat - 0.089 Gm

Rebecca Thompson Adkison

EASY TOMATO BISQUE

Serves: 4; Calories per serving: 135 (Protein 15%, Carbohydrate 57%, Fat 28%)

1 can tomato soup, undiluted
1/4 cup margarine
1 onion, chopped
1 (14-1/2-ounce) can tomatoes, drained
  and chopped, liquid reserved

1-1/3 cups milk
dash of basil
dash of thyme
dash of white pepper
dash of cayenne pepper

* Sauté onion in margarine until tender. Add soup, tomatoes, milk and seasonings.
* Heat thoroughly. If thinner consistency is desired, add reserved liquid from tomatoes.
* For more color, you may use less basil and substitute parsley.

Sodium - 762 Mg
Fiber-Dietary - 0.976 Gm
Cholesterol - 1.330 Mg

Fat - 4.423 Gm
Poly Fat - 1.807 Gm
Saturated Fat - 0.801 Gm

Pattie Bethune

BUSY DAY VEGETABLE SOUP

Serves: 8; Calories per serving: 191 (Protein 49%, Carbohydrate 39%, Fat 12%)

*1 pound lean ground top round or
    turkey
1 (46-ounce) can vegetable juice cocktail
    (can use hot and spicy flavor)
2 (16-ounce) cans Veg-all or 1 (16-ounce)
    bag frozen mixed vegetables*

*1 medium onion, chopped
1/4 teaspoon dried basil (optional)
1 (16-ounce) can tomatoes, undrained
1 teaspoon Worcestershire sauce
1/2 teaspoon instant beef bouillon granules
1/2 teaspoon salt (or to taste)*

* Brown meat and onion in large Dutch oven. Drain excess fat.
* Add all remaining ingredients. Simmer 45 minutes to 1 hour.

Sodium - 964 Mg
Fiber-Dietary - 4.627 Gm
Cholesterol - 50.705 Mg

Fat - 2.667 Gm
Poly Fat - 0.264 Gm
Saturated Fat - 0.845 Gm

Linda Jones, Mary Sue Patten, Laurie Guy

BLACK BEAN SOUP

Serves: 6; Calories per serving: 233 (Protein 19%, Carbohydrate 62%, Fat 20%)

*1-1/2 cups black dried beans
6 cups water
1 large onion, chopped
2 tablespoons oil
2 large cloves garlic, chopped
2 stalks celery, chopped (including tops)
1 potato, diced*

*1 carrot, diced
1 bay leaf
1 teaspoon oregano
1/4 teaspoon savory
1 teaspoon salt
1/8 teaspoon pepper
2 lemons (optional)*

* Wash beans. Bring to boil in 6 cups water; simmer 2-1/2 hours until beans are tender.
* Sauté onion in oil with garlic until soft. Add celery, potato and carrot; sauté slightly.
* Add vegetables to beans. Stir in seasonings. Simmer at least another hour. (Longer is better.) Add water as necessary.
* Puree half of the soup. Return to pot. Blend with remaining soup.
* If desired, juice 1 lemon; add just before serving. Garnish with slices of second lemon.

Sodium - 376 Mg
Fiber-Dietary - 5.848 Gm
Cholesterol - 0.000 Mg

Fat - 5.280 Gm
Poly Fat - 1.653 Gm
Saturated Fat - 0.506 Gm

Nancy Gaskin

SPICY BLACK BEAN SOUP

Serves: 9; Calories per serving: 264 (Protein 19%, Carbohydrate 61%, Fat 15%)

4 carrots, chopped
2 onions, chopped
1 clove garlic, minced
2 tablespoons olive oil
2 tablespoons cumin
1/2 teaspoon cayenne, or to taste
1-1/2 teaspoons ground coriander

4 cups beef broth
2 (16-ounce) cans black beans, including
  liquid
1/2 cup long grain rice
1/2 cup dry sherry
lowfat sour cream or nonfat yogurt
  (optional)

* In large heavy saucepan, cook carrots, onions and garlic in oil over medium heat, stirring until the vegetables are soft.
* Stir in seasonings; cook for 1 minute.
* Add the broth and beans; bring to a boil. Reduce heat and simmer for 15 minutes.
* Add rice; simmer for 15 to 20 minutes more.
* In a blender or food processor puree 1/2 the mixture. Return this to the saucepan with remaining soup. Stir in sherry.
* Garnish with sour cream or yogurt, if desired.

Sodium - 378 Mg
Fiber-Dietary - 5.490 Gm
Cholesterol - 0.250 Mg

Fat - 4.469 Gm
Poly Fat - 0.549 Gm
Saturated Fat - 0.711 Gm

Marilyn Thompson

HOMEMADE CHICKEN NOODLE SOUP

Serves: 6; Calories per serving: 234 (Protein 36%, Carbohydrate 42%, Fat 22%)

Stock:

1 whole chicken, 3 to 3-1/2 pounds	*1 bay leaf*
2 medium onions, peeled and quartered	*2 cloves garlic, minced*
2 carrots, peeled and cut thick	*1 tablespoon salt*
2 large ribs of celery with leaves	*pepper to taste*
3 sprigs of parsley	*3 quarts water*

Soup:

6 to 7 cups homemade stock	*1 cup cooked chicken*
1 carrot, peeled and cut into 1/4 slices	*1/2 cup fresh Parmesan cheese*
4 to 6 ounces spaghetti noodles, broken	

* To make stock, remove giblets from chicken.
* Place all ingredients in large pot. Bring to a simmer and cook uncovered, about 2-1/2 hours or until chicken is done.
* Strain stock through a colander into a bowl.
* Discard vegetables. Skim fat from the stock.
* When cool, cut chicken into small pieces or shreds to make 1 cup.
* To make soup, place stock in heavy saucepan and bring to a boil.
* Add spaghetti and carrots. Cook 10 to 12 minutes.
* Reduce heat and add chicken. Heat thoroughly.
* Garnish with 1-1/2 tablespoons Parmesan cheese per 1 cup serving.

Sodium - 1085 Mg	Fat - 5.644 Gm
Fiber-Dietary - 0.383 Gm	Poly Fat - 0.789 Gm
Cholesterol - 26.250 Mg	Saturated Fat - 2.411 Gm

Betty Rosbottom

HEARTY PEA SOUP

Serves: 8; Calories per serving: 197 (Protein 19%, Carbohydrate 63%, Fat 18%)

1 onion, diced	*2 teaspoons salt*
2 tablespoons oil	*dash pepper*
1 bay leaf	*1 carrot, chopped*
1 teaspoon celery seeds	*3 stalks celery, chopped*
1 cup dried green split peas	*1/2 cup chopped fresh parsley*
1/4 cup dried barley	*1 potato, diced*
1/2 cup dried lima beans	*1/2 teaspoon basil*
2 quarts water	*1/2 teaspoon thyme (optional)*

* In Dutch oven, sauté onion in oil until soft. Add bay leaf and celery seeds.
* Stir in peas, barley and limas.
* Add 2 quarts water; bring to a boil.
* Cook on low partially covered for about 1-1/2 hours.
* Add salt, pepper, vegetables and herbs.
* Simmer 45 minutes to 1 hour longer.
* Thin with additional water or stock as you like.

Sodium - 570 Mg	Fat - 4.085 Gm
Fiber-Dietary - 3.784 Gm	Poly Fat - 1.276 Gm
Cholesterol - 0.000 Mg	Saturated Fat - 0.356 Gm

Nancy Gaskin

BLACK BEAN CHILI

Serves: 12; Calories per serving: 251 (Protein 23%, Carbohydrate 66%, Fat 12%)

4 cups dried black turtle beans
1 cup chopped red onion
1/4 cup (packed) minced fresh cilantro
1 cup minced fresh or canned tomatoes
1/4 teaspoon salt
1/2 cup (packed) minced fresh parsley
5 to 6 cloves garlic, crushed
1 to 2 teaspoons ground cumin
2-1/4 teaspoons salt
black pepper to taste

2 teaspoons dried basil
1/2 teaspoon dried oregano
crushed red pepper or cayenne, to taste
1 tablespoon fresh lime juice
2 medium bell peppers, chopped
2 tablespoons virgin olive oil
1/2 cup tomato puree
1-2 (4-ounce) cans diced green chilies
lowfat Cheddar cheese and light sour cream
*   for garnish*

* Soak beans in plenty of water overnight. Drain. Cook in fresh boiling water, partly covered, until tender (1 to 1-1/2 hours). Check the water level during cooking and add more as necessary.
* Combine next 5 ingredients and let stand at room temperature while cooking beans.
* Transfer cooked beans to a large kettle or saucepan. Include about 2 to 3 cups of the cooking water.
* In heavy skillet, sauté garlic, seasonings, lime juice and bell pepper in olive oil over medium-low heat until the peppers are tender.
* Add the red onion mixture to cooked beans and cook until tender.
* Add the sautéed mixture along with the tomato puree and minced green chilies. Simmer covered over very low heat, stirring occasionally for about 45 minutes.
* Serve with grated Cheddar cheese and sour cream for toppings.

Sodium - 522 Mg
Fiber-Dietary - 7.353 Gm
Cholesterol - 0.000 Mg

Fat - 3.304 Gm
Poly Fat - 0.599 Gm
Saturated Fat - 0.539 Gm

Nancy Gaskin

QUICK TEX-MEX VEGETARIAN SOUP
Serves: 6; Calories per serving: 208 (Protein 19%, Carbohydrate 61%, Fat 19%)

soft tortillas, cut in strips
2 (28-ounce) cans peeled tomatoes
1 tablespoon minced garlic
1/2 cup chopped onion
1 package taco seasoning mix

1-1/2 teaspoons chili powder
6 cups water
1 (16-ounce) bag mixed vegetables
1 cup grated mozzarella cheese

* Place tortilla strips on baking sheet and bake at 350° for 10 minutes or until crispy.
* Place all other ingredients except cheese in large pot. Bring to boil. Reduce heat; simmer vegetables until completely cooked.
* Sprinkle with tortilla chips and cheese; serve hot.

Sodium - 1150 Mg
Fiber-Dietary - 5.827 Gm
Cholesterol - 10.648 Mg

Fat - 4.789 Gm
Poly Fat - 0.415 Gm
Saturated Fat - 2.031 Gm

Maya Shenoy

SOUTHWEST VEGETABLE CHILI
Serves: 4; Calories per serving: 281 (Protein 16%, Carbohydrate 78%, Fat 6%)

1 cup coarsely chopped onions
1 medium bell pepper, coarsely chopped
2 cloves garlic, minced
1/2 cup water
2 beef bouillon cubes
1/4 teaspoon salt
1 tablespoon chili powder

1/2 teaspoon cumin (optional)
1/4 cup wine vinegar
1 (15-ounce) can kidney beans, drained
1 (14-1/2-ounce) can tomatoes, chopped
1 can whole kernel corn, drained
hot cooked rice

* In 3-quart saucepan, combine first 7 ingredients; cover and simmer 5 minutes.
* Stir in vinegar, beans, tomatoes and corn. Bring mixture to boil; simmer uncovered 30 minutes, stirring occasionally.
* To serve, spoon into bowls; top with rice.

Sodium - 1290 Mg
Fiber-Dietary - 9.264 Gm
Cholesterol - 0.072 Mg

Fat - 2.119 Gm
Poly Fat - 0.459 Gm
Saturated Fat - 0.215 Gm

Linda Jones

ITALIAN FISH STEW

Serves: 7; Calories per serving - 312 (Protein 44%, Carbohydrate 26%, Fat 27%)

1/4 cup olive oil
1 cup chopped onions
1/2 cup chopped green pepper
3 cloves garlic, minced
1 (28-ounce) can Italian plum tomatoes
1 cup water
1/2 cup white wine
2 cups diced potatoes, peeled or
  unpeeled

1 teaspoon salt
1/4 teaspoon freshly ground pepper
1/2 teaspoon oregano
1/2 teaspoon basil
1/2 teaspoon thyme
2 pounds fresh or frozen fish (haddock or
  cod), cut into 2-inch chunks
Parmesan cheese

* Heat oil in large saucepan or Dutch oven.
* Sauté onions, green pepper and garlic for 5 minutes.
* Mash tomatoes slightly with spoon. Add to sautéed vegetables. Stir in water, wine, potatoes, salt and pepper.
* Simmer covered for 30 minutes.
* Add oregano, basil, thyme and fish.
* Cook about 10 minutes longer until fish flakes easily.
* Ladle into soup bowls. Serve with grated Parmesan cheese.

Sodium - 608 Mg
Fiber-Dietary - 2.573 Gm
Cholesterol - 95.904 Mg

Fat - 9.325 Gm
Poly Fat - 1.219 Gm
Saturated Fat - 1.328 Gm

Gina Clegg

BRUNSWICK STEW

Serves: 12; Calories per serving: 458 (Protein 56%, Carbohydrate 39%, Fat 4%)

1 (4 to 5 pound) turkey breast
2 (1-quart) cans crushed tomatoes
2 onions, chopped
2 (10-ounce) packages frozen baby limas
8 potatoes, peeled

2 (16-ounce) cans white kernel corn,
  drained
1/4 to 1/2 bottle Worcestershire sauce
hot sauce to taste
salt and pepper to taste

* Stew turkey in 6 cups of water. Reserve broth.
* Cool turkey. Remove meat from bone; shred or cut into small pieces.
* Place broth in large pot. Add onions, tomatoes and meat. Cook slowly for 1 hour.
* Add limas. Cook 45 minutes.
* Add potatoes. Cook until done. Remove potatoes. Press through potato masher or slotted spoon. Return to stew to thicken.
* Add corn, hot sauce, salt and pepper. Stir in Worcestershire sauce.
* Simmer until ready to serve. If stew is not thick enough, add a few instant potato flakes.

Sodium - 759 Mg
Fiber-Dietary - 6.653 Gm
Cholesterol - 157 Mg

Fat - 2.259 Gm
Poly Fat - 0.754 Gm
Saturated Fat - 0.604 Gm

Joy Litaker

HAM BREAKFAST SANDWICH

Serves: 3; Calories per serving: 249 (Protein 21%, Carbohydrate 57%, Fat 22%)

1 ounce light cream cheese
4 teaspoons fat-free peach yogurt
6 slices raisin bread

3 lean ham slices
1 Granny Smith apple cored, sliced into
  rounds

* Blend cream cheese and yogurt. Spread mixture on bread.
* Place ham slice and apple round on 3 slices of bread. Top with remaining bread slices.

Sodium - 863 Mg
Fiber-Dietary - 1.910 Gm
Cholesterol - 20.111 Mg

Fat - 6.457 Gm
Poly Fat - 0.439 Gm
Saturated Fat - 0.429 Gm

Linda Jones

APPLE-NUT BREAD OR MUFFINS

Serves: 18; Calories per serving: 153 (Protein 6%, Carbohydrate 64%, Fat 30%)

4 tablespoons light margarine
1 cup brown sugar, packed
2 egg whites
2 cups flour
1 teaspoon baking soda
1/4 teaspoon salt

1/2 teaspoon lemon zest
1 teaspoon cinnamon
1/4 teaspoon nutmeg
1 large apple, grated
1/2 cup buttermilk
3/4 cup pecans (optional)

* Cream margarine and sugar together.
* Add egg whites, one at a time, beating well after each addition.
* Combine dry ingredients and mix with grated apple.
* Add alternately with buttermilk to creamed mixture.
* Stir in nuts.
* Cook in 9x5x3-inch loaf pan or in muffin tins sprayed with non-stick vegetable spray.
* Bake loaves at 350° for 55 to 60 minutes. (Muffins take less time, so check after 20 minutes.)
* Cool in pan for 10 minutes before removing.

Sodium - 124 Mg
Fiber-Dietary - 0.803 Gm
Cholesterol - 0.250 Mg

Fat - 5.212 Gm
Poly Fat - 1.288 Gm
Saturated Fat - 0.715 Gm

Joanna Fox

BANANA-DATE BRAN MUFFINS

Serves: 12; Calories per serving: 195 (Protein 10%, Carbohydrate 67%, Fat 23%)

1-1/2 cups whole bran cereal
1 cup skim milk
1 tablespoon vinegar
2 eggs or 1/2 cup egg substitute
1/4 cup vegetable oil
1/3 cup oat bran
2/3 cup flour

1/3 cup brown sugar
2 teaspoons baking powder
1/2 teaspoon baking soda
3/4 cup dates or raisins
3 very ripe bananas (best if frozen and then
   thawed)

* Combine bran and milk. Add vinegar and let stand for 3 minutes.
* Stir in eggs and oil. Set aside.
* Stir together oat bran, flour, brown sugar, baking powder and baking soda. Stir in dates and mashed bananas.
* Add bran mixture to cereal mixture. Stir just until moistened.
* Bake at 400° for 20 to 25 minutes. (10 to 15 minutes for smaller muffins.)

Sodium - 235 Mg
Fiber-Dietary - 5.138 Gm
Cholesterol - 0.438 Mg

Fat - 5.536 Gm
Poly Fat - 1.593 Gm
Saturated Fat - 0.482 Gm

Betsy Mitchell

VIRGINIA'S OATMEAL BREAD

Serves: 32; Calories per serving: 111 (Protein 11%, Carbohydrate 83%, Fat 6%)

1 cup rolled oats
3 teaspoons salt
1 tablespoon butter or margarine
2 cups boiling water

1 package yeast
1/2 cup molasses
6 cups flour

* Pour boiling water over the oats, salt and butter. Stir well and let stand for 1 hour.
* Add yeast, softened in 1/4 cup warm water. Add molasses, flour; stir until well mixed.
* Let rise in warm place until doubled in size. Punch down; put into 2 greased loaf pans. Let rise until doubled again. Bake at 375° for 45 to 50 minutes.

Sodium - 206 Mg
Fiber-Dietary - 0.821 Gm
Cholesterol - 0.000 Mg

Fat - 0.744 Gm
Poly Fat - 0.296 Gm
Saturated Fat - 0.121 Gm

Pam Franklin

PEAR-OAT MUFFINS

Serves: 12; Calories per serving: 189 (Protein 7%, Carbohydrate 64%, Fat 29%)

3/4 cup whole wheat flour
1/2 cup plus 2 tablespoons packed dark
  brown sugar
1/3 cup finely chopped dates
1/4 cup raisins
1/4 cup rolled oats
3 tablespoons oat bran
3 tablespoons toasted wheat germ
1 teaspoon baking soda
1 teaspoon ground allspice

1/2 teaspoon baking powder
1/2 teaspoon salt
1/2 teaspoon ground ginger
5 tablespoons vegetable oil
1/3 cup shredded bran cereal
2 eggs
2 teaspoons vanilla
1 large pear, peeled, and finely chopped
1 cup grated, peeled sweet potato (about
  4 ounces)

* Mix first 12 ingredients in medium bowl.
* Combine oil, cereal, eggs and vanilla in large bowl. Let stand 3 minutes.
* Beat bran cereal mixture on high speed until thick.
* Blend in pear and sweet potato.
* Fold in dry ingredients; do not over mix.
* Pour into greased muffin tins. Bake at 375° for 25 minutes.

Sodium - 215 Mg
Fiber-Dietary - 3.332 Gm
Cholesterol - 0.000 Mg

Fat - 6.354 Gm
Poly Fat - 1.922 Gm
Saturated Fat - 0.493 Gm

The Hawk

YOGURT DILL BREAD
Serves: 8; Calories per serving: 141 (Protein 11%, Carbohydrate 63%, Fat 26%)

2 cups buttermilk biscuit baking mix　　*2 tablespoons minced onion*
1 (8-ounce) carton plain or lowfat yogurt　　*1 tablespoon dill*

* Mix all ingredients until soft dough forms.
* Spread in greased 9-inch pie plate or 8x8-inch pan.
* Bake at 400° for 20 minutes. Cool 10 minutes.
* Cut into wedges or squares.

Sodium - 373 Mg　　　　　　　　Fat - 4.073 Gm
Fiber-Dietary - 0.755 Gm　　　　Poly Fat - 0.004 Gm
Cholesterol - 0.500 Mg　　　　　Saturated Fat - 0.034 Gm

Francie López

ENGLISH MUFFIN LOAVES
Serves: 32; Calories per serving: 195 (Protein 13%, Carbohydrate 84%, Fat 3%)

5-1/2 to 6 cups flour　　　　　　*1/4 teaspoon baking soda*
2 packages active dry yeast　　　*2 cups milk*
1 tablespoon sugar　　　　　　　*1/2 cup water*
2 teaspoons salt　　　　　　　　*cornmeal*

* Combine 3 cups flour, yeast, sugar, salt and soda.
* Heat liquids until very warm (120° to 130°).
* Add to dry mixture and beat well. Stir in additional flour to make a stiff batter.
* Spoon into two 8-1/2x4-1/2-inch pans that have been greased and sprinkled with cornmeal. Let rise in a warm place for 45 minutes.
* Bake at 400° for 25 minutes. Remove from pans immediately and cool.

Sodium - 296 Mg　　　　　　　　Fat - 0.548 Gm
Fiber-Dietary - 1.656 Gm　　　　Poly Fat - 0.211 Gm
Cholesterol - 0.500 Mg　　　　　Saturated Fat - 0.113 Gm

Margaret Akers-Hardage
Lee Russo

FOOD PROCESSOR FRENCH BREAD

Serves: 32; Calories per serving: 103 (Protein 11%, Carbohydrate 79%, Fat 10%)

5-1/2 to 6-1/2 cups flour
2 (1/4-ounce) packages active dry yeast
1 tablespoon sugar
1 tablespoon salt
2 tablespoons vegetable oil

2-1/4 cups warm water (105°-115°)
vegetable oil
egg yolk (optional)
poppy seeds (optional)
sesame seeds (optional)

* Proof yeast by mixing both packages of yeast and 1 teaspoon sugar with 1/2 cup of very hot tap water until all is dissolved. If yeast is active, it will foam and start to rise within 5 to 10 minutes.
* Combine 3 cups flour sugar, salt and oil. Mix in processor with metal blade.
* Add yeast slowly.
* Add enough of the remaining flour alternately with the remaining warm water to make a soft dough that clings to the sides of the mixing bowl as it rotates.
* Beat for 1-1/2 minutes to knead.
* Cover processor bowl and let dough rise 20 minutes. Punch down.
* Divide dough in half. On a floured surface, roll each half in an 8x15-inch rectangle.
* Beginning with long side of rectangle, roll dough tightly and seal well. Taper ends of loaves.
* Place seam side down on a greased baking sheet. Brush with oil. Cover with plastic wrap and refrigerate for 2 to 24 hours.
* Heat oven to 400°. Remove bread from refrigerator, uncover and let stand 10 minutes.
* Brush loaves lightly with cold water.
* Bake 30 to 40 minutes. Remove from baking sheets and cool on wire racks.
* To make breadsticks, form large pinches of dough in cigar shapes; twist. Brush with egg yolk instead of water and sprinkle with choice of seeds.

Sodium - 201 Mg
Fiber-Dietary - 0.825 Gm
Cholesterol - 0.000 Mg

Fat - 1.099 Gm
Poly Fat - 0.357 Gm
Saturated Fat - 0.100 Gm

Judy Fahl
Sally Gabosch

WHOLE WHEAT BANANA BREAD
Serves: 12; Calories per serving: 200 (Protein 6%, Carbohydrate 63%, Fat 30%)

3-1/2 over-ripe bananas, mashed
6 tablespoons margarine, melted
3/4 cup brown sugar
1 egg or 1/4 cup egg substitute
1 cup whole wheat flour

1/2 cup all-purpose flour
1 teaspoon baking soda
3/4 teaspoon salt
1/4 cup nonfat yogurt or buttermilk
1/4 cup chopped nuts

* Using mixer, mash bananas. Add butter.
* Add sugar, egg, flour, soda, salt and yogurt. Mix well. Stir in nuts.
* Spray loaf pan with vegetable cooking spray. Add batter. Bake at 350° for 45 to 50 minutes.
* Cool bread in loaf pan 10 minutes. Remove to wire rack. Cool thoroughly.

Sodium - 283 Mg
Fiber-Dietary - 2.055 Gm
Cholesterol - 0.083 Mg

Fat - 7.049 Gm
Poly Fat - 3.002 Gm
Saturated Fat - 1.068 Gm

Betsy Mitchell

WHOLE WHEAT CRANBERRY BREAD
Serves: 16; Calories per serving: 158 (Protein 7%, Carbohydrate 65%, Fat 28%)

2 cups whole wheat flour
1 cup brown sugar
1-1/2 teaspoons baking powder
1 teaspoon salt
1 teaspoon orange rind (can use dried)

1/4 cup cooking oil
3/4 to 1 cup orange juice
1 egg, well beaten
1 cup whole cranberries
1/2 cup chopped walnuts

* Mix first 5 ingredients.
* Add oil, orange juice and egg; mix well. Stir in cranberries and walnuts.
* Pour batter into greased loaf pan. Bake at 350° for 50 to 55 minutes.
* Remove bread from pan. Cool on rack.

Sodium - 171 Mg
Fiber-Dietary - 2.098 Gm
Cholesterol - 0.000 Mg

Fat - 5.123 Gm
Poly Fat - 2.060 Gm
Saturated Fat - 0.382 Gm

Betsy Mitchell

PANCAKES

Serves: 8; Calories per serving: 122 (Protein 13%, Carbohydrate 60%, Fat 27%)

1-3/4 cups flour
2 tablespoons sugar
4 teaspoons baking powder
1/2 teaspoon salt

1-3/4 cups skim milk
1/2 cup egg substitute
3 tablespoons canola oil

* Sift flour, sugar, salt and baking powder into medium bowl.
* In another bowl, combine milk, egg substitute and oil. Beat lightly. Stir into flour mixture just until combined.
* Ladle approximately 1/4 cup batter onto hot griddle sprayed with non-stick spray.
* Turn when bubbles form on surface.

Variation: For blueberry pancakes, add one more tablespoon sugar to batter. Sprinkle each pancake with a few berries before turning.

Sodium - 218 Mg
Fiber-Dietary - 0.493 Gm
Cholesterol - 0.583 Mg

Fat - 3.648 Gm
Poly Fat - 1.085 Gm
Saturated Fat - 0.312 Gm

Sally Gaddy

FALL FRUIT SALAD

Serves: 8; Calories per serving: 79 (Protein 8%, Carbohydrate 90%, Fat 2%)

1 (16-ounce) can sliced peaches, drained
1 (16-ounce) can sliced pears, drained
2 unpeeled apples, cored and cut in thin
  wedges

1 cup pitted prunes or dates, quartered
1 cup plain nonfat yogurt
2 tablespoons honey
1 tablespoon grated orange peel

* Combine fruit in large bowl.
* Blend yogurt, honey and orange peel together.
* Toss gently with fruit to coat. Serve on lettuce greens.

Sodium - 16.522 Mg
Fiber-Dietary - 1.922 Gm
Cholesterol - 0.333 Mg

Fat - 0.208 Gm
Poly Fat - 0.048 Gm
Saturated Fat - 0.043 Gm

Maria Kleto

FRESH FRUIT COMPOTE
Serves: 8; Calories per serving: 89 (Protein 2%, Carbohydrate 81%, Fat 3%)

1 Red Delicious apple, unpeeled
1 pear, unpeeled
2 seedless oranges, peeled, sliced and
   quartered

1/2 fresh pineapple, cut in chunks
1/4 cup orange-flavored liqueur
2 tablespoons sugar
3 tablespoons lemon juice

* Core apple and pear. Cut in 1/2-inch cubes.
* Place all fruit in large serving bowl.
* Combine last 3 ingredients and stir until sugar is dissolved.
* Spoon mixture over fruit and toss gently.
* Cover and refrigerate until well chilled.
* Toss again before serving.

Sodium - 1.896 Mg
Fiber-Dietary - 2.071 Gm
Cholesterol - 0.000 Mg

Fat - 0.326 Gm
Poly Fat - 0.093 Gm
Saturated Fat - 0.031 Gm

Jean Webb

FROZEN CRANBERRY SALAD
Serves: 12; Calories per serving: 97 (Protein 8%, Carbohydrate 73%, Fat 19%)

1 (16-ounce) can whole cranberry sauce
1 cup nonfat yogurt or light sour cream
1/2 cup chopped walnuts

1 (8-1/2-ounce) can crushed pineapple,
   drained

* Blend cranberries with sour cream or yogurt.
* Fold in pineapple and nuts.
* Spoon into regular-sized paper-lined muffin pans.
* Cover with plastic wrap and freeze.

Sodium - 25.286 Mg
Fiber-Dietary - 0.553 Gm
Cholesterol - 0.333 Mg

Fat - 2.049 Gm
Poly Fat - 1.268 Gm
Saturated Fat - 0.147 Gm

Sue Kaliski

CUCUMBER SALAD WITH DILL

Serves: 3; Calories per serving: 42 (Protein 18%, Carbohydrate 71%, Fat 11%)

1 large or 2 small cucumbers
1 teaspoon salt
1/4 teaspoon pepper
3 to 4 tablespoons white vinegar

3 to 4 tablespoons lowfat yogurt
1 tablespoon finely chopped fresh dill or
  1 teaspoon dried dill

* Peel and thinly slice cucumbers.
* Add all other ingredients and mix well.
* Serve chilled.

Sodium - 729 Mg
Fiber-Dietary - 2.050 Gm
Cholesterol - 1.167 Mg

Fat - 0.574 Gm
Poly Fat - 0.112 Gm
Saturated Fat - 0.257 Gm

Gabriele Kellmann

COMPANY CARROT SALAD

Serves: 6; Calories per serving: 155 (Protein 5%, Carbohydrate 71%, Fat 25%)

3 to 4 medium carrots, shredded
1/3 cup pecan pieces
1 cup raisins

1 (16-ounce) can crushed pineapple
  (packed in own juice), drained
3 tablespoons fat-free mayonnaise

* Toast pecans in 300° oven until slightly browned; cool.
* Toss together carrots, raisins and drained pineapple.
* Add mayonnaise; mix thoroughly.
* Chill salad.
* Just before serving, toss with toasted pecans.

Sodium - 115 Mg
Fiber-Dietary - 3.548 Gm
Cholesterol - 0.000 Mg

Fat - 4.673 Gm
Poly Fat - 1.180 Gm
Saturated Fat - 0.408 Gm

Dougi O'Bryan

TWO-POTATO SALAD WITH MUSTARD DRESSING
Serves: 6; Calories per serving: 220 (Protein 5%, Carbohydrate 65%, Fat 29%)

1 pound white potatoes
1 pound sweet potatoes
1 tablespoon white wine vinegar
2 tablespoons Dijon mustard
3 tablespoons olive oil

1/4 cup finely chopped onion
1/4 cup finely chopped red bell pepper
2 tablespoons finely chopped sweet gherkin
  pickles
salt and pepper to taste

* Quarter potatoes lengthwise and cut crosswise into 3/4-inch pieces.
* In a steamer over boiling water layer white potatoes, then sweet potatoes. Cover and steam for 10 to 12 minutes or until just tender.
* Place in a bowl and let cool.
* Whisk together vinegar, mustard, salt and pepper. Add oil in a stream while whisking until blended.
* Add all ingredients to the potatoes and mix well.

Sodium - 534 Mg
Fiber-Dietary - 3.351 Gm
Cholesterol - 0.000 Mg

Fat - 7.251 Gm
Poly Fat - 0.650 Gm
Saturated Fat - 0.955 Gm

The Hawk

BABY PEA SALAD
Serves: 10; Calories per serving: 116 (Protein 7%, Carbohydrate 82%, Fat 1%)

1 cup sugar
1 cup cider vinegar
2 (16-ounce) cans tiny green peas
1 large red onion, sliced in thin rings

1 (2-ounce) jar chopped pimientos, drained
1 small stalk celery, chopped
1 green pepper, chopped
salt to taste

* Combine sugar and vinegar. Stir until sugar dissolves.
* Pour over all other ingredients. Chill overnight.
* Will keep in refrigerator several days.

Sodium - 331 Mg
Fiber-Dietary - 1.997 Gm
Cholesterol - 0.000 Mg

Fat - 0.226 Gm
Poly Fat - 0.100 Gm
Saturated Fat - 0.037 Gm

Leslie Gebert

TWO-BEAN RICE SALAD

Serves: 16; Calories per serving: 154 (Protein - 14%, Carbohydrate 64%, Fat 22%)

3 cups cold, cooked rice
1 (15-ounce) can pinto beans, rinsed
*   and drained*
1 (15-ounce) can black beans, rinsed
*   and drained*
1 (10-ounce) package frozen tiny peas,
*   thawed*
1 cup sliced celery

1 medium red onion, chopped
*   (approximately 1/2 cup)*
2 (4-ounce) cans diced green chilies,
*   drained*
1/4 cup snipped cilantro or parsley
1 recipe Garlic Dressing or 1 (8-ounce) jar
*   Italian salad dressing*

Garlic Dressing:

1/3 cup white wine vinegar
1/4 cup olive oil or salad oil
2 tablespoons water

3/4 teaspoon salt
1/2 teaspoon garlic powder
1/2 teaspoon pepper

* In a 2-1/2-quart covered container, combine cooked rice, pinto beans, black beans, peas, celery, onion, diced green chili peppers and cilantro or parsley.
* Combine dressing ingredients in screw-top jar. Cover; shake well to mix.
* Add dressing to the rice mixture; toss gently to mix. Cover and chill up to 24 hours.

Sodium - 287 Mg
Fiber-Dietary - 2.468 Gm
Cholesterol - 0.000 Mg

Fat - 3.834 Gm
Poly Fat - 0.462 Gm
Saturated Fat - 0.560 Gm

Linda Sanchez

BLACK BEAN SALAD

Serves: 6; Calories per serving: 470 (Protein 15%, Carbohydrate 64%, Fat 22%)

2 (15-ounce) cans black beans, drained
1 green pepper, diced
1 purple onion, chopped
Dressing:
1/4 cup sugar
1/4 cup oil

1 (4-ounce) can green chilies, chopped
2 small tomatoes, diced

1/4 cup vinegar

* Combine dressing ingredients.
* Combine vegetables and dressing. Marinate for 1 hour or more before serving.

Sodium - 486 Mg
Fiber-Dietary - 4.716 Gm
Cholesterol - 16.005 Mg

Fat - 11.145 Gm
Poly Fat - 2.455 Gm
Saturated Fat - 1.178 Gm

Pattie Bethune

VERMICELLI SALAD

Serves: 8; Calories per serving: 123 (Protein 14%, Carbohydrate 77%, Fat 9%)

8 ounces vermicelli, broken in pieces
1 tablespoon Season-All
1/4 cup fat-free Italian dressing
5 sliced green onions
1/4 to 1/2 green pepper, chopped

1 small cucumber, peeled, seeded and
chopped
12 small pimiento-stuffed olives, sliced
(optional)

* Cook vermicelli according to directions on package. Drain in a colander and rinse with cold water to cool.
* Remove to medium bowl. Add remaining ingredients and toss well.
* Chill for at least 8 hours.

Sodium - 597 Mg
Fiber-Dietary - 0.755 Gm
Cholesterol - 0.000 Mg

Fat - 1.306 Gm
Poly Fat - 0.265 Gm
Saturated Fat - 0.155 Gm

Joan Womack

STEPH'S LOW-CAL PASTA SALAD

Serves: 2; Calories per serving: 314 (Protein 21%, Carbohydrate 50%, Fat 28%)

1-1/2 cups cooked pasta bows
2 teaspoons olive oil, divided
2 cloves garlic, mashed
1/2 cup chopped onion
4 ounces smoked turkey sausage, cut
    into bite-sized pieces

1/2 cup chopped celery
1/2 cup chopped red bell pepper
2 tablespoons balsamic vinegar
1 tablespoon fresh basil, chopped
1 tablespoon fresh oregano, chopped
1/4 teaspoon fennel seeds (optional)

* Heat 1 teaspoon of oil in a medium frying pan. Add garlic and onion and sauté until transparent (about 5 minutes). Add sausage; sauté another 5 minutes.
* Pour mixture into a medium mixing bowl. Add celery, pepper and pasta.
* In a small bowl, combine remaining teaspoon of oil, vinegar and herbs.
* Pour dressing mixture over salad. Toss to blend.
* May be served immediately or refrigerated to serve cold.

Variation: Add other vegetables such as broccoli or mushrooms.

Sodium - 515 Mg
Fiber-Dietary - 2.594 Gm
Cholesterol - 71.060 Mg

Fat - 9.893 Gm
Poly Fat - 2.154 Gm
Saturated Fat - 2.016 Gm

Stephanie Fletcher

COLORFUL PASTA SALAD

Serves: 5; Calories per serving: 195 (Protein 17%, Carbohydrate 61%, Fat 23%)

3 cups cooked tri-colored rotini noodles
1/2 cup low-calorie Italian dressing
3/4 cup red pepper strips
1/2 cup sliced carrots
1/4 cup sliced green onions

1 (14-ounce) can artichoke hearts, drained
    and quartered
1/4 cup grated fresh Parmesan cheese
1/4 teaspoon dried basil
1/4 teaspoon pepper

* Mix rotini and 1/4 cup Italian dressing. Cover and chill.
* Mix other ingredients with 1/4 cup Italian dressing. Add rotini and toss. Serve chilled.

Sodium - 369 Mg
Fiber-Dietary - 1.709 Gm
Cholesterol - 34.000 Mg

Fat - 5.026 Gm
Poly Fat - 1.914 Gm
Saturated Fat - 1.434 Gm

Marilyn Thompson

SPINACH SALAD WITH ORANGE-POPPY SEED DRESSING
Serves: 8; Calories per serving: 71 (Protein 12%, Carbohydrate 81%, Fat 7%)

*1 pound fresh spinach, washed,
  thoroughly drained, and stems removed*
*2 small unpeeled red pears, cored and
  thinly sliced*

*1 (11-ounce) can mandarin oranges,
  drained*
1/2 cup alfalfa sprouts

Orange-Poppy Seed Dressing:

2/3 cup unsweetened orange juice
3 tablespoons water
2 tablespoons white wine vinegar
2 teaspoons cornstarch

2 teaspoons sweet-hot mustard
2 teaspoons honey
3/4 teaspoon poppy seeds

* Combine all ingredients for Orange-Poppy Seed Dressing except poppy seeds in saucepan; stir well.
* Bring mixture to a boil. Boil 1 minute or until thickened, stirring constantly.
* Stir in poppy seeds. Cover and chill before serving.
* Tear spinach into bite-sized pieces.
* Arrange on salad plates with pears, oranges and sprouts.
* Drizzle dressing over each salad.

Sodium - 63.999 Mg
Fiber-Dietary - 2.893 Gm
Cholesterol - 0.000 Mg

Fat - 0.630 Gm
Poly Fat - 0.222 Gm
Saturated Fat - 0.059 Gm

Judi Tingler

CHINESE CHICKEN SALAD AND DRESSING

Serves: 6; Calories per serving: 207 (Protein 31%, Carbohydrate 39%, Fat 30%)

*3 boneless chicken breasts, cooked
    and shredded*
1/4 cup slivered almonds
1 head romaine lettuce, broken in pieces
Chinese Chicken Salad Dressing:
1/2 cup sugar
2-1/2 teaspoons salt
1 teaspoon black pepper

*3 to 5 green onions, finely chopped (green
    part only)*
chopped fresh cilantro to taste
1 tablespoon sesame seeds

1/2 cup white vinegar
1 tablespoon sesame oil (no substitute)

* Toast almonds in ungreased skillet on top of stove or in a shallow pan in the oven at 375° for 10 to 15 minutes. Cool. Combine all ingredients in a large bowl.
* To make Chinese Chicken Salad Dressing, combine sugar, salt, pepper and vinegar in a small saucepan.
* Slowly heat and stir until the sugar is dissolved. Remove from heat and cool slightly.
* Add sesame oil and stir. Toss salad with warm dressing.

Sodium - 926 Mg
Fiber-Dietary - 2.144 Gm
Cholesterol - 36.500 Mg

Fat - 7.150 Gm
Poly Fat - 2.200 Gm
Saturated Fat - 1.086 Gm

Peggy Hamm

YOGURT DRESSING FOR FRUIT

Serves: 10; Calories per serving: 41 (Protein 11%, Carbohydrate 81%, Fat 8%)

1 cup lowfat yogurt
1 tablespoon lemon juice
1/4 cup honey

1/4 teaspoon nutmeg
1/4 teaspoon cinnamon

* Whisk together all ingredients. Chill. Serve over any fruit or use as a dip.

Sodium - 16.644 Mg
Fiber-Dietary - 0.029 Gm
Cholesterol - 1.400 Mg

Fat - 0.378 Gm
Poly Fat - 0.012 Gm
Saturated Fat - 0.242 Gm

Jane Gilbert

H. V. DRESSING

Serves: 30; Calories per serving: 14 (Protein 45%, Carbohydrate 45%, Fat 9%)

1 (12-ounce) carton lowfat cottage cheese *1/3 cup buttermilk*
1 package dry ranch dressing mix

* Blend all ingredients in blender until smooth.
* Cover tightly; store in refrigerator.
* Good on tossed salad, baked potatoes, broccoli and as a dip for vegetables.

Sodium - 150 Mg
Fiber-Dietary - 0.000 Gm
Cholesterol - 0.601 Mg

Fat - 0.139 Gm
Poly Fat - 0.004 Gm
Saturated Fat - 0.088 Gm

Becky Pickens

LAURA'S DELIGHTFUL FRUITFUL CHICKEN SALAD

Serves: 6; Calories per serving: 171 (Protein 50%, Carbohydrate 27%, Fat 22%)

3 cups diced cooked chicken breast
1 cup diced celery
1/4 cup minced onion (optional or to taste)
2 tablespoons lemon juice
1/4 teaspoon ground coriander (optional)

1/4 teaspoon salt
1/8 teaspoon pepper
1 (8-ounce) can unsweetened pineapple chunks, drained
1 cup seedless green grapes, halved
1/3 cup nonfat mayonnaise
3 tablespoons toasted, slivered almonds

* Combine chicken with celery, onion, lemon juice, coriander, salt and pepper.
* Chill thoroughly.
* Add pineapple, grapes and almonds.
* Add mayonnaise and toss lightly.
* Serve on lettuce leaves.

Sodium - 319 Mg
Fiber-Dietary - 1.138 Gm
Cholesterol - 53.789 Mg

Fat - 4.236 Gm
Poly Fat - 0.934 Gm
Saturated Fat - 0.840 Gm

Sarah Land

BLACK BEANS

Serves: 6; Calories per serving: 451 (Protein 17%, Carbohydrate 54%, Fat 29%)

8 ounces lean ham, cubed
2 (15-ounce) cans black beans or
   1 (15-ounce) can black beans and
   1 (15-ounce) can red beans
1/4 cup oil
1/2 large onion, chopped
2 green peppers, chopped

1 small clove garlic
1 bay leaf
1/4 cup red wine vinegar
4 cups cooked rice
garnishes: grated cheese, chopped
   tomatoes, chopped onion

* In a large pot, sauté onion and pepper in oil.
* Add remaining ingredients except vinegar and cook over medium heat 30 minutes.
* Stir in vinegar when ready to serve.
* Serve over rice. Top with grated cheese or chopped tomatoes and chopped onions.

Sodium - 646 Mg
Fiber-Dietary - 4.868 Gm
Cholesterol - 21.340 Mg

Fat - 14.477 Gm
Poly Fat - 3.169 Gm
Saturated Fat - 1.465 Gm

Jane Tilley, Laura Courter

CARROT-APPLE CASSEROLE

Serves: 6; Calories per serving: 186 (Protein 4%, Carbohydrate 85%, Fat 11%)

5 cups sliced carrots
5 cups sliced apples (unpeeled)
5 tablespoons sugar
2 tablespoons flour

cinnamon to taste
2 tablespoons margarine
1/2 cup orange juice

* Steam carrots in small amount of water until tender.
* Combine sugar, flour, cinnamon.
* Alternately layer carrots and apples in 9x9-inch square baking dish, sprinkling sugar
  mixture between layers. Place several pats of margarine on top.
* Pour orange juice over all. Bake covered at 350° for 45 minutes.

Sodium - 108 Mg
Fiber-Dietary - 6.937 Gm
Cholesterol - 0.000 Mg

Fat - 2.502 Gm
Poly Fat - 0.976 Gm
Saturated Fat - 0.404 Gm

Linda Sanchez

LEMON SOY CARROTS

Serves: 2; Calories per serving: 101 (Protein 7%, Carbohydrate 66%, Fat 26%)

4 carrots
1 tablespoon soy sauce
2 teaspoons lemon juice
1 teaspoon sugar

1/4 cup water
1/2 tablespoon unsalted butter (may
substitute diet margarine)
pepper to taste

* Half carrots lengthwise, then cut crosswise into quarter-inch slices.
* Stir carrots, soy sauce, lemon juice, sugar and water together in a 2-quart microwave-safe dish.
* Microwave on high 8 to 10 minutes until just tender. Stir once after 5 minutes.
* Dot with butter; add pepper to taste.
* Toss until butter melts.

Sodium - 567 Mg
Fiber-Dietary - 4.681 Gm
Cholesterol - 0.000 Mg

Fat - 3.154 Gm
Poly Fat - 1.065 Gm
Saturated Fat - 0.499 Gm

Elaine Quillman

EASY EGGPLANT PARMESAN

Serves: 6; Calories per serving: 80 (Protein 16%, Carbohydrate 53%, Fat 30%)

1 (16-ounce) can tomatoes
1 cup marinara sauce

1 large eggplant, washed and sliced
1/4 cup Parmesan cheese

* Combine tomatoes and marinara sauce.
* Layer unpeeled eggplant and sauce in baking dish.
* Bake at 350° for 40 minutes.
* Top with Parmesan cheese and bake until eggplant is tender.

Sodium - 465 Mg
Fiber-Dietary - 0.608 Gm
Cholesterol - 3.292 Mg

Fat - 2.969 Gm
Poly Fat - 0.543 Gm
Saturated Fat - 1.049 Gm

The Hawk

EASIEST, HEALTHIEST "FRENCH FRIES"
Serves: 4; Calories per serving: 225 (Protein 8%, Carbohydrate 89%, Fat 3%)

4 baking potatoes   *seasoned salt*
non-stick vegetable spray

* Wash baking potatoes (do not peel). Slice 1/8 to 1/4-inch thin.
* Spray baking sheet with vegetable spray and put potatoes on cookie sheet. Cover potatoes lightly with vegetable spray. Sprinkle potatoes with seasoned salt.
* Bake about 10 minutes at 400°; turn potatoes over and bake about 10 minutes more.
* Potatoes should be light brown when done. Serve with ketchup, if desired.

Sodium - 996 Mg   Fat - 0.802 Gm
Fiber-Dietary - 4.850 Gm   Poly Fat - 0.087 Gm
Cholesterol - 0.000 Mg   Saturated Fat - 0.052 Gm

Betsy Mitchell

SUMMER VEGETABLES WITH TARRAGON SAUCE
Serves: 6; Calories per serving: 60 (Protein 18%, Carbohydrate 55%, Fat 22%)

5 small yellow squash, sliced   *1 shallot, finely chopped*
12 asparagus spears   *1 teaspoon Dijon mustard*
2 tablespoons water   *1/2 teaspoon dried crushed tarragon*
1/2 cup chicken broth   *1/8 teaspoon pepper*
2 tablespoons dry white wine   *1 tablespoon margarine*
1 tablespoon cornstarch

* In 2-quart microwave casserole dish, place squash, asparagus and water. Cover and cook on 100% power in microwave for 5 to 7 minutes.
* Stir once and drain when cooked to crisp and tender.
* While vegetables are cooking, combine all other ingredients (except margarine) in a microwave-safe 2-cup measuring cup. Cook uncovered in microwave on high for 2 to 3 minutes. Stir every minute until thickened.
* Stir in margarine. Pour sauce over vegetables; toss and serve.

Sodium - 112 Mg   Fat - 1.667 Gm
Fiber-Dietary - 2.357 Gm   Poly Fat - 0.689 Gm
Cholesterol - 0.000 Mg   Saturated Fat - 0.316 Gm

Deborah McGovern

GARLIC OVEN POTATOES

Serves: 3; Calories per serving: 232 (Protein 7%, Carbohydrate 67%, Fat 26%)

3/4 pound new potatoes
6 cloves garlic, finely chopped
1 tablespoon olive oil

1/4 teaspoon rosemary
salt to taste
pepper to taste

* Cut potatoes into wedges.
* Place potatoes, garlic, rosemary, salt and pepper into 8-inch baking dish.
* Toss with oil.
* Bake at 450° for 45 minutes or until potatoes are slightly crispy, turning frequently during baking.

Sodium - 1076 Mg
Fiber-Dietary - 4.144 Gm
Cholesterol - 0.000 Mg

Fat - 6.996 Gm
Poly Fat - 0.665 Gm
Saturated Fat - 0.969 Gm

Nancy DeBiase

SWEET AND SOUR ZUCCHINI

Serves: 6; Calories per serving: 270 (Protein 13%, Carbohydrate 70%, Fat 17%)

2 tablespoons oil
1 onion, chopped
1 green pepper, chopped
2 cloves garlic, minced
2 teaspoons basil
1 pound zucchini, sliced into 2-inch pieces
1 (16-ounce) can kidney beans

1/2 to 1 teaspoon salt
2 tablespoons vinegar
1 tablespoon cornstarch
2 teaspoons sugar
3 cups cooked rice
soy sauce

* Sauté onion and pepper in oil until light brown.
* Add garlic and basil; cook over medium heat until browned.
* Add zucchini, beans and salt; simmer 15 minutes, stirring often.
* Blend vinegar, cornstarch and sugar. Add to vegetable mixture and cook until thickened. Serve over rice with soy sauce.

Sodium - 2412 Mg
Fiber-Dietary - 5.085 Gm
Cholesterol - 0.000 Mg

Fat - 5.212 Gm
Poly Fat - 1.494 Gm
Saturated Fat - 0.433 Gm

The Hawk

VEGETABLE MEDLEY
Serves: 4; Calories per serving: 64 (Protein 14%, Carbohydrate 56%, Fat 30%)

1-1/2 cups broccoli florets
1-1/2 cups sliced zucchini
1/2 cup red pepper strips
1 (8-ounce) can sliced water chestnuts

1/4 cup sliced green onions
2 teaspoons chicken bouillon granules
4 teaspoons margarine

* Combine first 5 ingredients in shallow microwave-safe 2-quart casserole.
* Sprinkle with bouillon granules and toss.
* Dot with butter, cover tightly with plastic wrap and vent 1 corner.
* Microwave on high 4 minutes, turning 1/4 turn after 2 minutes.
* Let stand covered 5 minutes before serving.

Sodium - 383 Mg
Fiber-Dietary - 2.128 Gm
Cholesterol - 0.228 Mg

Fat - 2.398 Gm
Poly Fat - 1.062 Gm
Saturated Fat - 0.437 Gm

Cindy Rawald

BROCCOLI RICE
Serves: 6; Calories per serving: 92 (Protein 20%, Carbohydrate 68%, Fat 12%)

1 (6-ounce) box long grain and wild rice
1 small head broccoli

1 (16-ounce) can kidney beans, drained

* Cook rice according to directions.
* While rice is cooking, chop broccoli florets into small pieces and place in
  microwave-safe cooking bowl. Add 1/4 cup water.
* Cover and microwave until tender crisp, shaking or stirring once or twice.
* Drain after cooking.
* Mix broccoli, beans and rice.
* Serve hot.

Sodium - 319 Mg
Fiber-Dietary - 3.485 Gm
Cholesterol - 2.465 Mg

Fat - 1.330 Gm
Poly Fat - 0.080 Gm
Saturated Fat - 0.610 Gm

Nancy Gaskin

CHEESY VEGETABLE ORZO

Serves: 2; Calories per serving: 109 (Protein 17%, Carbohydrate 60%, Fat 22%)

1/4 cup chopped onions
1 clove garlic, minced
1/2 cup chicken broth
1/4 cup diced carrot
1 tablespoon chopped fresh basil
1/8 teaspoon salt

1/8 teaspoon pepper
1/4 cup orzo
1/4 cup shredded zucchini
2 tablespoons shredded lowfat sharp
  Cheddar cheese

* Coat small saucepan with cooking spray and place over medium heat until hot.
* Add onion and garlic. Sauté for 2 minutes.
* Add broth and the next 4 ingredients and bring to a boil.
* Add orzo. Cover, reduce heat and simmer for 16 minutes.
* Remove from heat and stir in zucchini and cheese. Cover and let stand for 2 minutes.

Sodium - 444 Mg
Fiber-Dietary - 1.043 Gm
Cholesterol - 7.460 Mg

Fat - 2.667 Gm
Poly Fat - 0.189 Gm
Saturated Fat - 0.144 Gm

Erin Tilley

DILL POLO

Serves: 12; Calories per serving: 234 (Protein 9%, Carbohydrate 72%, Fat 19%)

3 cups rice, uncooked
1 (10-ounce) package frozen baby
  lima beans

2 tablespoons dried dill
1/4 cup oil
1/4 cup water

* Wash rice and cook with 10 cups water and 1 teaspoon salt for 15 minutes. Drain water and rinse the rice; put aside.
* Cook lima beans in 1 cup boiling water for 10 minutes; drain.
* Add beans to rice. Add dried dill to beans and rice and mix well.
* Stir oil and water together. Pour over the rice and bean mixture.
* Cook covered over low heat for 45 minutes until rice is done.

Sodium - 182 Mg
Fiber-Dietary - 0.462 Gm
Cholesterol - 0.000 Mg

Fat - 4.939 Gm
Poly Fat - 1.457 Gm
Saturated Fat - 0.423 Gm

Jamil Hosseinian

COMINO RICE

Serves: 8; Calories per serving: 174 (Protein 9%, Carbohydrate 70%, Fat 21%)

2 tablespoons olive oil
1 green pepper, diced
1 red pepper, diced
1 Spanish onion, diced
1 clove garlic, minced

1 teaspoon ground cumin
1-1/2 teaspoons salt
1-1/2 cups long grain rice
2 cups chicken broth

* Sauté diced pepper and onions in olive oil.
* Add garlic, cumin, salt and rice; stir until rice is coated.
* Add 2 cups chicken broth and heat to boiling.
* Cover and reduce heat to simmer; cook for 15 more minutes.
* Turn off heat and let stand covered 10 minutes longer.
* Fluff and serve.

Sodium - 597 Mg
Fiber-Dietary - 0.569 Gm
Cholesterol - 0.000 Mg

Fat - 4.002 Gm
Poly Fat - 0.423 Gm
Saturated Fat - 0.619 Gm

Francie López

CONFETTI RICE

Serves: 4; Calories per serving: 76 (Protein 9%, Carbohydrate 75%, Fat 15%)

1-1/3 cups cold water
1/3 cup long grain white rice
1/2 teaspoon salt
1/2 cup shredded zucchini

1/2 cup finely chopped broccoli
1/4 cup shredded carrot
1 tablespoon fresh lemon juice
1 teaspoon olive oil

* Combine water, rice and salt in heavy, medium saucepan. Bring to boil, stirring once.
* Reduce heat to low and cook covered 12 minutes.
* Stir in remaining ingredients.
* Cover, remove from heat and let stand 10 minutes.

Sodium - 274 Mg
Fiber-Dietary - 1.018 Gm
Cholesterol - 0.000 Mg

Fat - 1.310 Gm
Poly Fat - 0.160 Gm
Saturated Fat - 0.194 Gm

LuAnn Scruggs

STIR-FRIED BROWN RICE WITH VEGETABLES
Serves: 6; Calories per serving: 191 (Protein 11%, Carbohydrate 61%, Fat 28%)

1 cup brown rice
1 tablespoon chicken bouillon granules
3 tablespoons vegetable oil
1 cup thinly sliced carrots
3 green onions sliced, including tops
1 clove garlic, minced

1 large green pepper, thinly sliced
1 cup thinly sliced zucchini
1 cup thinly sliced mushrooms
1/2 cup slivered almonds
4 to 5 tablespoons soy sauce

* The day or morning before serving, cook rice according to package directions, adding chicken granules to water. Cool completely in refrigerator.
* Heat about 1 tablespoon oil over high heat. Add carrots and stir 1 minute. Add onions, garlic and pepper; stir-fry 1 more minute, adding more oil if needed.
* Add zucchini, mushrooms and almonds; cook 2 minutes more until tender crisp.
* Add rice and stir until heated. Season with soy sauce.

Sodium - 1249 Mg
Fiber-Dietary - 3.336 Gm
Cholesterol - 0.230 Mg

Fat - 6.083 Gm
Poly Fat - 1.672 Gm
Saturated Fat - 0.667 Gm

Marilyn Thompson

FETTUCCINE WITH TUNA SAUCE
Serves: 4; Calories per serving: 397 (Protein 22%, Carbohydrate 59%, Fat 19%)

2 tablespoons oil
1/2 cup chopped onions
1 clove garlic, minced
1 (29-ounce) can crushed tomatoes
1 tablespoon chopped fresh parsley

2 teaspoons sugar
1 teaspoon basil
1 (6-ounce) can water-packed tuna, drained
1 (8-ounce) package fettuccine

* Sauté garlic and onion in oil until tender but not brown.
* Add crushed tomatoes, parsley, sugar and basil. Cook uncovered about 20 minutes or until sauce thickens. Stir in tuna and heat thoroughly.
* Cook fettuccine according to directions on box. Serve tuna mixture over hot fettuccine.

Sodium - 680 Mg
Fiber-Dietary - 2.096 Gm
Cholesterol - 7.655 Mg

Fat - 8.332 Gm
Poly Fat - 2.576 Gm
Saturated Fat - 0.731 Gm

Francie López

239

LIGHT PASTA PRIMAVERA
Serves: 6; Calories per serving: 375 (Protein 14%, Carbohydrate 73%, Fat 12%)

2 cloves garlic, minced
1-1/2 tablespoons olive oil
3 carrots, sliced into rounds
1 small bunch broccoli, chopped
2 small zucchini, halved and sliced
3 green onions, sliced
1 (16-ounce) can crushed tomatoes

1 fresh tomato, chopped
1/4 teaspoon pepper
1/2 teaspoon basil
1/4 teaspoon salt
1 (16-ounce) package pasta, cooked and
   drained

* Sauté garlic in oil. Add carrots. Stir-fry until crisp-tender. Add broccoli. Stir-fry 2 to 3 minutes more. Add zucchini and onion. Stir-fry 1 to 2 minutes.
* Add crushed tomatoes, fresh tomato and seasonings. Simmer a few minutes.
* Serve over warm pasta.

Sodium - 254 Mg
Fiber-Dietary - 4.947 Gm
Cholesterol - 0.000 Mg

Fat - 5.235 Gm
Poly Fat - 1.062 Gm
Saturated Fat - 0.731 Gm

Nancy Gaskin

LINGUINE WITH CLAM SAUCE
Serves: 4; Calories per serving: 349 (Protein 18%, Carbohydrate 52%, Fat 25%)

2 (6-1/2-ounce) cans chopped clams
2 teaspoons minced garlic
2 tablespoons olive oil
1/2 cup dry white wine
1/4 teaspoon pepper

1/2 teaspoon crushed red pepper flakes
1 (8-ounce) package linguine
2 tablespoons minced fresh parsley
2 tablespoons or more Parmesan cheese

* Cook linguine according to package directions.
* Drain clams, reserving liquid.
* Bring liquid to boil; reduce heat and simmer until one half of liquid is left.
* Add garlic, olive oil, wine and pepper. Bring to boil; reduce heat; simmer 4 minutes.
* Mix all ingredients and toss. Sprinkle with parsley and cheese.

Sodium - 115 Mg
Fiber-Dietary - 0.206 Gm
Cholesterol - 59.892 Mg

Fat - 9.691 Gm
Poly Fat - 0.964 Gm
Saturated Fat - 1.860 Gm

The Hawk

SHRIMP LINGUINE

Serves: 10; Calories per serving: 344 (Protein 24%, Carbohydrate 45%, Fat 30%)

4-1/2 cups water
1-1/2 pounds fresh medium shrimp
in shells
1 (16-ounce) package linguine
1 (6-ounce) package frozen snow peas,
thawed
6 green onions, chopped
7 tablespoons olive oil

4 medium tomatoes, peeled, chopped and
drained
1/4 cup chopped fresh parsley
1/3 cup wine vinegar
1 teaspoon dried oregano
1-1/2 teaspoons dried basil
1/2 teaspoon garlic salt
1/4 teaspoon coarsely ground black pepper

* Bring water to a boil; add shrimp and cook 3 to 5 minutes.
* Drain well; rinse with cold water. Chill. Peel and devein shrimp; set aside.
* Cook linguine according to package directions, omitting salt. Drain. Rinse with cold water and drain again.
* Combine shrimp, linguine and remaining ingredients; toss gently.
* Cover and chill at least 4 hours.

Note: Omit tomatoes unless good fresh summer tomatoes are available.

Sodium - 214 Mg
Fiber-Dietary - 0.796 Gm
Cholesterol - 105 Mg

Fat - 11.560 Gm
Poly Fat - 1.636 Gm
Saturated Fat - 1.638 Gm

Laurie Guy

SALMON ALMONDINE PASTA

Serves: 8; Calories per serving: 360 (Protein 28%, Carbohydrate 42%, Fat 28%)

2 onions, thinly sliced
1 (8-ounce) can mushrooms, liquid
  reserved
1 clove garlic, minced
12 ounces linguine, cooked
6 tablespoons Parmesan cheese
3 tablespoons white wine
3 tablespoons light mayonnaise

3 tablespoons lowfat plain yogurt
juice of 1 lemon
grated nutmeg to taste
3 cups cooked salmon (or 1-2 large cans,
  drained and picked clean), flaked
1/2 to 1 teaspoon dried dill
6 tablespoons toasted, slivered almonds

* Spray non-stick skillet with cooking spray. Brown onions, mushrooms and garlic.
* Mix in linguine. Stir in mushroom liquid, Parmesan cheese, wine, mayonnaise, yogurt, lemon and nutmeg over low temperature until thoroughly heated.
* Top with salmon and sprinkle with dill. Cover and cook until heated throughout.
* Sprinkle with almonds before serving.

Sodium - 653 Mg
Fiber-Dietary - 1.179 Gm
Cholesterol - 49.075 Mg

Fat - 11.342 Gm
Poly Fat - 2.539 Gm
Saturated Fat - 2.531 Gm

Jane Tilley

CHICKEN-ZITI CASSEROLE

Serves: 6; Calories per serving: 397 (Protein 23%, Carbohydrate 47%, Fat 31%)

1 (30-ounce) jar spaghetti sauce
4 cups cooked ziti (6 ounces uncooked)
1-1/2 cups cooked chicken, cubed

1-1/2 cups shredded mozzarella cheese,
  divided
1 to 2 tablespoons grated Parmesan cheese

* In 2-quart casserole, stir sauce, chicken, ziti and 3/4 cup mozzarella.
* Top with remaining mozzarella and Parmesan cheese. Bake for 30 minutes at 350°.

Sodium - 846 Mg
Fiber-Dietary - 1.048 Gm
Cholesterol - 73.904 Mg

Fat - 13.657 Gm
Poly Fat - 2.947 Gm
Saturated Fat - 3.926 Gm

Betty Mullen

SPINACH AND CHICKEN MOSTACCIOLI CASSEROLE

Serves: 8; Calories per serving: 330 (Protein 31%, Carbohydrate 41%, Fat 28%)

10 ounces uncooked mostaccioli (may substitute rigatoni or other tubular pasta)
1 (10-ounce) package frozen chopped spinach, thawed
vegetable cooking spray
2 teaspoons vegetable oil
2/3 cup chopped onion
2 cloves garlic, minced

1 pound boneless chicken breasts, skinned and cut into 1-inch pieces
2 (14-1/2-ounce) cans whole tomatoes, undrained and coarsely chopped
3 tablespoons tomato paste
1-1/4 teaspoon dried basil
3/4 teaspoon dried oregano
1/4 teaspoon crushed red pepper
1/2 cup grated Parmesan cheese, divided

* Cook pasta according to package directions; drain.
* Place spinach on paper towels and squeeze to dry.
* Spray non-stick skillet with vegetable spray.
* Add oil and heat on medium high. Add onion and garlic; sauté until tender. Add chicken; cook until no longer pink.
* Stir in tomatoes and next 5 ingredients; bring to a boil. Reduce heat and simmer 5 more minutes.
* Combine pasta, spinach, chicken mixture and 1/4 cup cheese in a bowl.
* Spoon into a 13x9-inch baking dish sprayed with vegetable spray.
* Sprinkle with remaining cheese.
* Bake at 350° for 20 minutes or until thoroughly heated.

Sodium - 332 Mg
Fiber-Dietary - 1.693 Gm
Cholesterol - 55.563 Mg

Fat - 10.339 Gm
Poly Fat - 2.354 Gm
Saturated Fat - 2.717 Gm

Judi Tingler

Variation: For more tomato flavor, 2 (16-ounce) cans of tomatoes and 1 (6-ounce) can of tomato paste can be used. Also, Cheddar cheese is good sprinkled on top.

Betsy Mitchell

TOMATO-MOZZARELLA PASTA

Serves: 4; Calories per serving: 535 (Protein 20%, Carbohydrate 55%, Fat 25%)

1 pound ripe tomatoes
8 ounces mozzarella cheese
1/2 cup sliced fresh basil
6 tablespoons olive oil
6 tablespoons red wine vinegar
2 large cloves garlic, minced

1/4 teaspoon dried red pepper flakes
12 ounces fusilli or rotini pasta
1/4 cup pine nuts, toasted
salt to taste
pepper to taste

* Half and seed tomatoes. Cut tomatoes into 1/2-inch pieces and place in bowl.
* Mix basil, oil, vinegar, garlic and red pepper flakes. Season with salt and pepper. Pour over tomatoes. Let stand 30 minutes.
* Cook pasta until tender. Drain and return to pot. Add tomato mixture and cheese.
* Toss over low heat until cheese melts. Sprinkle with pine nuts to serve.

Sodium - 282 Mg
Fiber-Dietary - 1.718 Gm
Cholesterol - 31.944 Mg

Fat - 15.371 Gm
Poly Fat - 0.966 Gm
Saturated Fat - 5.975 Gm

Marilyn Thompson

APRICOT-MUSTARD CHICKEN

Serves: 8; Calories per serving: 289 (Protein 41%, Carbohydrate 30%, Fat 29%)

1 tablespoon margarine
2 tablespoons vegetable oil
8 chicken breasts, skinned
1/2 cup flour
salt to taste

1/2 cup apricot preserves
1 tablespoon Dijon mustard
1/2 cup nonfat yogurt
2 tablespoons slivered almonds, toasted

* Melt margarine and oil in large baking dish.
* Dredge chicken in flour and salt; shake off excess flour.
* Place single layer of chicken in prepared dish. Bake at 375° for 25 minutes.
* Combine apricot preserves, mustard and yogurt.
* Spread over chicken and bake an additional 30 minutes. Top with toasted almonds.

Sodium - 406 Mg
Fiber-Dietary - 0.578 Gm
Cholesterol - 73.250 Mg

Fat - 9.058 Gm
Poly Fat - 2.460 Gm
Saturated Fat - 1.455 Gm

Leslie Gebert

CHICKEN WITH BASIL AND MUSTARD

Serves: 4; Calories per serving: 170 (Protein 66%, Carbohydrate 3%, Fat 30%)

2 teaspoons olive oil
1-1/2 tablespoons Worcestershire sauce
2 teaspoons Dijon mustard

1-1/2 teaspoons dried basil
2 whole chicken breasts, split, skinned and boned

* Mix oil, Worcestershire sauce, mustard and basil.
* Marinate chicken in mixture overnight.
* Drain marinade and discard.
* Place breasts on prepared grill for 3 to 5 minutes until done.

Sodium - 181 Mg
Fiber-Dietary - 0.000 Gm
Cholesterol - 73.000 Mg

Fat - 5.485 Gm
Poly Fat - 0.850 Gm
Saturated Fat - 1.174 Gm

Deborah McGovern

CHICKEN CACCIATORE

Serves: 5; Calories per serving: 183 (Protein 62%, Carbohydrate 17%, Fat 17%)

5 skinless chicken breasts
6 ounces unsalted tomato juice
1/2 teaspoon dried rosemary
1/2 teaspoon oregano
1/2 teaspoon basil
1 bay leaf

1 teaspoon chopped garlic
1/2 cup chopped green onion tops
1/2 cup chopped green pepper
1 cup diced tomatoes (or 16-ounce can)
1/4 cup white wine

* Brown chicken on all sides in a hot pan, coated with non-stick spray.
* Add tomato juice, herbs, garlic and chopped vegetables.
* Cover and simmer until chicken is tender.
* Uncover and bring to boil to reduce sauce.
* Add wine and simmer briefly.

Sodium - 216 Mg
Fiber-Dietary - 1.578 Gm
Cholesterol - 73.000 Mg

Fat - 3.385 Gm
Poly Fat - 0.780 Gm
Saturated Fat - 0.914 Gm

Jane Gilbert

CHICKEN CURRY

Serves: 6; Calories per serving: 302 (Protein 66%, Carbohydrate 9%, Fat 25%)

2-3 pounds skinless chicken breasts
1/2 cup chopped onion
1 clove garlic
1 tablespoon cooking oil
2 tablespoons curry powder
1 teaspoon sugar

1 teaspoon salt
1 tablespoon cornstarch
1/3 cup water
1/4 cup yogurt, sour cream or milk
2 medium tomatoes, chopped
3 tablespoons cilantro, chopped

* In a 12x7x1/2-inch microwave-safe dish, microwave onion and garlic in oil uncovered for about 2 minutes on high until onion is tender.
* Cut up chicken pieces and arrange in dish.
* Combine curry powder, sugar, salt, cornstarch, cold water and yogurt.
* Stir in chopped tomatoes. Pour sauce over chicken.
* Cook covered on high for 25 to 28 minutes until chicken is done, turning chicken 3 times and spooning sauce over chicken.
* Sprinkle with chopped cilantro and serve with Saffron Rice (see Index).

Sodium - 124 Mg
Fiber-Dietary - 1.423 Gm
Cholesterol - 129 Mg

Fat - 8.140 Gm
Poly Fat - 1.898 Gm
Saturated Fat - 1.725 Gm

Shoba Rao

CHICKEN SCARPARELLO

Serves: 4; Calories per serving: 184 (Protein 64%, Carbohydrate 5%, Fat 21%)

Progresso banana peppers or Greek
  (salonica) peppers
4 chicken breasts, skinned and boned
butter

1/2 cup chicken broth
1/2 cup dry white wine
green olives with pits (optional)

* Brown chicken breasts in butter.
* Add chicken broth, dry white wine and peppers. Simmer. Add green olives, if desired.

Sodium - 330 Mg
Fiber-Dietary - 0.620 Gm
Cholesterol - 73.000 Mg

Fat - 4.164 Gm
Poly Fat - 0.763 Gm
Saturated Fat - 0.972 Gm

Tonia Fuller

CHICKEN KABOBS

Serves: 4; Calories per serving: 206 (Protein 56%, Carbohydrate 11%, Fat 30%)

4 chicken breasts, skinned and boned
2 tablespoons vegetable oil
1/4 cup soy sauce
1/4 cup white wine
2 tablespoons lemon juice
1/2 teaspoon garlic powder

1/2 teaspoon ground ginger
4 ounces fresh mushrooms
1 zucchini, cut into 1-inch pieces
1 red pepper, cut into pieces
pearl onions
3 tablespoons water

* Cut chicken breasts into 1-inch pieces.
* Combine oil, soy sauce, white wine, lemon juice, garlic powder and ginger. Mix well.
* Add the chicken. Cover and marinate 8 hours or overnight.
* Place vegetables and water in microwave-safe bowl. Microwave on high for 3 to 4 minutes. Drain and set aside.
* Drain chicken. Reserve marinade.
* Skewer chicken and vegetables. Baste with extra marinade.
* Bake at 350° about 30 minutes or cook on grill about 25 minutes or until chicken is done.

Sodium - 747 Mg
Fiber-Dietary - 1.102 Gm
Cholesterol - 73.000 Mg

Fat - 6.699 Gm
Poly Fat - 1.753 Gm
Saturated Fat - 1.145 Gm

Judy DuBose

CHICKEN TERIYAKI

Serves: 4; Calories per serving: 284 (Protein 44%, Carbohydrate 39%, Fat 11%)

4 chicken breasts, skinned and boned
1 green pepper, seeded and cut into
  julienne strips
Marinade:
2 tablespoons sugar
1/4 cup reduced sodium soy sauce
1/3 cup water
1/4 cup sherry

cooking oil
2 cups cooked brown or wild rice

1 teaspoon grated fresh ginger (or 1/2
  teaspoon powdered ginger)
1/8 teaspoon garlic powder
1/8 teaspoon white pepper

* Whisk together all marinade ingredients.
* Marinate chicken 2 hours or longer, turning occasionally.
* Brown chicken breasts on each side in cooking oil.
* Add marinade and simmer until tender (about 20 minutes).
* Add green pepper strips and cook until crisp tender.
* Serve over rice.

Sodium - 667 Mg
Fiber-Dietary - 1.610 Gm
Cholesterol - 73.000 Mg

Fat - 3.411 Gm
Poly Fat - 0.862 Gm
Saturated Fat - 0.921 Gm

Barbara Kane

Variation: Add 1 tablespoon toasted sesame seeds and 2 tablespoons honey to marinade. Flatten chicken breasts to 1/4-inch thickness and grill over hot coals for 6 minutes on each side, basting frequently.

Judy Thomas

GINGER-GLAZED CHICKEN

Serves: 8; Calories per serving: 350 (Protein 64%, Carbohydrate 20%, Fat 17%)

*2 broilers, halved or 6-8 chicken breast
  halves
1 (8-ounce) bottle Italian dressing, divided*

*1/2 cup orange marmalade
2 teaspoons ginger
1/8 teaspoon hot pepper sauce*

* Place chicken in single layer in pan. Pour 1/2 cup salad dressing over chicken. Turn to coat on all sides. Cover. Let stand 2 to 3 hours or refrigerate overnight.
* Combine remaining dressing with marmalade, ginger and hot pepper sauce. Brush chicken with mixture.
* Place chicken skin side up over hot coals. Grill slowly, basting often, 20 to 30 minutes. Turn; continue cooking 20 to 30 more minutes, basting often until golden and tender.

Sodium - 552 Mg
Fiber-Dietary - 0.208 Gm
Cholesterol - 144 Mg

Fat - 6.101 Gm
Poly Fat - 1.311 Gm
Saturated Fat - 1.729 Gm

Leslie Gebert

GARLIC-LIME CHICKEN

Serves: 4; Calories per serving: 177 (Protein 57%, Carbohydrate 10%, Fat 14%)

*4 chicken breast halves, skinned and
  boned
1/2 cup low-sodium soy sauce
1/4 cup fresh lime juice
1 tablespoon Worcestershire sauce*

*2 cloves garlic, minced
1/2 teaspoon dry mustard
1/2 teaspoon ground pepper
butter-flavored cooking spray*

* Mix soy sauce, lime juice, Worcestershire sauce, garlic and mustard.
* Pour over chicken; cover and marinate in refrigerator 30 minutes.
* Remove chicken from marinade and sprinkle with pepper.
* Spray skillet with butter-flavored cooking spray.
* Add chicken and cook over medium heat about 6 minutes on each side or until fork can be inserted in chicken with ease.

Sodium - 1208 Mg
Fiber-Dietary - 0.066 Gm
Cholesterol - 73.000 Mg

Fat - 3.237 Gm
Poly Fat - 0.640 Gm
Saturated Fat - 0.816 Gm

Linda Jones

GRILLED LEMON CHICKEN

Serves: 8; Calories per serving: 158 (Protein 72%, Carbohydrate 6%, Fat 22%)

1/2 cup lemon juice
1/4 cup Dijon mustard
3/4 teaspoon salt
1/4 teaspoon coarsely ground pepper
1/2 teaspoon thyme

1 teaspoon rosemary
1/2 teaspoon oregano
1 tablespoon parsley, chopped
juice of 1 lemon
8 chicken breasts, skinned and boned

* Stir together all ingredients except chicken. Pour marinade over chicken in glass dish.
* Marinate 2 to 4 hours in refrigerator.
* Grill chicken over medium heat 7 to 10 minutes on each side.

Sodium - 463 Mg
Fiber-Dietary - 0.101 Gm
Cholesterol - 73.000 Mg

Fat - 3.650 Gm
Poly Fat - 0.680 Gm
Saturated Fat - 0.882 Gm

Frances Fennebresque

HERB-PARMESAN CHICKEN

Serves: 10; Calories per serving: 274 (Protein 51%, Carbohydrate 25%, Fat 24%)

2 cups dry breadcrumbs
1 cup grated Parmesan cheese
1 teaspoon paprika
1 teaspoon garlic powder

1/2 teaspoon pepper
4 tablespoons parsley, chopped
5 whole chicken breasts, skinned
1/2 cup nonfat plain yogurt

* Mix first 6 ingredients in bowl. Dip chicken in yogurt, then roll in crumb mixture.
* Spray 13x9-inch pan with cooking spray.
* Place chicken breasts in pan so that they do not touch. Bake at 350° for 1 hour.

Sodium - 406 Mg
Fiber-Dietary - 0.827 Gm
Cholesterol - 81.100 Mg

Fat - 7.135 Gm
Poly Fat - 1.027 Gm
Saturated Fat - 3.000 Gm

Marilyn Thompson

LITE CHICKEN PICCATA

Serves: 4; Calories per serving: 246 (Protein 56%, Carbohydrate 14%, Fat 30%)

*4 boneless chicken breast halves,
   skinned*
1/4 cup flour
1/4 teaspoon salt
1/4 teaspoon pepper

1-1/2 tablespoons margarine
1/4 cup lemon juice
1/2 lemon, thinly sliced
2 tablespoons chopped fresh parsley
2 teaspoons capers (water packed), drained

* Place chicken between 2 sheets of wax paper and flatten to 1/4-inch thickness using a mallet or rolling pin. Cut each breast in 2 to 3 pieces.
* Combine flour, salt and pepper; dredge chicken in flour mixture.
* Coat large skillet with cooking spray. Add margarine and melt over medium heat.
* Add chicken and cook 3 to 4 minutes on each side or until golden brown.
* Remove chicken and drain on paper towels. Transfer to a platter and keep warm.
* Add capers and lemon juice to pan drippings in skillet. Cook until thoroughly heated, stirring occasionally.
* Pour lemon mixture over chicken and garnish with lemon slices and chopped parsley.

Sodium - 208 Mg
Fiber-Dietary - 0.503 Gm
Cholesterol - 87.139 Mg

Fat - 8.143 Gm
Poly Fat - 2.163 Gm
Saturated Fat - 1.781 Gm

Nancy Austin

LEMON CHICKEN

Serves: 4; Calories per serving: 479 (Protein 78%, Carbohydrate 2%, Fat 20%)

2-1/2 pounds skinless chicken pieces
1 teaspoon finely chopped garlic
1 tablespoon grated lemon rind
4 tablespoons lemon juice

4 tablespoons chicken broth
1 teaspoon oregano, crushed
1/2 teaspoon thyme, crushed
fresh parsley for garnish

* Choose pan large enough to hold chicken close together in 1 layer. Spray non-stick vegetable spray in pan. Rub garlic on chicken; place in pan. Sprinkle with lemon rind.
* Mix lemon juice and chicken broth; pour gently over chicken.
* Sprinkle with oregano and thyme.
* Bake at 400° for 20 minutes, basting every 10 minutes.
* Turn chicken; continue baking and basting until done. Garnish with parsley.

Sodium - 258 Mg
Fiber-Dietary - 0.134 Gm
Cholesterol - 241 Mg

Fat - 10.251 Gm
Poly Fat - 2.207 Gm
Saturated Fat - 2.902 Gm

Suzanne Allen

PEACHY CURRIED CHICKEN

Serves: 4; Calories per serving: 270 (Protein 42%, Carbohydrate 43%, Fat 15%)

1/2 cup water
1 tablespoon instant minced onion
1 (7/8-ounce) package chicken
  gravy mix

1/2 cup peach preserves
1 teaspoon curry powder
1 teaspoon dry mustard
4 chicken breast halves, skinned and boned

* Line 13x9-inch baking dish with foil.
* Combine water and onion in medium-sized bowl and let stand 5 minutes.
* Add remaining ingredients, except chicken, to water and onion. Stir until well-blended. Add chicken one piece at a time and turn to coat thoroughly.
* Place chicken in baking dish. Spoon remaining sauce over chicken.
* Bake uncovered at 350° for 30 minutes until chicken is golden brown. Baste with pan juices during cooking.

Sodium - 514 Mg
Fiber-Dietary - 0.166 Gm
Cholesterol - 73.000 Mg

Fat - 4.295 Gm
Poly Fat - 0.662 Gm
Saturated Fat - 0.871 Gm

Cathy Keane

TANDOORI OR INDIAN BARBEQUED CHICKEN
Serves: 6; Calories per serving: 195 (Protein 61%, Carbohydrate 13%, Fat 25%)

2 tablespoons chopped garlic
3 tablespoons chopped fresh ginger
1/2 cup lemon juice
1 teaspoon pepper
1 teaspoon salt
1 teaspoon cumin powder

1 teaspoon cayenne pepper
1 cup plain yogurt
2 pounds skinless chicken pieces
2 tablespoons oil or melted margarine
lemon slices, whole onions, tomato
    slices (optional)

* To make marinade, mix all ingredients except chicken and margarine in blender.
* Coat chicken with marinade. Cover and refrigerate for 24 hours.
* Remove chicken from marinade. Bake at 400° for 45 minutes or grill until chicken is
   done, basting occasionally with margarine and remaining marinade.
* Serve with pieces of lemon, grilled fresh onions and tomato slices.

Sodium - 497 Mg
Fiber-Dietary - 0.149 Gm
Cholesterol - 73.667 Mg

Fat - 5.354 Gm
Poly Fat - 1.586 Gm
Saturated Fat - 1.278 Gm

Maya Shenoy

MARINATED TURKEY STEAKS
Serves: 6; Calories per serving: 624 (Protein 61%, Carbohydrate 9%, Fat 30%)

1/2 cup reduced-sodium soy sauce
1/4 cup vegetable oil
1 tablespoon honey

3 cloves garlic, minced
1/2 teaspoon ginger
6 turkey breast cutlets

* Mix all marinade ingredients together and put into a large plastic bag.
* Add turkey and marinate in refrigerator for 8 hours or overnight.
* Cook over medium coals for 15 to 25 minutes or until done, turning to cook both sides.

Sodium - 1064 Mg
Fiber-Dietary - 0.397 Gm
Cholesterol - 251 Mg

Fat - 20.336 Gm
Poly Fat - 2.150 Gm
Saturated Fat - 3.172 Gm

Variation: To marinade add: 2 to 4 ounces pineapple juice; olive oil instead of
vegetable oil; 1/4 teaspoon dry mustard; 3 green onions, chopped.

Jean Moody, Pat Waldron

EASY FIVE-HOUR OVEN STEW

Serves: 12; Calories per serving: 195 (Protein 35%, Carbohydrate 37%, Fat 28%)

1-1/2 pounds lean stew beef
1 cup chopped celery
6 carrots, cut up
1 large onion, diced
4 medium potatoes, quartered

1 (16-ounce) can whole tomatoes
1 tablespoon sugar
2 tablespoons tapioca
salt and pepper to taste
garlic powder to taste

* Mix all ingredients in a large casserole. Cover tightly.
* Bake 5 hours at 250°. Do not peek while baking.

Sodium - 311 Mg
Fiber-Dietary - 2.208 Gm
Cholesterol - 38.022 Mg

Fat - 5.971 Gm
Poly Fat - 0.319 Gm
Saturated Fat - 2.509 Gm

Janet Anthony

E-Z BEEF BURGUNDY

Serves: 6; Calories per serving: 597 (Protein 55%, Carbohydrate 18%, Fat 23%)

3 pounds lean chuck, cubed
1 (10-1/2-ounce) can consommé
1 (11-1/2-ounce) can vegetable
  cocktail juice
1 cup burgundy wine
1/2 cup light brown sugar
1 (10-1/2-ounce) can onion soup
1/2 teaspoon onion salt

1 teaspoon oregano leaves
1/2 teaspoon celery salt
2 bay leaves
1/2 teaspoon thyme leaves
1 small can sliced mushrooms
1/3 cup water
3 tablespoons cornstarch

* Brown beef cubes in oil.
* Combine remaining ingredients except water and cornstarch and bring to a boil.
* Reduce heat and simmer for 2 hours.
* Combine water with cornstarch.
* Stir cornstarch mixture into hot stew. Cook over medium heat until thickened.

Sodium - 1377 Mg
Fiber-Dietary - 0.915 Gm
Cholesterol - 229 Mg

Fat - 15.053 Gm
Poly Fat - 0.853 Gm
Saturated Fat - 5.294 Gm

Georgia Draucker

CRANBERRY-GLAZED PORK ROAST

Serves: 12; Calories per serving: 314 (Protein 58%, Carbohydrate 20%, Fat 22%)

2 teaspoons cornstarch
1/8 teaspoon cinnamon
1/8 teaspoon salt

1/4 cup orange juice
1 (16-ounce) can whole cranberry sauce
2-4 pound boneless pork tenderloin roast

* Combine cornstarch, cinnamon, salt, orange juice and cranberry sauce; cook until thickened, stirring frequently.
* Place pork in shallow pan. Baste with sauce.
* Bake at 350° until meat thermometer registers 155° to 160° (about 45 minutes to 1 hour), basting several times.
* Serve roast with remaining sauce.

Sodium - 134 Mg
Fiber-Dietary - 0.142 Gm
Cholesterol - 140 Mg

Fat - 7.368 Gm
Poly Fat - 0.880 Gm
Saturated Fat - 2.509 Gm

Beth Blackwell

GRILLED BEER SHRIMP

Serves: 6; Calories per serving: 218 (Protein 59%, Carbohydrate 6%, Fat 31%)

3/4 cup beer
3 tablespoons oil
2 tablespoons snipped parsley
4 teaspoons Worcestershire sauce

1 clove fresh garlic, minced
1/2 teaspoon salt
1/8 teaspoon pepper
2 pounds large shrimp, peeled

* Mix together all ingredients, except shrimp, to make marinade.
* Add shrimp and allow to marinate in refrigerator for at least 3 hours.
* Allow to stand in marinade at room temperature for about 30 minutes.
* Thread shrimp on double-pronged skewers and brush with marinade.
* Grill about 2 to 3 minutes on each side. (May be broiled on well-oiled broiler if not grilled.)
* Shrimp are done when they turn bright pink and opaque. Do not over cook.

Sodium - 439 Mg
Fiber-Dietary - 0.140 Gm
Cholesterol - 233 Mg

Fat - 7.148 Gm
Poly Fat - 2.362 Gm
Saturated Fat - 0.822 Gm

Pattie Bethune

JACKSONVILLE SHRIMP CREOLE

Serves: 8; Calories per serving: 239 (Protein 43%, Carbohydrate 35%, Fat 22%)

5 large green peppers
5 large onions
1 bunch celery
2 tablespoons vegetable oil
1 tablespoon flour
salt and pepper to taste

1/4 teaspoon allspice or to taste
1 tablespoon sugar
1 (8-ounce) can tomato sauce
4 ounces tomato paste
2 pounds raw shrimp, peeled and deveined
8 cups cooked rice

* Cut green peppers, onions and celery into 1/2-inch chunks.
* Cook slowly in a skillet with oil and a light sprinkling of flour.
* Stir occasionally to keep from sticking.
* Season to taste with salt, pepper, allspice and sugar. Add tomato sauce and tomato paste.
* Cook over medium heat for 5 minutes, stirring occasionally. Add shrimp and cook about 15 minutes or until shrimp are tender.
* Serve over rice.

Sodium - 756 Mg
Fiber-Dietary - 3.109 Gm
Cholesterol - 175 Mg

Fat - 5.795 Gm
Poly Fat - 1.928 Gm
Saturated Fat - 0.672 Gm

Gail Latham

LO-CAL SWEET AND SOUR SHRIMP

Serves: 6; Calories per serving: 219 (Protein 59%, Carbohydrate 22%, Fat 20%)

2 pounds large shrimp, cooked and
  peeled
1 (15-ounce) can unsweetened
  pineapple chunks

1 tablespoon margarine
1 medium onion, chopped
1 green pepper, cut in strips
cooked rice

Sauce:

reserved pineapple juice
1/4 cup vinegar
1 tablespoon low-sodium soy sauce

1 tablespoon cornstarch
1/2 teaspoon dry mustard

* Drain pineapple, reserving juice.
* Spray a 10-inch skillet with vegetable oil spray. Over medium heat, sauté onion and pepper in margarine.
* To make sauce, combine pineapple juice, vinegar, soy sauce, cornstarch and dry mustard in medium-size bowl. Use whisk to blend.
* Add sauce to vegetable mixture in skillet. Cook until thickened over low heat.
* Gently add shrimp and pineapple chunks. Heat thoroughly.
* Serve over rice.

Sodium - 352 Mg
Fiber-Dietary - 0.885 Gm
Cholesterol - 233 Mg

Fat - 4.677 Gm
Poly Fat - 1.816 Gm
Saturated Fat - 0.809 Gm

Suggestion: This can also be made with chicken, cut in chunks.

Pamela Cooke

OVEN-CRISPED FISH
Serves: 4; Calories per serving: 189 (Protein 48%, Carbohydrate 22%, Fat 27%)

1/2 cup unseasoned breadcrumbs	1 pound catfish fillets (or any fish fillet)
1/2 teaspoon paprika	3 tablespoons lemon juice
1/4 teaspoon dried thyme leaves	2 tablespoons white wine
1/8 teaspoon garlic powder	salt

* Combine breadcrumbs and spices. Set aside.
* Rinse and dry fish.
* Combine wine and lemon juice in shallow pan. Dip each fillet in lemon mixture.
* Sprinkle with salt on both sides. Roll in seasoned breadcrumbs, coating well.
* Place fish in 13x9-inch pan which has been sprayed with non-stick vegetable spray.
* Bake at 425° for 20 to 25 minutes, until fish flakes easily when tested with a fork.

Sodium - 700 Mg	Fat - 5.524 Gm
Fiber-Dietary - 0.491 Gm	Poly Fat - 1.343 Gm
Cholesterol - 65.372 Mg	Saturated Fat - 1.250 Gm

Linda Jones

TUNA GLAZED WITH GINGER AND LIME
Serves: 6; Calories per serving: 125 (Protein 67%, Carbohydrate 10%, Fat 23%)

6 (1-inch) tuna steaks	3 teaspoons grated fresh ginger
3 tablespoons fresh lime juice	3 teaspoons oriental sesame oil
2 tablespoons low-sodium soy sauce	1/2 teaspoon crushed red pepper flakes
3 cloves garlic, crushed	1 teaspoon sugar

* Arrange fish in shallow glass baking dish.
* Whisk remaining ingredients together in small bowl and pour over fish.
* Cover and marinate for 30 minutes at room temperature or 1 hour in refrigerator. Turn fish once or twice.
* Grill about 15 minutes, basting several times. Turn once.

Sodium - 235 Mg	Fat - 3.160 Gm
Fiber-Dietary - 0.057 Gm	Poly Fat - 1.211 Gm
Cholesterol - 38.300 Mg	Saturated Fat - 0.536 Gm

Variation: Mahi Mahi may be substituted for the tuna steaks.

Lynda Dobbins

HEALTHY POUND CAKE

Serves: 16; Calories per serving: 252 (Protein 5%, Carbohydrate 63%, Fat 32%)

2-1/2 cups flour
2 cups sugar
1/2 teaspoon salt
1/2 teaspoon baking soda

1 cup light margarine, room temperature
1 teaspoon vanilla or almond extract
1 cup plain lowfat yogurt
3 egg whites

* Mix all ingredients together in a large bowl.
* Beat with mixer at high speed for 3 to 4 minutes.
* Pour into a 10-inch Bundt pan coated with non-stick vegetable spray.
* Bake at 350° for 1 hour. (Test for doneness - may need to cook longer.)
* Cool upright for at least 30 minutes. Invert pan, remove cake and serve.

Sodium - 256 Mg
Fiber-Dietary - 0.528 Gm
Cholesterol - 0.875 Mg

Fat - 9.111 Gm
Poly Fat - 2.187 Gm
Saturated Fat - 1.972 Gm

Joanna Fox

BLUEBERRY-CHERRY CRISP

Serves: 6; Calories per serving: 185 (Protein 5%, Carbohydrate 73%, Fat 22%)

1/4 cup lowfat sour cream
1 tablespoon plus 1 teaspoon brown sugar
Topping:
1/2 cup flour
2 tablespoons sugar

2 cups fresh blueberries
2 cups fresh cherries, pitted

2 tablespoons brown sugar
2 tablespoons margarine, softened

* Mix sour cream and brown sugar, stirring well. Cover and chill at least 30 minutes.
* Combine blueberries and cherries in 8-inch square pan. Toss well.
* To make topping, mix flour and next 3 ingredients until crumbly. Sprinkle over fruit.
* Bake at 375° for 40 minutes.
* Top with sour cream mixture.

Sodium - 56.323 Mg
Fiber-Dietary - 2.155 Gm
Cholesterol - 0.583 Mg

Fat - 4.726 Gm
Poly Fat - 1.796 Gm
Saturated Fat - 0.848 Gm

Erin Tilley

AMARETTO-CHOCOLATE SILK PUDDING

Serves: 6; Calories per serving: 197 (Protein 7%, Carbohydrate 75%, Fat 10%)

3/4 cup granulated sugar　　　　　　*1/4 cup amaretto liqueur*
1/4 cup unsweetened cocoa powder　　*2 tablespoons margarine*
1/4 cup cornstarch　　　　　　　　　*3/4 teaspoon vanilla*
2 cups skim milk　　　　　　　　　　*1/8 teaspoon almond extract*

* Sift sugar, cocoa powder and cornstarch together in a heavy saucepan and whisk.
* Heat milk and amaretto together until hot but not boiling. As soon as little bubbles begin to appear on the surface, remove from heat.
* Slowly pour the hot liquid over dry ingredients.
* Whisk well and bring to a boil over medium-low heat, whisking continually, until the mixture thickens and comes to a boil. Increase heat and boil for a minute more.
* Remove from heat. Stir in margarine until it melts; stir in vanilla and almond extracts.
* Pour into 6 individual serving dishes. Place a piece of wax paper over the top of each portion. Chill for at least 2 hours before serving. Best served same day.

Sodium - 88.573 Mg　　　　　　　　Fat - 2.395 Gm
Fiber-Dietary - 0.048 Gm　　　　　　Poly Fat - 0.873 Gm
Cholesterol - 1.333 Mg　　　　　　　Saturated Fat - 0.430 Gm

Linda Sanchez

MICROWAVE VANILLA CUSTARD

Serves: 6; Calories per serving: 96 (Protein 18%, Carbohydrate 80%, Fat 2%)

1/3 cup sugar　　　　　　　　　　　*1 egg*
3 tablespoons cornstarch　　　　　　*2-1/2 cups milk*
1/4 teaspoon salt　　　　　　　　　*1/2 teaspoon vanilla*

* Combine sugar, cornstarch and salt. Add egg. Beat with whisk.
* Add milk and beat until smooth.
* Microwave on high for 4 minutes. Beat thoroughly.
* Continue on high 3 minutes until desired consistency. Whip in 1/2 teaspoon vanilla.

Sodium - 155 Mg　　　　　　　　　　Fat - 0.186 Gm
Fiber-Dietary - 0.036 Gm　　　　　　Poly Fat - 0.008 Gm
Cholesterol - 1.667 Mg　　　　　　　Saturated Fat - 0.120 Gm

Ruth Fitzpatrick

LEMON OATMEAL COOKIES

Serves: 40; Calories per serving: 41 (Protein 7%, Carbohydrate 70%, Fat 22%)

1/4 cup margarine, softened
3/4 cup sugar
1 tablespoon grated lemon rind
1 teaspoon fresh lemon juice
1/4 teaspoon salt
1/4 teaspoon ground allspice

1 egg
1 cup flour
1/2 teaspoon baking soda
1/4 teaspoon cream of tartar
1 cup quick oats

* Cream margarine. Gradually add sugar, beating at medium speed.
* Add lemon rind, lemon juice and next 3 ingredients; beat well.
* Combine flour, baking soda and cream of tartar. Gradually add to margarine
  mixture, beating well. Add oats and mix.
* Drop by rounded teaspoons onto cookie sheets sprayed with non-stick cooking spray.
* Bake at 350° for about 12 minutes.

Sodium - 40.084 Mg
Fiber-Dietary - 0.180 Gm
Cholesterol - 0.000 Mg

Fat - 1.030 Gm
Poly Fat - 0.270 Gm
Saturated Fat - 0.208 Gm

Abbey Rawald

FROZEN APPLE YOGURT

Serves: 22; Calories per serving: 51 (Protein 8%, Carbohydrate 74%, Fat 17%)

2 red apples
half-gallon vanilla frozen yogurt,
  softened
1 teaspoon ground cinnamon

1/2 teaspoon nutmeg
2 packets artificial sweetener
1 tablespoon lemon juice
4 teaspoons apple brandy or apple cider

* Peel, core and grate apples.
* Mix yogurt, apples, cinnamon, nutmeg, sweetener and lemon juice.
* Stir in apple brandy or apple cider.
* Place in covered container and refreeze.

Sodium - 8.356 Mg
Fiber-Dietary - 0.223 Gm
Cholesterol - 2.418 Mg

Fat - 1.015 Gm
Poly Fat - 0.012 Gm
Saturated Fat - 0.010 Gm

Carroll Thompson

LEMON SHERBET

Serves: 8, Calories per serving: 99 (Protein 15%, Carbohydrate 83%, Fat 1%)

1 envelope unflavored gelatin
3 cups skim milk, divided
1/4 cup sugar

1 (6-ounce) can frozen lemonade
    concentrate, thawed and undiluted
1/2 teaspoon grated lemon rind

* Sprinkle gelatin over 1/2 cup skim milk in a medium saucepan; let stand 1 minute.
* Add sugar. Cook over low heat until gelatin dissolves, stirring constantly.
* Remove from heat. Stir in 2-1/2 cups milk and remaining ingredients; mixture will curdle. Pour into an 8-inch square pan.
* Freeze 3 hours or until mixture is firm but not frozen.
* Spoon chunks of sherbet mixture into food processor. Process until smooth.
* Return mixture to pan. Freeze 4 hours or until firmly frozen.
* Let stand 10 minutes before serving.

Sodium - 48.706 Mg
Fiber-Dietary - 0.544 Gm
Cholesterol - 1.500 Mg

Fat - 0.165 Gm
Poly Fat - 0.006 Gm
Saturated Fat - 0.108 Gm

Elaine Quillman

FRUIT CRISP

Serves: 6; Calories per serving: 216 (Protein 6%, Carbohydrate 74%, Fat 20%)

1 cup blueberries
3 apples, peeled and sliced
1 tablespoon lemon juice
1/4 cup apple juice
2 tablespoons sugar
1 teaspoon cinnamon

1/8 cup apple juice
1 cup oatmeal
1/3 cup whole wheat flour
1/4 cup brown sugar
2 tablespoons margarine

* Layer blueberries, then apples in a 1-1/2-quart casserole.
* Pour lemon juice and 1/4 cup apple juice over fruit. Sprinkle with cinnamon and sugar.
* In food processor, combine remaining ingredients; process until mixed.
* Sprinkle on top. Bake at 350° for 30 minutes.

Sodium - 50.480 Mg
Fiber-Dietary - 3.274 Gm
Cholesterol - 0.000 Mg

Fat - 5.102 Gm
Poly Fat - 1.979 Gm
Saturated Fat - 0.821 Gm

Sally Burris

POULTRY

AUNT ETHEL'S CHICKEN BREAST SUPREME
Knock-out good

Serves: 12

12 chicken breasts, skinned and boned
2 cups sour cream (do not use light)
1/4 cup lemon juice
4 teaspoons Worcestershire sauce
4 teaspoons celery salt
2 teaspoons paprika

4 cloves garlic, finely chopped
2 teaspoons salt
1/4 teaspoon pepper
1-3/4 cups dry breadcrumbs
1/2 cup margarine, melted
1/4 cup shortening, melted

* Wash and dry chicken breasts.
* Whisk together next 8 ingredients in a large, deep bowl. Add chicken, covering well with the mixture.
* Cover bowl with plastic wrap. Marinate overnight or at least 10 hours.
* Roll each breast in breadcrumbs, coating well. Place in a 13x9-inch baking pan sprayed with non-stick vegetable spray.
* Combine margarine and shortening and spoon half the mixture over the chicken.
* Cover with foil. Bake at 350° for 45 minutes.
* Drizzle remaining margarine-shortening mixture over chicken. Bake uncovered 10 to 15 minutes, or until brown.

Jane Gilbert

BAKED CHICKEN IN WINE

Easy   Serves: 6-8

6 to 8 chicken breasts, skinned
1/2 cup white wine
2 cans cream of mushroom soup
1 can sliced mushrooms, drained
1/4 cup chopped red onion

1-1/4 cups sour cream
paprika
parsley
hot, cooked rice

* Place chicken breasts in a 13x9-inch baking dish.
* Mix wine, mushroom soup, mushrooms, onion and sour cream. Pour over chicken.
* Sprinkle onion and paprika over the sauce.
* Bake at 350° for 1 hour. Sprinkle with parsley. Serve with rice.

Marjori Carroll, Pam Wilcox

2/16/08
Tasted good, but very anemic appearance.

BARBEQUED CHICKEN

Serves: 6

6 chicken breasts
1 onion, finely chopped
1 clove of garlic, minced
1/2 green pepper, finely chopped
3 tablespoons butter
3 tablespoons Worcestershire sauce
1 cup water

2 tablespoons vinegar
4 tablespoons brown sugar
1 cup ketchup
1 teaspoon mustard
1/2 cup chopped celery
1/2 teaspoon salt
1/4 cup lemon juice

* Place chicken in a baking dish.
* Sauté onion, garlic and green pepper in butter until golden. Add remaining ingredients except lemon juice.
* Simmer for 30 minutes. Add lemon juice.
* Pour sauce over chicken. Cover with foil.
* Bake at 350° for 1 hour and 15 minutes.

Patsy Burns

BIRDS OF PARADISE

Serves: 8

4 whole chicken breasts, skinned,
    boned and halved
salt to taste
1 stick butter or margarine
3 eggs
1 tablespoon milk

1/2 cup grated Parmesan cheese
1 cup sherry
cooked wild rice
green grapes
toasted pecans

* Salt chicken breasts.
* Beat eggs and milk together.
* Dip chicken in egg mixture, then roll in Parmesan cheese.
* Melt butter in skillet. Brown chicken on both sides.
* Lower heat to simmer. Add sherry. Cook covered 45 minutes, basting frequently.
* Serve on a bed of wild rice. Garnish with green grapes and pecans.

Hilda Rutherford
Jean Wilkinson

10/28/07 Very good.

BREAST OF CHICKEN WITH CAPERS

Serves: 4

4 chicken breast halves, boned and
 skinned
salt and pepper to taste
1 teaspoon paprika, preferably Hungarian
2 tablespoons butter

1/4 cup finely chopped onion
1/4 cup dry vermouth
2/3 cup heavy cream
2 tablespoons capers, drained

* Sprinkle chicken breasts on both sides with salt, pepper and paprika.
* Heat butter in large skillet or electric fry pan. Cook chicken over moderate heat for 5 to 6 minutes on one side, turn and cook 2 minutes.
* Scatter onions around chicken. Cover tightly and cook over low heat about 8 minutes.
* Transfer to warm platter and cover with foil.
* Add wine to skillet, stirring to dissolve brown particles clinging to sides and bottom.
* Cook until most of wine evaporates. Add cream and capers. Bring to boil over high heat. Add any juices that have accumulated around chicken on platter.
* Cook, stirring, until reduced to about 3/4 cup. Spoon sauce over chicken and serve.

Virginia Golding

CHICKEN AND ARTICHOKES
Great company meal!

Easy

Serves: 6

2 cans cream of chicken soup
1/2 cup white wine
1/8 teaspoon salt
1/8 teaspoon pepper
6 chicken breast halves, skinned and boned
1 can sliced water chestnuts, drained

1 to 2 (14-ounce) cans artichoke hearts,
 drained and quartered
1/2 pound fresh mushrooms, sliced
1 cup packaged, seasoned herb stuffing
1/4 cup butter or margarine
hot cooked rice

* Mix together soup, wine, salt and pepper. Pour 1/3 of the mixture into a buttered 13x9-inch baking dish.
* Add chicken. Cover with water chestnuts, artichoke hearts and mushrooms.
* Pour remaining soup and wine mixture over chicken. Cover with stuffing. Dot with butter. Cover with foil and bake at 350° for 45 minutes.
* Remove foil and bake an additional 30 minutes. Serve with rice.

Katrina Hidy

CHICKEN BREASTS WITH HAM

Serves: 6

6 chicken breast halves, skinned and
  boned
salt and pepper to taste
6 tablespoons butter
6 slices cooked ham
1 cup canned sliced mushrooms,
  drained, reserving liquid

1/4 teaspoon each rosemary, savory and
  thyme
1/2 cup dry sherry
1/4 cup white wine
1 tablespoon cornstarch
1 cup heavy cream
6 slices toast

* Season chicken with salt and pepper. Sauté in 4 tablespoons butter for 10 minutes or
  until golden brown.
* Add liquid from mushrooms to chicken. Add herbs. Cover and cook for 20 minutes.
* Add sherry and wine. Simmer 10 minutes.
* Dissolve cornstarch in cream. Pour into pan, stirring constantly.
* Add mushrooms. Simmer 5 minutes or until sauce is thickened, stirring often.
* Sauté ham in remaining 2 tablespoons butter.
* Place 1 slice ham on each piece of toast. Top with chicken. Spoon sauce over all.

Lorren Grandle

CHICKEN FILLETS WITH LEMON-BUTTER SAUCE

Easy

Serves: 8

8 chicken breasts, skinned and boned
3 eggs
3/4 cup flour
1 cup milk
Lemon-Butter Sauce:
6 tablespoons butter

1/2 teaspoon salt
1/4 teaspoon pepper
2 cups fresh breadcrumbs
butter

2 to 3 tablespoons fresh lemon juice

* Pound chicken breasts between 2 sheets of wax paper until 1/4-inch thick.
* Mix eggs, flour, milk, salt and pepper. Soak breasts in batter overnight in refrigerator.
* Dredge breasts lightly in breadcrumbs. Fry in butter, about 4 minutes per side.
* Melt butter for Lemon-Butter Sauce in small pan. Add lemon juice.
* Spoon sauce over chicken and serve.

Mary Ann Little, Susan Hill

CHICKEN FINGERS WITH PLUM SAUCE

Serves: 10-12

6 whole chicken breasts, boned and cut
   into strips
1-1/2 cups buttermilk
2 tablespoons lemon juice
2 teaspoons Worcestershire sauce
1 teaspoon soy sauce
1 teaspoon paprika
1 tablespoon Greek seasoning
Plum Sauce:
1-1/2 cups red plum jam
1-1/2 tablespoons horseradish

1 teaspoon salt
1 teaspoon pepper
2 cloves garlic, minced
4 cups plain breadcrumbs
1/4 cup sesame seeds
1/4 cup butter or margarine, melted
1/4 cup shortening, melted

1-1/2 tablespoons mustard
1-1/2 teaspoons lemon juice

* Marinate chicken plus next 8 ingredients in buttermilk overnight. Drain.
* Coat chicken with breadcrumbs and sesame seeds. Refrigerate 1 hour.
* Place chicken on jellyroll pan. Do not crowd.
* Brush chicken with butter-shortening mixture. Bake at 400° for 20 to 30 minutes.
* To prepare Plum Sauce, combine all ingredients; heat until warm. Serve with chicken.

Sally Gabosch

COMPANY CHICKEN

Easy

Serves: 6

6 chicken breasts, skinned and boned
6 slices ham or dried beef
8 ounces fresh mushrooms, sliced
6 slices Swiss cheese

1 can cream of mushroom soup
1 cup sour cream
1/2 soup can dry sherry (optional)
paprika

* Pound chicken between 2 pieces wax paper to flatten.
* Top each chicken breast with a slice of ham and cheese. Roll up.
* Place in casserole. Top with mushrooms.
* Mix together soup, sour cream and sherry. Spoon over mushrooms. Sprinkle with paprika.
* Cover with foil. Bake at 325° for 1 hour. Sauce is wonderful served with wild rice.

Joy Litaker, Peggy Stokes
Dottie Kirkland, Lori Spears

CHICKEN MACADAMIA

Serves: 4-6

*2 pounds chicken breasts, skinned and
    boned, cut into 1-1/2-inch pieces*
vegetable oil
Marinade:
2 eggs, beaten
2 tablespoons soy sauce
1 tablespoon grated fresh ginger
1/4 teaspoon pepper
2 tablespoons brandy
Sweet and Sour Sauce:
1/2 cup sugar
1/3 cup vinegar
1 teaspoon freshly grated ginger

1 small jar macadamia nuts
2 tablespoons butter

1 tablespoon vegetable oil
1/2 cup flour
1/4 cup cornstarch
2 tablespoons water
1 small onion, minced

1 tablespoon cornstarch
1/4 cup water or pineapple juice

* Combine marinade ingredients. Pour over chicken in glass bowl. Refrigerate at least 2 hours.
* Toast nuts in butter in 350° oven several minutes. Watch carefully, these burn easily.
* Remove chicken from marinade. Fry chicken in vegetable oil, transferring to warm oven until all chicken pieces are cooked. Sprinkle toasted nuts over chicken.
* Combine Sweet and Sour Sauce ingredients in small saucepan. Bring to a boil. Cook 1 to 2 minutes, or until thickened. Pour over chicken and serve.

Pattie Bethune

CHICKEN PALAISE

Easy

Serves: 4

1 whole chicken, quartered and skinned
butter
1 medium onion, sliced
1 green pepper, sliced

1 garlic clove, crushed
sliced mozzarella cheese
fresh basil (optional)

* Brown chicken and garlic in butter.
* Add onions and green peppers. Cover and simmer for 30 minutes.
* Place a slice of cheese over each chicken piece and heat until melted.

Lynda Dobbins

CHICKEN MARSALA

Serves: 6

6 chicken breast halves, skinned and
   boned
1 egg, beaten
1/4 cup milk
1/4 cup flour
1-1/2 teaspoons salt
1/4 teaspoon pepper
3 tablespoons olive oil
3 tablespoons butter or margarine

1 green pepper, cut into strips
1 onion, sliced
8 ounces fresh mushrooms
1 clove garlic, crushed
1 cup Marsala wine
1 envelope instant chicken broth
1 cup water
lemon slices

* Combine egg and milk in shallow dish. Combine flour, salt and pepper on wax paper. Dip chicken in egg mixture; roll in flour to coat all sides. Refrigerate 2 to 3 hours.
* Heat oil and butter in large skillet. Brown chicken on both sides. Remove to platter. Keep warm.
* Sauté green pepper, onion, mushrooms and garlic in same skillet until tender. Spoon over chicken.
* Add wine to skillet. Stir in instant chicken broth and 1 cup water. Simmer uncovered 10 minutes to reduce liquid.
* Return chicken and vegetables to pan. Heat. Serve topped with lemon slices.

Karen Jackson

CHICKEN PICCATA

Easy

Serves: 4

4 boneless chicken breasts
1/4 cup flour
1/8 teaspoon garlic powder
salt and pepper to taste
1/2 stick margarine

chopped parsley
1 cup fresh mushrooms, sliced
juice of 1 lemon
1/4 cup dry white wine

* In bag mix flour, garlic powder, salt and pepper. Shake chicken in bag to coat.
* Sauté chicken in margarine until lightly browned.
* Sprinkle with parsley. Add mushrooms, lemon juice and wine.
* Cover and simmer on low for 20 minutes.

Joy Litaker

CHICKEN PINEAPPLE

Serves: 4-6

4 large chicken breasts, skinned and
  boned
1/3 cup flour
1 teaspoon salt
1/2 teaspoon pepper
1 clove garlic, minced
1/4 cup chopped onion

hot oil for frying
12 ounces unsweetened pineapple juice
1/3 cup chopped green pepper
1/2 teaspoon dry mustard
1 tablespoon soy sauce
1/3 cup chili sauce

* Cut chicken into bite-sized pieces. Mix flour, salt and pepper.
* Roll chicken in flour. Fry in oil to cook slightly, but not long enough to brown.
* Remove chicken from pan. Drain all but 1 tablespoon oil from pan. Add garlic, onion and pepper. Sauté 5 minutes.
* Add 1 cup pineapple juice. Stir. Add remaining ingredients. Stir. Simmer 5 minutes.
* Place chicken in 3-quart casserole. Pour sauce over chicken. Bake covered at 350° for 30 minutes. Add more pineapple juice if needed while cooking.
* Serve over rice. Freezes well.

Lillian Worthy

CHICKEN SPARACINO

Serves: 6

6 large chicken breasts, boned and
  skinned
salt and pepper to taste
1/2 cup butter, melted
1 tablespoon parsley
1 teaspoon marjoram

1/2 teaspoon thyme
1/4 pound mozzarella cheese
1/2 cup flour
2 eggs, well beaten
1 cup Italian breadcrumbs
1 cup dry white wine

* Pound chicken breasts to 1/8-inch thickness between sheets of wax paper. Sprinkle with salt and pepper. Blend butter, parsley, marjoram and thyme; set aside.
* Cut cheese into 6 sticks and wrap 1 inside each breast. Secure with a toothpick. Roll breasts in flour, then egg, then breadcrumbs. Place in baking dish.
* Pour butter and herb mixture evenly over chicken rolls.
* Bake at 350° for 15 minutes. Add wine. Bake 15 minutes more. Baste with drippings.

Nancy DeBiase

CHICKEN VIRGINIA

Serves: 6

2 eggs, beaten	6 slices mild cheese
1 tablespoon water	3 whole chicken breasts, split, skinned
1 cup breadcrumbs	and boned
1/4 teaspoon white pepper	1/2 cup flour
1/4 teaspoon dried parsley	oil
1/4 teaspoon coriander	1 cup seedless green grapes
6 slices Virginia baked ham	

* Mix eggs with water in a shallow pan; set aside.
* Mix breadcrumbs with pepper, parsley and coriander; set aside.
* Pound chicken breast between wax paper to even thickness.
* Place slice of ham and cheese on each piece of chicken.
* Carefully coat each chicken serving with flour, egg and crumb mixture. Let dry for 20 minutes. Heat oil in skillet. Sauté chicken 2 to 3 minutes on each side.
* Put in lightly greased baking dish. Bake at 425° for 20 minutes. Garnish with green grapes.

Bobbie Stelluto

JOY'S CHICKEN

Serves: 5-6

3/4 cup rosé wine	1 teaspoon ginger
1/4 cup soy sauce	1/2 teaspoon oregano
1/8 cup oil	1 tablespoon brown sugar
2 tablespoons water	8 to 10 chicken pieces, skinned
1 clove garlic, minced	

* Mix first 8 ingredients.
* Place chicken in a 13x9-inch glass or metal roasting pan.
* Pour mixture over skinned chicken.
* Bake at 350° for 45 minutes, turning chicken pieces halfway through baking time.

Carol Harris

COQ AU VIN

Serves: 4-6

4 ounces fresh mushrooms, sliced
4 to 8 small shallots or green onions,
   sliced
2 to 3 ounces butter or oil
1 chicken, cut into pieces
1 clove garlic, crushed
2 tablespoons flour

2 cups red wine or 1-1/2 cups chicken stock
   and 1/2 cup red wine
1/4 teaspoon rosemary
1/2 teaspoon salt
1/4 teaspoon black pepper
4 ounces bacon, diced, cooked and drained

* Sauté mushrooms with onions in butter until onions are golden brown.
* Remove vegetables from pan. Add chicken. Cook 10 minutes or until brown.
* Remove chicken from pan. Add garlic and flour. Cook 3 to 4 minutes.
* Gradually add red wine or stock and wine, stirring constantly.
* Stir in seasonings. Bring just to a boil. Simmer until sauce is smooth.
* Return chicken, mushrooms and onions to the sauce. Add bacon.
  Simmer chicken approximately 30 minutes or until chicken is tender.
* Serve with hot rice or noodles.

Joan Bolton
Gail Bell

GARLIC CHICKEN
Deliciously different

Serves: 8-10

16 to 20 pieces of chicken (thighs and
   legs)
2 whole garlic bulbs, unpeeled, broken
   into cloves

6 large potatoes, unpeeled, cubed
2 tablespoons oil
1/4 cup maple syrup

* Arrange chicken and potatoes in a large roasting pan.
* Layer garlic cloves on top of chicken.
* Pour oil over all.
* Bake at 350° for 1 hour.
* Pour maple syrup over all. Bake an additional 15 minutes.

Alice Michelin

MEXICAN CHICKEN BREASTS
Favorite of children

Easy   Serves: 8

1 cup Cheddar cracker crumbs
2 tablespoons taco seasoning mix
8 chicken breast halves, skinned
   and boned
2 tablespoons margarine
4 green onions, chopped

2 cups evaporated skim milk
1 cup shredded mozzarella cheese
1 cup lowfat Cheddar cheese
1 (4-ounce) can chopped green chilies
1/2 teaspoon chicken bouillon granules

* Mix cracker crumbs and seasoning mix.
* Roll chicken breasts in mixture and place in greased 13x9-inch baking dish.
* Sauté onions in margarine.
* Stir in evaporated skim milk. Add remaining ingredients.
* Pour over chicken. Bake uncovered at 350° for 45 minutes.

Nancy Dykes

ORANGE CHICKEN WITH GRAPES
Treat for family or guests

Easy   Serves: 8

8 skinless, boneless chicken breast
   halves
salt and pepper to taste
1/2 stick margarine
2/3 cup frozen orange juice concentrate

2/3 cup chicken broth
2 tablespoons white wine vinegar
1/2 teaspoon ginger
1 cup seedless grapes, halved
1 orange, sectioned

* Sprinkle chicken breasts with salt and pepper.
* Melt margarine in 10-inch skillet until hot. Brown chicken on both sides and remove
   from pan. Pour off any remaining margarine.
* Mix all other ingredients and pour into hot skillet.
* Return chicken to pan and cook in sauce 5 to 8 minutes or until done.
* Serve over rice.

Hilda Rutherford

PECAN CHICKEN WITH DIJON SAUCE

Serves: 4

4 chicken breast halves, boned and
   skinned
8 tablespoons melted butter or
   margarine, divided
3 tablespoons Dijon mustard,
   divided

2 tablespoons olive oil
6 ounces finely chopped pecans
2/3 cup sour cream or plain yogurt
1/2 teaspoon salt
1/4 teaspoon pepper

* Pound chicken breasts until 1/4-inch thick.
* Combine 6 tablespoons butter and 2 tablespoons mustard.
* Dip chicken breasts in butter mixture. Roll in chopped pecans.
* Sauté 3 minutes on each side in 2 tablespoons butter and 2 tablespoons olive oil.
* Place sautéed chicken in lightly greased baking pan. Bake at 300° for 15 to 20 minutes.
* Remove chicken from pan and deglaze pan with sour cream. Add remaining mustard and seasonings. Spoon small amount of sauce over each piece of chicken and serve.

Sally Gabosch

SHERRY CHICKEN

Easy

Serves: 8

8 skinless chicken breasts
1/4 cup flour
1 teaspoon salt
1 teaspoon pepper
1/4 cup margarine

1 tablespoon marjoram (or to taste)
1 (14-ounce) jar whole onions, drained
1 (10-1/2-ounce) can beef consommé
1/2 cup sherry
2 to 4 stalks celery, including tops

* Shake chicken breasts with flour, salt and pepper in a plastic bag. Place chicken in 13x9-inch pan.
* Dot each piece of chicken with margarine; sprinkle with marjoram. Add onions.
* Mix beef consommé with sherry and add to chicken. Top with celery stalks.
* Cover with foil; bake at 425° for 30 minutes. Uncover chicken; bake at 325° for an additional 30 minutes. Remove celery stalks before serving.

Note: If chicken is ready before you are, just add more sherry and turn heat to low.

Beth Love

STUFFED CHICKEN BREASTS

Easy   Serves: 4

4 chicken breast quarters   4 slices prosciutto or ham
1 (10-ounce) package frozen broccoli,   garlic powder
  thawed and chopped   lemon-pepper or Greek seasoning
4 slices Muenster cheese

* Cut a pocket in the side of each chicken breast, running parallel to the ribs.
* Place cheese on the prosciutto slice and top with 1/4 cup broccoli; roll up and stuff into the chicken pocket.
* Sprinkle with garlic powder, lemon-pepper or Greek seasoning.
* Bake in a greased casserole covered with foil at 350° for 45 minutes.
* Remove the foil and brown for 5 minutes under broiler.

Sally Gabosch

SUE'S CHICKEN DISH

Easy   Serves: 4

2 pounds chicken breasts, skinned   1/2 stick butter, melted
  and boned   6 slices Swiss cheese
1 can cream of chicken soup   1/4 cup chopped onion
1/2 cup milk   1 stalk celery, chopped
1 cup packaged stuffing mix

* Place chicken in glass baking dish.
* Arrange cheese slices on top.
* Add milk to soup and pour over chicken.
* Melt butter in saucepan; sauté onion and celery lightly. Add crumbs.
* Sprinkle mixture over chicken.
* Bake at 350° for 1 hour.

Christine Schaeffer
Lee Russo

ANNA'S BIRMINGHAM CHICKEN

Serves: 8

6 to 8 chicken breasts
5 ounces vermicelli or linguine
1 can cream of mushroom soup
1 can cream of chicken soup
1 large onion, chopped

1 stick butter or margarine, melted
1/4 cup sherry
1 (16-ounce) carton sour cream
Parmesan cheese
paprika

* Cook chicken breasts and cut in bite-sized pieces. Reserve broth.
* Cook noodles in chicken broth according to package directions. Drain.
* Sauté onion in melted butter. Mix with all other ingredients except cheese and paprika.
* Place in 13x9-inch baking dish and top with Parmesan cheese. Sprinkle with paprika.
* Bake at 350° for 45 minutes or until bubbly. Can be frozen.

Judy DuBose

BAKED CHICKEN REUBEN

Delicious served with crusty French bread and a fresh fruit salad

Serves: 8

4 whole chicken breasts, halved and
    boned
1/4 teaspoon salt
1/4 teaspoon pepper

1 (16-ounce) can sauerkraut, drained well
sliced Swiss cheese
1-1/4 cups Thousand Island salad dressing
1 tablespoon chopped parsley

* Place chicken breasts in greased 13x9-inch baking pan. Sprinkle with salt and pepper.
* Cover chicken with sauerkraut and top with cheese slices. Pour salad dressing evenly over cheese.
* Cover pan with foil and bake at 325° for 1-1/2 hours.

Linda Williams

CHICKEN À LA MARIA

Serves: 12

3/4 cup seasoned breadcrumbs
1/4 cup Parmesan cheese
6 whole chicken breasts, skinned, boned
   and halved
1/2 cup sliced onion
2 tablespoons butter

2 tablespoons flour
1 cup milk
1 (10-ounce) package frozen chopped
   spinach, thawed and well drained
4 ounces boiled ham, diced

* Combine crumbs and cheese. Dip chicken in crumb mixture to coat lightly.
* Arrange in a 13x9-inch baking dish. Set remaining crumb mixture aside.
* In saucepan, cook onion in butter. Blend in flour. Add milk. Cook and stir until thick and bubbly.
* Stir in spinach and ham. Spoon spinach mixture over chicken; sprinkle with crumb mixture. Bake uncovered at 350° for 40 to 45 minutes or until done.

Irene Kelly

HOT CHICKEN SALAD

Serves: 4-6

2 cups cooked chicken, diced
2 hard-boiled eggs, chopped
1 cup chopped celery
2 teaspoons minced onion
1/2 cup mayonnaise

1 tablespoon lemon juice
1/2 cup sliced water chestnuts
1 can cream of mushroom soup
salt and pepper to taste
1/2 cup Parmesan cheese

* Combine all ingredients except Parmesan cheese. Put in a greased 1-1/2-quart casserole. Sprinkle with cheese.
* Bake at 375° for 30 minutes, or until bubbly.

Pat Kelly

Variations: Can substitute 1/2 cup slivered almonds for water chestnuts, and cream of chicken soup for cream of mushroom soup. Can top casserole with small can chow mein noodles or 1/2 cup grated Cheddar cheese instead of Parmesan cheese.

Shirley Griffin, Colleen Huber

CHICKEN CASHEW CASSEROLE

Serves: 8

1 cup chopped celery
1/2 cup chopped onions
2 tablespoons margarine
2 cans cream of mushroom soup
3/4 cup chicken broth

4 tablespoons soy sauce
1 chicken, cooked and boned
3 cups cooked rice
1 large can Chinese noodles
1 cup cashews

* Cook celery and onions in margarine. Add soup, broth and soy sauce.
* Cook for 2 minutes. Add chicken and rice.
* Heat in 13x9-inch baking dish for 15 minutes at 350°.
* Remove from oven; add noodles and nuts.
* Return to oven until heated through (about 2 to 5 minutes).

Pat Viser

CHICKEN OLIVIA

Serves: 6

3 cups cooked chicken, cut in large pieces
2 cups chopped celery
1 cup cooked rice
3/4 cup mayonnaise
2 to 3 teaspoons chopped onion
1 teaspoon lemon juice

1 can cream of chicken soup
1 can sliced water chestnuts
3 hard-boiled eggs, chopped
1 stick butter, melted
1 cup crushed corn flakes
1/2 cup sliced almonds

* Mix all ingredients except butter, corn flakes and almonds in a large casserole.
* Combine butter, cornflakes and almonds. Spoon over casserole.
* Bake at 350° for 30 minutes.

Susan Basini
Gail Dings

CHICKEN WITH PHYLLO

Serves: 6

1/3 cup white wine
1/3 cup Worcestershire sauce
2 cups cubed chicken, uncooked
1/4 cup butter or margarine
1/4 cup flour
2 tablespoons Dijon mustard
1 teaspoon salt
1/4 teaspoon pepper
2 cups milk

1 (8-ounce) package cream cheese, cut into
   1/2-inch pieces
1 (10-ounce) package frozen green peas
2 medium stalks celery, sliced
1/2 cup sliced green onions, with tops
1 (6-ounce) can sliced water chestnuts,
   drained
6 frozen phyllo sheets, thawed
1/4 cup butter or margarine, melted

* Stir-fry chicken in white wine and Worcestershire sauce.
* Melt 1/4 cup margarine in 3-quart saucepan. Stir in flour, mustard, salt and pepper. Cook, stirring constantly, until smooth and bubbly. Remove from heat.
* Stir in milk. Return to heat. Boil 1 minute, stirring constantly. Remove from heat.
* Add cream cheese. Beat until smooth.
* Rinse frozen peas under running cold water to separate. Drain.
* Stir peas, chicken, celery, onions and water chestnuts into sauce. Spread in ungreased 8x8-inch baking dish.
* Cut phyllo sheets crosswise into halves. Cover with damp towel to keep from drying out.
* Carefully separate 1/2 sheet phyllo. Place on chicken mixture, folding edges under to fit dish. Brush with melted margarine. Layer remaining phyllo using same method, brushing each layer with margarine.
* Score top of phyllo into 6 sections.
* Bake at 375° for 45 minutes or until golden brown.
* Let stand 10 minutes before serving.

John Leistler

CHICKEN REYNARD

Serves: 4

4 chicken breast halves, cooked,
  boned and shredded
Sauce:
3 tablespoons butter
1/2 cup sliced celery
1 cup sliced fresh mushrooms
1 small onion, diced
1-1/4 cups heavy cream

1 pan freshly baked cornbread

2 tablespoons cornstarch
1/2 teaspoon salt
pepper to taste
1-1/4 cups chicken broth

* Sauté onions, mushrooms and celery in butter until tender.
* Mix cornstarch with cream. Add to sautéed mixture. Add chicken broth, salt and pepper. Bring to boil and simmer until thickened.
* Cut cornbread into 3-inch squares. Slice open. Place shredded chicken on each half and cover generously with sauce. Serve open-faced.

Linda Battle

Variation I: Add chicken to sauce and heat. Serve over rice.
Variation II: May add peas and/or carrots to sauce. Serve over hot biscuits.

Jean Smith

BAKED CHICKEN

Easy

Serves: 2

2 chicken breasts, skinned
1/4 stick margarine, softened
dash garlic salt
dash lemon pepper seasoning
dash oregano

dash paprika
dash parsley
1 medium onion, chopped
1/4 cup grated Parmesan cheese

* Spread margarine on each piece of chicken.
* Sprinkle with garlic salt, lemon pepper, oregano, paprika and parsley. Top with onion.
* Bake uncovered at 375° for 30 to 35 minutes or until tender.
* Top chicken with cheese. Broil 3 to 5 minutes or until crisp.

Ann Marie Ware

MAMA'S CHICKEN POT PIE

Serves: 6

1 cup chopped onion
1 cup chopped celery
1 cup chopped carrots
1 (10-ounce) package frozen peas
  (optional)
1/3 cup margarine
1/2 cup all-purpose flour

2 cups chicken broth
1 cup half-and-half or evaporated milk
1 teaspoon salt
1/4 teaspoon pepper
4 cups cooked, chopped chicken (preferably
  breasts)
2 unbaked deep-dish pie shells

* Sauté onion, celery and carrots in margarine for 10 minutes.
* Add flour, stir and cook for 1 minute.
* Add chicken broth and half-and-half. Stir well. Add peas.
* Stir and cook over medium heat until thick and bubbly.
* Add salt, pepper and chicken. Simmer on lowest heat.
* Pour chicken pie filling into one pie shell. Top with second crust. Seal edges. Prick top
  with fork. Bake at 400° for 45 minutes.

Len Efird, Sue Moss Patton
Laura Courter, Patsy Burns

MAINSTAY INN CHICKEN PIE

Serves: 6-8

3 cups cooked chicken, cut into
  bite-sized pieces
1/2 cup milk
1/2 cup sour cream
3 cups cooked vegetables of choice
1 can cream of chicken soup

3/4 cup buttermilk biscuit mix
1/4 cup cornmeal
3/4 cup milk
1 egg
2 cups shredded Cheddar cheese
paprika

* Thoroughly heat chicken, 1/2 cup milk, sour cream and soup. Add cooked vegetables.
* Spoon mixture into individual baking dishes or a 13x9-inch casserole.
* Beat together remaining ingredients except cheese until almost smooth.
* Pour evenly over hot chicken mixture. Sprinkle with cheese and paprika.
* Bake at 375° uncovered until top is set and liquid bubbles around edges, about 20 to
  25 minutes.

Marge McWilliams

CHICKEN TETRAZZINI

Serves: 6-8

4 large chicken breasts
2 cups chicken broth
1-1/2 cups chopped celery
1 medium onion, diced
8 ounces sliced mushrooms
4 tablespoons flour
2-1/2 teaspoons salt
1/4 teaspoon pepper

5 tablespoons butter
1 cup whipping cream
2-1/2 tablespoons dry sherry
1 (8-ounce) package vermicelli, cooked and
   drained
3/4 cup breadcrumbs
5 tablespoons grated Parmesan cheese

* Cook chicken until tender. Drain, reserving 2 cups broth. Bone and chop into
  bite-sized pieces.
* Sauté celery, onions and mushrooms in butter. Add flour, salt and pepper.
* Slowly add chicken broth and whipping cream. Stir constantly until thickened.
* Add chicken and sherry to the sauce.
* Place vermicelli in greased 13x9-inch baking dish. Top with chicken mixture.
* Sprinkle with breadcrumbs, Parmesan cheese and dot with butter.
* Bake at 350° for 40 minutes or until light brown and bubbly.

Teresa Ernsberger

STUFFED CHICKEN BREASTS WITH AVOCADO

Serves: 6

2 cups fresh mushrooms, sliced
1/2 cup butter or margarine, divided
6 chicken breast halves, skinned and
   boned
3/4 cup flour

1 teaspoon salt
1/2 teaspoon pepper
1/2 cup Parmesan cheese
3 ripe avocados, peeled, seeded and sliced

* Sauté mushrooms in 1/4 cup butter. Remove from skillet.
* Place chicken breasts between sheets of wax paper and pound gently.
* Coat chicken in mixture of flour, salt and pepper.
* Cook chicken in same skillet with remaining butter 3 minutes per side, or until tender.
* Place chicken on broiler pan. Top chicken with mushrooms and avocado slices;
  sprinkle with Parmesan cheese. Broil lightly until cheese melts.

Terry Casto

283

CHICKEN CHIMICHANGAS

Yields: 8 individual chimichangas

2-1/2 cups chopped, cooked chicken
2/3 cup medium-hot picante sauce
1/3 cup chopped green onions
1 teaspoon ground cumin (or to taste)
1/2 teaspoon oregano (or to taste)
1/2 teaspoon salt

1 (4-ounce) can chopped green chilies
8 (7-inch) flour tortillas
1/4 cup margarine, melted
1 cup shredded Monterey Jack cheese
optional garnishes: sour cream,
    guacamole, picante sauce

* Combine first 7 ingredients in saucepan. Cook over medium heat until most of the moisture has evaporated. Set aside.
* Barely dampen 2 paper towels. Heat tortillas one at a time between towels for 10 seconds in microwave.
* After each tortilla is heated brush 1 side with melted margarine and turn over. Put 1/3 cup chicken mixture and 2 tablespoons cheese in center.
* Fold edges and overlap in center to form a square package.
* Place packages in a greased 13x9-inch baking dish. Bake at 475° for 10 to 15 minutes, or until crisp.
* Serve with optional garnishes.

Rizzie Baldwin

FRANCIE'S FAJITAS

Easy

Serves: 8

smoked salt
2 pounds boneless chicken, cut in strips
olive oil
3 bell peppers, cut in strips (use red,
    yellow and green for color)

1 medium onion, cut in rings
large flour tortillas
1 to 2 diced tomatoes
guacamole
picante sauce

* Season chicken strips with smoked salt.
* Sauté chicken in olive oil over medium-high heat until lightly browned.
* Add peppers and onions. Continue stir-frying until vegetables are crisp tender.
* Serve with tortillas, chopped tomatoes, guacamole and picante sauce.

Francie López

PAULA'S CHICKEN FIESTA

Easy   Serves: 4

4 boneless chicken breasts   1 (4-ounce) can chopped green chilies
1 package taco seasoning mix   1 cup sour cream
breadcrumbs   2 to 3 scallions, chopped
1 cup grated Monterey Jack cheese   1 package Cajun style rice, cooked

* Roll chicken breasts in taco seasoning and then in breadcrumbs. Place in a greased baking dish. Cover with cheese.
* Combine chilies, sour cream and scallions. Pour over chicken.
* Bake at 350° for 45 minutes. Serve with Cajun rice.

Parkie Thomas

CHICKEN ENCHILADA CASSEROLE

Serves: 8

3 to 4 chicken breasts   1 can cream of mushroom soup
1 bottle prepared Italian salad dressing   1 can cream of chicken soup
1 (10-ounce) bag tortilla chips, broken   1 cup sour cream
1 small onion, chopped   1-1/2 cups shredded Cheddar cheese
1 (4-ounce) can diced green chilies   dash of chili powder
1 to 2 tablespoons diced jalapeño peppers

* Marinate chicken in salad dressing for 30 minutes; then grill or sauté.
* Chop chicken into bite-sized pieces. Layer chips in bottom of 13x9-inch baking dish. Layer chicken on top of chips.
* Combine all other ingredients except Cheddar cheese and chili powder. Pour mixture over chicken. Top with cheese and sprinkle with dash of chili powder.
* Bake at 350° for 40 minutes or until bubbly.

Rebecca Thompson-Adkison

Variation: Cook chicken in water seasoned with 1 onion, 2 stalks celery, salt and pepper. Cut into bite-sized pieces. Substitute 1 can cream of celery soup for mushroom soup. Omit sour cream. Add 1 (10-ounce) can tomatoes.

Linda Sanchez, Karen Peters

EASY ENCHILADAS

Serves: 4-6

3/4 pound chicken, boned, skinned,
  and cut into strips, or peeled shrimp
3 slices bacon
1-1/2 cups picante sauce
1 can black beans, undrained
1 large red pepper, chopped
2 cloves garlic, minced

1 teaspoon ground cumin
1/2 cup sliced green onions
10 (7-inch) flour tortillas
1-1/2 cups shredded Monterey Jack cheese
toppings: sour cream, avocado slices,
  shredded lettuce

* Cook bacon in skillet until crisp. Drain on paper towels.
* Cook and stir chicken (or shrimp) in drippings with the garlic until it is no longer pink.
* Stir in 1/2 cup picante sauce, beans, red pepper and cumin. Simmer until thickened, about 7 minutes, stirring occasionally. Stir in bacon and onions.
* Spoon heaping 1/4 cup of mixture down center of each tortilla. Top with 1 tablespoon cheese. Roll up and place seam side down in lightly greased 13x9-inch casserole.
* Spoon remaining cup of picante sauce over tortillas.
* Bake at 350° for 15 minutes. Top with additional cheese; return to oven and bake until melted, about 3 minutes.

Pat Waldron

TEX-MEX MEAT LOAF

Easy

Serves: 6

1-1/2 pounds ground turkey
1 (16-ounce) can red kidney beans or
  pintos, drained and rinsed
1-1/2 cups picante or taco sauce, divided
1 medium onion, chopped
1 clove garlic, minced

1/2 cup dry breadcrumbs
2 eggs
1-1/2 teaspoons ground cumin
3/4 teaspoon salt
2 tablespoons brown sugar

* Combine all ingredients except 1/2 cup of picante sauce and brown sugar.
* Mix well and press into a 9x5-inch loaf pan. Bake at 350° for 1 hour.
* Carefully pour off drippings. Combine remaining picante sauce and brown sugar; spread over meat loaf. Bake an additional 15 minutes.
* Let stand for 10 minutes before serving.

Francie López

AUTUMN CORNISH HENS

Serves: 8

8 Cornish hens (approximately 1 pound
   each)
12 cloves garlic, finely minced
4 tablespoons dried oregano
salt and pepper to taste
1 cup red wine vinegar or balsamic
   vinegar
1/2 cup olive oil

1 cup pitted prunes
1 cup dried apricots
1 cup pitted green olives
1/2 cup capers, plus a little juice
8 bay leaves
1 cup brown sugar
1 cup dry white wine
4 tablespoons chopped Italian parsley

* Clean hens under cold water and pat dry.
* Combine next 10 ingredients to make marinade. Divide hens among large zip-lock
  bags. Pour equal amounts of marinade into bags. Close bags. Refrigerate overnight.
* Remove hens from bags and arrange in shallow roasting pan. Spoon marinade over
  hens. Sprinkle with brown sugar and pour wine around them.
* Bake at 350° for 1-1/4 hours, basting frequently, until golden brown.
* Transfer hens and other ingredients to serving platter. Moisten with pan juices and
  sprinkle with parsley. Pass remaining juices in sauceboat.

Camilla Turner

CORNISH HENS WITH FRUIT

Easy - Must be prepared ahead

Serves: 4

4 Cornish game hens
1 cup chopped celery
1 cup chopped apple
1 cup chopped onion
1/2 cup raisins

1 cup chopped, peeled orange
1 cup whole seedless grapes
1 cup orange juice
1 cup Madeira wine

* Marinate fruit and vegetables in the orange juice and wine for 8 hours or overnight.
* Drain and reserve marinade. Salt and pepper hens inside and out.
* Stuff hens with approximately 1/4 cup of fruit and vegetable mixture. Tie legs
  together to hold in stuffing.
* Bake uncovered at 350° about 2 hours. While cooking, baste with reserved marinade.

Pamela Cooke

SOUTHERN-STYLE QUAIL OR DOVES

Easy   Serves: 6

12 quail   6 tablespoons flour
salt, pepper and flour for dredging   4 cups chicken broth
2 sticks butter   1 cup sherry

* Clean and wash quail. Salt, pepper and flour the birds.
* Brown the quail in a heavy skillet in butter. Remove and place birds in a baking dish.
* Blend flour with butter left in skillet. Add chicken broth, sherry, salt and pepper. Stir until smooth.
* Pour gravy over quail. Cover baking dish.
* Bake at 350° for about 1 hour. Boneless chicken breasts may be substituted for quail.

Ann Houck

ELEGANT TURKEY OR VEAL ROLLS
Great company dish

Serves: 4

4 veal or turkey cutlets   1/2 cup fine dry breadcrumbs
1 (4-1/2-ounce) can deviled ham   3/4 cup water
1 tablespoon instant minced onion   1 (11-1/2-ounce) package mushroom gravy
1 (3-ounce) package cream cheese   mix
2 tablespoons butter or margarine, melted   1/4 cup dry sherry

* Pound cutlets thin. Mix ham with onion flakes and spread over cutlets just to edge.
* Slice cream cheese into 12 narrow strips and place 3 strips on each cutlet.
* Roll up firmly and fasten with toothpick.
* Dip cutlets in melted butter and coat with breadcrumbs. Arrange in a 10x6-inch microwave-safe dish which has been sprayed with non-stick spray.
* In small glass bowl combine gravy mix, water and sherry.
* Microwave on high for 2 minutes, stirring after 1 minute; pour over cutlet rolls. Cover with plastic wrap, turning back one corner to vent.
* Microwave on high 13 to 15 minutes, rotating 1/2 turn every 5 minutes. (Meat should be tender and filling set.)
* Cutlets can be refrigerated and reheated later.

Susan Grove

ROAST TURKEY

Prepare ahead

1 turkey	1 onion, cut in half
1 tablespoon dry mustard	1 stalk celery
1 tablespoon Worcestershire sauce	1/4 bunch fresh parsley
1 tablespoon olive oil	2 strips bacon
salt and pepper	2 cups chicken stock
1 teaspoon vinegar	1 stick butter

* Combine dry mustard, Worcestershire sauce, olive oil, salt, pepper and vinegar to make a soft paste. Rub turkey well inside and out with paste a few hours before cooking (preferably the day before).
* When ready to bake, place onion, celery and parsley inside the turkey. Lay 2 strips bacon across turkey breast. Place pats of butter between the drumstick and the body.
* Soak a dish towel or cheesecloth in olive oil and place over turkey.
* Place turkey in open roaster. Add 2 cups chicken stock.
* Bake at 300° according to size of turkey. Baste once or twice during baking.

7-10 pounds - 30 minutes per pound
10-15 pounds - 20 minutes per pound
15-18 pounds - 18 minutes per pound
18-20 pounds - 15 minutes per pound
20-23 pounds - 13 minutes per pound

Nancy Dykes

BARBEQUE SAUCE FOR CHICKEN AND PORK

Yields: 1 cup

3 tablespoons ketchup	3 tablespoons brown sugar
2 tablespoons vinegar	1 teaspoon salt
1 tablespoon lemon juice	1 teaspoon mustard
2 tablespoons Worcestershire sauce	1 teaspoon paprika
4 tablespoons water	1/2 teaspoon hot sauce
2 tablespoons butter	1 teaspoon chili powder

* Mix all ingredients in pan over low heat. Use for basting while baking or grilling meat.

Ann Houck

HANK'S CHICKEN MARINADE

Great marinade for chicken to be grilled, stir-fried or baked

Easy   Yields: 3/4 cup

1/2 cup soy sauce   *1/2 teaspoon garlic powder*
4 tablespoons honey   *dash of pepper*
2 tablespoons white vinegar   *hot pepper sauce to taste*
1/2 teaspoon onion powder

* Mix all ingredients.
* Let stand for at least 30 minutes before using to give the flavors time to blend.

Mary Jane Bennett

WHITE TARRAGON SAUCE FOR CHICKEN

Easy   Yields: 1-1/3 cups

1 cup light mayonnaise   *4 tablespoons lemon juice*
3 tablespoons tarragon vinegar   *2 tablespoons sugar*
1 tablespoon coarsely ground pepper

* Mix all ingredients.
* Divide sauce. Use half for basting. Use remaining sauce for dipping when chicken is
  served.

Kim Martin

MEATS

BAR-B-Q BEEF
Tender, juicy and flavorful

Easy - Prepare ahead   Serves: 4-6

1 (1-ounce) package dry onion   1 beef brisket
    soup mix   1 pint prepared coleslaw, if desired, as
1 (12-ounce) can of beer   topping
1 (12-ounce) bottle chili sauce

* Mix onion soup mix, beer and chili sauce.
* Place brisket in casserole. Add sauce. Cover and bake at 325° for 2-1/2 to 3 hours.
* Remove brisket from sauce and slice.
* Chill sauce and remove fat. Return sliced brisket to sauce and refrigerate overnight.
* Reheat and serve on crusty roll or bun.
* Top with spoonful of sauce and prepared coleslaw, if desired.

Janifer Ruhl

BBQ CHUCK ROAST
An old family recipe

Serves: 6-8

1 (4 to 5) pound chuck roast, 2 inches thick   2 tablespoons brown sugar
2 teaspoons salt   1/2 teaspoon dry mustard
1/4 teaspoon pepper   1/4 cup lemon juice
1/2 cup water   1/4 cup vinegar
1 (8-ounce) can tomato sauce   1/4 cup ketchup
2 to 3 medium onions, sliced   1 tablespoon Worcestershire sauce
2 cloves garlic, chopped

* Salt and pepper roast and brown in Dutch oven on all sides in small amount of oil.
* Add water, tomato sauce, onion and garlic to meat.
* Cover; cook at 325° for 1-1/2 hours.
* Mix remaining ingredients and pour over roast. Cook an additional 1-1/2 hours.
* Juices can be thickened with cornstarch or flour to make a BBQ gravy to serve with
  meat. (Dissolve 2 tablespoons flour or cornstarch in 3/4 cup water and add to juices;
  cook, stirring, until juices thicken to desired consistency.)

Meg Clarke

COMPANY POT ROAST

Easy   Serves: 10

1 (4-pound) eye of round   *2 beef bouillon cubes*
2 tablespoons vegetable oil   *1/4 teaspoon pepper*
1/4 pound mushrooms, sliced   *2 bay leaves*
2 medium onions, sliced   *1/3 cup tomato paste*
1 large carrot, halved   *1 cup water*
1 stalk celery, halved   *2 tablespoons flour*
2 cloves garlic, minced   *3 tablespoons water*
1-1/4 teaspoons salt   *1 pound wide egg noodles*

* Brown roast in oil in Dutch oven. Remove meat; drain fat.
* Combine next eleven ingredients in Dutch oven; heat to boiling. Add roast. Cover and simmer 4 hours. Remove roast to platter.
* Blend flour with 3 tablespoons water. Stir flour mixture into tomato paste mixture. Stir until mixture boils for 1 minute.
* Cook egg noodles according to package directions. Drain and toss with a small amount of gravy. Serve roast with noodles and gravy.

Sandy Hibberd

GRANDMA DORIE'S BRISKET

Serves: 4-6

1 (2-1/2 to 3-pound) brisket, trimmed   *oil*
2 to 3 large onions, chopped   *seasoned salt*
1 (8-ounce) can tomato-mushroom sauce   *garlic powder*
4 cloves fresh garlic, finely chopped   *pepper*

* Brown onions slowly in a small amount of oil.
* Put onions in bottom of roasting pan. Cover with sauce and chopped garlic.
* Season meat with seasoned salt, garlic powder and pepper.
* Place meat on top of sauce (do not baste with sauce until after the first 1/2 hour).
* Cover pan with foil. Put on the lower rack of oven.
* Bake at 350° to 375°, basting with sauce every 1/2 hour until done. Test with two-prong fork. Meat is done if the fork goes in and out easily.
* May add peeled carrots and small red potatoes to the pan in the last hour.

Ann Able

HELEN'S MARINATED FLANK STEAK
A five-star recipe

Easy   Serves: 4

1 medium onion, chopped   *1 tablespoon Italian seasoning*
1/4 cup salad oil   *salt and pepper to taste*
1/2 cup soy sauce   *1-1/2 pounds flank steak*
1 drop hot pepper sauce

* Mix first 6 ingredients to make marinade.
* Marinate steak at least 6 hours.
* Grill to desired doneness.

Susan Hill

PEPPER STEAK

Serves: 4

1/4 cup butter or margarine   *1 tablespoon cornstarch*
1-1/2 pounds round or sirloin steak,   *1 teaspoon sugar*
  cut in strips   *2 tablespoons water*
1/8 teaspoon garlic powder   *2 tablespoons soy sauce*
1/3 cup chopped onion   *1/2 teaspoon salt*
1-1/2 whole green peppers, cut in strips   *3 cups cooked and drained wide noodles*
1 (16-ounce) can tomatoes   *1 cup shredded Cheddar cheese*
1 beef bouillon cube

* Melt butter in skillet. Add beef; sprinkle with garlic. Sauté, stirring, until brown.
* Remove meat from skillet. Add onion and pepper; sauté 2 minutes.
* Return meat to skillet. Add tomatoes and bouillon.
* Simmer 20 minutes if using round steak (5 minutes for sirloin).
* Blend cornstarch, sugar, water, soy sauce and salt. Add to meat. Cook until sauce is
  thickened, stirring constantly. Reduce heat; simmer 10 minutes.
* Toss cooked noodles with cheese. Spoon steak and sauce over noodles.

Marilyn Nasekos

BESSIE'S STIR-FRY TRUE DELIGHT

Easy   Serves: 6-8

1 pound sirloin, cut in thin strips   *1/4 cup soy sauce*
1 bunch broccoli, cut in small pieces   *2 tablespoons Worcestershire sauce*
1 medium onion, cut in rings   *dash of garlic salt*
1 (8-ounce) package mushrooms, sliced   *cooked rice*
1/2 cup oil

* Combine oil, soy sauce, Worcestershire sauce and salt. Pour over steak and set aside for 30 minutes or more.
* Drain meat and drop into hot wok. Cook until meat turns brown.
* Remove from wok (with juice) and set aside.
* Heat a small amount of oil in wok and stir-fry vegetables approximately 3 minutes.
* Return meat and juice to pan and cook 5 minutes. Serve over cooked rice.

Kay Simpson

FILLET STEAK AND SAVORY BUTTER

Easy   Serves: 4-6

1-1/2 pounds fillet steak   *salt*
small amount of oil for searing steak   *freshly ground pepper*
Savory Butter:
1/2 cup soft butter   *1 tablespoon fresh oregano or 1 large pinch*
1/2 teaspoon Dijon mustard   * dried oregano*
2 cloves garlic, crushed   *1/2 teaspoon Worcestershire sauce*
1 tablespoon chopped chives

* Prepare butter by creaming all ingredients together. Roll into a sausage shape, wrap in wax paper and chill.
* Cut fillet into 3/4-inch slices. Sear steaks over high heat in a heavy frying pan just smeared with oil for about 15 seconds per side. Be careful not to pierce steaks when turning. Remove to ovenproof serving platter and cover loosely.
* Fifteen minutes before serving, season steaks lightly with salt and pepper and top each slice with a round of Savory Butter.
* Bake at 425° for about 10 minutes. Remove and keep warm, allowing about 5 minutes for juices to settle. Serve with the buttery juices spooned over meat.

Jean Bestal

STEAK MOUTARDE FLAMBÉ

Easy   Serves: 4

1 tablespoon butter   *4 teaspoons Dijon mustard*
4 fillets of beef, 1-1/2-inches thick *4 teaspoons herb-flavored or mild brown*
salt   *mustard*
coarsely ground pepper   *1/4 teaspoon paprika*
1/4 teaspoon rosemary   *2 tablespoons sour cream*
1/2 teaspoon crumbled sage leaves   *1/2 cup cream*
1/4 cup cognac

* In skillet, heat butter and sauté beef fillets over high heat for 4 to 5 minutes. Turn and sprinkle with salt, pepper, rosemary and crumbled sage leaves. Cook 4 to 5 minutes more for rare, or to desired doneness. Pour off excess fat from skillet.
* Warm cognac in microwave. Sprinkle over fillets.
* Ignite cognac and transfer fillets to a warmed platter when flame burns out. Keep warm.
* Add mustards and paprika to skillet. Combine sour cream and cream. Stir mixture into the mustards in skillet. Cook for 1 minute. Pour over fillets and serve immediately.

Nancy Austin

BEEF STROGANOFF

Serves: 4-6

2 pounds beef kabobs   *1 (10-ounce) can cream of chicken soup*
4 tablespoons butter or margarine   *1 (10-ounce) can cream of mushroom soup*
2 large onions, minced   *4 tablespoons ketchup*
2 to 3 cups water   *2 tablespoons dried parsley flakes*
salt and pepper to taste   *1 teaspoon garlic salt*
1 (8-ounce) can sliced mushrooms,   *1 (8-ounce) carton sour cream*
* drained*

* Brown meat with onion in butter. Cover with water. Simmer until tender. Add salt and pepper. Add other ingredients and simmer for 15 minutes.
* Just before serving, stir in sour cream and heat. Do not boil.
* Serve over noodles or rice.

Roberta McKenzie

PRIME RIB
A rare treat!

Easy   Serves: 6-8

1 (4 to 6 pound) standing rib roast,   lemon-pepper seasoning
   nicely trimmed
Horseradish Sauce:
1 (3-ounce) package lemon gelatin   dash of pepper
3/4 teaspoon salt   1 cup sour cream
1 teaspoon (or more) grated onion   1/2 to 1 cup slightly drained horseradish
1 tablespoon vinegar

* Remove roast from refrigerator about 1 hour before baking.
* Wipe surfaces with damp paper towel.
* Sprinkle with lemon pepper, pressing into top surface.
* Place on rack in roasting pan.
* Preheat oven to 500° to 550°.
* Place roast in oven and immediately reduce temperature to 350°.
* Roast for 20 minutes per pound for rare.
* Use a meat thermometer to check for doneness.
* While roast is cooking, prepare Horseradish Sauce. Dissolve salt and gelatin in 1 cup boiling water. Add vinegar and pepper. Chill until slightly thickened.
* Add sour cream, horseradish and onion. Chill to set.
* Remove roast from oven and allow to stand 10 minutes.
* Slice horizontally from bone and cut into 1/2 to 3/4-inch slices.
* Serve with Horseradish Sauce.

Pattie Bethune

BEEF TENDERLOIN WITH MADEIRA SAUCE

Serves: 10-12

1 whole beef tenderloin, well trimmed (about 7 pounds)
Madeira Sauce:

2 beef bouillon cubes	*6 tablespoons butter, divided*
1-1/2 cups hot water	*4 tablespoons flour*
1-1/2 pounds mushrooms, thinly sliced	*1/2 cup Madeira wine*
1 small onion, thinly sliced (optional)	*salt and pepper to taste*

* Cook tenderloin in 500° oven for 5 minutes per pound for rare (6 minutes per pound for medium rare). Turn off oven; let stand at least 1 hour.
* Dissolve bouillon cubes in hot water.
* Sauté mushrooms and onion in 2 tablespoons butter. Reserve. Melt remaining butter in skillet. Add 4 tablespoons flour. Stir until mixed.
* Slowly add dissolved bouillon. Stir until sauce is thickened.
* Add Madeira wine, onion and mushrooms.
* Season to taste with salt and pepper. Serve over sliced tenderloin.

Frances Fennebresque

BEEF TENDERLOIN WITH TARRAGON BUTTER

1 beef tenderloin (allow 6 to 8 ounces per person), trimmed and tied
Marinade:

1/2 cup soy sauce	*1/4 cup apple cider vinegar*
3/4 cup Burgundy or Chianti wine	*4 cloves garlic, minced or mashed*
1/2 teaspoon ground ginger	*2 tablespoons chopped fresh parsley*

Tarragon Butter:

2 medium shallots	*1/2 teaspoon dried tarragon, crumbled*
2 tablespoons chopped fresh parsley	*1/2 teaspoon freshly ground pepper*
4 teaspoons tarragon vinegar	*1/2 cup chilled butter, cut into small pieces*

* Combine marinade ingredients, mixing well. Marinate tenderloin overnight.
* To prepare Tarragon Butter, combine shallots, parsley, vinegar, tarragon and pepper in food processor; mince by pulsing several times. Add butter and blend well.
* Preheat oven to 325°. Place tenderloin in roasting pan. Bake until meat thermometer registers rare to medium-rare, according to your preference.
* Slice and spread generously with Tarragon Butter. Serve immediately.

Virginia Golding

CIDER STEW
Very nice flavor

Easy   Serves: 6-8

2 pounds stew beef, cut in 1-inch   2 cups apple cider or apple juice
  cubes   1/2 cup water
3 tablespoons flour   1-2 tablespoons vinegar
2 teaspoons salt   3 medium potatoes, peeled and quartered
1/4 teaspoon pepper   4 medium carrots, quartered
1/4 teaspoon crushed dried thyme   2 medium onions, diced
3 tablespoons cooking oil   1 stalk celery, sliced

* Combine flour, salt, pepper and thyme. Coat meat with flour mixture.
* In a Dutch oven, brown meat in hot cooking oil. Skim off fat.
* Stir in apple cider, water and vinegar.
* Bring to a boil. Reduce heat; cover and simmer about 1-1/4 hours or until meat is nearly tender.
* Stir in potatoes, carrots, onions and celery.
* Cover; simmer 30 minutes or more until meat and vegetables are tender.

Elaine Hoffmann

OVEN-BAKED BEEF STEW
A great meal served with fresh hot bread

Easy   Serves: 8

2 pounds stew beef cut in 1/2-inch cubes   1 (16-ounce) can stewed tomatoes
2 stalks celery, cut in chunks   1 can beef bouillon soup
6 carrots, cut in chunks   2 teaspoons salt
4 potatoes, cut in chunks   1 tablespoon sugar
2 small onions, cut in chunks   4 tablespoons cornstarch

* Mix all ingredients in large roasting pan. Cover tightly with foil.
* Bake at 325° for 3 hours or at 250° for 4 hours. Do not uncover.

Lynne Greenoe
Mae Mae Cook

BEEF AND BEAN CASSEROLE
Serve with hot bread.

Easy

Serves: 12 or more

1-1/2 pounds lean ground beef
1/2 cup chopped onion
2 (16-ounce) cans tomato sauce
1 (15-ounce) can kidney beans, drained
1 (15-ounce) can pork and beans

1 (15-ounce) can lima beans, drained
1/2 cup brown sugar
2 tablespoons vinegar
1 teaspoon pepper

* Brown meat and onions. Drain.
* Add all other ingredients to meat and onions. Stir well. Pour into a large casserole.
* Bake uncovered at 350° for 1-1/2 hours.

Noreen Moody

BEEF PIE
Add a salad and bread for a great meal.

Easy

Serves: 8

1 (10-ounce) package cut green beans
1 tablespoon butter or margarine
1 medium onion, thinly sliced
1/4 cup chopped bell pepper
1 pound ground chuck or 1 pound
   ground turkey
3-1/2 teaspoons salt

1 teaspoon pepper
8 ounces evaporated milk (may use skim
   evaporated milk)
4 ounces canned mushrooms, drained
1 small can tomato paste
1 (10-inch) unbaked pie crust
cheese slices or shredded cheese

* Cook or steam green beans until crisp tender. Set aside.
* Melt butter; brown onions and pepper.
* Add meat and brown. Drain.
* Add remaining ingredients and cook until bubbly. Add green beans.
* Pour into pie crust. Top with cheese.
* Bake at 350° for 30 minutes.

Irene Kelly

BUFF'S MEAT, NOODLE AND TOMATO CASSEROLE
A great casserole for busy nights!

Easy   Serves: 6

1-1/2 pounds lean ground beef
1 tablespoon vegetable oil
1 cup chopped onions
1 cup chopped celery, including leaves
1-1/2 large carrots, grated
1 (28-ounce) can Italian tomatoes
1 tablespoon salt

3/4 teaspoon oregano
1/2 teaspoon pepper
1/2 teaspoon garlic powder
1 (12-ounce) package elbow macaroni
1 (10-ounce) package frozen chopped
   spinach. slightly thawed
Parmesan cheese, grated

* In large Dutch oven, brown meat in oil.
* Add onion, celery and carrots to browned meat and cook about 5 minutes.
* Stir in tomatoes and spices. Bring to a boil. Lower heat. Cover and simmer for 1 hour.
* Cook noodles according to package directions until al dente; drain.
* Add pasta and spinach to meat sauce. Mix thoroughly.
* Pour mixture into 13x9-inch casserole. Cover with Parmesan cheese.
* Bake at 350° for 30 minutes.

Bobbie Cloud

BARBEQUE MEATBALLS
Freezes nicely! Tastes even better the next day!

Serves: 4-6

1 pound ground beef
1 cup soft breadcrumbs
1/2 cup milk
1 teaspoon salt
pepper to taste
1/2 cup ketchup

1/2 cup water
1/4 to 1/2 cup vinegar
1-1/2 tablespoons Worcestershire sauce
1/4 cup chopped green pepper
1/2 cup chopped onions
1 tablespoon sugar

* Mix beef, breadcrumbs, milk, salt and pepper. Shape into meatballs, usually about 8.
* Place meatballs in a 13x9-inch baking dish.
* Mix remaining ingredients and pour over meatballs.
* Bake at 375° for 30 minutes, then turn meatballs over.
* Spoon sauce over meatballs and continue baking until done (15 to 30 minutes more).

Myra Chandler

MEXICAN BEEF CASSEROLE
Very spicy and filling

Easy   Serves: 8-10

1 pound ground chuck or 1 pound   *2 tablespoons chili powder (or less)*
   ground turkey   *4 ounces shredded Cheddar cheese*
1 medium onion, chopped   *1 (16-ounce) can pinto beans, undrained*
2 cloves garlic, minced   *1 (6-ounce) package Mexican cornbread*
salt and pepper to taste   *mix*
2 (8-ounce) cans tomato sauce

* Brown meat with onion, garlic, salt and pepper; drain. Add tomato sauce and chili powder; stir. Pour into 13x9-inch greased casserole. Top with cheese.
* Spoon beans over cheese and spread evenly. May refrigerate overnight at this point.
* Prepare cornbread mix as directed on package. Spread cornbread evenly on top of cheese. Bake at 400° in preheated oven for 25 minutes or until cornbread is crusty.

Janet Povall

TACO PIE
Teenagers love this!

Easy   Serves: 6-8

1 (16-ounce) can refried beans   *3/4 cup water*
1 (8-ounce) jar taco sauce, divided   *1 baked (9-inch) deep-dish pastry shell*
1 pound ground beef or 1 pound   *2 cups shredded sharp Cheddar cheese,*
   ground turkey   *divided*
1 medium onion, chopped   *1 cup crushed corn chips*
1 package taco seasoning mix

* Combine refried beans and 1/3 cup taco sauce. Set aside.
* Brown ground meat with onion. Drain. Add taco seasoning mix and water. Stir well and bring to a boil. Reduce heat and simmer 20 minutes, stirring occasionally.
* Spoon half of bean mixture into baked pastry shell. Top with half the meat mixture, half the cheese and all the corn chips. Repeat layers with remaining bean and meat mixtures. Top with remaining cheese.
* Bake at 400° for 20 to 25 minutes. Garnish as desired.

Gail Dings

SOUTH-OF-THE-BORDER LASAGNA

2 pounds ground meat
1 onion, chopped
1 clove garlic, minced
2 tablespoons chili powder
3 cups tomato sauce
1 teaspoon sugar
vegetable oil

1/2 cup sliced black olives
1 (4-ounce) can chopped green chilies
12 corn tortillas
2 cups cottage cheese
1 egg, beaten
8 ounces Monterey Jack cheese, grated
1 cup grated Cheddar cheese

* Brown meat. Drain. Add onions and garlic and cook until soft.
* Sprinkle chili powder over meat and mix well.
* Add tomato sauce, sugar, salt, olives and green chilies. Simmer for 15 minutes.
* While mixture simmers, cook soft tortillas in hot oil.
* Beat together cottage cheese and eggs. Set aside.
* In a 13x9-inch casserole, layer 1/3 meat mixture, 1/2 Monterey Jack cheese, 1/2 cottage cheese and 1/2 tortillas. Repeat the process ending with sauce.
* Cover with grated Cheddar cheese. Bake at 350° for 30 to 40 minutes.

B. J. Dengler

VITELLO AL LIMONE

Serves: 4

1-1/2 cups flour
1 tablespoon salt-free lemon-herb
  seasoning
2 pounds lean veal, preferably from
  leg, cut into 8 thin slices
1/2 cup olive oil

2 teaspoons unsalted butter or margarine
1/4 cup dry white wine
1/2 cup chicken broth
1 teaspoon lemon juice
2 teaspoons chopped parsley
lemon slices (optional)

* Pound veal slices lightly with a mallet.
* On wax paper, combine flour and lemon-herb seasoning. Coat veal with the mixture.
* Heat oil in heavy skillet over medium-high heat. Sauté veal in oil until lightly browned on both sides; set aside. Discard remaining oil; wipe skillet clean.
* Add butter, wine, broth and lemon juice to skillet. Bring to a boil.
* Add veal. Reduce heat; simmer 10 minutes or until sauce is thickened and veal is tender. Serve with a garnish of parsley and lemon slices.
* Boneless chicken breast may be substituted for veal.

Judy Kennedy

VEAL MOZZARELLA

Easy

Serves: 4

1 egg, slightly beaten
2 tablespoons milk
1 teaspoon salt
1 (1-pound) veal cutlet, 1/2-inch thick
  (or 1/2 pound veal scallopini)
1/2 cup dry seasoned breadcrumbs
1/4 cup olive oil
1 small onion, chopped
1/4 cup chopped green pepper

1 (16-ounce) can tomato sauce
1/2 cup white cooking wine
1/2 cup water
1 teaspoon garlic salt
1/8 teaspoon pepper
1/8 teaspoon marjoram
1/8 teaspoon oregano
4 ounces sliced mozzarella cheese
cooked noodles

* Combine egg, milk and salt. Dip meat into mixture; roll in crumbs.
* Brown meat in oil in a large skillet. Remove to 12x8-inch baking dish.
* Sauté onion and green pepper in skillet. Stir in tomato sauce, wine, water and remaining spices and herbs. Simmer 10 minutes.
* Pour sauce over cutlets.
* Bake at 350° for 30 minutes.
* Place cheese over meat; return to oven until cheese melts (2 to 3 minutes).
* Serve with hot noodles.

Laurie Guy

MARINATED PORK TENDERLOIN

Easy

Serves: 6-8

6 tablespoons oil
2 tablespoons soy sauce
1 tablespoon Worcestershire sauce
1-1/2 teaspoons dry mustard
1/2 teaspoon salt
1/2 teaspoon pepper

2 tablespoons wine vinegar
1/2 teaspoon parsley
1/4 teaspoon garlic powder
1 tablespoon lemon juice
1 (3 to 4 pound) pork tenderloin

* Mix all ingredients and marinate pork overnight.
* Grill for 20 minutes, basting with marinade.
* Finish cooking in microwave oven for 10 minutes at medium power, if necessary.

Linda Sanchez

OLD FAITHFUL

Serves: 4

4 thick pork chops
2 tablespoons butter or margarine
6 tablespoons rice, uncooked
1 large onion, thinly sliced
2 ripe tomatoes, thinly sliced
1/2 green pepper, thinly sliced

salt and pepper to taste
1 can consommé or 1 cup water and 1 beef
   bouillon cube
1 pinch marjoram
1 pinch thyme

* Brown pork chops in butter in skillet.
* While chops brown put rice in bottom of greased 9x9-inch casserole. Place chops on rice.
* Top each chop with slices of onion, tomato and green pepper.
* Add salt and pepper to taste. Pour consommé over top.
* Sprinkle with marjoram and thyme.
* Cover. Bake at 350° for 1 hour, undisturbed.

Brandon Chapman

ORANGE PORK CHOPS
An easy favorite

Serves: 6

6 pork chops, 1/2-inch thick
1/2 cup orange juice
1 teaspoon salt

1/4 teaspoon pepper
1/2 teaspoon dry mustard
1/4 cup brown sugar

* Place pork chops in a greased 13x9-inch baking dish.
* Mix other ingredients well and pour over top.
* Bake at 350° until tender, about 1 hour.
* Baste frequently during cooking.

Ellen Knott

OVEN B-B-Q
Great taste and aroma

Must be done ahead   Serves: 8-10

4 to 5 pound Boston Butt or fresh ham   1/4 teaspoon black pepper
  (can also be made with beef)   1 garlic clove, crushed
1 large onion, chopped   1 cup vinegar
3 tablespoons brown sugar   1-1/2 cups water
3 tablespoons powdered mustard   1/2 cup ketchup
1/2 teaspoon red pepper flakes   1/2 cup Worcestershire sauce

* Place meat in roasting pan.
* Mix remaining ingredients and pour over meat. Cover tightly.
* Bake at 325° for 5 to 6 hours until meat is so tender it falls from bones.
* Cool and refrigerate. When cold, remove fat from top. Chop meat and reheat in sauce.
* Can double sauce recipe to have extra at serving time.
* Freezes well.

Donna Penzell

HOPPIN' JOHN SQUARES
A distinctive Southwestern flavor

Serves: 6

1/2 cup chopped green pepper   1-1/4 cups milk
2 tablespoons finely chopped onion   1 cup shredded Cheddar cheese, divided
2 tablespoons butter or margarine   1 (15-ounce) can black-eyed peas, drained
2 tablespoons flour   1 cup cooked brown rice
3/4 teaspoon chili powder   3/4 cup diced cooked ham
1/4 teaspoon ground cumin   2 eggs, beaten

* Cook pepper and onion in butter until tender.
* Stir in next 3 ingredients; add milk. Cook and stir until bubbly. Remove from heat.
* Stir in 3/4 cup of cheese and remaining ingredients.
* Turn into a well-greased 8x8-inch baking dish.
* Bake in 350° oven for 30 minutes or until set.
* Top with remaining cheese. Let stand for 5 minutes. Cut into squares to serve.

Janet Anthony

GOUGÈRE WITH MUSHROOMS AND HAM
For a special lunch or brunch

Serves: 5-6

Pâté à Choux:

1 cup sifted flour	*1/2 cup butter or margarine*
salt and pepper to taste	*4 eggs*
1 cup water	*1/2 cup diced sharp Cheddar cheese*

Filling:

4 tablespoons butter or margarine	*1 teaspoon instant chicken bouillon*
1 cup chopped onions	*1 cup hot water*
1/2 pound sliced mushrooms	*2 large tomatoes, cut in thin strips (may be*
1-1/2 tablespoons flour	*peeled and seeded)*
1 teaspoon salt	*1-1/2 cups ham, cut in thin strips*
1/4 teaspoon pepper	*2 tablespoons shredded Cheddar cheese*

* To prepare Pâté à Choux, sift flour with salt and pepper onto a sheet of wax paper.
* In a large saucepan heat water and butter. When butter melts, turn up heat and bring to a boil.
* Add flour mixture all at once. Stir vigorously until mixture forms a ball in center of the pan (about 1 minute).
* Turn off heat and allow mixture to cool for 5 minutes.
* Add eggs, one at a time, beating well with wooden spoon after each addition (this beating is important as the gougère will not puff otherwise).
* Stir in diced cheese.
* To prepare filling, melt the butter in a large skillet.
* Sauté the onion until soft but not browned.
* Add mushrooms. Continue cooking for 2 minutes.
* Sprinkle with flour, salt and pepper. Mix and cook an additional 2 minutes.
* Add instant chicken broth and water. Mix well.
* Bring to boil, stirring constantly. Simmer 4 minutes.
* Remove sauce from heat. Add ham and tomatoes. Stir well.
* Butter a round 10 or 11-inch ovenproof baking dish or pie pan.
* Spoon Pâté à Choux in a ring around the edge of pan, leaving the center open.
* Pour filling into center.
* Sprinkle top with cheese.
* Bake at 400° for 40 minutes, or until gougère is puffed and brown and filling is bubbly.
* Serve at once, cut into wedges as for a pie.

Mary Lou Stafford

BEVERLY DRIVE CASSEROLE

Easy   Serves: 6

6 medium potatoes, washed and   1 (8-ounce) carton sour cream
  unpeeled   1 teaspoon dried parsley flakes
1 (8-ounce) jar pasteurized processed 1 pound package little smoked sausages,
  cheese spread, at room temperature   sliced

* Slice potatoes into boiling water. Cook until tender. Drain.
* Combine remaining ingredients. Place 1/2 potatoes in buttered casserole. Pour 1/2 sausage mixture over potatoes. Repeat layers. Bake at 350° for 30 minutes.

Dottie Hollowell

BOURBON-WHITE WINE MARINADE

Easy - Must be done ahead   Yields: 1-3/4 cups

1/2 cup white wine   1/4 cup Worcestershire sauce
1/2 cup bourbon   2 tablespoons brown sugar
1/4 cup olive oil   2 chopped shallots or spring onions
1 teaspoon Dijon mustard

* Stir all ingredients together. Pour over skinless chicken breasts or pork chops.
* Marinate covered at least 2 hours or overnight in refrigerator. Grill.

Leslie Gebert

EASTERN NORTH CAROLINA-STYLE BARBEQUE SAUCE

Yields: 1 pint

1 pint vinegar   2 teaspoons cayenne pepper
2 tablespoons brown sugar   2 teaspoons salt

* Combine all ingredients in saucepan. Cook until sugar dissolves. Cool.
* Use for basting pork or chicken. This is thin sauce that adds flavor but does not burn.
* Sauce keeps well in tightly closed bottle. No need to refrigerate.

Hilda Rutherford

MILD MARINADE FOR BEEF

Easy   Yields: 2-1/2 cups

12 ounces pineapple juice   *1 teaspoon garlic powder*
1/2 cup soy sauce   *1/4 cup sugar*
2-1/2 tablespoons red wine vinegar   *3 ounces sherry*
1/2 teaspoon Accent

* Combine ingredients. Place meat in a shallow dish. Pour marinade over meat.
* Marinate for 3 to 8 hours, turning meat every hour. Can remain in marinade overnight.

Debbie Whelchel

NO-VINEGAR MARINADE FOR LONDON BROIL/BEEF RIBS

Easy   Yields: 1/2 cup

1/4 cup salad oil   *1 teaspoon garlic powder or 1 clove garlic,*
1/4 cup light soy sauce   * minced or mashed*
1 to 2 tablespoons lemon juice   *salt and pepper to taste*
1 teaspoon paprika

* Combine all ingredients. Marinate meat overnight.
* Grill or broil meat according to preference. Do not reuse marinade.

Lee Russo, Libby Cathcart

SESAME MARINADE

Easy   Yields: 2-3/4 cups

1 cup red wine   *6 cloves garlic*
3/4 cup red wine vinegar   *3 tablespoons grated fresh ginger*
1/4 cup sesame oil   *3 teaspoons dried thyme*
1/2 cup olive oil

* Mix all ingredients in a jar and shake. Pour over steak (flank steak is great).
* Marinate overnight. Grill steak.

Irene Kelly

BORDELAISE SAUCE

Easy   Yields: 1-3/4 cups

1/3 stick butter
2 heaping tablespoons flour
1 teaspoon beef stock base
1 cup hot water

1 heaping tablespoon chives
1/3 cup Burgundy
1 (4-ounce) can sliced mushrooms, drained
*   or 1/2 cup sliced fresh mushrooms*

* Brown butter and flour. Add chives and stir.
* Dissolve beef base in water. Add to butter mixture. Stir over low heat until thickened.
* Add Burgundy and mushrooms. Serve immediately.

Betty Mullen

MARVELOUS LAMB MARINADE AND SAUCE

Easy   Yields: 3/4 cup

2 large cloves garlic
1/2 teaspoon salt
2 tablespoons Dijon mustard
1 tablespoon soy sauce

2 tablespoons lemon juice
2 tablespoons (or more) fresh rosemary,
*   chopped*
1/4 cup olive oil

* Press garlic through garlic press or mash garlic into a paste.
* Add salt, mustard, soy sauce, lemon juice and rosemary.
* Whisk in oil to form an emulsion (or shake all ingredients in a jar).
* Can be used as an overnight marinade and as a sauce over lamb chops or lamb roast.

Pattie Bethune

MOM'S MUSTARD SAUCE

3 tablespoons dry mustard
1/2 cup sugar

1 egg
1/3 cup white vinegar

* Put all ingredients in the top of a double boiler over boiling water.
* Beat with mixer until thick (about 10 minutes). Store in jar in refrigerator. Keeps well.

Donna Penzell

SEAFOOD

PAELLA VALENCIA

A simplified version of the traditional Spanish dish

Serves: 6

3 (14-1/2-ounce) cans clear chicken
  broth
1/3 cup olive oil
1 whole chicken breast, skinned,
  boned and cut into 1-inch pieces
2 boneless pork chops, cut into
  1-inch pieces
1 small onion, chopped

1 small red bell pepper, sliced
salt and pepper to taste
1 medium tomato, peeled and chopped
2 cloves garlic, minced
1 cup frozen peas
1 (16-ounce) package saffron rice mix
1 pound raw shrimp, peeled and deveined

* Bring chicken broth to boil. Lower heat and simmer.
* In a large skillet, heat olive oil until very hot; watch carefully.
* Add chicken, pork, onions and red pepper. Salt and pepper mixture lightly and brown for 5 minutes, stirring briskly.
* Lower heat to medium. Stir in tomato, garlic and peas.
* Add uncooked rice. Continue stirring until rice has browned slightly. Add warm broth. Stir to mix.
* Cook on medium-high for 5 minutes, stirring constantly. Lower heat to medium. Continue cooking and stirring 20 minutes more. During the last 4 to 5 minutes, stir in shrimp and cook until heated thoroughly.

The Latin Spanish Department

CHICKEN AND SEAFOOD JAMBALAYA CASSEROLE
Wonderful party dish

Serves: 8

3 onions, chopped
1 cup sliced green onions
4 tablespoons butter
1 (14-ounce) can tomatoes, undrained
1 (6-ounce) can tomato paste
1/4 cup water
4 cloves garlic, chopped
2 stalks celery, chopped
1/2 bell pepper, chopped

2 tablespoons parsley, chopped
1/4 teaspoon thyme
1 bay leaf
1/4 teaspoon ground cloves
2 pounds raw shrimp, peeled and deveined
1 pound hot sausage, cooked and drained
3-1/2 cups cooked rice
1-1/2 cups chicken, cooked and diced
salt, pepper and cayenne pepper

* Sauté onions in butter for 5 minutes until transparent.
* Add tomatoes, tomato paste and water. Cook for 5 minutes, stirring constantly.
* Add garlic, celery, bell pepper, parsley, thyme, bay leaf and cloves. Stir well.
* Add shrimp and sausage. Cook 30 minutes, stirring often.
* Remove bay leaf. Stir in rice and season to taste with salt, pepper and cayenne pepper.
* Add chicken. Stir and turn into buttered 13x9-inch casserole.
* Bake at 325° until hot and bubbly, about 30 minutes.

Barbara Henson

EASY OVEN JAMBALAYA

Serves: 6-8

2-1/4 cups water
1-1/2 cups uncooked white rice
1 (10-ounce) can cream of celery soup
1 (10-ounce) can cream of shrimp soup
1 (10-ounce) can tomatoes and green
    chilies, undrained and chopped

1/2 cup chopped celery
1/2 cup chopped bell pepper
1/2 cup chopped onion
1 pound smoked sausage, or andouille
    sausage, sliced 1/2-inch thick
1 pound raw shrimp, peeled and deveined

* Lightly grease a shallow 3-quart baking dish.
* Combine all ingredients except shrimp in baking dish.
* Cover and bake at 350° for 45 minutes, stirring several times to mix rice as it cooks.
* Stir in shrimp. Cover and bake another 15 to 20 minutes or until rice is done.

Rizzie Baldwin

SHRIMP AND SAUSAGE JAMBALAYA

Serves: 12

1 pound smoked sausage, thinly sliced
3 tablespoons olive oil
2/3 cup chopped green pepper
2 cloves garlic, minced
3/4 cup chopped fresh parsley
1 cup chopped celery
2 (16-ounce) cans tomatoes, undrained
   and chopped
2 cups chicken broth
1 cup chopped green onions
1-1/2 teaspoons thyme

2 bay leaves
2 teaspoons oregano
1 teaspoon to 1 tablespoon Creole
   seasoning (depending on spiciness
   desired)
1/2 teaspoon salt
1/4 teaspoon cayenne pepper
1/4 teaspoon black pepper
2 cups uncooked rice
3 pounds raw medium shrimp, peeled and
   deveined

* Sauté sausage in 4-quart heavy pot. Remove with slotted spoon.
* Add oil to drippings and sauté green pepper, garlic, parsley and celery for 5 minutes.
* Add tomatoes with liquid, broth and onions to pot; stir in spices.
* Add rice after washing and rinsing 3 times.
* Add sausage and cook for 30 minutes covered over low heat, stirring occasionally.
* After most liquid has been absorbed by rice, add shrimp and cook until shrimp turns pink. Transfer mixture to a 13x9-inch or larger casserole.
* Bake at 350° for 20 to 25 minutes.

Judi Tingler

SEAFOOD CASSEROLE SUPREME

Serves: 12

1 box chicken-flavored rice-vermicelli
1 cup sour cream
1 cup mayonnaise
1-1/2 pounds crabmeat

1-1/2 pounds shrimp, cooked, peeled and
   deveined
1-1/2 pounds sautéed scallops
1 cup grated Cheddar cheese

* Cook rice-vermicelli mix according to directions on box.
* Mix sour cream and mayonnaise with rice. Add seafood.
* Place mixture in a 13x9-inch baking dish. Top with cheese.
* Bake at 350° for 30 minutes.

B. J. Dengler

MARTY'S CHEESE 'N SEAFOOD RAVIOLI

Serves: 2

1 (8-ounce) package commercial cheese
   ravioli
4 tablespoons dry sherry, divided
2 tablespoons minced onion
1 teaspoon butter
1 tablespoon flour
salt and pepper to taste

1/4 teaspoon ground nutmeg
1 cup skim milk
2 tablespoons grated Parmesan cheese
1/2 cup cooked shrimp
1/2 cup cooked scallops
1 tablespoon minced parsley
paprika (optional)

* Cook ravioli according to package directions.
* While ravioli is boiling, combine 2 tablespoons sherry, onion and butter in a non-stick skillet. Cook over moderate heat until wine has evaporated.
* Mix flour, salt, pepper, nutmeg, milk and rest of sherry in a separate bowl, blending well. Add to skillet and cook over low heat until simmering.
* Stir in cheese until melted. Add shrimp and scallops, stirring until heated thoroughly.
* Spoon over drained ravioli, adding parsley and paprika, if desired.

Marty Viser

SEAFOOD MEDLEY

Serves: 12-15

1 stick butter or margarine
2 cups milk
2 cups half-and-half
2 egg yolks, beaten
3 tablespoons cornstarch
2 teaspoons salt
1 teaspoon black pepper
dash red pepper
3 tablespoons white wine

1 pound crabmeat
1 pound cleaned and cooked shrimp
2 cups diced cooked chicken
1/2 pound sea scallops
1 large can mushrooms with liquid
1 large jar chopped and drained pimientos
2 tablespoons chopped parsley
puff pastry shells or cooked rice

* Melt butter in double boiler over medium heat. Combine egg yolks, milk and half-and-half. Add to butter in double boiler.
* Add cornstarch mixed with a little water, stirring constantly. When mixture thickens, add remaining ingredients. Serve hot with puff pastry or over rice. Can be frozen.

Diddy Irwin

ROYAL SEAFOOD CASSEROLE

May be prepared ahead and frozen   Serves: 8-10

2 (10-1/2-ounce) cans condensed cream
of shrimp soup
1/2 cup mayonnaise
1 small onion, chopped
3/4 cup milk
salt
white pepper
seasoned salt
ground nutmeg
cayenne pepper

3 pounds shrimp, cooked, peeled and
deveined
1 (7-1/2-ounce) can crabmeat, drained
1 (5-ounce) can sliced water chestnuts,
drained
1-1/2 cups diced celery
3 tablespoons minced fresh parsley
1-1/3 cups cooked long grain white rice
paprika
slivered almonds

* Blend soup into mayonnaise in a large bowl. Stir until smooth. Add onion and milk.
* Add seasonings generously. Combine remaining ingredients except paprika and almonds. Add a few tablespoons of milk if mixture is dry.
* Turn into large, shallow, buttered casserole. Sprinkle with paprika. Scatter almonds generously over top. Bake uncovered at 350° for 30 minutes.

Manetta Latham

SHRIMP AND CRABMEAT COMPANY CASSEROLE

Serves: 12-16

2 pounds shrimp, cooked, peeled and
deveined
2 pounds backfin crabmeat, picked
over for cartilage and shell
1 large onion, finely chopped
2 large green peppers, diced
4 to 5 large celery ribs, diced
1 cup mayonnaise

1 bottle Durkee's Sauce
salt and pepper to taste
dash hot pepper sauce
fresh breadcrumbs (6 French rolls
processed in food processor until
coarse crumbs)
1/2 cup melted butter

* Combine shrimp, crabmeat, vegetables, mayonnaise and Durkee's in large mixing bowl, stirring to combine. Divide and place into two 13x9-inch glass casseroles.
* Sprinkle fresh breadcrumbs over top. Drizzle melted butter over the crumbs.
* Bake at 375° for 20 minutes, or until hot.

Pattie Bethune

CRAZY CRAB CASSEROLE

Serves: 4

6 tablespoons butter or margarine
3 tablespoons flour
1/8 teaspoon nutmeg
dash paprika
1/2 teaspoon salt
3 tablespoons sherry

1-1/2 cups light cream or half-and-half
1 (8-ounce) can crabmeat, cleaned
1/2 cup sliced mushrooms (or stems and
  pieces)
grated cheese (optional)
cooked rice or Chinese noodles

* In double boiler, melt butter. Stir in flour, nutmeg, paprika, salt, sherry and cream.
* Add crab and stir until thickened. Add mushrooms.
* Divide into 4 individual casseroles. Sprinkle grated cheese over each.
* Place under broiler until cheese melts and mixture bubbles.
* Serve with rice or Chinese noodles.

Pat Viser

CRABMEAT LASAGNA

Serves: 8-10

2 tablespoons butter
1 (4-ounce) can mushrooms, drained
1 tablespoon parsley
1/4 teaspoon oregano
1 teaspoon salt
1/4 cup chopped onions
1 clove garlic, minced
1/2 teaspoon dill weed

2 (15-ounce) cans tomato sauce
1/8 teaspoon basil
2 (6-1/2-ounce) cans crabmeat
10 to 12 lasagna noodles
1 cup sour cream
2 (8-ounce) packages mozzarella cheese
2 cups grated sharp Cheddar cheese

* Melt butter. Add onions, mushrooms and garlic. Cook until tender.
* Stir in tomato sauce and all seasonings. Cover and simmer for 20 minutes.
* Stir in crab and remove from heat.
* Cook noodles and drain. Arrange half the noodles in 13x9-inch baking dish.
* Pour half the sauce over noodles and spread half the sour cream over that.
* Sprinkle half the cheeses and repeat layers.
* Cover and bake at 350° for 1 hour.

Nancy Higgins

CRAB MORNAY

Great to do ahead - very versatile

Yields: 5 entrees or appetizers for 16-20

1/4 cup chopped green onions
1 stick butter, melted
2 tablespoons flour
1 pint half-and-half

1/2 cup chopped fresh parsley
1 pound lump crabmeat
salt and pepper to taste

* Sauté green onions, including tops, in melted butter.
* Add flour, half-and-half and parsley. Cook over medium heat, stirring until thickened.
* Add crabmeat and heat. Season with salt and pepper.
* Serve over toasted English muffins with a piece of broiled Canadian bacon, in individual dishes topped with breadcrumbs, or as an appetizer in chafing dish with melba toast and phyllo cups.
* Freezes well.

Betty Mullen

CRAB WITH PROSCIUTTO

From The Coach House in New York City

Easy

Serves: 6

24 thin slices prosciutto
1 pound fresh lump crabmeat
1-1/2 sticks unsalted butter
1 teaspoon Worcestershire sauce

1/2 teaspoon hot pepper sauce
juice of 1 lemon
2 tablespoons finely chopped parsley
freshly ground black pepper

* Arrange prosciutto slices on a flat surface.
* Place a heaping tablespoon of crabmeat in the center of each slice.
* Roll the prosciutto over the crabmeat, cigar style.
* Repeat with the remaining prosciutto and crabmeat.
* Heat the butter in a large skillet. When foaming add prosciutto rolls.
* Cook until ham begins to sizzle and crab is heated through, turning once.
* Transfer to hot platter. Add Worcestershire sauce, hot pepper sauce and lemon juice to the skillet. Heat.
* Pour over crab rolls. Serve hot. Top with parsley and pepper.

Crickett Byler-Martyn

REAL CHESAPEAKE BAY CRAB CAKES
Almost as good as being there!

Serves: 8

2 slices white bread soaked in small
    amount of milk
1 egg, beaten
1/4 teaspoon Old Bay seasoning
2 tablespoons mayonnaise
2-1/2 tablespoons prepared mustard

1 pound crabmeat
salt and pepper
dried minced onion flakes
parsley
vegetable oil

* Mix first 6 ingredients with fork.
* Add salt, pepper, minced onion and parsley to taste.
* Shape into cakes (will feel soggy).
* Refrigerate at least 1 hour to help hold shape when cooking.
* Fry in vegetable oil until brown.
* Serve on buns if desired.

Betty Thalinger

FRIED OYSTERS AND COCKTAIL SAUCE

Serves: 2

1 pint raw oysters
salt and pepper to taste
1 to 1-1/2 cups cracker meal
Sauce:
1/2 cup ketchup
1/2 cup chili sauce
juice of 1 lemon

2 eggs, beaten
oil for frying

1 tablespoon horseradish
1 dash hot pepper sauce (optional)

* Wash oysters well, feeling for shell.
* Sprinkle with salt and pepper.
* Alternately roll oysters in cracker meal, eggs, then cracker meal.
* Cook in hot oil over medium heat, watching carefully to avoid over cooking.
* Drain on paper towels.
* Mix sauce ingredients. Serve sauce with hot oysters.

Marie Higgins Mullen

MY MOTHER'S SCALLOPED OYSTERS

Easy   Serves: 4-6

1 stick butter   salt and pepper
1 cup crushed round buttery crackers   paprika
1 pint oysters, drained thoroughly   6 tablespoons heavy cream

* Grease a 9 to 10-inch pie plate with vegetable cooking spray.
* Melt butter and toss with cracker crumbs.
* Cover bottom of pie plate with a few cracker crumbs.
* Place 1/2 of oysters in pie plate and cover with 1/2 of crumbs.
* Dust with salt, pepper and paprika.
* Repeat layer with remaining ingredients.
* Drizzle cream on top.
* Bake at 400° for 20 to 30 minutes.

Jennie Sheppard

SCALLOPS IN WHITE WINE
Easy and impressive

Serves: 6

1-1/2 pounds scallops   2 teaspoons lemon juice
4 tablespoons butter   1 teaspoon salt
1/2 pound fresh mushrooms, sliced   freshly ground pepper to taste
1/4 cup finely chopped onion   2 tablespoons parsley
2 tablespoons flour   1 cup buttered crumbs
1 cup dry white wine   paprika

* Wash and dry scallops (if large, cut in half).
* Heat butter in skillet. Sauté mushrooms and onions until tender.
* Stir in flour and cook several minutes.
* Stir in wine, lemon juice, salt, pepper and parsley. Bring to a boil.
* Add scallops.
* Spoon into large shallow casserole or 6 individual casseroles.
* Sprinkle with buttered crumbs and paprika.
* Bake at 400° for 25 minutes (large casserole) or 15 minutes (individual casseroles).

Gail Madara

SHRIMP CREOLE

Serves: 4

4 slices bacon
1/2 cup chopped bell pepper
1/2 cup chopped onion
1/2 cup chopped celery
2 cups tomatoes or 28-ounce can
  whole tomatoes, drained and chopped

1/2 cup chili sauce
1 tablespoon Worcestershire sauce
1/4 teaspoon black pepper
1 teaspoon salt
3 to 4 shakes hot pepper sauce
1 pound boiled shrimp, peeled and deveined

* Fry bacon and remove from pan to drain.
* Put onion, celery and bell pepper in bacon fat and brown lightly.
* Add tomatoes, chili sauce, Worcestershire sauce, black pepper, salt and hot pepper sauce.
* Cook slowly until thick, stirring occasionally.
* Add shrimp 10 to 15 minutes before serving.
* Break bacon into small pieces and add.
* Add more seasoning if needed, perhaps even a pinch of sugar.
* Serve over rice.

Ann Houck

ELEGANT SHRIMP LINGUINE

Easy

Serves: 4-6

8 ounces linguine
1/2 cup Italian dressing
1/2 to 1 pound raw shrimp, peeled and
  deveined
1 yellow squash, cut in julienne strips
1 zucchini, cut in julienne strips

1 carrot, cut in julienne strips
3 green onions, cut in strips
1 clove garlic, minced
1/4 cup chopped fresh parsley
1 teaspoon salt
dash cayenne pepper

* Prepare linguine as package directs; drain.
* Heat Italian dressing in medium skillet.
* Add remaining ingredients except linguine.
* Cook and stir 8 to 10 minutes.
* Add linguine and toss.

Pam McLean

MARINATED SHRIMP WITH ORANGE

Serves: 8-10

3 pounds large raw shrimp, peeled and
   deveined
4 oranges, peeled and sectioned
4 medium white onions, sliced
1-1/2 cups cider vinegar
1 cup vegetable oil
2/3 cup fresh lemon juice
1/2 cup ketchup

1/4 cup sugar
2 tablespoons drained capers
2 tablespoons minced parsley
2 teaspoons salt
2 teaspoons mustard seed
1 teaspoon celery seed
1/4 teaspoon pepper
2 cloves garlic, crushed

* Cook shrimp in boiling water only 2 minutes. Rinse with cold water until thoroughly chilled. Drain.
* Combine shrimp, oranges and onions in large bowl.
* Mix remaining ingredients and pour over shrimp mixture.
* Cover and refrigerate 8 hours or overnight, stirring occasionally.
* Drain and serve in individual shells or on a bed of lettuce.

Catherine Whittington

SHRIMP AND ARTICHOKES

Serves: 6

2 (14-1/2-ounce) cans artichoke hearts,
   drained
1 pound shrimp, cooked, peeled and
   deveined
White Sauce:
4 tablespoons butter
4 tablespoons flour
1-1/2 cups milk

1/2 pound fresh mushrooms, sliced
1/4 cup grated Parmesan cheese
fresh parsley
paprika

salt and pepper
1 tablespoon Worcestershire sauce
1/4 cup dry sherry

* Layer artichokes, shrimp and mushrooms in a buttered 13x9-inch casserole.
* Melt butter in saucepan. Stir in flour. Add milk. Cook until thickened.
* Season with salt and pepper, Worcestershire sauce and sherry. Pour over casserole.
* Sprinkle with cheese and paprika. Bake at 375° for 30 to 40 minutes. Garnish with parsley.

Frances Fennebresque

SHRIMP WITH ASPARAGUS
Elegant but easy

Serves: 6

1-1/2 pounds fresh asparagus
1/4 cup melted butter or margarine
1 large clove garlic, crushed
2 teaspoons grated lemon rind
1-1/2 tablespoons fresh lemon juice

1/4 teaspoon salt
2 pounds raw medium shrimp, peeled and
    deveined
6 thinly cut lemon slices

* Spray 13x9-inch baking dish with non-stick vegetable spray.
* Trim asparagus; cut into 2-inch pieces. Steam 3 minutes. Rinse in cold water. Drain and set aside.
* Combine butter, garlic, lemon rind, lemon juice and salt. Stir well and set aside.
* Arrange asparagus spears in baking dish. Place shrimp over asparagus.
* Spoon butter-lemon mixture evenly over shrimp. Top with lemon slices. Cover with aluminum foil.
* Bake at 400° for 10 to 15 minutes. Serve over hot cooked rice.

Laurie Guy

SHRIMP WITH FETA CHEESE
You must try this!

Serves: 4

1 medium onion, thinly sliced
1/4 cup olive oil
3 tomatoes, peeled, seeded and chopped
1/2 cup dry white wine
1/2 cup chopped fresh parsley

1 clove garlic, minced
1 teaspoon salt
pepper to taste
1 pound shrimp, peeled and deveined
6 ounces feta cheese

* Cook onion in olive oil until soft.
* Add tomatoes, wine, parsley, garlic, salt and pepper. Bring to boil. Reduce heat and simmer partially covered for 30 minutes.
* Let cool. Stir in shrimp. Spoon into 1-quart baking dish.
* Sprinkle with crumbled feta cheese.
* Bake at 450° for 10 to 20 minutes until cheese is melted and bubbly.

Barbara Henson

SPICY SHRIMP BAKE

Easy   Serves: 6-8

1-1/2 cups margarine, melted   3 teaspoons salt
3 pounds raw medium shrimp, in shells   2-1/2 tablespoons coarsely ground black
1/2 cup Italian salad dressing   pepper
2 tablespoons Worcestershire sauce   juice of 3 lemons
1 tablespoon soy sauce   1 tablespoon paprika
3 cloves garlic, minced   2 tablespoons hot pepper sauce
2 bay leaves

* Melt margarine in a 13x9-inch baking dish. Add shrimp (do not attempt to marinate
  the shrimp, as this will make them mealy) and all other ingredients.
* Bake at 350° for 15 to 20 minutes if shrimp is at room temperature; 30 to 40 minutes if
  shrimp is very cold. Stir several times during cooking. Do not over cook as shell will
  stick to shrimp. Shrimp is done when it has curled up.
* French bread for dipping in sauce and a tossed salad complete the meal.

Peggy Buchanan

SHRIMP WITH TOMATO SAUCE

Serves: 4

1 pound raw shrimp, peeled and deveined   1 tablespoon chopped fresh ginger
1 egg white   2 tablespoons sliced green onion
1 teaspoon white wine   3 tablespoons ketchup
1 teaspoon salt   1 teaspoon sugar
1 tablespoon cornstarch   1/2 teaspoon salt
4 cups oil for deep-frying   3 tablespoons water
2 tablespoons oil   2 teaspoons cornstarch dissolved in 2
1 tablespoon chopped garlic   teaspoons water

* Marinate shrimp in egg white, wine, salt and 1 tablespoon cornstarch for 1/2 hour.
* Heat frying oil. Deep-fry shrimp until color changes to pink. Remove and drain shrimp
  on paper towels.
* Put 2 tablespoons oil in pan and stir-fry garlic, ginger and green onion.
* Add ketchup, sugar, salt, water and cornstarch paste. Bring to a boil for a few seconds.
* Add shrimp to tomato sauce mixture; stir thoroughly and serve.

Yuh Hui Lee

BROILED SOLE

Easy   Serves: 4

2 pounds sole fillets (or other mild fish)   3 tablespoons mayonnaise
2 tablespoons lemon juice   3 tablespoons chopped onion
1/2 cup grated Parmesan cheese   chopped parsley
4 tablespoons butter, melted   lemon wedges

* Preheat broiler.
* Place fillets in flat baking dish. Brush with lemon juice. Let stand 20 minutes.
* Combine cheese, butter, mayonnaise and onion.
* Broil fillets for 6 to 10 minutes or until flaky.
* Spoon mayonnaise mixture on top of fillets.
* Broil 3 minutes.
* Garnish with parsley and lemon wedges.

Kathy Gately

DAD'S FISH

Easy   Serves: 4

1 medium onion, chopped   1-1/2 to 2 pounds fish (dolphin or any
1 green pepper, chopped   sturdy white fish)
2 tablespoons butter   1 beaten egg
1 (15-ounce) can stewed tomatoes   seasoned flour
curry to taste   1 stick butter

* Sauté onion and green pepper in 2 tablespoons butter.
* Add stewed tomatoes and curry. Let simmer.
* Dip fish in egg, then flour.
* Cook in hot skillet with melted butter.
* Turn fish after golden crust has formed
* Cook second side until crust has formed.
* Add tomato mixture. Cook a few minutes to blend flavors.

Marwen McDowell

PEPPERED FISH WITH CRISPY SLAW

Serves: 4

1 cup finely shredded Napa cabbage
1/2 cup matchstick-size snow peas strips
1/2 cup matchstick-size carrots
4 (1/2-inch thick) swordfish steaks
2 teaspoons coarsely ground pepper
3 tablespoons peanut oil
Soy Vinaigrette:
2 tablespoons dark soy sauce
1 tablespoon vegetable oil
1 tablespoon rice vinegar
1 tablespoon mirin (sweet rice
   cooking wine)

2 tablespoons matchstick-size fresh ginger
   strips
2 matchstick-size strips of Wonton
   wrappers
2 small tomatoes, cut into wedges

1 tablespoon fresh lime juice
1-1/2 teaspoons sugar
1 teaspoon grated fresh ginger
1 teaspoon oriental sesame oil
1 clove garlic, minced

* Combine first 3 ingredients in small bowl.
* Sprinkle both sides of fish with pepper.
* Cover and refrigerate the vegetables and fish separately for 1 to 4 hours.
* To prepare the Soy Vinaigrette, combine all ingredients in small bowl. Cover and refrigerate 1 to 4 hours. (Can be prepared up to 2 days ahead.)
* Heat 2 tablespoons of oil in small skillet over medium-high heat.
* Add ginger and fry for 30 seconds until golden brown. Transfer with a slotted spoon to paper towels.
* Add wonton strips and fry until crisp (about 1 minute). Transfer to paper towels to drain.
* Heat remaining tablespoon of oil in a large skillet until quite hot.
* Add fish and fry until brown and cooked through (about 2-1/2 minutes per side).
* Transfer fish to plates.
* Add 1/2 of vinaigrette to vegetables and toss well.
* Divide vegetable slaw among plates.
* Sprinkle ginger and wonton strips over the slaw.
* Spoon the remaining vinaigrette over fish.
* Garnish with tomatoes.

Note: If preferred, can stir-fry slaw for 1 minute to wilt.

Pat Waldron

SALMON GRILL

People who do not care for salmon will like this.

Easy   Serves: 4

4 (1 to 1-1/4-inch) salmon steaks or   1/4 cup butter, melted
   fillets   2 tablespoons soy sauce
1/4 cup firmly packed dark brown sugar   2 tablespoons dry sherry

* Combine sugar, butter, soy sauce and sherry in a small saucepan.
* Cook until dissolved and well blended.
* Cool to room temperature.
* Wash steaks in cold water and pat dry with paper towels.
* Place each steak in heavy-duty foil which has been sprayed with non-stick spray.
* Turn foil edges up to make a dish.
* Brush with 1/2 the soy sauce mixture.
* Refrigerate for 15 minutes.
* Turn steaks. Brush with the remaining mixture.
* Using a second piece of foil over steaks, seal each in a tent.
* Refrigerate until grill is ready.
* Place over hot coals and cook for 10 to 12 minutes.

Dougi O'Bryan

SALMON WITH SAFFRON BUTTER

Elegant dinner served with angel hair pasta and broccoli

Serves: 4

1 pound salmon fillet   1/8 teaspoon saffron
2 tablespoons water   4 tablespoons butter
2 tablespoons white wine   3/4 cup whipping cream

* Cut salmon on a deep bias angle and away from the skin into very thin slices.
* Combine water, wine and saffron in skillet.
* Bring to a boil and reduce almost completely.
* Add butter; stir until melted.
* Sauté salmon about 1 minute per side; remove to a plate.
* Add whipping cream to skillet and heat. Pour over salmon.

Kathy Yarmey

DILL SAUCE
Excellent with salmon!

Yields: 1 cup

4 tablespoons butter, divided
2 tablespoons flour
1 teaspoon fresh dill
1 teaspoon shallots, minced

1/2 cup dill pickle juice
1/2 cup whipping cream
salt and pepper to taste

* Melt 2 tablespoons butter over medium heat. Stir in flour. Cook 1 to 2 minutes, stirring constantly. Do not brown.
* Clean and mince dill.
* Sauté dill and shallots in remaining 2 tablespoons of butter in saucepan.
* Add pickle juice and cream. Bring to a boil.
* Add flour and butter mixture in small amounts until thickened.
* Add salt and pepper.

Scott Spaulding

MUSTARD SAUCE FOR STONE CRABS
A delicious accompaniment to any shellfish

Easy

Yields: 1-1/4 cups

3-1/2 teaspoons dry mustard
1 cup mayonnaise
2 teaspoons Lea & Perrins (do not
   substitute) Worcestershire sauce

1 teaspoon A-1 sauce
1/8 cup whipping cream
dash salt

* Beat together dry mustard and mayonnaise.
* Add other ingredients. Chill.
* Serve in small dish with stone crabs.

Leslie Gebert

ROTISSERIE DRESSING
Fabulous with shrimp or crab

Yields: 4 cups

1 cup vegetable oil
1 cup mayonnaise
3 tablespoons Worcestershire sauce
dash of hot pepper sauce
1/2 cup ketchup
1/4 cup chili sauce
1 tablespoon dry mustard

1 tablespoon grated onion
1 clove garlic, mashed
1 grated lemon rind
juice of 1/2 lemon
1 teaspoon salt
1/2 teaspoon pepper

* Put all ingredients in jar and shake well. Refrigerate overnight.
* Serve as a dip for shrimp or other seafood. Also good served over salad greens.

Betty Mullen

GRANDPA'S FISH BASTING SAUCE

Easy   Yields: 3/4 cup

1/4 cup white wine
1/4 cup lemon juice
1/4 cup butter or margarine

white pepper to taste
chervil to taste
garlic powder to taste

* Heat wine, lemon juice and butter until butter melts. Add spices. Stir well.
* Baste fish before cooking and several times during cooking.

Suzanne Allen

ITALIAN DRESSING MARINADE FOR GRILLED FISH

commercial Italian dressing

* Marinate fish in any commercial Italian dressing. Fresh fish can also be frozen in the dressing.
* When thawed, fish is ready to grill.

Lucy Anderson

MOUNTAIN TROUT MARINADE

Easy   Yields: 1-1/4 cups

1/2 cup soy sauce   *1 clove garlic, crushed*
1/2 cup sherry   *1/4 cup salad oil*
1 tablespoon lemon juice

* Mix all ingredients. Pour over fish in baking dish.
* Marinate fish for 1 hour.
* Baste fish as they are grilled.
* Makes enough marinade for two 10 to 12-inch trout.

Jean Webb

SALMON MARINADE

A good marinade for mackerel or salmon

Easy   Yields: 1 cup

1/4 cup soy sauce   *3/4 to 1 teaspoon ground ginger*
1/4 cup teriyaki sauce   *1 tablespoon chopped onion*
1/4 cup white wine   *1/2 teaspoon black pepper*
1/2 teaspoon sugar   *2 garlic cloves, crushed (optional)*
3 tablespoons olive oil

* Mix all ingredients and refrigerate.
* Marinate fillets or steaks at least 1/2 hour before grilling or baking.
* Grill fillets 5 to 10 minutes on each side, depending on thickness of fish, or bake at
  350° for 20 to 25 minutes.
* Discard used marinade.
* Unused marinade will keep up to a month refrigerated.

Wendy Helms

CAKES

APFELKUCHEN (GERMAN APPLECAKE)
Great for a neighborhood coffee

Serves: 8

1 stick butter
3 eggs
1 teaspoon vanilla
4 to 5 apples
1/2 cup sugar

6 drops lemon flavoring
1-3/4 cups flour
1 teaspoon baking powder
1/2 cup powdered sugar

* Grease a 9-inch springform pan and set aside.
* In a large bowl beat together butter and sugar.
* Beat in eggs, lemon flavoring and vanilla until light and fluffy.
* Sift in flour and baking powder. Mix well. Pour into prepared pan.
* Peel, quarter and core apples. Cut into rounded side of each quarter making several lengthwise incisions so that quarters fan.
* Place prepared apple quarters on top of pastry, sliced side up. Press slightly into pastry. Bake at 350° for 40 to 50 minutes or until done.
* Let cool, remove from pan and dust lightly with powdered sugar.

Annette Schulte

FRESH APPLE CAKE
Wonderful served at breakfast!

Serves: 16

3 cups flour
1-1/3 cups vegetable oil
2-1/2 cups sugar
1 teaspoon salt
1 teaspoon baking soda
3 eggs

2 teaspoons vanilla
2 teaspoons cinnamon
dash of ground cloves
3 cups diced apples
1 to 2 cups chopped pecans or walnuts

* Mix flour, oil, sugar, eggs, salt, baking soda and vanilla by hand.
* Add cinnamon, cloves, apples and nuts. Mix well.
* Pour into greased and floured tube or Bundt pan. Bake at 350° for 1-1/2 hours.

Lynne Greenoe, Alice Nance
Becky Tomsyck

APPLE-NUT CAKE

Easy   Serves: 12-16

1 cup chopped walnuts   *1 teaspoon salt*
2 cups sugar   *2 teaspoons baking soda*
2 cups flour   *2 eggs*
2 teaspoons cinnamon   *1/2 cup vegetable oil*
1 teaspoon nutmeg   *1 (20-ounce) can apple pie filling*
1 teaspoon ground cloves   *1-1/2 teaspoons vanilla*

* Mix flour, sugar, spices, salt and baking soda.
* Add eggs, oil, pie filling and vanilla. Mix thoroughly. Stir in nuts.
* Bake in greased and floured 10-inch tube pan at 350° for 1 hour.
* Allow to remain in the pan until completely cooled (about 2 hours).

Irene Kelly

FRAULEIN ADERHOFF'S GERMAN APPLE CAKE
Not too sweet

Serves: 12-16   OR - edges burnt, bottom burnt
                              sweet cake

Filling:
3 medium apples, peeled and thinly   *1/4 cup sugar*
*   sliced*   *1 tablespoon cinnamon*
Batter:
3 cups flour   *1/4 cup orange juice*
2 cups sugar   *1 teaspoon salt*
1 tablespoon baking powder   *1 cup vegetable oil*
4 eggs   *1 tablespoon vanilla*

* Toss apples, 1/4 cup sugar and cinnamon together. Set aside.
* To make batter, combine flour, sugar, baking powder and salt in large mixing bowl.
* Stir remaining ingredients into dry mixture a little at a time. Batter will be thick.
* Spoon 1/3 of batter into greased, floured 10-inch tube pan. Top with 1/2 apple filling. Repeat layering, ending with batter on top.
* Bake at 350° for 1 hour and 15 minutes or until tester inserted in center comes out clean. Cool in pan 10 to 15 minutes.
* Shake pan to loosen. Remove; cool completely; sprinkle with powdered sugar.

Pam Funderburk

APRICOT CAKE

Serves: 12-15

1/2 cup shortening
1 cup sugar
2 eggs, well beaten
1 teaspoon vanilla

1-3/4 cups cake flour
1/2 teaspoon salt
2-1/2 teaspoons baking powder
1/2 cup milk

Apricot Filling and Meringue:

2 cups dried apricots
2 cups water
1 cup sugar
1/4 teaspoon salt

1 teaspoon grated lemon rind
2 egg whites
2 tablespoons sugar
1 teaspoon lemon juice

* Cream shortening and sugar.
* Add beaten eggs, and beat until light. Add vanilla.
* Sift together flour, salt and baking powder.
* Add to creamed mixture alternately with milk, beginning and ending with dry ingredients.
* Beat well.
* Pour batter into two 8-inch layer cake pans that have been greased, lined with wax paper, and greased again.
* Bake at 375° for 25 to 30 minutes.
* Let stand 5 minutes, then turn out on racks to cool.
* To make Apricot Filling, simmer apricots in water in a covered saucepan until tender, about 30 minutes. Put through a sieve or puree in blender.
* Return to saucepan. Add 1 cup sugar, salt and lemon rind.
* Cook slowly until thick, stirring constantly.
* Split cake layers crosswise.
* Reserve 2/3 cup of the apricot mixture for the meringue.
* Spread the rest between the cake layers.
* Beat the egg whites until foamy.
* Gradually add 2 tablespoons sugar and continue to beat until meringue is thick and reaches the soft-peak stage.
* Fold in remaining 2/3 cup apricot puree and 1 teaspoon lemon juice.
* Frost top and sides of cake with Apricot Meringue.
* Serve as soon as possible, as meringue does not hold up well. Refrigerate any leftovers.

Linda Pickens

BANANA CAKE

Serves: 10

2 sticks butter
1 cup sugar
2 eggs
1 cup mashed bananas (approximately
   3 bananas)
Frosting:
8 ounces cream cheese, softened
6 tablespoons butter, softened
3 cups powdered sugar, sifted

1-3/4 cups flour
1/2 teaspoon salt
2/3 teaspoon soda
5 tablespoons buttermilk
1 teaspoon vanilla

1 teaspoon vanilla
juice of 1/2 lemon
1 large banana, sliced

* Cream butter and sugar. Add eggs, one at a time. Add bananas.
* Mix flour, salt and soda. Add to batter.
* Add buttermilk and vanilla. Mix 1 minute.
* Pour into 2 round 8 or 9-inch pans. Bake at 350° for 25 to 30 minutes.
* Cool 10 minutes in pan; then cool 2 hours on rack.
* To prepare frosting, mix all but banana until spreading consistency.
* Frost first layer. Top with sliced banana. Top with second layer.
* Frost top and sides. Can sprinkle with chopped nuts if desired.

Jane Tilley

BANANA-PINEAPPLE CAKE

Serves: 12-15

3 cups flour
1 teaspoon soda
1 teaspoon cinnamon
2 cups sugar
1 teaspoon salt
1-1/2 cups vegetable oil

1 (8-ounce) can crushed pineapple,
   undrained
1-1/2 teaspoons vanilla
3 eggs
2 cups pureed bananas

* Grease and flour 10-inch Bundt pan.
* Mix all ingredients together until well blended.
* Pour batter into pan. Bake at 350° for 1-1/4 hours. Check after 1 hour for doneness.
* Cool and frost with your favorite cream cheese frosting.

Terry Casto

WAYSIDE INN CARROT CAKE

Serves: 12-16

2 cups sugar
4 eggs
1-1/2 cups vegetable oil
2 cups self-rising flour

1-1/2 teaspoons baking soda
2 teaspoons cinnamon
2 (6-ounce) jars baby food carrots
1/2 cup walnuts (optional)

Icing:

1 stick margarine or butter
1 (8-ounce) package cream cheese
1 teaspoon vanilla

1 box powdered sugar
1/4 to 1/2 cup coconut
chopped nuts to sprinkle on top, if desired

* Beat sugar, eggs, and oil thoroughly and slowly.
* Add flour, baking soda and cinnamon; mix well.
* Fold in carrots and add nuts, if desired.
* Bake in a lightly greased 13x9-inch pan at 350° for 40 minutes or three 8-inch round pans at 325° for 20 to 25 minutes. Cool.
* Prepare icing by creaming margarine and cream cheese together. Add vanilla.
* Mix in sugar and coconut until smooth. Spread on cake and sprinkle with nuts.

Janet Mercer, Nancy DeBiase

CHOCOLATE DECADENCE CAKE
Very rich and dense

Serves: 16 *5/4/08 Disaster. Edges burnt like charcoal center was not cooked through*

8 ounces bittersweet or semi-sweet
  chocolate, chopped
1/3 cup brewed coffee
2 sticks unsalted butter
1 tablespoon vanilla

6 large eggs, separated
1 cup dark brown sugar, firmly packed
1/2 cup sugar
1/3 cup flour
powdered sugar

* Melt chocolate, and butter with coffee in a saucepan over medium heat.
* Remove from heat. Stir in vanilla.
* Beat egg yolks with both sugars. Add to chocolate mixture. Blend in flour.
* Beat egg whites until stiff. Fold into chocolate mixture.
* Pour batter into greased 10-inch springform pan. Bake at 350° for 45 minutes.
* Cool completely. To serve, invert on plate. Sprinkle with powdered sugar.

Jamil Hosseinian

BLACK FOREST TORTE
Wonderfully different

Serves: 8-10

1-1/2 cups toasted hazelnuts, grated
1/4 cup flour
1/2 cup butter or margarine
1 cup sugar
4 ounces semi-sweet chocolate,
  melted and cooled

6 tablespoons kirsch, divided
6 eggs, separated
3 cups heavy cream chilled
1/3 cup powdered sugar
chocolate curls

Cherry Filling:
1 (16-ounce) jar red marashino cherries
4 teaspoons kirsch

1-1/2 teaspoons cornstarch
1 teaspoon lemon juice

* Grease and lightly flour an 8-inch springform pan.
* Blend grated hazelnuts and flour and set aside.
* Cream butter and gradually add sugar.
* Add egg yolks one at a time, mixing after each.
* Blend in chocolate and 2 tablespoons kirsch.
* Stir in nut-flour mixture until blended.
* Beat egg whites until stiff peaks form. Fold egg whites into batter. Turn this mixture into prepared pan.
* Bake at 375° about 1 hour. Cool 10 minutes, remove from pan and continue to cool.
* To make Cherry Filling, drain cherries, reserving 1/2 cup syrup.
* Set aside 13 cherries for decoration. Slice remaining cherries.
* Combine reserved syrup and kirsch in a saucepan. Gradually blend in cornstarch and lemon juice. Stir over medium heat for 1 minute.
* Stir in sliced cherries and cool.
* Cut torte into 3 layers.
* Place top layer inverted on cake plate.
* Spread with cherry filling.
* Whip cream, gradually adding half the powdered sugar and remaining kirsch.
* Spread some of the whipped cream over the cherry filling.
* Cover with second layer and remaining cherry filling.
* Spread with whipped cream and top with third layer of torte.
* Frost entire torte with remaining whipped cream.
* Decorate torte with reserved cherries and chocolate curls.

Rosi Weber

CHOCOLATE UPSIDE-DOWN CAKE

Serves: 8-9

1 cup flour
1/4 teaspoon salt
3/4 cup sugar
2 teaspoons baking powder
1-1/2 tablespoons cocoa
Sauce:
1/2 cup sugar
1/2 cup brown sugar

1/2 cup milk
2 tablespoons butter or margarine, melted
1 teaspoon vanilla
1/2 cup chopped nuts

5 tablespoons cocoa
1 cup hot water

* Mix dry ingredients and stir in nuts.
* Mix milk, butter and vanilla and combine with dry ingredients.
* Pour into a well-greased 9x9-inch or 8x8-inch pan.
* Mix sauce ingredients and pour over cake batter. Bake at 350° for 30 minutes.
* Cut in squares. Serve inverted on individual plates. Spoon excess sauce over servings.

Sally Gabosch

HERSHEY CHOCOLATE CAKE

Easy

Serves: 12-16

1 stick margarine, softened
1 cup sugar
4 eggs
1 cup flour
Icing:
1/2 stick margarine
1 cup sugar

1 (16-ounce) can chocolate syrup
1 teaspoon vanilla
1 teaspoon baking powder

1/3 cup evaporated milk
1/2 cup chocolate chips

* Cream margarine and sugar together.
* Add eggs, flour, syrup, vanilla and baking powder.
* Pour into greased 13x9-inch pan. Bake at 350° for 25 to 30 minutes. Cool.
* To prepare icing, bring margarine, sugar and evaporated milk to boil for 2 minutes.
* Add chocolate chips. Pour over cooled cake.

Mildred Thompson
Mae Mae Cook, Laura Courter

TUNNEL OF FUDGE CAKE

Serves: 12-16

1-3/4 cups margarine or butter, softened
1-3/4 cups sugar
6 eggs
2 cups powdered sugar
2-1/4 cups flour
Glaze:
3/4 cup powdered sugar
1-1/2 to 2 tablespoons milk

3/4 cup cocoa
1/2 teaspoon salt
2 cups chopped nuts (walnuts, pecans or
   almonds)
1 teaspoon vanilla

1/4 cup cocoa

* Grease and flour a 12-cup Bundt pan or 10-inch tube pan.
* In large bowl, beat margarine and sugar until light and fluffy.
* Add eggs one at a time, beating well after each addition.
* Gradually add powdered sugar and blend well.
* Lightly spoon flour into measuring cup. Level off.
* Stir in remaining cake ingredients until well blended. Spoon batter into prepared pan.
* Bake at 350° for 58 to 62 minutes. (Toothpick test cannot be used as center will be fudgy.) Cool upright in pan on wire rack for 1 hour. Turn onto plate. Cool well.
* To make glaze, combine all glaze ingredients until well blended.
* Spoon over cooled cake, allowing some to run down sides. Store tightly covered.

Vernie Pickens

EGGNOG CAKE

Serves: 12-16

1 large angel food cake
5 egg yolks
1/2 cup bourbon
2 sticks butter

1 box powdered sugar
4 ounces slivered almonds
12 large macaroon cookies, crushed
1/2 pint whipping cream, whipped

* Beat egg yolks until thick. Add bourbon.
* Cream butter and sugar together. Combine butter mixture with egg mixture.
* Stir in almonds and macaroons.
* Slice cake horizontally into 3 layers. Frost with bourbon-cream mixture.
* Fill center hole with whipped cream. Serve each slice with a dollop of the cream.

Gigi Walthall

WALDORF-ASTORIA CAKE

Serves: 15

1 stick butter	2 cups cake flour
2 cups sugar	2 teaspoons baking powder
4 squares unsweetened chocolate	1/2 teaspoon salt
2 eggs	1 teaspoon vanilla
1-1/2 cups milk	1 cup chopped nuts
Icing:	
2 squares unsweetened chocolate,	1/4 teaspoon salt
melted	1 teaspoon vanilla
1 box powdered sugar	1 cup chopped nuts
1 stick butter	3 to 4 tablespoons cream
2 teaspoons lemon juice	

* Cream sugar and butter until light and fluffy.
* Melt chocolate. Add to sugar mixture.
* Add eggs, one at a time, beating thoroughly after each addition.
* Sift baking powder, salt and flour together.
* Add milk alternately with flour mixture. Blend well. Add vanilla and nuts.
* Bake in 3 prepared cake pans at 350° for 30 minutes. Cool completely before icing.
* Mix all icing ingredients until smooth. Spread over cake.

Erma Rogers

WORLD'S EASIEST GINGERBREAD

Serves: 12

2 cups flour	1 cup sour milk (add 1 tablespoon vinegar
1 cup sugar	to plain milk and let stand 15 minutes)
1 cup dark molasses	1 teaspoons baking soda
1 cup vegetable oil	1 teaspoon ginger
2 eggs	dash of nutmeg
4 teaspoons cinnamon	

* Mix together all ingredients and pour into a greased and floured 13x9-inch pan.
* Bake at 350° for 35 minutes.
* When cool, top with powdered sugar, whipped topping or lemon sauce.

Meg Clarke

GINGERBREAD AND GINGERBREAD SAUCE

1 cup dark molasses
1/2 cup sugar
1/2 cup melted margarine
2 teaspoons ground ginger
2 teaspoons ground cloves or allspice
Sauce:
1 cup sugar
1 tablespoon flour
1 cup boiling water

1/2 teaspoon baking soda
1 cup boiling water
2-1/2 cups sifted flour
2 eggs, well beaten

juice and grated rind of 1 lemon
2 tablespoons butter

* Mix molasses, sugar, margarine, ginger and cloves.
* Dissolve baking soda in boiling water and add to mixture. Add flour and eggs.
* Pour batter (batter will be thin) into greased and floured 13x9-inch pan.
* Bake at 375° for 30 minutes. Serve with sauce.
* To make sauce, mix first 3 ingredients and bring to a boil. Allow to boil for several minutes. Add lemon juice and rind.
* When slightly thickened, remove from heat and add butter. Serve over cake squares.

Alice Nance

BASIC LAYER CAKE

Serves: 12

1 cup butter (at room temperature)
2 cups sugar
5 eggs
3 cups flour
2 teaspoons baking powder

1/4 teaspoon salt
1 cup milk
1 teaspoon almond extract
1 teaspoon vanilla
1 teaspoon lemon flavoring

* Cream butter and sugar until light and fluffy.
* Add eggs one at a time, beating well after each addition.
* Sift together flour, baking powder and salt. Add to butter mixture alternately with milk, beginning and ending with dry ingredients. Blend in flavorings.
* Divide batter among 3 greased and floured 9-inch cake pans.
* Bake at 350° for 30 minutes or until done. Let layers stand a few minutes in pans before turning out onto racks to cool. Ice as desired.

Dougi O'Bryan, Pam Richey

WILLIAMSBURG ORANGE CAKE

Serves: 9-12

1/2 cup margarine, softened
1 cup sugar
2 eggs
1 teaspoon vanilla
1-2/3 cups unsifted flour
1 teaspoon baking soda
Orange-Wine Icing:
2 cups unsifted powdered sugar
1 tablespoon grated orange peel

1/2 teaspoon salt
1 cup fresh buttermilk
1 cup dark raisins
1 cup coarsely chopped English walnuts
1 teaspoon grated orange peel
1/4 cup orange juice

1/3 cup softened margarine
2 tablespoons cream sherry

* In large bowl, cream margarine and sugar until light and fluffy.
* Beat in eggs and vanilla.
* In small bowl, blend flour, baking soda and salt.
* Add flour mixture to creamed mixture alternately with buttermilk, blending after each addition. Stir in raisins, walnuts and orange peel.
* Pour into greased 8x8-inch baking pan. Bake at 350° for 50 minutes.
* Cool in pan 10 minutes and turn onto rack.
* Punch cake several times with fork. Pour orange juice over cake. Cool.
* To prepare icing, combine sugar, margarine and orange peel in small bowl.
* Add sherry and beat until smooth. Ice cake.

Donna Penzell

SOUTH CAROLINA FRESH PEACH CAKE

Easy

Serves: 16

3 eggs, well beaten
1-3/4 cups sugar
1 cup vegetable oil
2 cups flour
1 teaspoon soda
1 teaspoon salt

1 teaspoon cinnamon
2 cups sliced fresh peaches or 1 pound bag
    frozen
1/2 cup chopped pecans
1/4 cup orange juice
1 teaspoon vanilla

* In a large bowl mix all ingredients thoroughly by hand.
* Pour into a greased and floured 13x9-inch baking pan. Bake at 375° for 50 minutes.

Hilda Rutherford

POPPY SEED CAKE WITH LEMON ICING
Wonderful cake, freezes well

Serves: 15

1 cup butter
1/2 cup shortening
3 cups sugar
1 teaspoon vanilla
5 eggs
3-1/3 cups flour
Icing:
6 tablespoons butter
3 cups powdered sugar
1-1/2 tablespoons milk
1/2 tablespoon lemon juice

1/2 teaspoon baking powder
1/2 teaspoon salt
1 cup milk
2 teaspoons lemon juice
1/3 cup poppy seeds

1-1/2 teaspoons vanilla
1/8 teaspoon yellow food coloring
grated rind of 1 lemon
1 tablespoon poppy seeds

* Cream butter and shortening. Add sugar and beat well.
* Add vanilla then eggs, one at a time, beating well after each addition.
* Mix flour, baking powder and salt in separate bowl.
* Add to butter mixture alternately with milk. Mix well.
* Stir in lemon juice and poppy seeds.
* Pour batter into buttered and floured 10-inch tube pan.
* Bake at 350° for 1 hour and 40 minutes.
* To make icing, cream butter. Gradually add 1 cup sugar, vanilla, milk and lemon juice.
* Beat in remaining sugar until light and fluffy.
* Mix in food coloring.
* Stir in lemon rind and poppy seeds.

Martha Schmitt

Variation: Substitute 1-1/2 teaspoons almond extract for lemon juice. Top with glaze instead of icing.

Glaze:
3/4 cups sugar
1/4 cup orange juice
1 tablespoon butter

1/2 teaspoon vanilla
1/2 teaspoon almond extract

* Heat all ingredients in saucepan until sugar is dissolved.
* Pour glaze over warm cake.

Linda Battle

SUWANNEE RIVER PRESERVES CAKE

Serves: 16

3 eggs
1/2 teaspoon salt
2 cups sugar
1 teaspoon vanilla
3/4 cup oil
1 cup buttermilk

2 cups flour
1 teaspoon nutmeg
1 teaspoon baking soda
3/4 cup nuts (optional)
1 (8 to12-ounce) jar fruit preserves

* Mix all ingredients except preserves in order given using an electric mixer.
* Fold in jar of preserves. Pour into well-greased (not floured) tube or Bundt pan.
* Bake at 350° for 1 to 1-1/2 hours or until tester comes out dry.
* This cake forms its own chewy icing.

Irene Kelly

PRUNE CAKE

Easy

Serves: 20

1 cup vegetable oil
1-1/2 to 2 cups sugar
3 eggs
2 cups flour
1/2 to 1 teaspoon salt
1 teaspoon soda
1 teaspoon nutmeg
Topping:
1 tablespoon corn syrup
1 cup sugar
1/2 teaspoon soda

1 teaspoon cinnamon
1 teaspoon allspice
1 cup buttermilk
1 teaspoon vanilla
1 cup cooked prunes, chopped (or 1 large
    or 2 small jars baby food prunes)
1 cup pecans, chopped (optional)

1/2 cup buttermilk
1 stick margarine
1 teaspoon vanilla

* Combine oil, sugar and eggs.
* Add dry ingredients and mix. Add remaining ingredients and blend thoroughly.
* Pour mixture into 13x9-inch greased and floured pan.
* Bake at 350° for 40 to 60 minutes.
* To prepare topping, combine all ingredients.
* Cook over moderate heat for 5 minutes, stirring constantly. Pour over hot cake.

Peggy Dickerson

PUMPKIN PIE CAKE

Serves: 20-24

1 (16-ounce) can pumpkin
1 (13-ounce) can evaporated milk
3 eggs
1 teaspoon nutmeg
1/2 teaspoon ginger
2 teaspoons cinnamon

1/2 teaspoon cloves
1-1/4 cups sugar
1/2 teaspoon salt
1 (18-1/2-ounce) box yellow cake mix
1 cup nuts, chopped
1-1/2 sticks butter or margarine, melted

* Blend together pumpkin, milk, eggs, nutmeg, ginger, cinnamon, cloves, sugar and salt.
* Pour mixture into well-greased 13x9-inch pan.
* Sprinkle yellow cake mix over mixture. Gently pat down.
* Sprinkle nuts over cake mix.
* Drizzle melted butter over all.
* Bake at 350° for 50 minutes.
* Cool in pan.
* When cold, run knife around edge of pan. Turn cake onto plate.

Penny Pezdirtz

HOLIDAY PUMPKIN CAKE

Serves: 16-20

4 eggs
2 cups sugar
1 cup vegetable oil
2 cups flour, sifted
2 teaspoons baking soda

2 teaspoons cinnamon
1/2 teaspoon salt
1 (16-ounce) can pumpkin
1 teaspoon vanilla
Luscious Cream Cheese Frosting

* Combine eggs and sugar.
* Add oil and mix in remaining ingredients.
* Pour batter into 3 greased and floured cake pans. Bake at 350° for 35 to 40 minutes.
* Frost cooled cake with Luscious Cream Cheese Frosting (see Index).

Ann Howell

RED VELVET CAKE

Serves: 12-16

1/2 cup shortening
1-1/2 cups sugar
2 eggs
2 teaspoons cocoa
2 ounces red food coloring
1 tablespoon vanilla
Icing:
3 tablespoons flour
1 dash salt
1 cup milk
1 stick butter or margarine

1 cup buttermilk
2-1/4 cups flour
1/2 teaspoon salt
1 tablespoon white vinegar
1 teaspoon baking soda

1/2 cup shortening
1-1/2 teaspoons vanilla
1-1/2 cups sugar

* Cream shortening and sugar. Add eggs.
* In a measuring cup, make paste of cocoa and red food coloring. Add to sugar mixture.
* Add vanilla. Sift flour and salt together.
* Add flour and buttermilk alternately to mixture. Beat well.
* Fold in soda and vinegar.
* Pour into a greased tube pan or 3 greased 9-inch cake pans.
* Bake at 300° (1 to 1-1/2 hours for tube pan, 45 minutes to 1 hour for 9-inch cake pans).
* Cool in pan for 10 minutes. Turn out on plate and cool completely.
* To prepare icing, combine flour, salt and milk. Cook on low heat, stirring constantly until very thick. Let cool.
* Cream together shortening, butter, sugar and vanilla. Add to cooked mixture.
* Blend until creamy and smooth. Ice cake.

Beth Crigler

SAD CAKE

Serves: 12-16

1 box brown sugar
2 cups buttermilk biscuit baking mix
4 eggs
Icing:
1 (8-ounce) package cream cheese
1 box powdered sugar
1/2 stick margarine

2 cups chopped pecans
1 teaspoon vanilla

1 teaspoon vanilla
milk to spreading consistency

* Mix sugar and baking mix; add remaining ingredients.
* Pour into 13x9-inch greased pan. Bake at 325° for 30 minutes.
* Mix icing ingredients . Ice cooled cake.

Charlotte Hagar

GRANDMOTHER'S STRAWBERRY SHORTCAKE

A good company dessert, especially when fresh strawberries are in season

Serves: 12-16

2 cups flour
3 teaspoons baking powder
1/4 teaspoon salt
1 cup sugar
2 eggs, separated

3/4 cup milk
1/2 teaspoon vanilla
1/2 cup margarine, melted
frozen whipped topping
strawberries

* Sift flour, baking powder, salt and 3/4 cup of sugar 3 times.
* Beat egg whites until stiff and gradually beat in the remaining 1/4 cup sugar.
* Beat egg yolks in a separate bowl; add milk, vanilla and melted margarine.
* Pour egg yolk mixture into flour mixture and beat until batter is smooth.
* Fold in beaten egg whites.
* Bake in a 13x9-inch pan at 350° for 20 to 25 minutes. Bake at 325° if using a glass dish.
* Cut into squares and serve with sliced strawberries and frozen whipped topping.

Joan Erwin

LUSCIOUS STRAWBERRY CAKE
Can be prepared ahead - keeps well in refrigerator

Serves: 12-16

1 prepared angel food cake
1 (8-ounce) container frozen whipped
 topping
1 (8-ounce) container vanilla yogurt
1 (8-ounce) container sour cream

1 (5-ounce) can light evaporated milk
1/2 cup powdered sugar
1 quart strawberries, sliced (reserve a few
 whole strawberries for decoration)
1/3 package strawberry glaze

* Slice cake horizontally into 3 layers.
* Blend frozen whipped topping, yogurt, sour cream, sugar and milk. (May not need entire can of milk.)
* Slice strawberries and mix with glaze.
* Layer cake, creamy mixture and berries to make 3 layers.
* Decorate top with whole berries.

Carol Landers

CHOCOLATE POUND CAKE
Old family recipe

Serves: 16

2 sticks margarine
3 cups sugar
3 cups flour
1/2 cup cocoa
1 teaspoon baking powder

1/4 teaspoon salt
5 eggs
1 cup milk
1 teaspoon vanilla

* Cream margarine and sugar well.
* Sift flour, cocoa, baking powder and salt together 3 times; set aside.
* Add eggs one at a time to sugar and margarine, mixing well.
* Mix milk and vanilla together. Add alternately with flour mixture to egg mixture.
* Pour mixture into a greased and floured tube pan.
* Bake at 350° for 1 hour.

Alice Nance

CHOCOLATE-KAHLÚA POUND CAKE

Can also be made as cupcakes or a sheet cake

Serves: 12-15

1 box devil's food cake mix with
   pudding
1/2 cup sugar
1/3 cup vegetable oil
3 eggs
Icing:
1/2 stick butter
1 cup sugar

3/4 cup water
1/4 cup bourbon
1/2 cup kahlúa
3/4 cup black coffee, double strength
2 teaspoons cocoa

1/3 cup evaporated milk
1 cup chocolate chips

* Put all ingredients in bowl of electric mixer and beat for 4 minutes.
* Bake in greased Bundt pan at 350° for 50 minutes.
* Let cool for 10 minutes, then remove from pan and ice.
* To prepare icing, heat butter, sugar and milk. Boil 2 minutes, stirring constantly.
* Remove from heat. Stir in chocolate chips. Beat until smooth. Add more milk if necessary. Pour over cake.

Ann Houck

FRANKLIN POUND CAKE

A favorite holiday cake

Serves: 16-20

2 sticks butter
2 sticks margarine
2 cups sugar
6 eggs
4 cups flour
1 teaspoon baking powder

1/4 teaspoon salt
1/2 pound chopped candied red cherries
1/2 pound chopped candied pineapple
1 pound chopped pecans
1 tablespoon vanilla

* Cream butter, margarine and sugar. Add eggs one at a time.
* Sift 3 cups flour with baking powder and salt. Mix remaining cup of flour with fruit and nuts. Stir both into egg mixture and mix well.
* Add vanilla and mix well. Pour into a greased 10-inch tube pan.
* Bake at 250° for 3 hours. Check after 2 hours and 45 minutes. Cool in pan.

Ellen Knott

MARILYN'S ICED LEMON POUND CAKE

Serves: 16-20   5/4/08 OK.
Very sweet

2 sticks margarine, softened
3 cups sugar
1/2 teaspoon salt
1/2 cup shortening
2 tablespoons lemon extract

5 eggs
1 cup milk
3 cups flour, divided
1/2 teaspoon baking powder

Icing:

1/2 stick margarine, softened
1 box powdered sugar

grated rind and juice of 2 medium lemons

* Allow refrigerated ingredients to reach room temperature.
* In large bowl, cream margarine, sugar, salt, shortening and lemon extract together.
* Add one egg at a time. Add 2 cups flour and milk alternately, beating well.
* In a small bowl, mix baking powder into remaining cup of flour.
* Slowly add to batter until moistened (do not over beat).
* Pour into a 10-inch tube pan that has been lightly coated with cooking spray.
* Place on middle rack of cold oven. Set oven at 325° and bake for 1-1/2 hours.
* To prepare icing, cream margarine and sugar in processor or mixing bowl.
* Add grated rind and juice. Process or mix until correct spreading consistency is achieved. (If more liquid is needed, add a small amount of water or milk.)

Stephanie Fletcher

OLD-FASHIONED POUND CAKE

Serves: 16-20

1-1/2 cups shortening
3 cups sugar
6 eggs
3-1/2 cups flour

1 teaspoon salt
1 cup milk
1/2 teaspoon lemon extract
1/2 teaspoon vanilla

* Cream shortening and sugar until light and fluffy. Add eggs, beating after each one.
* Mix flour with salt. Add flour and milk alternately, beginning and ending with flour.
* Stir in vanilla and lemon extract.
* Spray a 10-inch tube pan with non-stick cooking spray. Turn batter into pan; bake at 325° for 1 hour 25 minutes or until done. Let cake sit 10 minutes; remove from pan.

Linda Oelschlaeger

PINEAPPLE POUND CAKE

Serves: 16-20

1/2 cup vegetable shortening
2 sticks butter
3 cups sugar
5 extra large eggs
3 cups flour
Glaze:
1/2 stick butter
2 cups powdered sugar

1 teaspoon baking powder
2 teaspoons vanilla
1 teaspoon lemon extract
1 (8-ounce) can crushed pineapple
1/4 cup milk

1/2 cup crushed pineapple

* Grease or spray and flour a tube pan.
* Cream shortening, butter and sugar until light and fluffy. Add eggs, one at a time.
* Fold in flour, mixed with baking powder. Mix well. Add milk and flavorings.
* Add pineapple and mix well for 2 to 3 minutes. Bake at 325° for 1-1/2 hours.
* To prepare glaze, melt butter and stir in powdered sugar.
* Add crushed pineapple; cook over medium-low heat until thick. Spread over hot cake.

Betsy Knott Dross

SWEDISH POUND CAKE

Serves: 16

1 cup margarine
2 cups sugar
5 eggs
2 cups flour
Glaze:
3/4 cup sugar
3/4 cup water

1 teaspoon vanilla
1 cup coconut
1 cup pecans

1 stick margarine
1 teaspoon almond extract

* Cream margarine and sugar. Add eggs, one at a time. Beat well.
* Stir in flour until well blended. Add vanilla, coconut and nuts. Mix well.
* Bake in greased and floured tube pan at 350° for 1 hour.
* To prepare glaze, combine sugar and water in pan and boil for 3 minutes.
* Remove from heat and add margarine and almond extract. Stir.
* Poke holes in warm cake. Pour glaze over while cake is still warm.

Susan Knott Floyd

SOUR CREAM POUND CAKE

Serves: 16

1-1/2 cups butter, room temperature
3 cups sugar
6 large eggs, room temperature
1 cup sour cream
3 cups flour

1/2 teaspoon soda
1/8 teaspoon salt
1 teaspoon vanilla (and/or lemon extract,
    and/or almond extract)
powdered sugar

* Butter and flour tube pan.
* Cream butter in food processor. Add sugar, 1 tablespoon at a time.
* Add eggs, one at a time. Stir in sour cream.
* Sift flour, soda and salt together. Add flour mixture 1/2 cup at a time, processing until just blended. Stir in extract. Pour into tube pan. Bake at 325° for 1-1/4 to 1-1/2 hours.
* Cool on rack in pan 15 minutes. Remove; sprinkle with powdered sugar when cool.

Mary Edwards, Louise Lucas
Parkie Thomas, Debbie Ferguson

THREE-FLAVOR POUND CAKE

Serves: 16

3 cups sugar
2 sticks margarine
1/2 cup vegetable shortening
5 eggs
1 teaspoon coconut flavoring
Glaze:
1 cup sugar
1/2 cup water

1 teaspoon rum flavoring
1/2 teaspoon baking powder
1/4 teaspoon salt
3 cups flour
1 cup milk

1 tablespoon almond extract

* Cream sugar, margarine and vegetable shortening. Add eggs one at a time.
* Mix dry ingredients into the flour. Add the flavorings to the milk. Add flour mixture to the egg mixture, alternating with milk.
* Put in a large tube pan that has been sprayed with non-stick vegetable spray.
* Bake at 325° for 1-1/2 hours. Cool for 15 minutes and remove from pan.
* Combine glaze ingredients; boil until sugar is dissolved. Spoon over warm cake.

Joy Litaker

BUTTERMILK POUND CAKE

Serves: 16

3 sticks butter
3 cups sugar
5 eggs
4 cups sifted cake flour

1/2 teaspoon salt
1/2 teaspoon baking soda
1 cup buttermilk (fresh, not powdered)
1 teaspoon vanilla

* Cream butter and sugar. Add eggs one at a time, beating after each egg.
* Sift together flour and salt.
* Dissolve soda in buttermilk; add alternately with flour mixture.
* Add vanilla and mix well.
* Pour batter into a lightly greased tube pan ; put into cold oven and bake at 325° for 1 hour and 15 minutes. (Can bake in 13x9-inch pan for about 1 hour.)

Donna Penzell, Frances Fennebresque

AMARETTO CHEESECAKE

Prepare ahead

Serves: 16

1-1/2 cups graham cracker crumbs
1/3 cup sugar
1/2 cup butter, melted
2 pounds cream cheese, softened
1-1/2 cups sugar
2 teaspoons vanilla
Topping (optional):
6 ounces chocolate chips

1/4 cup amaretto
2 whole eggs, slightly beaten
2 egg yolks, slightly beaten
1/4 cup cream
1 to 2 cups chocolate chips

1/4 cup cream

* Mix together graham cracker crumbs, sugar and butter.
* Press into bottom of 10-inch springform pan.
* Cream together cream cheese and sugar. Add vanilla and amaretto.
* Blend in eggs, egg yolks and cream to make a smooth batter. Fold in chocolate chips.
* Pour batter into crust. Bake at 425° for 15 minutes.
* Reduce oven temperature to 350°. Bake an additional 45 minutes.
* Turn oven off. Open oven door slightly. Leave cake in oven for about 10 minutes.
* For topping, if desired, melt chocolate chips with cream. Pour over cheesecake.
* Refrigerate until thoroughly chilled.

John Leistler

CHOCOLATE CHIP CHEESECAKE

Prepare ahead   Serves: 16

25 to 28 chocolate chip cookies, finely   1 teaspoon grated orange rind
  crushed   1/2 teaspoon vanilla
2-1/2 tablespoons sugar   5 whole eggs
5 tablespoons butter, melted   2 egg yolks
5 (8-ounce) packages cream cheese,   1/4 cup sour cream
  softened   1 cup semi-sweet chocolate chips, chopped
1-1/4 cups sugar   or 1 cup mini-chocolate morsels
3 tablespoons flour
Topping:
1 cup sour cream   1 teaspoon vanilla
2 tablespoons sugar

* Combine cookie crumbs, sugar and butter. Mix well.
* Press cookie crumbs into bottom of well-greased 9-inch springform pan. Place pan in freezer.
* Beat cream cheese in large bowl until smooth.
* Add sugar, flour, orange rind and vanilla to cream cheese. Beat just enough to blend.
* Add eggs and yolks, one at a time, blending well.
* Stir in sour cream.
* Fold in chocolate chips.
* Pour mixture into chilled crust.
* Bake 15 minutes at 450°.
* Reduce oven temperature to 250°. Bake for 1 hour more or until set. (May take longer, depending on oven.)
* To make topping, blend sour cream, sugar and vanilla.
* Spread evenly over top of cake.
* Bake at 450° for an additional 8 minutes. Remove to wire rack. Cool.
* Refrigerate at least 24 hours; 48 hours is best.
* Serve plain or garnished with chocolate curls.

Sylvia Knapp
Nancy DeBiase

RICK'S FUDGE TRUFFLE CHEESECAKE
Chocolate lovers beware!

Prepare ahead   Serves: 12

1-1/2 cups vanilla wafer crumbs
1/2 cup powdered sugar
1/3 cup cocoa
1/3 cup butter or margarine, melted
1 (12-ounce) package semi-sweet
  chocolate chips

3 (8-ounce) packages cream cheese,
  softened
1 (14-ounce) can sweetened condensed milk
4 eggs
2 teaspoons vanilla

* Combine vanilla wafer crumbs, powdered sugar, cocoa and butter.
* Press firmly in bottom of 9-inch springform pan.
* Melt chips in heavy saucepan, over very low heat, stirring constantly. Remove from heat.
* Beat cheese until fluffy. Gradually add sweetened condensed milk, beating until smooth.
* Add eggs one at a time, beating well after each addition. Stir in vanilla.
* Add melted chips. Blend well. Pour into crust.
* Bake at 300° for 60 to 70 minutes or until center is set.
* Cool to room temperature, then chill several hours before serving.

Sally Teden

PRALINE CHEESECAKE

Must prepare ahead   Serves: 12

1 cup chocolate cookies, crushed   *3 eggs*
1/4 cup butter, melted   *1 cup chopped pecans*
1-1/2 pounds cream cheese   *2 tablespoons flour*
1-1/4 cups firmly packed brown sugar   *1-1/2 teaspoons vanilla*
Topping:
1/2 cup firmly packed brown sugar   *12 pecan halves*
1/4 cup butter

* Combine crushed cookies and 1/4 cup melted butter. Mix well.
* Press evenly in bottom of a 9-inch springform pan.
* Blend cream cheese and 1-1/4 cups brown sugar in a large bowl until smooth.
* Add eggs one at a time, beating well after each addition.
* Stir in chopped pecans, flour and vanilla. Mix thoroughly.
* Pour batter into prepared crust. Bake at 350° for 50 to 55 minutes or until set.
* Cool to room temperature. Cover and refrigerate overnight.
* To make topping, combine brown sugar and butter in small saucepan. Cook over low heat, stirring occasionally, until smooth and thickened, about 5 minutes.
* Pour hot topping evenly over chilled cake. Remove springform pan.
* Arrange pecan halves around edge. Serve chilled or at room temperature.

Pam Funderburk
Carol Lawing

PUMPKIN-PECAN CHEESECAKE

An elegant and different dessert for the fall holidays

Must prepare ahead

Serves: 12

1-1/2 cups graham cracker crumbs
1/4 cup sugar
6 tablespoons butter, melted
3 (8-ounce) packages of cream cheese
  at room temperature
3/4 cup sugar
3/4 cup packed light brown sugar
Topping:
3/4 cup packed light brown sugar
6 tablespoons chilled butter

5 large eggs
1 (1-pound) can solid-pack pumpkin
1/2 cup whipping cream
1/2 teaspoon ground cinnamon
1/2 teaspoon ground nutmeg
1/4 teaspoon ground cloves

1-1/2 cups chopped pecans

* Prepare crust by mixing crumbs, sugar and butter in medium bowl.
* Press mixture in bottom and up sides of a 9-inch springform pan. Chill.
* Using electric mixer, beat cream cheese in large bowl until smooth.
* Add sugar and brown sugar.
* Add eggs one at a time and beat until fluffy.
* Blend in pumpkin, cream, cinnamon, nutmeg and cloves.
* Pour into crust and bake at 325° until center no longer moves when pan is shaken, about 1-1/2 hours.
* To prepare topping, add butter to brown sugar and cut in until mixture resembles coarse meal.
* Stir in pecans.
* When cheesecake is finished baking, remove from oven and sprinkle topping over cheesecake.
* Return cheesecake to oven and bake 15 minutes more.
* Cover and refrigerate overnight. Should be served cold.

Jewel Freeman

WHITE CHOCOLATE CHEESECAKE

Prepare ahead   Serves: 12-16

3/4 cup blanched almonds, ground
3/4 cup quick-cooking oats
3/4 cup graham cracker crumbs
1-1/4 cup sugar, divided
1/4 cup plus 2 tablespoons butter or
* margarine, melted*
2 (8-ounce) packages cream cheese,
* softened*

1 (16-ounce) carton sour cream
1 teaspoon vanilla
8 ounces white chocolate, melted
4 egg whites
1/8 teaspoon cream of tartar
1 tablespoon powdered sugar

* Combine almonds, oats, graham cracker crumbs, 1/4 cup sugar and butter. Blend well.
* Press into bottom and 2 inches up the side of a 10-inch springform pan.
* Bake at 350° for 5 minutes. Cool.
* Combine cream cheese and 1 cup sugar. Beat at medium speed until fluffy.
* Add sour cream and vanilla. Stir in white chocolate.
* Beat egg whites with cream of tartar to form soft peaks. Add powdered sugar. Beat until stiff.
* Fold egg whites into cheese mixture.
* Pour batter into crust.
* Bake at 325° for 55 minutes. Turn oven off. Leave cheesecake in oven for 30 minutes.
* Partially open oven door. Leave cheesecake in oven another 30 minutes.
* Remove from oven. Chill at least 8 hours.
* Garnish with shaved chocolate and white chocolate curls.

Judy DuBose

MRS. WOHLBRUCK'S FAVORITE CHOCOLATE CHIP CAKE

Serves: 12

1 (18-1/2-ounce) box yellow cake mix
1 small box instant vanilla pudding
1 cup sour cream
1/2 cup vegetable oil
1/2 cup water

4 eggs, beaten
1 bar grated German chocolate
1 (12-ounce) bag semi-sweet chocolate
  chips

* Mix cake mix, pudding, sour cream, oil, water and eggs until well blended.
* Fold in chocolate chips and grated chocolate.
* Pour batter into well-greased, floured Bundt pan. Bake at 350° for 55 to 60 minutes.
* Good served with chocolate, vanilla or peppermint ice cream.

Mae Mae Cook, Parkie Thomas

Variation: Bake as 3-layer cake. Ice with Luscious Cream Cheese Frosting (see Index).

The Hawk

YUMMY COCONUT LAYER CAKE

Easy - Prepare ahead

Serves: 16

1 (12-ounce) carton frozen whipped
  topping
1/2 pint sour cream
3/4 cup sugar

2 (6-ounce) packages frozen coconut
  (save a little for top)
1 teaspoon vanilla
1 package yellow cake mix

* Mix together whipped topping, sour cream, coconut, sugar and vanilla. Refrigerate.
* Bake cake according to package directions for 2 layers. When completely cool, slice each layer in half horizontally, forming 4 layers.
* Fill and frost layers with refrigerated mixture. Sprinkle with reserved coconut.
* Refrigerate several days before serving.

Mary Gregory

Variation: Substitute orange juice for water in cake mix directions. Use three 6-ounce packages coconut in icing.

Patricia Raad

DARK CHOCOLATE CAKE

Easy   Serves: 12

1 box Devil's Food cake mix   4 eggs
1 small package instant chocolate   1/2 cup vegetable oil
  pudding   1/2 cup water
1 cup sour cream   1-1/2 cups semi-sweet chocolate morsels
Glaze:
1 (6-ounce) package semi-sweet   1/2 cup butter
  chocolate morsels   powdered sugar (optional)

* Combine all ingredients. Pour into well-greased and floured tube pan.
* Bake at 350° for 40 to 45 minutes.
* To prepare glaze, melt chocolate and butter, stirring until smooth and slightly cooled.
* Spoon over cake while mixture is still warm.
* If desired, may sprinkle with powdered sugar when cooled.

Ann Kendrick

CRUMB CRUMB CAKE
Delicious for a morning coffee

Serves: 12

1 box butter cake mix   2/3 cup vegetable oil
4 eggs   2/3 cup milk
Butter Crumbs:
4 cups flour   2/3 cup sugar
2/3 cup brown sugar   1 tablespoon vanilla
1/2 pound margarine   1 tablespoon cinnamon
1/4 pound butter   powdered sugar (optional)

* Mix all batter ingredients until smooth. Pour into prepared 12x8-1/2-inch pan.
* Bake at 350° for 20 minutes. Remove from oven and cool completely.
* To prepare Butter Crumbs, mix all ingredients with your hands. Make crumbs as large as you like. Spread over cooled cake, using hands to even out crumbs.
* Bake at 350° an additional 20 minutes.
* Sprinkle with powdered sugar when cool.

Irene Kelly, Nancy DeBiase

POPPY SEED CAKE

Easy   Serves: 10-12

1 box yellow cake mix   *1/3 cup vegetable oil*
4 eggs   *1/3 cup poppy seeds*
1 cup sour cream   *2/3 cup sherry*
1 large box instant vanilla pudding

* Blend all ingredients together and beat 2 to 3 minutes on medium speed.
* Pour into greased and floured Bundt pan.
* Bake at 325° for 45 minutes.

Diane Thomas,
Mary Gregory, Patricia Raad

PINEAPPLE-APRICOT CAKE WITH LEMON GLAZE

Easy   Serves: 12

1 box Pineapple Supreme cake mix   *1 cup apricot nectar*
1/2 cup sugar   *4 eggs*
1/2 cup oil
Lemon Glaze:
1 heaping cup powdered sugar   *2 to 3 tablespoons lemon juice*

* Combine all ingredients.
* Beat for 2 minutes until smooth.
* Pour into well-greased and floured tube pan.
* Bake at 350° for 35 to 40 minutes.
* Let cool in pan for 5 minutes.
* While cake is cooling, prepare glaze.
* Mix all ingredients.
* After cake is removed from pan, punch holes in the top with a toothpick.
* While the cake is still a little warm, spoon Lemon Glaze over the top.

Libby Ehmann

LEMON-GLAZED BUNDT CAKE

Easy

Serves: 12-16

1 box yellow cake mix
1 small package lemon jello
4 eggs
Glaze:
juice of 1 lemon

2/3 cup vegetable oil
2/3 cup water
1/2 to 1 teaspoon lemon extract

1 cup powdered sugar

* Mix cake mix with jello.
* Add eggs, oil, water and extract to dry ingredients, beating well.
* Pour batter into greased and floured Bundt pan. Bake at 350° for 40 minutes.
* Combine lemon juice and powdered sugar, stirring well.
* Pour half the glaze on cake while hot and still in pan. Cool thoroughly.
* Turn cake onto cake plate. Drizzle with remaining glaze.

Sallye Wentz, Kay Simpson

PLANTATION RUM CAKE
Delicious and moist

Easy

Serves: 12

1 box yellow cake mix with
   pudding
1/2 cup water
1/2 cup vegetable oil
Topping:
1 stick margarine or butter
1 cup sugar

1/2 cup light rum
4 eggs
1/2 cup chopped walnuts or pecans

1/4 cup water
1/2 cup rum

* Mix cake mix, water, oil and rum in large mixing bowl.
* Mix in 4 eggs, one at a time, beating well after each addition.
* Sprinkle chopped nuts in bottom of well greased, floured Bundt pan. Pour in batter.
* Bake at 375° for 45 to 50 minutes.
* To prepare topping, melt margarine, add other ingredients and boil for 2 minutes.
* Pour hot topping over cake as soon as you take it out of the oven. Pour slowly to keep from running over edge of pan. Let cake stay in pan until topping soaks in.

Susan Davenport, Lynn Wheeler

RAVE REVIEWS CAKE

1 box yellow cake mix with pudding
1-1/3 cups water
4 eggs
1/4 cup vegetable oil
Cream Cheese-Coconut Frosting:
2 cups coconut
2 tablespoons butter
1 (8-ounce) package cream cheese
2 tablespoons butter

2 cups coconut
1 cup chopped pecans
2 teaspoons vanilla
1 teaspoon almond extract

3-1/2 cups powdered sugar
2-3 teaspoons milk
1 teaspoon vanilla
1 teaspoon almond extract

* Combine cake mix, water, eggs and oil. Beat 4 minutes.
* Stir in coconut, pecans and flavorings. Pour into three 9-inch layer pans.
* Bake at 350° for 35 minutes. Cool 15 minutes. Remove from pans; cool on wire rack.
* To prepare frosting, sauté 2 cups coconut in 2 tablespoons butter until golden brown. Turn onto paper towel to drain.
* Cream 2 tablespoons butter with 8 ounces cream cheese.
* Add 3-1/2 cups powdered sugar and 2 to 3 teaspoons milk.
* Stir in 1 teaspoon vanilla, 1 teaspoon almond extract and 1-3/4 cups sautéed coconut.
* Spread between layers of cake, on sides and top. Sprinkle with 1/4 cup coconut.

Nancy Martin

STRAWBERRY CAKE

1 box white cake mix
1 small box strawberry gelatin
2 tablespoons flour
1 cup vegetable oil
Icing:
1 stick butter or margarine
1 box powdered sugar

1/2 cup water
4 eggs
1 (10-ounce) package frozen strawberries,
  thawed and divided (4 ounces for icing)

4 ounces frozen strawberries (thawed)

* Combine all batter ingredients except strawberries and mix well.
* Stir in 6 ounces of strawberries. Pour batter into 3 prepared 8-inch baking pans.
* Bake at 350° for 30 minutes. Cool on wire racks.
* To make icing, mix butter (or margarine) with powdered sugar.
* Add strawberries a little at a time until creamy. Frost cake.

Marie Bazemore

SNICKERS CAKE
Rich and delicious

Serves: 16-20

1 box German Chocolate cake mix
1 (14-ounce) package caramels
1/2 cup evaporated milk
1 stick butter
Icing (optional):
1 cup sugar
6 tablespoons milk

6 large Snickers bars
1 cup chocolate chips
1/2 cup chopped pecans

6 tablespoons margarine
1 cup chocolate chips

* Mix cake batter according to directions.
* Pour half of batter into 13x9-inch pan. Bake at 350° for 20 minutes.
* Melt caramels, milk and butter. Pour over hot cake.
* Slice Snickers bars thinly and space evenly over cake. Sprinkle with chocolate chips and pecans.
* Pour remaining batter on top. Bake at 350° for 25 to 30 minutes. Let cool in pan.
* To prepare icing, melt sugar, margarine and milk in saucepan. Boil 1 minute.
* Stir in chocolate chips. Ice cooled cake if desired.

Beth Wiener

AUNT ANN'S CHOCOLATE CUPCAKES

1 cup vegetable oil
2 eggs
1 cup cocoa
1 cup buttermilk
2 cups sugar
1/2 teaspoon salt

2 teaspoons baking soda dissolved in 1 cup
     boiling water
2 cups sugar
1 teaspoon vanilla
2 cups flour

* Combine all ingredients. Beat 3 minutes with electric mixer (batter will be very thin).
* Pour batter into 24 muffin tins, lined with baking cups.
* Bake at 350° for 25 to 30 minutes. Test for doneness.

Note: Batter also makes 13x9-inch cake (bake 35 to 45 minutes).

Donna Penzell

ORANGE-DATE CUPCAKES

Yields: 18 cupcakes

1/4 pound butter
1 cup sugar
2 cups sifted flour
1/2 teaspoon baking soda
1 teaspoon baking powder
Glaze:
1 cup sugar
juice of 2 oranges

2 eggs, beaten
2/3 cup buttermilk
1 cup chopped dates
1/2 cup lightly toasted chopped pecans
 (optional)

grated rind of 1 orange

* Cream butter and sugar until fluffy.
* Sift flour with baking soda and baking powder.
* Add to creamed mixture, mixing thoroughly.
* Add eggs and buttermilk and mix thoroughly.
* Fold in dates and nuts.
* Bake in muffin tins at 375° for 20 to 25 minutes or until light brown.
* For glaze, boil sugar, orange juice and rind for about 5 minutes.
* While cupcakes are still warm, pour a teaspoon of hot glaze over each or brush on with pastry brush. Cool before removing cakes from muffin tins.

Sara Rose

SURPRISE CUPCAKES

Easy

Yields: 24 cupcakes

1 box chocolate cake mix
8 ounces cream cheese, softened
1 egg

1/2 cup sugar
1/8 teaspoon salt
1 cup chocolate chips

* Prepare cake mix according to box directions.
* Pour into 24 cupcake tins lined with papers.
* Combine cream cheese, egg, sugar and salt. Beat well.
* Fold in chocolate chips. Drop by spoonfuls into cake batter.
* Bake at 350° for 30 minutes. Cool.
* May frost with buttercream or other favorite icing.

Dottie Hollowell

GEORGIA CARAMEL ICING

This icing never fails!

3 cups firmly packed light brown sugar
3/4 cup butter
pinch of salt

3/4 cup evaporated milk or half-and-half
1-1/2 teaspoons vanilla

* Combine sugar, butter, salt and evaporated milk in saucepan.
* Stir constantly over low heat until dissolved.
* Let mixture boil, stirring often, until it reaches soft ball stage.
* Remove from heat. Beat until cool. To cool icing more rapidly, place saucepan in a shallow pan of cool water while beating.
* Add vanilla.
* This is enough icing for the top and sides of a 2-layer cake.

Pam Richey

EASY CHOCOLATE ICING

A good frosting for brownies

Yields: Enough icing for a 13x9-inch pan

3 tablespoons butter
2 tablespoons cocoa
1-1/2 cups of powdered sugar

2 tablespoons milk
1 teaspoon vanilla

* Melt butter in saucepan.
* Stir in cocoa; add sugar, milk and vanilla; stir until blended.

Yvonne Rayburn

LUSCIOUS CREAM CHEESE FROSTING

1 box powdered sugar
1 (8-ounce) package cream cheese

1 stick margarine, softened
1 teaspoon vanilla

* Mix all ingredients until smooth.

The Hawk

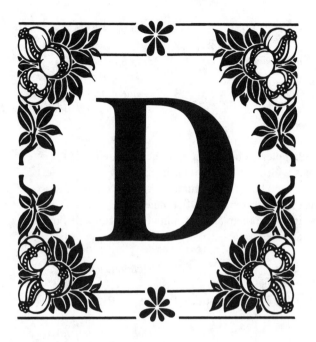

Desserts
and
Pastries

APPLE CRISP

Easy - Prepare Ahead   Yields: 4-6 servings

4 cups apple chunks, peeled and cored   *3/4 cup flour*
1/4 cup water   *1/3 cup softened butter (not melted) or*
1 teaspoon cinnamon   ·   *margarine*
1/2 teaspoon salt   *1 cup chopped nuts (optional)*
1 cup light brown sugar

* Place prepared apples on bottom of an 8-inch square pan.
* Sprinkle apples with water, cinnamon and salt.
* Mix sugar, flour and butter until crumbly. Spread over apples.
* Bake uncovered at 350° for about 40 minutes.
* If nuts are desired, add them after 35 minutes and continue baking for 5 minutes.
* Serve warm with ice cream.

Donna Lomax

Variation I: Substitute 2/3 cup oatmeal for nuts.

Debbie Fitzpatrick

Variation II: Add 1 teaspoon lemon juice to water. Substitute 3/4 cup sugar for brown
sugar. Add 3/4 cup grated Cheddar cheese to topping and omit nuts. Serve warm.

Janet Gollup

BANANA FLAMBÉ

Easy   Serves: 4

1 tablespoon butter   *1 pint vanilla or cinnamon ice cream*
2 tablespoons orange juice   *2 tablespoons Galliano liqueur*
1/2 cup brown sugar   *dash of cinnamon*
2 bananas

* Cook first 3 ingredients over low heat until slightly thickened. Pour over bananas.
* Heat Galliano until it steams; light with a match. Pour over bananas.
* Add ice cream while liqueur flames.

Steve Spaulding

EASY BANANA PUDDING

Serves: 8-12

1 (14-ounce) can sweetened condensed
  milk
1-1/2 cups cold water
1 small package instant vanilla pudding

2 cups frozen whipped topping, thawed
vanilla wafers
3 to 5 bananas, sliced

* In large mixing bowl combine condensed milk and water.
* Add pudding and mix until well blended.
* Chill for 5 minutes.
* Fold in whipped topping.
* In large bowl, alternate layers of vanilla wafers, sliced bananas and pudding mixture.

Jean Skidmore

SOUTHERN BANANA PUDDING
The real thing!

Serves: 4

1/2 cup sugar
1 egg, slightly beaten
2 tablespoons flour
1 cup milk

1 teaspoon vanilla
vanilla wafers
bananas, sliced

* Combine sugar and flour in saucepan. Add egg. Stir until well blended.
* Add milk and vanilla. Mix well.
* Cook over medium heat, stirring constantly until pudding thickens and coats spoon.
* Line bottom and sides of 8x8-inch glass dish with vanilla wafers.
* Top with layer of sliced bananas.
* Spoon pudding over bananas.
* Serve warm.

Debbie Whelchel

FRESH BLUEBERRY CRUNCH

Easy   Serves: 6

4 cups fresh blueberries   1/2 cup butter or margarine
1 cup firmly packed brown sugar   3/4 cup rolled oats, uncooked
3/4 cup flour

* Place blueberries in greased 2-quart baking dish.
* Put sugar, flour and butter in food processor. Pulse until crumbled.
* Stir in uncooked oats.
* Spoon mixture over blueberries.
* Bake at 350° for 45 minutes.

Leslie Fischer

AMARETTO DESSERT CAKE
A pretty make-ahead dessert

Easy - Prepare ahead   Serves: 8-10

2 packages Stella D'oro Almond Toast   3/4 cup amaretto
1 small package vanilla pudding   1 (12-ounce) container frozen whipped
1 small package chocolate pudding   topping
3-1/2 cups milk

* Combine vanilla pudding with 1-3/4 cups milk and 1/2 cup amaretto.
* Cook over medium heat until smooth and thickened.
* Line bottom of 10-inch springform pan with 1 package of almond toast.
* Pour vanilla pudding over toast and cover with second package of almond toast.
* Combine chocolate pudding with remaining 1-3/4 cups milk and 1/4 cup amaretto.
* Cook over medium heat until smooth and thickened.
* Pour over second layer of almond toast.
* Refrigerate at least 24 hours.
* Remove rim from springform pan.
* Frost with thawed whipped topping.
* At this point, dessert can be served or refrigerated for serving later.

Dougi O'Bryan

CHERRY OR BLUEBERRY TORTE

Easy

Serves: 6-8

1 cup margarine, softened
1 cup plus 1 tablespoon sugar
1 egg, beaten
2 teaspoons vanilla

4 cups flour
4 teaspoons baking powder
2 (21-ounce) cans blueberry or cherry pie
   filling

* Mix first 6 ingredients until crumbly.
* Use 3/4 of mixture to line bottom and sides of 13x9-inch pan, patting in place.
* Pour pie filling on top, spreading evenly.
* Sprinkle remaining crumbs on top.
* Bake at 350° for 30 to 40 minutes (keep a watchful eye).

Helen Dargay

CHERRY PUDDING TORTE

A memory of my childhood and my grandmother

Serves: 8

1 cup sugar
1 cup flour
1 teaspoon soda
1 teaspoon cinnamon
Sauce:
1 cup cherry juice
1 tablespoon cornstarch
1/2 teaspoon salt

2 cups canned sour cherries, drain and
   reserve juice
1 tablespoon butter, melted
1 egg, beaten

1/2 cup sugar
1 tablespoon butter

* Mix all cake ingredients. Put in greased 9x9-inch pan. Bake at 350° for 30 to 45 minutes.
* Mix sauce ingredients in saucepan and cook until thickened.
* At serving time, cut cake into individual squares and pour warm sauce over each.

Julie Jackson

CHOCOLATE MOUSSE TORTE
Can be made a day ahead - fabulous!

Prepare ahead   Serves: 8

8 squares semi-sweet chocolate   *2-1/2 teaspoons vanilla*
1 tablespoon instant coffee   *1/8 teaspoon salt*
1/4 cup boiling water   *fine breadcrumbs*
8 eggs, separated   *1-1/2 cups whipping cream*
2/3 cup sugar   *1/4 cup powdered sugar*

* Dissolve coffee in boiling water. Add to chocolate in microwave-safe bowl.
* Cook on 50% power for 2 minutes, then stir with whisk.
* Continue heating at 1 minute intervals until melted and can be whisked smooth.
* Beat egg yolks until thick. Gradually beat in sugar until mixture is thick.
* Slowly beat in chocolate. Add 1 teaspoon vanilla.
* Beat egg whites and salt until stiff, but not dry.
* Stir 1/4 of egg whites into chocolate mixture. Fold in remaining whites until blended.
* Dust a buttered 9-inch pie plate with breadcrumbs.
* Fill plate with part of mousse mixture so that it is level with the edge.
* Bake at 350° for 25 minutes.
* Turn oven off, but leave mousse in 5 minutes longer. Remove and cool completely.
* Refrigerate remaining uncooked mousse.
* When shell is cooled, fill with chilled uncooked mousse, mounding it up like pie filling. Chill.
* Beat the cream, 1-1/2 teaspoons vanilla and sugar until stiff. Spread over pie.
* Refrigerate until ready to serve.

Marilyn Thompson

WHITE CHOCOLATE FONDUE

Easy

1 pound white chocolate   *2 teaspoons white corn syrup*
1/2 cup half-and-half   *1 tablespoon Frangelico*

* Put ingredients in saucepan. Warm until chocolate melts (about 10 minutes). Stir.
* Serve with fresh fruit (strawberries, cherries, pineapple, pears and apples) for dipping.

Jane Coley

INDIVIDUAL BITTERSWEET CHOCOLATE SOUFFLÉS

Serves: 8

8 ounces bittersweet chocolate
1 tablespoon unsalted butter
1 tablespoon flour
1/2 cup milk
3 egg yolks
1 teaspoon vanilla
4 egg whites

1/8 teaspoon cream of tartar
1/4 cup sugar
2 to 3 tablespoons powdered sugar (for dusting)
lightly sweetened whipped cream (for garnish)

* Lightly butter 8 (6-ounce) ramekins. Dust well with sugar.
* Place on baking sheet and set aside.
* In top of double boiler over barely simmering water, melt the chocolate, stirring occasionally, until smooth (can melt in a microwave at 50% power for about 3-1/2 minutes. Stir until smooth). Remove from heat.
* In small saucepan, melt butter over moderate heat.
* Stir in flour and cook until thickened, but not browned, 1 to 2 minutes.
* Add milk and whisk briskly until smooth and thick, about 3 minutes.
* Remove from heat, add melted chocolate and whisk until smooth.
* Whisk in egg yolks and vanilla. Set aside.
* In medium bowl, beat egg whites and cream of tartar with electric beater at medium speed until soft peaks form, about 1 minute.
* Gradually sprinkle sugar on top. Beat at high speed until whites are stiff, but not dry.
* Using rubber spatula, fold 1/4 whites into chocolate mixture; then fold in remaining whites.
* Spoon mixture into prepared ramekins, filling them about 3/4 full. (The soufflés can be prepared to this point up to 1 day ahead. Cover and refrigerate.)
* Bake the soufflés for 15 to 17 minutes, until puffed and slightly cracked and a tester inserted in the center indicates the soufflé is moist, but not runny.
* Dust soufflés with powdered sugar and serve immediately in ramekins with the whipped cream. Can be served with hot fudge sauce if desired.

Rose Hegele

DEATH BY CHOCOLATE

Serves: 12-15

1 box chocolate cake mix
1 cup kahlúa
2 large packages instant chocolate
  pudding
chocolate curls, if desired

4 to 5 (1.4-ounce) chocolate-covered toffee
  candy bars, crumbled
2 (12-ounce) containers frozen whipped
  topping, thawed

* Prepare cake according to package directions. Bake in 13x9-inch prepared pan. Cool.
* Pierce cake with fork and drizzle with kahlúa. Refrigerate overnight.
* Prepare pudding according to package directions. Set aside.
* Break cake into small chunks.
* In a trifle bowl, layer ingredients in this order: cake, pudding, candy, whipped topping. Repeat, making 2 or 3 layers.
* To prepare chocolate curls, melt 1/2 cup chocolate chips in microwave. Spread on wax paper. When hardened, use vegetable peeler or cheese slicer to make curls. Garnish.

Marge Aultman, Margo Colasanti

DIRT DESSERT

Serves: 12

1/2 stick butter or margarine,
  softened
1 (8-ounce) package cream cheese,
  softened
1 cup powdered sugar
3-1/2 cups milk

2 small packages instant vanilla or
  chocolate pudding
1 (12-ounce) container frozen whipped
  topping, thawed
2 (20-ounce) packages cream-filled
  chocolate sandwich cookies

* Cream butter, cream cheese and powdered sugar in large bowl.
* In another bowl mix milk, pudding and whipped topping. Combine mixtures.
* Crush cookies (not too fine) in food processor.
* Put 1/3 of crushed cookies in bottom of foil-lined clay pot or plastic sand pail.
* Add 1/2 pudding mixture.
* Layer 1/3 crushed cookies and remaining filling. Top with remaining crumbs.
* Can add plastic greens or flowers. Serve with garden spade or sand shovel.

Irene Kelly, Mary Gregory

GABINO SONTELINO'S WHITE CHOCOLATE MOUSSE

Must prepare ahead   Serves: 12

12 ounces white chocolate   *2 teaspoons vanilla*
2 cups whipping cream, well-chilled   *4 egg whites*
1 cup warm milk, divided   *pinch of salt*
1 envelope unflavored gelatin   *1/2 teaspoon lemon juice*
Raspberry Sauce:
1 (10-ounce) package frozen raspberries   *1 tablespoon kirsch (optional)*
3 tablespoons sugar

* Chop white chocolate in small pieces.
* Melt chocolate in 3/4 cup milk in the top of double boiler over hot not boiling water, stirring until smooth.
* Remove double boiler from heat and let chocolate stand.
* Soften gelatin in the remaining 1/4 cup of milk, stirring until smooth.
* Add softened gelatin to melted chocolate and mix thoroughly.
* Remove top of double boiler. Add vanilla.
* Allow chocolate mixture to cool to room temperature.
* Beat egg whites until foamy.
* Add salt and continue beating until almost stiff peak stage.
* Fold egg whites into chocolate mixture in thirds.
* Whip cream to soft mounds.
* Fold cream into chocolate mixture in thirds.
* Add lemon juice.
* Pour mixture into a stainless steel bowl and allow to chill for several hours before serving.
* To prepare Raspberry Sauce, thaw, puree and strain raspberries. Add sugar and kirsch, stirring until sugar is dissolved. Refrigerate.
* To serve, place a pool of raspberry sauce on individual dessert plates.
* Using an ice cream scoop, place 2 or 3 mounds of mousse in the sauce.

Catherine Whittington

DESSERT PIZZA

A lovely dessert using seasonal fruit

Easy   Serves: 12-16

1 package refrigerated sugar cookie
  dough or chocolate chip cookie dough
1 (8-ounce) package cream cheese,
  softened

1 (8-ounce) container frozen whipped
  topping, thawed
1 cup powdered sugar

Topping:
sliced fresh fruit of your choice (grapes
  strawberries, blueberries, kiwi)

lemon juice

* Spread cookie dough evenly on pizza pan.
* Bake at 350° for 20 minutes or until lightly browned.
* Beat cream cheese until smooth.
* Add powdered sugar and whipped topping; beat until smooth. Spread on cooled crust.
* Dip fruit pieces in lemon juice to keep fresh color. Arrange fruit on top.
* Refrigerate until ready to serve.

Linda Jones
Len Efrid

EGGNOG CREAM

Easy   Serves: 4

1-1/2 cups eggnog
1 small package instant vanilla pudding

1/2 pint whipping cream, whipped
nutmeg (optional)

* Combine eggnog and pudding mix. Beat at low speed until thick.
* Fold in whipped cream.
* Chill 30 minutes.
* Can sprinkle with nutmeg before serving.

Leslie Gebert

LEMON PUDDING CAKE
A cake which makes its own lemon sauce

Easy   Serves: 4

2 tablespoons butter, softened   3 tablespoons flour
1/2 cup sugar   2 eggs, separated
3 tablespoons lemon juice   1 teaspoon lemon zest
1 cup milk   whipped cream

* Cream butter and sugar. Add flour, lemon juice, zest, slightly beaten egg yolks and milk.
* Fold in stiffly beaten egg whites. Turn into greased 1-quart casserole.
* Place a larger pan on oven rack and set the smaller casserole in it. Add 1 inch of hot water to the larger pan.
* Bake at 350° for 40 minutes, or until top is golden and springs back when touched. (Note: There will be a cake-like top layer over a very thin sauce.)
* Spoon cake into bowls, topping with sauce.
* Serve hot with whipped cream.

Joanna Fox

ORANGE CHARLOTTE

Prepare ahead   Serves: 6

1 tablespoon gelatin (softened in 1   3 tablespoons lemon juice
  tablespoon cold water)   1 cup orange juice with pulp
1/3 cup cold water   3 egg whites
1/3 cup boiling water   1/2 pint whipping cream
1 cup sugar

* Add 1/3 cup cold water and then 1/3 cup boiling water to softened gelatin. Stir well.
* Add sugar, lemon juice, orange juice and pulp. Chill.
* When mixture begins to thicken, beat until frothy.
* Stiffly beat egg whites. Beat whipping cream.
* Gently fold egg whites and whipped cream into orange mixture.
* Pour into mold and chill until firm.
* Garnish with orange wedges or a sprig of mint.

Georgia Draucker

MERINGUE CAKE WITH CARAMEL-STRAWBERRY SAUCE

Gorgeous - looks like an angel food cake

Prepare ahead   Serves: 12

superfine sugar   *1/4 teaspoon almond extract*
8 egg whites, room temperature   *2 tablespoons hot water*
1/4 teaspoon cream of tartar   *2 tablespoons light corn syrup*
1/8 teaspoon salt   *1/2 cup superfine sugar*
1 cup superfine sugar
Strawberry Sauce:
1/4 cup sugar   *2 tablespoons framboise or Triple Sec*
20 ounces frozen strawberries, thawed   *liqueur*
strawberries for garnish

* Sprinkle sugar in generously buttered 12-cup Bundt pan. Tap out excess sugar.
* Cut parchment paper to cover top of pan. Butter paper on one side.
* In a large bowl, beat egg whites until frothy.
* Add cream of tartar and salt, beating until soft peaks form. Gradually add sugar, beating until whites are stiff.
* Stir in almond extract.
* Carefully spoon mixture into Bundt pan, smoothing surface. Cover with parchment, buttered side down.
* Place Bundt pan in a deep roasting pan. Add enough boiling water to roasting pan to submerge Bundt pan half way.
* Bake in a pre-heated 350° oven until top of meringue rises about 1 inch above edge of pan and is lightly colored, about 30 minutes.
* Remove Bundt pan to a rack to cool thoroughly.
* When meringue is cool, remove parchment from top. Submerge Bundt pan in warm water for several seconds. Invert onto serving plate.
* In a small saucepan, combine hot water and corn syrup. Add sugar.
* Cook over low heat, stirring occasionally until sugar dissolves. Increase heat and boil until caramel colored.
* Remove from heat and cool until slightly thickened. Drizzle over meringue.
* In food processor, combine sauce ingredients and puree.
* Strain and refrigerate.
* Just before serving, fill center of meringue with berries.
* Spoon strawberry sauce around meringue.
* Meringue may be baked 2 days ahead, covered with plastic wrap and refrigerated.

Pat Kelly

PAVLOVA
Very light, but impressive and a family favorite

Prepare ahead   Serves: 8-10

4 egg whites (at room temperature)   2 teaspoons cornstarch
pinch of salt   2 cups whipped cream
1 cup sugar   fruit to garnish (strawberries, bananas, kiwi
1 teaspoon white vinegar   or raspberries
1/2 teaspoon vanilla

* Beat egg whites with pinch of salt until stiff.
* Gradually add sugar, vinegar and vanilla.
* Sift cornstarch and fold in lightly.
* Place foil on tray; grease and dust lightly with cornstarch.
* Heap mixture onto foil in a circle.
* Place in preheated 400° oven. Immediately reduce temperature to 250°. Bake
  undisturbed for 1-1/2 hours.
* Cool and top with whipped cream and sliced fruit.

Variation: Flavor whipped cream with 1 teaspoon of instant coffee and sprinkle with
shaved chocolate if fruits are not available.

Viv Buszko

PEACH CRISP

Easy   Serves: 4-6

4 cups peaches, peeled and sliced   1 cup flour
3/4 cup sugar   1 stick margarine, softened
1/2 teaspoon cinnamon   ice cream

* Place peaches in greased 1-quart baking dish.
* Spoon half of sugar and the cinnamon over peaches.
* Cut butter into flour. Add remaining sugar. Mixture should be crumbly.
* Spoon mixture over peaches.
* Bake at 375° for 30 to 40 minutes.
* Serve warm with ice cream.

Marwen McDowell

PUMPKIN ROLL

This will become a holiday tradition.

Serves: 8-10

3 eggs
1 cup sugar
2/3 cup canned pumpkin
1 teaspoon lemon extract
3/4 cup flour
1/2 teaspoon salt
Filling:
1 (8-ounce) package cream cheese,
  softened
4 tablespoons margarine, softened

1 teaspoon ginger
2 teaspoons cinnamon
1/2 teaspoon nutmeg
1 teaspoon baking soda
1 cup chopped walnuts

1 cup powdered sugar
1 teaspoon vanilla

* Beat eggs 5 minutes, slowly adding sugar. Add pumpkin and lemon extract.
* Combine dry ingredients and add to pumpkin mixture.
* Pour into greased and floured 15x10-inch jellyroll pan. Bake at 375° for 15 minutes.
* Turn out on towel sprinkled with powdered sugar. Beginning at short end, roll up cake and towel together. Set aside to cool.
* Beat cream cheese and margarine together until smooth. Add sugar and mix well. Add vanilla and beat until smooth.
* Unroll cake. Remove towel. Spread filling on cake. Roll up again. Slice to serve.

Carol Lawing, Kathryn Smith

BERRIES "N" CREAM

1 (15-ounce) can sweetened
  condensed milk
1/3 cup lemon juice
1 tablespoon grated lemon rind

1 pint fresh strawberries
1 cup heavy cream
8 ladyfingers, split

* Combine first 3 ingredients. Fold in berries.
* Whip 1/2 cup cream until stiff. Fold into berry mixture.
* Line 9x5-inch loaf pan with ladyfinger halves.
* Pour berry mixture into pan.
* Refrigerate until firm, at least 4 hours. Invert on plate.
* Whip remaining cream. Spread on top and sides of cake. Decorate with extra berries.

Barbara Kane

RAISIN-APPLE MERINGUE

Serves: 4

1 pound peeled and cored cooking
    apples
4 ounces seedless raisins
1/4 cup sugar

juice of 1 orange
1 tablespoon rum or orange juice
2 egg whites
1/2 cup sugar

* Slice the apples. Put apples, raisins, 1/4 cup sugar, orange juice and rum (or extra orange juice) in a shallow 2-quart baking dish.
* Cover with lid and cook at 300° for 30 to 40 minutes until apples are tender. Remove from oven.
* Whisk egg whites until stiff. Whisk in 1/4 cup sugar, then fold in remaining 1/4 cup sugar. Pile or pipe meringue over apples.
* Return to oven for 35 minutes until meringue is set or golden color.
* Serve hot or cold with whipped cream.

Joan Bolton

SNOWBALL DESSERT
Attractive and delicious

Easy - Must be prepared ahead

Serves: 10-12

2 envelopes unflavored gelatin
1 cup boiling water
1 cup sugar
1 (20-ounce) can crushed pineapple,
    undrained

juice of 1 lemon
1 (12-ounce) carton frozen whipped topping
1 angel food cake, torn into pieces
1 (3-1/2-ounce) can flaked coconut

* Sprinkle gelatin over boiling water and stir.
* Add sugar, pineapple and lemon juice. Stir. Refrigerate until slightly thickened.
* Add 1/2 of whipped topping to gelatin mixture.
* Place a layer of cake pieces into 2-1/2-quart mold or dish. Top with a layer of gelatin mixture.
* Repeat until all cake and gelatin mixture is used.
* Refrigerate until set. Unmold cake.
* Frost with remaining whipped topping and sprinkle with coconut.

Karen Barry

HAWAIIAN TRIFLE

An elegant dessert - wonderful at Christmas

Must be prepared ahead   Serves: 16-20

2 frozen purchased pound cake loaves
1 (10 or 15-ounce) package coconut
  cookies, crumbled
1-1/2 cups cream sherry, divided
1/4 cup plus 2 tablespoons brandy,
  divided
2/3 cup guava jelly
Pastry Cream:
12 egg yolks
1 cup sugar
1 cup flour

2/3 cup pineapple preserves
1-1/2 cups shredded sweetened coconut,
  toasted
1 cup whipping cream
2 tablespoons powdered sugar
1 teaspoon cream sherry
1/2 cup macadamia nuts (optional)

4 cups hot milk
2 tablespoons butter
1 tablespoon vanilla

* Prepare Pastry Cream first by combining egg yolks and sugar in top of double boiler. Beat until mixture thickens.
* Add flour, stir until well blended.
* Gradually add hot milk, beating constantly.
* Cook over boiling water, stirring constantly until thickened and smooth.
* Remove from heat. Add butter and vanilla. Stir until butter melts and vanilla is blended.
* Cover with plastic wrap, pressing directly onto pudding (this step is very important).
* Cool completely.
* Slice cakes into 1/4-inch slices.
* Line bottom of 16-cup trifle bowl with enough cake slices to cover.
* Evenly spread half the cookie crumbs on top.
* Spoon 3/4 cup sherry and 3 tablespoons brandy over crumbs.
* Spread with guava jelly and 1/3 of the pastry cream.
* Repeat layers using pineapple preserves and topping with 1/2 of the toasted coconut.
* Put third layer of cake on coconut, spread with last 1/3 of pastry cream.
* Whip the cream, adding powdered sugar and sherry. Spoon over pastry cream. Sprinkle with remaining coconut.
* Garnish with finely chopped macadamia nuts if desired.
* Chill.

Dougi O'Bryan

RASPBERRY-ANGEL TRIFLE
A feast for the eyes as well as the palate

Must be prepared ahead   Serves: 12-15

1 cup whipping cream
1 small package instant vanilla pudding
1 teaspoon almond extract
1 medium size angel food cake, torn
   into 1-inch pieces (8 to 10 cups)

1 (16-ounce) jar seedless raspberry
   preserves
1 cup raspberries (fresh if available)
1/2 cup slivered almonds

* Beat well-chilled whipping cream in chilled bowl until stiff.
* Prepare pudding as directed on package.
* Fold whipped cream and almond extract into pudding.
* Alternate 3 layers each of cake pieces, raspberry jam and pudding mixture in a 3-quart trifle bowl or deep glass bowl.
* Toast slivered almonds in shallow baking dish in 350° oven for approximately 5 minutes. Cool.
* Sprinkle toasted almonds over trifle and garnish with fresh raspberries.
* Refrigerate at least 5 hours before serving.

Lea Tsahakis

APPLE CRUMB PIE

Easy   Yields: 1 pie

2/3 cup shortening
1 teaspoon salt
1/4 cup boiling water
1-1/2 cups flour
6 apples, pared, cored, sliced
1/4 to 1/2 cup sugar

1 teaspoon cinnamon
pinch of salt
1/3 cup butter
1/4 to 1/2 cup sugar
3/4 cup flour

* Cream shortening with salt. Add boiling water and mix well. Add flour and mix well.
* Press into 9 to 10-inch pie plate.
* Place apple slices evenly over crust. Sprinkle sugar, cinnamon and salt over apples.
* Cream butter with sugar and flour. Spoon mixture over apples.
* Bake pie at 450° for 10 minutes. Reduce temperature to 350° and bake an additional 30 minutes or until topping begins to brown.

Laurie Guy

FRENCH APPLE PIE

Yields: 1 pie

6 cups tart apples, sliced
1-1/4 teaspoons ground cinnamon
1-1/4 teaspoons ground nutmeg
1 cup sugar
3/4 cup milk
2 eggs

2 tablespoons butter, softened
1 cup biscuit baking mix
1/2 cup chopped nuts
1/3 cup brown sugar
3 tablespoons butter

* Grease 10-inch deep-dish pie plate.
* Mix apples, cinnamon, nutmeg and sugar. Spoon into pie plate.
* Beat milk, eggs and butter until smooth. Pour over apples.
* Mix remaining ingredients until crumbly and sprinkle over pie.
* Bake at 325° for 55 to 60 minutes.

Lynda Dobbins

GOURMET APRICOT PIE

Prepare ahead

Yields: 1 pie

1/2 cup firmly packed light brown sugar
1/3 cup flour
1/4 cup butter
2 cups sour cream
1 cup sugar
4 tablespoons flour

1/4 teaspoon salt
1 teaspoon almond extract
2 eggs
3/4 cup dried apricots, cut in small pieces
1/2 cup water
1 (9-inch) unbaked pie shell

* Using fork or pastry blender, mix first 3 ingredients until crumbly. Set aside.
* Combine apricots and water. Cook over medium heat until tender. Drain any excess water. Cool slightly.
* Combine sour cream, sugar, flour, salt, almond extract and eggs. Beat well with electric mixer. Fold in apricots. Pour mixture into pie shell.
* Bake at 400° for 25 minutes.
* Remove from oven; sprinkle topping on pie.
* Return to oven and bake for 20 minutes. Cool.
* Chill and serve with whipped cream.

Dougi O'Bryan

CHOCOLATE CHESS PIE

Easy   Yields: 2 pies

1-3/4 cups sugar   1/4 cup evaporated milk
1/3 cup cocoa   1 teaspoon vanilla
1-1/4 cups butter or margarine, melted   2 (9-inch) unbaked pie shells
4 eggs, beaten

* Combine sugar, cocoa and melted butter. Mix well.
* Add eggs, evaporated milk and vanilla. Mix well.
* Pour mixture into 2 pie shells. Bake at 350° for 40 to 50 minutes or until middle is set.

Rose Hegele
Karen Pritchett

CHOCOLATE FRENCH SILK PIE

Easy - Prepare ahead   Yields: 1 pie

2 egg whites   1/4 pound butter
1/8 teaspoon salt   2/3 cup sugar
1/8 teaspoon cream of tartar   2 eggs
1/2 cup sugar   1 teaspoon vanilla
1/2 cup broken pecans   1/2 pint heavy cream, whipped
1/2 teaspoon vanilla (or rum)   grated chocolate
1 square unsweetened chocolate

* Beat egg whites until foamy. Add salt and cream of tartar.
* Add sugar gradually and beat until very stiff. Fold in pecans and vanilla. Spread over
  bottom and up sides of greased 9-inch pie plate.
* Bake at 300° for 55 minutes. Cool.
* Melt chocolate and let cool.
* Cream butter and sugar together.
* Add eggs one at a time, beating 5 minutes after each egg is added.
* Stir in cooled chocolate and vanilla.
* Pour into meringue shell. Chill overnight.
* When served, top with whipped cream and grated chocolate.

Mary Lou Stafford
Judy Fahl, Happy Rogers

CHOCOLATE MOUSSE PIE

A drop-dead-delicious dessert for dinner parties

Prepare ahead   Serves: 10-12

3 cups chocolate wafer crumbs   *4 egg yolks*
1/2 cup butter, melted   *3 cups whipping cream, separated*
1 pound semi-sweet chocolate   *4 egg whites, beaten until stiff*
2 whole eggs   *6 tablespoons powdered sugar*

* Combine crumbs and melted butter. Press into springform pan and chill.
* Melt chocolate in top of double boiler; cool to lukewarm.
* Add whole eggs, mix well. Add yolks, beat well.
* Whip 2 cups of the cream until firm.
* Fold small amount into chocolate to lighten.
* Fold chocolate mixture into whipped cream, then fold in beaten egg whites.
* Pour into crust and chill 6 hours or more.
* Whip remaining 1 cup cream. Add sugar to taste and spread on top.
* Chill or freeze.

Dottie Hollowell

GERMAN CHOCOLATE PIE

Yields: 4 pies

6 eggs   *1/2 teaspoon almond extract*
1 stick margarine, melted   *1 medium can coconut*
4 cups sugar   *3/4 cup chopped nuts*
4 tablespoons flour   *1 (12-ounce) can evaporated milk*
1/2 cup cocoa   *4 frozen pie shells*
1 tablespoon vanilla

* Mix all ingredients together, beating well after each addition.
* Pour in equal parts into 4 pie shells.
* Bake at 325° for 50 minutes or until pies are set and tops begin to crack.

Note: Recipe can be halved. Good to make one for family and give others to friends.
Almond flavoring gives a little different taste.

Ellen Knott

MOM'S CHOCOLATE MERINGUE PIE

An old recipe and a favorite of my family

Easy   Yields: 2 pies

3 cups milk   *1/2 stick butter*
5 eggs, separated   *1 tablespoon vanilla*
2 cups sugar   *2 (9-inch) pie shells, baked and cooled*
1/2 cup cocoa   *10 tablespoons sugar*
6 tablespoons flour

* Scald milk. Beat egg yolks. Add to milk.
* Sift flour, 2 cups sugar and cocoa together.
* Add dry ingredients to milk and eggs; mix on low speed with electric mixer until well blended.
* Cook over medium heat until mixture thickens. This only takes a few minutes, so stir constantly. Remove from heat. Add butter and vanilla.
* Allow to cool until butter melts. Stir mixture well. Pour into pie shells.
* Beat reserved egg whites until fluffy, gradually adding sugar. Spread meringue over pie. Bake at 350° about 10 minutes or until slightly golden.
* Cool and serve.

Karen Peters

FUDGE PIE

Yields: 1 pie

1/4 pound butter   *1/4 teaspoon salt*
2 squares unsweetened chocolate   *1 teaspoon vanilla*
2 eggs   *1/3 cup chopped pecans*
1 cup sugar   *vanilla or coffee ice cream*
1/4 cup flour

* Melt butter and chocolate over low heat.
* Combine eggs and sugar.
* Add chocolate mixture, flour, salt, vanilla and nuts, mixing well.
* Pour into a 9-inch pie pan. Bake at 350° for 30 minutes.
* Just before serving, top with vanilla or coffee ice cream.
* Can be made ahead and frozen.

Jan Tucker

OLD-FASHIONED LEMON CHESS PIE

Easy   Yields: 1 pie

1 unbaked 9-inch pie crust   *1/3 cup milk*
2 cups sugar   *1/4 cup butter, melted*
4 eggs   *1/4 cup lemon juice*
1 tablespoon flour   *2 teaspoons grated lemon rind*
1 tablespoon cornmeal

* Combine sugar, flour and cornmeal.
* Add eggs and mix well.
* Gradually add milk, lemon juice, melted butter and lemon rind.
* Pour into unbaked pie shell.
* Bake at 375° for 45 minutes.

Mildred Thompson

ENGLISH PIE
Good with holiday meals

Yields: 2 pies

4 large eggs   *1 cup raisins*
2 cups sugar   *1/2 teaspoon cinnamon*
1/2 stick butter, melted   *1/2 teaspoon nutmeg*
1 tablespoon vinegar   *1/2 teaspoon allspice*
1 tablespoon vanilla   *2 (8-inch) unbaked pie shells*
1 cup chopped pecans   *1 pint whipping cream, whipped*

* Separate yolks and egg whites and beat separately, beating yolks about 1 minute and whites until soft peaks form.
* Add sugar and butter to yolks, mixing about 30 seconds.
* Add vinegar, vanilla, pecans, raisins and spices to yolk-sugar mixture, stirring well.
* Fold in egg whites.
* Pour into pie shells.
* Bake at 350° for 35 to 45 minutes. Top will be crusty.
* Top with whipped cream to serve.

Janet Povall

OATMEAL PIE

Easy   Yields: 1 pie

1/2 stick butter or margarine   *2/3 cup rolled oats*
2 eggs, beaten   *1 teaspoon vanilla*
2/3 cup dark corn syrup   *1 (10-inch) unbaked pie shell*
2/3 cup sugar

* Mix ingredients in order listed. Pour into unbaked pie shell.
* Bake at 325° for 40 minutes or until firm. Cool before serving.

Martha Schmitt

ORANGE-APPLE TART
(Tarte aux Pommes et aux Oranges)

Serves: 6

1 large unbaked deep-dish pie shell   *3 to 4 Red or Golden Delicious apples*
2 pounds tart cooking apples, peeled,   *3 to 4 tablespoons apricot jam*
  cored and quartered   *1/2 teaspoon cinnamon*
1/2 cup white wine   *5 to 6 whole cloves*
1 strip lemon rind   *2 thin-skinned oranges, thinly sliced*
4 tablespoons butter   *1/2 cup water*
1 cup sugar, divided

* Put apple quarters in saucepan with wine, a strip of lemon rind, butter and 1/4 cup sugar, as well as all spices. Cover and simmer until tender.
* Remove lemon rind and cloves. Puree apples in sieve or blender.
* Place apple puree in unbaked pie shell.
* Peel and thinly slice the Delicious apples and place overlapping slices on top of puree.
* Sprinkle with 1/4 cup sugar and bake at 375° until crust is brown.
* To make orange glaze, combine 1/2 cup sugar and 1/2 cup of water in saucepan and bring to boil.
* Add orange slices to sugar water. Poach until tender.
* Remove orange slices and place on top of cooked apple tart.
* Boil remaining syrup until it begins to thicken. Add apricot jam and glaze top of tart.
* Cool and serve.

Frederick King

PEACH PIE
A family favorite for generations

Easy   Yields: 1 pie

1 unbaked pie shell   *2 eggs*
3 to 4 peaches (or equivalent frozen peach *juice of 1 lemon*
* halves), peeled and halved*   *1/2 teaspoon vanilla*
1 cup sugar   *4 tablespoons butter*
2-1/2 tablespoons flour   *whipped cream*

* Line uncooked pie shell with peach halves.
* Mix all ingredients (except butter) and pour over pie.
* Dot with butter.
* Bake 325° for 1 hour or until set.
* Serve with whipped cream.

Note: I freeze peach halves on cookie sheet, then place in baggies to use all winter.

Betty Mullen

PEANUT BUTTER PIE
Rave reviews

Easy   Yields: 2 pies

24 chocolate sandwich cookies, crushed   *2 cups powdered sugar*
1 stick margarine, melted   *1 (16-ounce) carton frozen whipped*
1 cup peanut butter, smooth or crunchy   * topping, thawed*
1 (8-ounce) package cream cheese,   *1 jar chocolate ice cream topping*
* softened*

* Mix together cookie crumbs and margarine. Press into 2 deep-dish pie pans sprayed with non-stick vegetable spray.
* Mix peanut butter, cream cheese and powdered sugar together until well blended. Fill pie shells.
* Spread 1/2 of whipped topping on each pie. Swirl chocolate topping over pie.
* Can be frozen.

Diddy Irwin

EASY PEAR TART

Serves: 6-8

1 package frozen commercial puff
    pastry sheets, thawed
5 firm pears

4 tablespoons sugar
2 tablespoons kirsch
1/2 cup pear preserves

* Arrange 1 puff pastry sheet flat on a cookie sheet.
* Cut remaining sheet into 1-inch strips and using water, glue to edges of flat sheet to form a raised border.
* Chill thoroughly.
* Peel and core the pears. Cut pears in half and slice into paper-thin slices.
* Arrange the pear slices in overlapping rows on the chilled pastry.
* Sprinkle with sugar and kirsch.
* Bake at 400° for 15 to 20 minutes until sugar caramelizes and pastry is brown.
* Heat pear preserves in saucepan over low heat. Brush preserves over tart.
* Serve warm.

Steve Horsley

CARAMEL PECAN PIE
Very creamy with a wonderful flavor

Easy

Yields: 1 pie

1/2 cup sugar
1/2 cup firmly packed brown sugar
1 tablespoon flour
1/3 cup butter, melted
1/3 cup milk

1 tablespoon vanilla
1 egg, slightly beaten
1 to 1-1/2 cups coarsely chopped pecans
1 (9-inch) pie crust, unbaked

* Mix sugars together. Stir in flour.
* Add butter, milk, egg and vanilla.
* Fold in pecans. Pour into pie shell.
* Bake at 300° for 40 to 50 minutes or until firm.
* May be served warm or at room temperature.

Dougie O'Bryan
Linda Pickens

PECAN FUDGE PIE

Easy - Prepare ahead   Yields: 1 pie

1 (9-inch) unbaked pastry shell
2 squares unsweetened chocolate
1/4 cup margarine or butter
1 (14-ounce) can sweetened condensed
   milk
1/2 cup hot water

2 eggs, well beaten
1 teaspoon vanilla
1/8 teaspoon salt
1-1/2 cups pecan pieces
vanilla ice cream (optional)
whipped cream (optional)

* Melt chocolate and margarine in medium saucepan over low heat.
* Stir in condensed milk, hot water and eggs. Mix well.
* Remove from heat and stir in other ingredients.
* Pour into pie shell. Bake at 350° for 40 to 45 minutes. Cool.
* Chill 3 hours.
* Serve with vanilla ice cream or whipped cream.

Pam McLean

REALLY LETHAL PECAN PIE

Yields: 2 pies

1-1/4 cups dark corn syrup
1 cup firmly packed light brown sugar
4 tablespoons unsalted butter
4 large eggs
1 teaspoon vanilla

2-1/2 cups pecans, broken into coarse
   pieces
1/4 teaspoon salt
2 (9-inch) unbaked pie shells

* Combine corn syrup and sugar in 1-quart saucepan.
* Stir over moderate heat until sugar has dissolved. Bring to boil and cook 2 to 3
  minutes.
* Remove from heat and stir in butter.
* In 2-quart mixing bowl, beat eggs well with wire whisk or electric mixer.
* Continue to beat while slowly pouring in syrup mixture.
* Stir in vanilla, pecans and salt. Pour mixture into pie shells.
* Place on center rack of oven. Bake at 350° for 45 to 50 minutes, or until filling has set.
* You may want to cover crust with foil to prevent burning.

Elaine Hoffmann

LILLIAN'S PRALINE PUMPKIN PIE
Will be the hit of any holiday dinner

Easy

Yields: 1 pie

1 (9-inch) unbaked pie shell
1/3 cup ground pecans
1 cup firmly packed brown sugar,
    divided
2 tablespoons butter or margarine,
    softened
2 eggs, well beaten

1 cup pumpkin (cooked or canned)
2/3 cup firmly packed brown sugar
1 tablespoon flour
1/2 teaspoon pumpkin pie spice
1/4 teaspoon cinnamon
1 cup undiluted evaporated milk

* Combine pecans, 1/3 cup brown sugar and butter. Press firmly into bottom of pie shell.
* Bake at 450° for 10 minutes.
* Combine eggs, pumpkin, remaining brown sugar, flour and spices.
* Blend in evaporated milk, beating until mixture is smooth and creamy. Pour into pie shell.
* Reduce oven temperature to 325°. Return pie to oven. Bake 50 to 60 minutes.

Karen Ignatz

FRENCH RHUBARB PIE

Yields: 1 pie

1 (9-inch) pie shell
1 cup sugar
2 tablespoons flour
1 egg, well beaten
Topping:
1/3 cup butter
1/2 cup brown sugar

1/2 teaspoon vanilla
2 cups rhubarb (or apples cut in small
    pieces)

3/4 cup flour

* Mix flour and sugar; stir in egg; add vanilla and rhubarb.
* Spoon rhubarb mixture into pie shell.
* To prepare topping, cream butter and sugar together.
* Work in flour with pastry blender or cut it with edge of spoon. Sprinkle over rhubarb.
* Bake at 400° for 15 minutes. Reduce heat to 350° and bake 30 minutes or until done.
* Watch carefully as this pie browns very quickly; reduce heat if necessary.

Pat Kelly

SHERRY CHIFFON PIE

Prepare ahead   Yields: 2 pies

2 graham cracker pie crusts   *1/2 teaspoon salt*
1 tablespoon gelatin   *4 eggs, separated*
1/4 cup water   *1 cup heavy cream, whipped*
1 cup sugar, divided   *1/3 cup sherry*
1/2 cup milk   *macadamia nuts, crushed*

* Dissolve gelatin in water.
* In top of a double boiler, combine 1/2 cup sugar, milk, salt and egg yolks; cook and stir until thickened. Cool. Stir in dissolved gelatin.
* In separate bowl, whip egg whites until stiff. Slowly beat in 1/2 cup sugar.
* After custard has cooled, beat it with whisk until fluffy.
* Fold egg whites into custard; fold in whipped cream.
* Stir in sherry and spoon into pie shells.
* Chill thoroughly. Sprinkle with nuts before serving.

Lillian Worthy

SQUASH PIE

A surprising use for summer squash while it is so abundant

Easy   Yields: 2 pies

2 cups cooked yellow squash   *1 stick margarine, melted*
1-1/2 cups sugar   *1 tablespoon lemon flavoring*
3 tablespoons flour   *1 tablespoon coconut flavoring*
3 eggs, beaten   *2 (9-inch) uncooked pie shells*

* Drain cooked squash thoroughly and mash in mixer or food processor.
* Combine sugar and flour and add to squash.
* Stir in eggs, margarine and flavorings.
* Prick pie crusts sparingly on bottom and sides.
* Cook crusts at 400° for 4 to 5 minutes. Remove from oven. Pour in squash filling.
* Return to oven and cook at 400° for 15 minutes.
* Reduce temperature to 300° and bake until thoroughly set and golden brown.
* If crust browns too rapidly, cover with aluminum foil lightly placed on top of pies.

Margaret Melton

SWEET POTATO PIE

Prepare ahead   Serves: 12

2 cups crushed pretzels
1-1/2 sticks margarine, melted
3 cups cooked sweet potatoes
1 cup sugar
1 teaspoon vanilla

1 stick margarine, melted
1 (8-ounce) package cream cheese, softened
1 (8-ounce) container frozen whipped
   topping, thawed
1 cup sugar

* Mix pretzel crumbs and melted margarine.
* Press into 13x9-inch pan.
* Bake at 325° for 15 minutes. Cool.
* Mix together sweet potatoes, sugar, vanilla and melted margarine.
* Spread on top of crust.
* Combine cream cheese and sugar; beat well. Fold in whipped topping.
* Spread on top of potato mixture. Chill.

Vernie Pickens

JARRETT HOUSE VINEGAR PIE
House dessert at Jarrett House in Dillsboro, N. C.

Yields: 1 pie

1-1/2 cups sugar
1/2 cup butter or margarine, melted
   and cooled
3 beaten eggs

2 tablespoons flour
2 tablespoons cider vinegar
1 tablespoon vanilla
1 (9-inch) unbaked pie shell

* In large bowl, beat first 5 ingredients with electric mixer on high speed about 1 minute until smooth. Stir in vanilla.
* Pour into pie shell.
* Bake at 300° for 50 minutes, or until top forms pale golden crust (inside will be slightly liquid). Cool.
* Serve at room temperature.

Ellen Knott

BEST EVER PRALINES AND CREAM

No one can resist this ice cream dessert.

Must prepare ahead   Serves: 12

1/2 cup rolled oats
1/2 cup firmly packed brown sugar
2 sticks butter
1 cup chopped pecans

2 cups flour
2 (12-ounce) jars of caramel or
    butterscotch topping
1/2 gallon vanilla ice cream, softened

* Mix first 5 ingredients.
* Bake in 13x9-inch greased pan at 350° for 20 minutes.
* Stir every 5 minutes. Mixture will be crumbly.
* Cool and divide mixture in half.
* Put half of crumbs in bottom of 13x9-inch pan.
* Pour 1 jar of caramel topping over crumbs.
* Put softened ice cream on topping.
* Pour other jar of topping over ice cream.
* Sprinkle with rest of crumbs.
* Freeze.

Ellen Knott

FROZEN GRAND MARNIER CREAM

Easy - Must prepare ahead   Serves: 4-6

2 egg whites
salt (pinch)
6 tablespoons sugar, divided

1 cup whipping cream
1/4 cup Grand Marnier
fresh fruit

* Beat egg whites with salt until soft peaks form.
* Beat in 3 tablespoons sugar until egg whites are stiff and shiny.
* Whip cream with 3 tablespoons sugar.
* Add to egg whites and fold in Grand Marnier.
* Freeze for several hours.
* Serve in compotes with fresh raspberries, sliced strawberries, peaches or blueberries.

Jean Wilkinson

KAHLÚA FREEZE DELIGHT

Easy - Must prepare ahead   Serves: 12

28 chocolate sandwich cookies, crushed   4 squares semi-sweet chocolate
1/4 cup margarine, melted   6 tablespoons margarine
1/2 gallon coffee ice cream, softened   4 tablespoons kahlúa
1/3 cup kahlúa   1 (16-ounce) carton frozen whipped
1 cup sugar   topping, thawed
1 (5-ounce) can evaporated milk   1 cup pecans, lightly toasted, buttered and
1 teaspoon vanilla   lightly salted

* Mix cookie crumbs and margarine together and spread in greased 13x9-inch pan.
* Beat ice cream and 1/3 cup kahlúa. Spread on top of cookie crust. Freeze.
* Place sugar, milk, vanilla, chocolate and margarine in saucepan. Boil for 1 minute. Cool.
* Add remaining kahlúa.
* Pour over ice cream and refreeze.
* Stir toasted nuts into the whipped topping. Spread on top of chocolate. Freeze.

Variation: Substitute vanilla ice cream for coffee ice cream and amaretto for kahlúa. Spread 1 (16-ounce) jar of raspberry preserves on top of ice cream.

Anonymous

FROZEN LEMON CRÈME

Must prepare ahead   Serves: 4-5

1 cup milk   juice of 2 large lemons
1 cup heavy cream   grated rind of 2 lemons
1 cup sugar   4 to 5 large lemons, hollowed (optional)

* Stir together milk, heavy cream and sugar until dissolved.
* Pour into pan and freeze until mushy.
* Add grated rind and lemon juice.
* Beat with rotary beater and freeze again about 2 hours (until mushy).
* Beat again thoroughly and freeze until solid.
* Can serve in hollowed whole lemon shells.

Donna Penzell

TURKISH DELIGHT

My version of the Sea Island Golf Club's Turkish Cassada

Must prepare ahead   Serves: 10-12

1 box brownie mix   *1 jar fudge sauce*
1/2 gallon coffee ice cream, softened   *chopped pecans to garnish*
1 jar caramel sauce

* Prepare brownie mix according to package directions and pour into well-greased 10-inch springform pan.
* Bake until done. Cool thoroughly in pan.
* Mound ice cream on top of brownie and freeze.
* Spoon thin layer of caramel sauce on top of ice cream and freeze.
* Spoon thin layer of fudge sauce on top of caramel sauce. Sprinkle with pecans.
* Freeze until ready to serve.
* When ready to serve, remove from pan and slice in wedges.

Lee Russo

CRANBERRY SHERBET

Easy   Serves: 12

1 pound cranberries   *1 (6-ounce) can frozen orange juice,*
4 cups water   *thawed*
1-1/2 to 2 cups sugar   *2 egg whites*
1 small package orange-flavored gelatin

* Cook cranberries in water until soft. Force mixture through foley mill or strainer. Discard hulls.
* Add gelatin and sugar to cranberry liquid, stirring until dissolved. Add orange juice.
* Freeze until soft-frozen. Beat mixture.
* Beat egg whites until soft peaks form. Add to cranberry mixture.
* Freeze thoroughly. Cover with plastic wrap when frozen.
* Keeps frozen for several weeks.

Lynn Frankenfield

POP'S LEMON SHERBET
Serve with pretzels.

Yields: 3 quarts

1-1/3 cups lemon juice (about 12 lemons)   2 cups sugar
grated rind of 3 lemons   2 quarts milk

* Mix lemon juice, grated rind and sugar.
* Place in 1 gallon ice cream churn.
* Churn until frosty and icy.
* Add 2 quarts milk and churn until frozen.
* Remove dasher and pack down for awhile in can to ripen.
* Serve with pretzels.

Becky Pickens

REPUBLICAN ICE CREAM CAKE

Easy - Must prepare ahead   Serves: 10-12

1/2 gallon vanilla ice cream, softened   1/2 cup sugar
30 chocolate sandwich cookies, crushed   1 (5-ounce) can evaporated milk
1/2 stick butter, melted   peanuts
2 bars German sweet chocolate

* Mix crushed cookies with melted butter. Press into ungreased 13x9-inch pan.
* Spread softened vanilla ice cream over cookie mixture. Place in freezer.
* Melt chocolate bars, sugar and evaporated milk over low heat. Stir and bring to a boil.
* Remove from heat immediately. Cool.
* Pour over ice cream. Sprinkle with chopped nuts.
* Return to freezer.

Laura Courter

AMARETTO ICE CREAM PIE

Easy - Must prepare ahead   Yields: 1 pie

1 quart vanilla ice cream, softened   *1 (9-inch) chocolate pie crust*
4 ounces amaretto liqueur

* Mix ice cream and amaretto in a blender or food processor.
* Spoon into pie shell.
* May sprinkle extra cookie crumbs on top.
* Cover pie with plastic wrap and refreeze at least 4 hours or overnight.

Terry Casto

Variation: Use 2 to 4 tablespoons crème de menthe syrup in place of amaretto.

Jean Moody

MISSISSIPPI PIE
One of our family's favorite desserts

Must prepare ahead   Serves: 12

1 cup flour   *1/4 cup dark brown sugar*
1/2 cup butter, softened   *1/2 gallon vanilla ice cream, softened*
1/2 cup chopped pecans
Caramel Sauce:
1/2 cup butter   *2 tablespoons corn syrup*
1-1/2 cups dark brown sugar   *1/2 cup milk or half-and-half*
1/8 teaspoon salt

* Mix flour, butter, sugar and pecans; spread in buttered 13x9-inch pan.
* Bake at 375° for 15 minutes or until lightly browned. Cool.
* Crumble crust with fork. Spread ice cream on crumbled crust and freeze.
* Cook sauce ingredients over medium heat about 15 minutes or until moderately
  thickened. Cool to room temperature.
* Pour over ice cream and refreeze.
* To serve, cut into squares.

Frances Fennebresque

PEANUT ICE CREAM PIE

Easy   Yields: 1 pie

1 (9-inch) graham cracker crust   *1/2 cup creamy peanut butter*
1 quart vanilla ice cream, softened   *2/3 cup chopped dry roasted salt-free*
1/2 cup light corn syrup   *   peanuts*

* Press half of ice cream in crust.
* In small bowl, stir corn syrup and peanut butter until well blended.
* Pour half of mixture over ice cream. Sprinkle with half of peanuts.
* Repeat layering. Freeze until firm, about 5 hours.
* Let pie stand at room temperature for 5 minutes for easy cutting.

Shirley Griffin

FROZEN STRAWBERRY PIE

Easy - Must prepare ahead   Yields: 1 pie

Crust:
1/2 cup butter, softened   *2 tablespoons sugar*
1 cup flour
Filling:
1 (10-ounce) package frozen   *2 teaspoons lemon juice*
*   strawberries, partially thawed*   *1/2 cup whipping cream*
1/2 cup sugar   *strawberry halves for garnish*
1 egg white

* Combine 1/2 cup butter with 2 tablespoons sugar (do not cream). Add 1 cup flour. Mix until dough forms.
* Crumble 1/4 to 1/3 cup of mixture in small pan.
* Press remaining dough in 9-inch pie pan.
* Bake both pans at 375° until brown. (Crumbs bake about 10 to 12 minutes.)
* Combine strawberries, sugar, egg white and lemon juice.
* Beat at highest speed until soft mounds form.
* Beat whipping cream until thickened. Fold into strawberry mixture.
* Spoon into pie shell, sprinkle with crumbs and decorate with strawberry halves.
* Freeze until firm, about 4 to 6 hours.

Mary Ann Little

BET'S WONDERFUL SAUCE

Easy

chocolate syrup
corn syrup

plain or crunchy peanut butter

* Mix ingredients in equal amounts. Serve over ice cream or pound cake.

Ellen Knott

CHOCOLATE SYRUP

Easy

Yields: 3 cups

6 squares unsweetened chocolate
2 cups sugar
1 stick margarine or butter

1 (12-ounce) can evaporated milk
1 teaspoon vanilla
dash of salt

* Melt chocolate squares in 1-quart pan. Add sugar, butter and salt; bring to boil.
* Add evaporated milk and vanilla. Return to boil. Remove from heat. Cool.
* Store in refrigerator.
* Serve warm over ice cream or use in making chocolate milk or hot chocolate.

Tonia Fuller

HOT FUDGE SAUCE

Easy

Yields: 12 servings

3 squares unsweetened chocolate
3/4 cup sugar
2 tablespoons flour
salt (pinch)

1/2 to 1 cup boiling water
1 teaspoon vanilla
1 tablespoon butter (optional)

* Mix first 5 ingredients. Add 1/2 cup boiling water; stir. Add more water if necessary. Cook slowly, stirring until desired thickness.
* Add vanilla (and butter if desired) after mixture is cooked.
* Serve warm. Store in refrigerator.

Louise Lucas, Donna Penzell

COOKIES
AND
CONFECTIONS

BRILLIANT CANDY SLICES

A lovely Christmas cookie!

Yields: 3 dozen

1 cup butter, softened	2-1/2 cups sifted flour
1 cup powdered sugar	1 cup walnut halves
1 egg	1 cup green candied cherries, halved
1 teaspoon vanilla	1 cup red candied cherries, halved

* Cream butter and sugar. Blend in egg, vanilla and flour.
* Stir in nuts and both candied cherries.
* Shape batter into small rolls and chill at least 3 hours.
* Cut rolls into 1/8-inch slices and place on ungreased cookie sheet.
* Bake at 350° for 12 to 15 minutes.
* Cool on wire rack.

Variation: Sprinkle with granulated sugar.

Betsy Chapman

YUMMY BUTTERSCOTCH COOKIES

Easy   Yields: 6 dozen

1 cup sugar	2 eggs, slightly beaten
1 cup powdered sugar	3-1/2 cups self-rising flour
1 cup margarine or butter, softened	1 cup whole wheat flour
1 cup vegetable oil	1 teaspoon cream of tartar
1 tablespoon almond extract	2 cups sliced almonds
1 tablespoon vanilla	1 (12-ounce) package butterscotch chips

* In large bowl mix both sugars, margarine and oil.
* Add flavorings and eggs. Mix well.
* Lightly spoon flour into measuring cup; level off.
* Stir together both flours and cream of tartar. Blend well with egg-sugar mixture.
* Stir in almonds and chips. Chill 2 hours.
* Drop by teaspoonfuls onto non-stick cookie sheet.
* Bake at 350° for 10 to 12 minutes or until lightly golden brown around the edges.

Dougi O'Bryan

EASY CHOCO-CHIPPER COOKIES

Not your basic chocolate chip cookies

Easy   Yields: 3-1/2 dozen

1 package deluxe white cake mix   *1 (6-ounce) package semi-sweet chocolate*
1/2 cup vegetable oil   *chips*
2 tablespoons water   *1/2 cup chopped pecans*
2 eggs

* Blend cake mix, oil, water and eggs.
* Stir in chocolate chips and nuts.
* Drop from teaspoon onto ungreased cookie sheet.
* Bake at 350° for 10 to 12 minutes. (Top of cookies will look pale.)
* Cool on cookie sheet for about 1 minute.
* Remove to rack to finish cooling.

Sandy Pettyjohn
Penny Pezdirtz

CHOCOLATE DREAM COOKIES

Yields: 2 dozen

2 tablespoons margarine   *1 cup self-rising flour*
1 (12-ounce) package chocolate chips   *1/2 cup chopped pecans*
1 (14-ounce) can sweetened condensed   *1 teaspoon vanilla*
* milk*

* Melt margarine and chocolate chips in top of double boiler.
* Stir in sweetened condensed milk.
* Remove from heat; add flour, nuts and vanilla.
* Drop by teaspoonfuls on cookie sheet covered with foil.
* Bake at 325° for 8 to 10 minutes. Do not overbake.
* Allow to cool before removing from foil.

Sharon Edge
Sally Teden

STUFFED DATE DROPS
A bit time-consuming, but different and delicious

Yields: 5-1/2 dozen

1 pound pitted dates (about 70)
1 (8-ounce) package pecan halves
1/4 cup shortening
3/4 cup brown sugar, packed
1 egg
Golden Icing:
1/2 cup butter
3 cups powdered sugar, sifted

1-1/4 cups flour, sifted
1/2 teaspoon baking powder
1/2 teaspoon baking soda
1/4 teaspoon salt
1/2 cup sour cream

3/4 teaspoon vanilla
3 tablespoons water

* Stuff dates with nuts. (Dates can be stuffed with nuts and refrigerated the night before baking.)
* Cream together shortening and sugar until light. Beat in egg.
* Sift together dry ingredients; add alternately with sour cream. Gently fold in dates.
* Drop onto greased cookie sheet (a date per cookie).
* Bake at 350° for 10 minutes. Cool and top with Golden Icing.
* To prepare icing, lightly brown butter. Remove from heat.
* Gradually beat in powdered sugar and vanilla.
* Slowly add water, 1 tablespoon at a time, until spreading consistency.

Dianne Blanke

PECAN DELIGHTS

Easy

Yields: 6-8 dozen

1 cup margarine
4 tablespoons powdered sugar
2 teaspoons vanilla

2 cups finely chopped pecans
2 cups sifted flour

* Beat margarine until soft.
* Add powdered sugar and mix until creamy. Add vanilla.
* Stir pecans and flour into batter.
* Shape into oblong rolls or balls. Bake at 300° for 45 minutes or until slightly brown.
* Roll in powdered sugar while hot and again when cooled.

Marie Bazemore

ELAINE'S RUBY COOKIES

Yields: 4-5 dozen

1 stick butter
3 tablespoons powdered sugar
1 cup sifted flour

1-1/2 teaspoons vanilla
1 cup finely ground pecans
seedless raspberry jam

* Cream butter and sugar. Stir in flour just until mixed to form soft dough.
* Add vanilla and nuts. Chill until firm.
* Roll dough into balls about the size of marbles or slightly larger.
* Place about 2 inches apart on ungreased cookie sheet.
* Use thumb or forefinger to make a hollow in the center of each.
* Fill hollow with jam (about 1/4 to 1/2 teaspoonful).
* Bake at 300° for 20 minutes or until lightly browned.
* Remove from cookie sheet at once. Cool completely on racks.

Pam Richey

FRUITCAKE COOKIES
A Christmas tradition

Yields: 7-8 dozen

2 pounds candied mixed fruit
3 cups flour, divided
1/2 cup butter or margarine, softened
1 cup brown sugar, firmly packed
4 eggs, beaten
3 tablespoons milk
1 teaspoon nutmeg

3 teaspoons baking soda
1 teaspoon cinnamon
1 teaspoon allspice
1 pound muscat raisins
1 pound coarsely chopped pecans
4 ounces whiskey

* Mix fruit with 1-1/2 cups flour.
* Cream butter with sugar. Add eggs and milk.
* Mix together remaining flour, nutmeg, baking soda, cinnamon and allspice.
* Add to butter mixture.
* Add fruit, nuts and whiskey. Stir well.
* Drop by teaspoonfuls onto greased cookie sheet.
* Bake at 325° for 15 to 20 minutes. Do not overbake. Cool on wire rack.

Sarah Howard

GINGER COOKIES
A good Christmas cookie

Easy   Yields: 4 dozen

2 cups flour   3/4 cup shortening
2 teaspoons ginger   1 cup sugar
2 teaspoons baking soda   1 egg
1 teaspoon cinnamon   1/4 cup molasses
1/2 teaspoon salt

* Sift together flour, ginger, baking soda, cinnamon and salt. Set aside.
* Cream shortening and sugar. Add egg and molasses. Mix well with flour mixture.
* Roll dough into teaspoon-sized balls. Roll each ball in sugar.
* Place on ungreased cookie sheet. Bake at 350° for 12 to15 minutes.

Alice Nance, Kathryn Smith

JUMBLE COOKIES
Better than chocolate chip cookies

Yields: 3-1/2 dozen

1-1/4 cups flour   1 teaspoon vanilla
1/2 teaspoon baking soda   2 cups crispy rice cereal
1/4 teaspoon salt   1 (6-ounce) package semi-sweet chocolate
1/2 cup margarine, softened   chips
1 cup sugar   1 cup raisins
1 egg

* Sift dry ingredients and set aside.
* Beat margarine and sugar until smooth. Blend in egg.
* Add dry mixture and blend well. Add vanilla. Stir in cereal, chocolate bits and raisins.
* Drop by teaspoonfuls onto greased cookie sheet. Bake at 350° for 10 to 12 minutes.

Betty Thalinger

Variation: Use 1/2 cup each brown sugar and granulated sugar. Omit raisins and add 1/2 cup rolled oats.

Jean Webb

LEMON YUMMIES

Easy   Yields: 6 dozen

1 cup shortening
1/2 cup firmly packed brown sugar
1/2 cup sugar
1 egg, well beaten
2 tablespoons lemon juice

1 tablespoon lemon rind, grated
2 cups flour
1/4 teaspoon soda
1/2 teaspoon salt
1/2 cup chopped pecans or walnuts

* Cream shortening, gradually adding both sugars. Beat until light and fluffy.
* Add egg, lemon juice and lemon rind. Beat mixture well.
* Combine dry ingredients. Add to creamed mixture. Stir in chopped nuts.
* Drop by teaspoonfuls onto lightly greased cookie sheet.
* Bake at 400° for 8 to 10 minutes.
* Cool on cookie sheet about 1 minute, then remove to wire rack and cool completely.

Laurie Guy

MACADAMIA NUT ANGELS

Yields: 48 bars

2 cups flour
1-1/3 cups sugar, divided
3/4 cup butter
3 eggs, separated
3/4 cup cake flour
1-1/2 teaspoons baking powder

1/4 teaspoon salt
1/4 cup oil
1/3 cup milk
1 teaspoon vanilla
1/2 cup macadamia nuts

* Combine flour and 1/2 cup sugar. Cut in butter until crumbly. Press mixture in bottom of a 13x9-inch pan.
* Bake at 350° for 15 minutes.
* Beat egg whites until frothy. Gradually add 1/2 cup sugar; continue beating until stiff.
* Sift cake flour, 1/3 cup sugar, baking powder and salt into a bowl.
* Make a well in this mixture and pour in oil, milk, egg yolks and vanilla. Mix well.
* Beat egg whites and fold into mixture. Fold in nuts.
* Pour batter over baked crust. Bake at 350° for 35 minutes. Cool.
* Sprinkle with powdered sugar and cut into bars.

Susan Basini

MINT CHOCOLATE COOKIES

Yields: 2-3 dozen

2/3 cup margarine, softened
2/3 cup sugar
1/3 cup brown sugar
1 egg
1 teaspoon vanilla

2 squares unsweetened chocolate, melted
  and cooled
1-1/2 cups flour
1 (6-ounce) package mint chocolate chips

* Cream margarine and sugars.
* Add egg, vanilla and melted chocolate.
* Beat at medium-high speed until fluffy.
* Add flour. Stir in mint chocolate chips.
* Drop by teaspoonfuls onto greased cookie sheet.
* Bake at 375° for 10 to 12 minutes.

Nancy Wohlbruck

AUNT MARY ANN'S SUPER COOKIES
You can't eat just one!

Yields: 8-9 dozen

1 cup sugar
1 cup firmly packed brown sugar
1 cup shortening
2 eggs
2 teaspoons vanilla
1 tablespoon milk
2 cups flour

1 teaspoon baking powder
1 teaspoon soda
1 teaspoon salt
3 cups rolled oats
1 (6-ounce) package chocolate chips
1 cup raisins

* Combine first 6 ingredients in large bowl.
* Sift together flour, baking powder, soda and salt; stir into sugar mixture.
* Add oats, chips and raisins, mixing well.
* Drop by teaspoonfuls 2 inches apart on a greased cookie sheet.
* Bake at 350° for 12 minutes.

Mary Ann Kempert Dzuree

LACY OATMEAL COOKIES

Yields: 3 dozen

2 cups rolled oats
1 cup firmly packed brown sugar
2 teaspoons baking powder

1 stick butter, melted
1 egg

* Mix all ingredients together.
* Line cookie sheet with wax paper.
* Drop dough by teaspoonfuls onto cookie sheet.
* Bake at 350° for 8 to 10 minutes.

Variation: While still warm, roll each cookie into tube shape and slightly press outer edge. Makes a pretty party cookie.

Mary Edwards

MAMA'S OATMEAL COOKIES

"My mother mailed these cookies to her brother in the service during World War II."

Yields: 5 dozen

3/4 cup shortening
1 cup firmly packed light brown sugar
1/2 cup sugar
1 egg
1/4 cup water
1 teaspoon vanilla
1 cup sifted flour

1 teaspoon salt
1/2 teaspoon baking soda
1 teaspoon ground cinnamon
1/2 teaspoon ground nutmeg
1/2 teaspoon ground cloves
3 cups quick oats (uncooked)

* Beat shortening, sugars, egg, water and vanilla until creamy.
* Sift together flour, salt, soda and spices.
* Add to creamed mixture; blend well. Stir in oats.
* Drop by teaspoonfuls onto greased cookie sheet.
* Bake at 350° for 12 to 15 minutes.

Variations: Add chopped nuts, raisins, chocolate chips or coconut, as desired.

Maria Kleto, Hanna Kane

411

OATMEAL RAISIN COOKIES

Yields: 3 dozen

1 egg
1-1/2 cups firmly packed brown sugar
1/4 cup water
1 teaspoon vanilla
3/4 cup vegetable oil
1/2 cup dry milk

1 teaspoon salt
1/2 teaspoon soda
2 cups rolled oats
1 cup wheat germ
1/2 cup raisins

* Combine egg, sugar, water, vanilla and oil; beat thoroughly.
* Stir together dry milk, salt and soda. Add to batter, mixing well.
* Stir in oats, wheat germ and raisins. Drop by teaspoonfuls onto cookie sheet.
* Bake at 350° for 12 to 15 minutes.

Variation: Use nuts or chocolate chips instead of raisins.

Buffy Crothers

TEXAS MILLIONAIRE COOKIES

Yields: 7 dozen

1/2 cup butter, softened
1/2 cup shortening
1 cup sugar
1 cup firmly packed brown sugar
2 eggs
1 teaspoon vanilla
2 cups flour
1/2 teaspoon salt

2-1/2 cups oatmeal, ground in blender or
*   processor*
1 teaspoon baking powder
1 teaspoon baking soda
1 (12-ounce) package chocolate chips
1 (4-ounce) milk chocolate bar, grated
1-1/2 cups chopped nuts

* Cream butter, shortening and both sugars. Add eggs and vanilla.
* Mix together flour, oatmeal, salt, baking powder and baking soda. Add to creamed mixture.
* Add chocolate chips, chocolate bar and nuts.
* Roll into balls. Place 2 inches apart on cookie sheets. Bake at 375° for 6 minutes.

Debbie Fitzpatrick, Marilyn McNulty

NUT GOODIE BARS

Yields: 100

1 (12-ounce) package chocolate chips
1 (12-ounce) package butterscotch chips
2 cups peanut butter
1/2 pound butter, melted
1/2 cup evaporated milk

1 small package vanilla pudding mix
2 pounds powdered sugar
1 teaspoon vanilla
1 pound salted nuts

* Melt together chocolate chips, butterscotch chips and peanut butter in saucepan.
* Pour half the mixture into 15x10-inch jellyroll pan; reserve remaining half for topping.
* Combine melted butter, pudding mix and milk; cook over low heat for 1 minute.
* Add powdered sugar and vanilla. Beat with electric mixer until well blended.
* Spread over chocolate layer and refrigerate for 10 minutes.
* Add salted peanuts to reserved chocolate mixture and spread over second layer.
* Bars keep for long time in refrigerator.

Judy Fahl, Judy Beise

CHOCOLATE RASPBERRY SHORTBREAD

Yields: 48 squares

1 cup butter (no substitute)
1/2 cup sugar
2 egg yolks
2-1/2 cups flour

1 (10-ounce) jar seedless raspberry jam
1 cup semi-sweet mini-chocolate chips
4 egg whites (at room temperature)
1 cup sugar

* Cream butter. Gradually add 1/2 cup sugar, beating well on medium speed with an electric mixer.
* Add egg yolks one at a time, beating well after each addition. Stir in flour.
* Press mixture evenly into a lightly greased 15x10-inch jellyroll pan.
* Bake at 350° for 15 to 20 minutes or until lightly browned.
* Remove from oven, spread jam over crust, sprinkle with chocolate chips and set aside.
* Beat egg whites on high speed until foamy.
* Add 1 cup sugar (1 tablespoon at a time) while beating on high speed until stiff peaks form and sugar is dissolved.
* Carefully spread meringue over morsels, sealing to edge of crust.
* Bake at 350° for 25 minutes or until golden brown. Cut into bars immediately.

Dougi O'Bryan

413

PECAN SHORTBREAD COOKIES

Yields: approximately 3 dozen

2 sticks butter, softened
1/4 cup sugar
1 teaspoon vanilla

2 cups flour
1 cup chopped nuts
powdered sugar

* Cream butter and sugar. Add vanilla and blend well.
* Fold in flour, working with hands if necessary to blend.
* Stir in nuts.
* Drop by teaspoonfuls onto greased cookie sheet.
* Bake at 300° for about 25 minutes (check at 20 minutes) until very lightly browned.
* Cool cookies several minutes. Remove from pan. Roll in powdered sugar.

Sally Gabosch

PEPPERMINT CRISPIES

Yields: 4 dozen

1 cup butter, softened
1 cup sugar
2 eggs
2 teaspoons vanilla
2-1/3 cups sifted flour

1 teaspoon baking powder
1/2 teaspoon baking soda
1/2 teaspoon salt
2/3 cup crushed candy canes
powdered sugar

* Cream butter and sugar together in large bowl. Add eggs and vanilla. Blend well.
* Combine flour, baking powder, soda and salt. Add to sugar mixture.
* Chill dough thoroughly.
* Roll dough into small balls. Place on greased cookie sheet. Flatten slightly with greased bottom of glass dipped in sugar.
* Sprinkle generously with crushed candy.
* Bake at 350° for 6 to 8 minutes.
* Sift powdered sugar over baked cookies.

Margaret Akers-Hardage

RICOTTA COOKIES

Yields: 8-10 dozen

1 pound butter, softened
2 cups sugar
3 eggs
1 pound ricotta cheese
Frosting:
2 tablespoons butter, melted
2 cups powdered sugar

2 teaspoons vanilla
1 teaspoon salt
4 cups flour
1 teaspoon baking soda

2 tablespoons milk
food coloring (optional)

* Cream together butter and sugar.
* Combine eggs, cheese, vanilla and salt. Add to butter mixture.
* Sift flour and baking soda together. Add to creamed mixture.
* Spoon dough onto cookie sheet in small mounds.
* Bake at 350° for 12 minutes. Do not allow to brown. Cool.
* To prepare frosting, mix butter, sugar and milk in bowl until smooth.
* Add several drops of food coloring, if desired.
* Frost cooled cookies. Cookies freeze well.

Lee Russo

SNICKERDOODLES
Great Christmas cookies!

Yields: 5 dozen

1/2 cup butter, softened
1/2 cup shortening
1-1/2 cups sugar
2 eggs

2-3/4 cups self-rising flour
2 tablespoons sugar
2 teaspoons cinnamon

* Cream together butter, shortening, sugar and eggs. Add flour.
* Roll dough into balls the size of small walnuts. Roll balls in sugar-cinnamon mixture.
* Place 2 inches apart on an ungreased cookie sheet.
* Bake at 400° for 8 to 10 minutes until lightly browned but still soft.
* Cool and store in airtight container.

Katrina Hidy

SUGAR COOKIES

Yields: 5-6 dozen

2 cups sugar
1 cup shortening
2 eggs
1 teaspoon lemon extract
4-1/2 cups flour

2 teaspoons baking powder
1 teaspoon salt
1/2 cup milk
paste food coloring (optional)

* Cream shortening and sugar. Add eggs and lemon extract. Beat well.
* Stir flour, baking powder and salt together.
* Alternately add flour mixture and milk to creamed mixture, stirring well after each addition.
* Chill several hours or overnight. (May also be made a day or two in advance.)
* Roll dough out to 1/4-inch thickness on floured surface. Roll dough out slightly thinner if a crisper cookie is desired.
* Cut out cookies using desired cookie cutters.
* Bake on ungreased cookie sheet at 350° for 8 to 10 minutes.

Kathryn Smith
Maxine Starner

VANILLE KIPFERL

Yields: 5-6 dozen

3 cups flour
1 cup vanilla sugar
Vanilla Sugar:
3-inch piece of vanilla bean, crushed

1/2 cup ground almonds
1-1/2 cups butter or shortening

2 cups sugar

* Put all the ingredients including Vanilla Sugar on a board and work together until the mixture does not stick.
* Form dough into a large ball. Cut the dough ball into 4 pieces.
* Roll each piece into a long roll. Slice 30 pieces from each roll.
* Form each slice into a crescent shape.
* Bake at 350° until set but not brown (about 10 to 12 minutes).
* Remove from cookie sheet while still warm and roll gently in more vanilla sugar.

Rosi Weber

BATES REUNION BROWNIES

Everyone asked for the recipe!

Easy   Yields: 15 large brownies

4 squares unsweetened chocolate   *2 teaspoons vanilla*
2 sticks margarine   *1 cup flour*
2 cups sugar   *1 cup chopped pecans*
4 eggs

* Spray 13x9-inch glass baking dish with non-stick vegetable spray.
* Melt chocolate and margarine in large saucepan over low heat.
* Remove from heat. Stir in sugar. Whisk in eggs. Add remaining ingredients.
* Pour into glass baking dish and bake at 325° for 40 minutes. Brownies will be crusty but sticky in middle. Cool 10 minutes.
* Cut into 15 pieces and place in freezer uncovered until completely cooled. Remove and place in covered container.

Betty Mullen

BOURBON BROWNIES

A most requested recipe

Yields: 6 dozen

1 package family size brownie mix   *1-1/2 teaspoons almond extract*
1 cup chopped pecans   *2 cups sifted powdered sugar*
1/3 cup bourbon   *1 (12-ounce) package chocolate chips*
1 stick margarine, softened   *1 tablespoon shortening*

* Mix brownie mix according to package directions.
* Add nuts. Pour into jellyroll pan. Bake at 350° for 25 minutes.
* Pour bourbon over hot brownies. Refrigerate.
* Cream margarine, extract and sugar. Spread on cold brownies and refrigerate.
* Melt chocolate chips and shortening in microwave.
* Spread over top. Let sit. Cut into bars.

Variation: Omit bourbon and increase almond extract to 2 tablespoons.

Marilyn Thompson,
Penny Strack, Parkie Thomas

417

CARAMEL BROWNIE SQUARES

Yields: 36-48 squares

1 box German chocolate cake mix
1 (14-ounce) package caramels
2/3 cup evaporated milk, divided

3/4 cup margarine, melted
1 cup chopped pecans or walnuts
1 (6-ounce) package mini-chocolate chips

* Combine caramels and 1/3 cup evaporated milk in small saucepan over low heat, stirring constantly until caramels melt.
* Combine remaining 1/3 cup evaporated milk, melted margarine and cake mix in a large bowl. Stir well.
* Press half the cake mixture into a 13x9-inch baking dish; bake 6 to 8 minutes at 325°.
* Remove from oven; pour caramel mixture evenly over brownie crust.
* Sprinkle nuts and chips over caramel.
* Put the remaining cake mixture on top and spread, using your fingers as best you can.
* Bake an additional 22 minutes. Allow to cool and cut into squares.

Pattie Bethune, Stephanie Fletcher
Maria Kleto, Nancy DeBiase

CRUNCHY BROWNIE BARS

Yields: 24 large bars

3/4 cup sifted flour
1/4 teaspoon baking soda
1/4 teaspoon salt
1-1/2 cups quick-cooking rolled oats
3/4 cup light brown sugar
3/4 cup butter or margarine, melted

1 large package chewy brownie mix
1-1/2 ounces unsweetened chocolate
3 tablespoons butter or margarine
2-1/4 cups sifted powdered sugar
1-1/2 teaspoons vanilla
3 tablespoons very hot water

* Combine flour, soda and salt. Stir in oats and brown sugar. Add butter.
* Pat mixture into ungreased 13x9-inch baking pan. Bake at 350° for 10 minutes.
* Prepare brownie mix according to package directions. Spread brownie batter over crunchy partially baked layer. Return to oven; bake at 350° for 40 to 45 minutes. Cool.
* Melt chocolate and butter in small saucepan.
* Remove from heat. Stir in powdered sugar, vanilla and 2 tablespoons hot water.
* Stir until smooth. Add remaining tablespoon hot water. Stir.
* Spread over brownies while frosting is still hot. Let sit until firm. Cut into squares.

Georgia Draucker

CHOCOLATE STICKS

No cooking - and everybody loves them.

Easy   Yields: 48 sticks

2 cups crushed vanilla wafers   1 (14-ounce) can sweetened condensed milk
2 cups chopped nuts   1 teaspoon vanilla
1/8 teaspoon salt   powdered sugar
4 squares unsweetened chocolate

* Crush vanilla waters. Put in large bowl.
* Add chopped nuts and salt. Toss mixture.
* Melt chocolate in saucepan with the condensed milk.
* Pour mixture over vanilla wafers and nuts. Add vanilla.
* Mix thoroughly (it will be thick) until all crumbs are coated with chocolate.
* Place in buttered 13x9-inch pan. Chill.
* Cut into sticks and roll in powdered sugar.

Myra Chandler

SINFULLY DELICIOUS CARAMEL BARS

Quick and easy

Yields: 24-30 bars

1 (14-ounce) jar caramel topping or   1 cup salted peanuts
  1 (14-ounce) package caramels   1 (6-ounce) package semi-sweet chocolate
  melted in 3 tablespoons water   chips
5 cups crispy rice cereal   1 (6-ounce) package butterscotch chips

* Melt caramels with water in microwave, stirring several times until sauce is smooth or
  use jar of caramel topping.
* Pour caramel sauce over cereal and nuts in a bowl and toss until well coated.
* With greased fingers, press mixture into greased 13x9-inch pan.
* Melt chips. Stir together. Spread over cereal mixture.
* Cool thoroughly. Cut into bars.

Nancy Pierce

CHEESE BLINTZ

Good pick-ups for morning coffees

Prepare ahead - Freezes well

Yields: 7 dozen

2 (8-ounce) packages cream cheese
2 egg yolks
1/2 cup sugar
2 loaves thin-sliced white bread

1 pound butter, melted
1 box brown sugar
cinnamon to taste

* Cream together cream cheese, egg yolks and sugar.
* Remove crusts from bread. With rolling pin, roll each slice as thinly as possible.
* Spread each slice with the cheese mixture and roll up jellyroll fashion.
* Dip each blintz in butter, allowing excess to drain. Roll in brown sugar mixed with cinnamon.
* Cut each rolled bread slice into thirds. (This is easier if you freeze for about 10 minutes.)
* Bake on ungreased baking sheet at 350° for 15 to 20 minutes.
* These can be frozen in ziploc bags before they are baked.

Jean Moody
Mary Helen Bowman

CRUNCHY BARS

As good as a granola bar!

Easy

Yields: 16 bars

2 sticks margarine
1 tablespoon corn syrup
1 teaspoon baking powder
1 cup sugar

2 cups rolled oats
1-1/2 cups all-purpose flour
1/2 to 1 cup raisins (optional)

* Melt margarine in saucepan. Add syrup and raisins. Bring almost to boil.
* Remove from heat. Mix in baking powder.
* Add sugar, oats and flour.
* Mix well and turn into greased 9-inch square cake pan. Press down until smooth.
* Bake at 400° for 20 to 25 minutes or until golden.
* Cool and cut into squares. Store in airtight container.

Joan Bolton

GERMAN CHEWS
Rich, chewy and irresistible

Yields: about 30

2 cups flour
1 cup unsalted butter
2-1/2 cups brown sugar, divided
1 cup coarsely chopped pecans

2 eggs
1 teaspoon vanilla
1/2 teaspoon baking powder

* Mix flour, butter and 1 cup brown sugar until crumbly.
* Spread in 15x10-inch jellyroll pan.
* Bake at 300° for 10 minutes.
* Mix 1-1/2 cups brown sugar with remaining ingredients.
* Spread this mixture evenly over the prepared crumb crust.
* Return to oven and bake at 300° until light brown, about 30 to 40 minutes.
* Cool and cut into fingers.

Gabriele Kellmann

HUMDINGERS
Quick and yummy

Easy

Yields: 24 squares

2 rolls refrigerated chocolate chip
    cookie dough
2 (8-ounce) packages cream cheese,
    softened

2 eggs
2 teaspoons vanilla
1 cup sugar

* Put cookie dough in freezer for about 10 minutes for easier slicing.
* Lightly grease a 13x9-inch baking pan.
* Slice 1 roll of dough and place slices on bottom of pan (28 to 30 slices are needed).
* Beat cream cheese, eggs, vanilla and sugar together until smooth and creamy. Spread on cookie slices in pan.
* Slice other roll of dough and place slices on top of creamed mixture.
* Bake at 350° for 35 to 40 minutes or until filling is set.
* Cool. Refrigerate to store.
* Cut into 2-inch squares. Serve at room temperature.

Mary Helen Bowman

POUND CAKE BARS

Easy   Yields: 4-5 dozen

1 box yellow cake mix   *1 (8-ounce) package cream cheese,*
1 stick butter, melted   *softened*
2 eggs beaten   *2 eggs, beaten*
1 box powdered sugar   *1 teaspoon vanilla*

* Add cake mix to melted butter. Add eggs and mix well.
* Spread into a greased 15x10-inch jellyroll pan. Mixture will be thick.
* Mix remaining ingredients and spread over cake mixture.
* Bake at 350° for 35 minutes. Cool completely before cutting.

Marilyn Thompson

Variation: Use lemon cake mix and lemon extract for Lemon Stickies.

Gretchen Downer

MONICA'S PUMPKIN BARS

Easy   Yields: 3 dozen bars

4 eggs   *1 teaspoon baking soda*
1 cup vegetable oil   *1/2 teaspoon salt*
2 cups sugar   *2 teaspoons cinnamon*
1 (15-ounce) can pumpkin   *1/2 teaspoon ground ginger*
2 cups flour   *1/2 teaspoon ground cloves*
2 teaspoons baking powder   *1/2 teaspoon ground nutmeg*
Icing:
1/2 stick butter, softened   *1 box powdered sugar*
1 tablespoon milk   *4 ounces cream cheese, softened*
1 teaspoon vanilla

* Mix first 4 ingredients. Combine dry ingredients. Add to egg mixture.
* Pour into greased and floured 18x12-inch pan. Bake at 350° for 25 to 30 minutes.
* Cool. Frost. Cut into 1-inch squares.
* To prepare icing, combine butter, milk, vanilla, sugar and cream cheese in mixing
  bowl. Blend with electric mixer until smooth.

Margo Colasanti

PUMPKIN CHEESECAKE BARS

Cut in small squares, it's a great cookie - in larger squares, a delicious dessert!

Yields: 48 small bars

1 (16-ounce) package pound cake mix
3 eggs
2 tablespoons butter or margarine,
* melted*
4 teaspoons pumpkin pie spice
1 (8-ounce) package cream cheese,
* softened*

1 (14-ounce) can sweetened condensed milk
1 (16-ounce) can pumpkin
1 cup finely chopped nuts
1-1/2 cups sour cream
1/3 cup sugar
1 teaspoon almond extract

* Combine cake mix, 1 egg, margarine and 2 teaspoons pumpkin pie spice.
* Mix with electric mixer until crumbly.
* Press evenly on bottom of 15x10-inch jellyroll pan.
* Using same bowl in which crust was prepared, beat cream cheese until fluffy.
* Gradually beat in condensed milk, remaining 2 eggs, pumpkin and remaining 2 teaspoons pumpkin pie spice and pour over crust. Sprinkle with nuts.
* Bake at 350° for 30 to 35 minutes or until set. Remove from oven.
* Mix together sour cream, sugar and almond extract. Spread evenly over pumpkin.
* Bake at 450° for 5 minutes. Cool, then chill. Cut into bars or squares.

The Hawk

SCOTCH SHORTBREAD

Toasty, buttery and deliciously tender

Yields: 8-12 wedges

1-1/4 cups flour
3 tablespoons cornstarch

1/3 cup sugar
1/2 cup butter, cut into chunks

* Combine all ingredients in food processor and process until mixture is very crumbly with no large particles. Press dough into a firm ball with your hands.
* Press dough firmly and evenly into a 9-inch springform pan.
* Press edge of dough with a fork to make decorative border. Prick surface evenly.
* Bake at 325° about 40 minutes or until pale golden brown.
* Remove from oven. Cut into wedges with a sharp knife while still warm.
* Sprinkle with 1 tablespoon sugar. Cool and store in airtight container. Can be frozen.

Judy Fahl

ROCKY ROAD FUDGE BARS
Worth the effort!

Step 1:

1/2 cup butter	1/2 cup chopped nuts
1 ounce unsweetened chocolate	1 teaspoon baking powder
1 cup sugar	1 teaspoon vanilla
1 cup flour	2 eggs

* Melt chocolate and butter. Pour in large bowl.
* Add remaining ingredients. Mix until smooth.
* Spread in bottom of a 13x9-inch greased pan.

Step 2:

1 (6-ounce) cream cheese, softened	1 egg
1/4 cup butter, softened	1 teaspoon vanilla
1/2 cup sugar	1/4 cup chopped nuts
2 tablespoons flour	1 (6-ounce) package chocolate chips

* Beat all ingredients except chocolate chips with electric mixer until fluffy.
* Spread over first layer. Sprinkle chocolate chips on top.
* Bake at 350° for 20 to 25 minutes or until brown.

Step 3:

2 cups miniature marshmallows

* When mixture in Step 2 has baked, spread marshmallows on top and put back in oven for 2 minutes.

Step 4:

1/4 cup butter	1/4 cup milk
2 ounces cream cheese	1 box powdered sugar
1 square unsweetened chocolate	

* While bars are baking, melt butter, cream cheese and chocolate with milk in saucepan. Add sugar. Beat until smooth.
* While bars are hot, pour chocolate icing over melted marshmallows and swirl to cover.
* When thoroughly cooled, cut into squares.

Terry Casto

VAMINO BARS
Rich and delicious

First Layer:

1/2 cup butter or margarine
1/4 cup sugar
5 tablespoons cocoa
1 teaspoon vanilla

1 egg
2 cups crushed graham crackers
1/2 cup shredded coconut
1/2 cup chopped nuts

Second Layer:

1/2 cup butter or margarine, melted
6 tablespoons milk

4 tablespoons vanilla pudding mix
4 cups powdered sugar

Third Layer:

4 ounces semi-sweet chocolate chips

4 tablespoons butter or margarine

* Boil first 4 ingredients over low heat for 2 minutes. Cool.
* Add egg while stirring.
* Blend in graham cracker crumbs, coconut and nuts.
* Spread in 13x9-inch pan.
* Cool thoroughly.
* Combine second layer ingredients and spread over first layer in pan. Chill.
* Melt third layer ingredients together.
* Spread over second layer in pan.
* Refrigerate. Cut into bars.

Sabra Leadbitter

AMARETTO KISSES

Yields: 4-5 dozen

1 (6-ounce) package chocolate chips
1/2 cup sugar
3 tablespoons corn syrup
1/2 cup amaretto

2-1/2 cups crushed vanilla wafers
1 cup finely chopped pecans
sugar

* Melt chocolate chips. Stir in 1/2 cup sugar and corn syrup.
* Add amaretto and blend well.
* In separate bowl mix vanilla wafers and nuts. Stir into the chocolate mixture.
* Form into 1-inch balls and roll in sugar. Store in airtight container.

The Hawk

BEREA BALLS

Yields: 4 dozen

1/2 cup butter, softened
2 cups sifted powdered sugar
1 (6-ounce) package semi-sweet
  chocolate chips
2 squares unsweetened chocolate

1/4 cup dark rum or amaretto
1 teaspoon freeze-dried coffee
1 tablespoon boiling water
cocoa
1/2 cup finely chopped pecans

* Cream butter and powdered sugar until smooth; set aside.
* In top of double boiler melt chocolate morsels and unsweetened chocolate. Add rum.
* Dissolve coffee in boiling water; add to chocolate mixture, stirring until well blended.
* Pour chocolate mixture into creamed mixture and blend thoroughly. Add pecans.
* Chill 30 minutes or until mixture can be rolled into balls.
* Shape into teaspoon-sized balls and roll in cocoa.
* Chill at least 1-1/2 hours.
* Must store in refrigerator.

Leslie Gebert

BUTTER BRICKLE CUPS

Yields: 60-80 pieces

1 pound bulk candy-making chocolate
8 to 10 chocolate-covered toffee bars,
  crushed

petit four paper cups

* Melt chocolate in top of double boiler.
* Mix crushed candy with chocolate.
* Spoon into paper cups.
* Let stand until set, about 15 minutes.
* Store in cool place or freeze.

Note: May substitute coconut, chopped nuts or raisins for toffee bars.

Margo Colasanti

CHOCOLATE PEANUT BUTTER CUPS

Yields: 30 candy cups

3/4 cup creamy peanut butter
1/2 cup margarine
1/3 cup sugar
1/3 cup light brown sugar
1 egg
1 teaspoon vanilla

2 tablespoons milk
1/2 teaspoon baking soda
1-1/3 cups all-purpose flour
30 miniature chocolate-covered peanut
    butter cups

* Cream peanut butter and margarine together. Add sugar and light brown sugar.
* Add egg, vanilla and milk. Gradually add baking soda and flour.
* Using mini-muffin pans lined with paper cups, place dough in cups until 3/4 full.
* Bake at 350° for 5 minutes.
* Remove from oven and push candy cup into each cookie.
* Return to oven. Bake 3 to 5 minutes more.
* Allow to cool on counter top.
* Once set, store in freezer or keep at room temperature.

Clara Irwin

CHOCOLATE TRUFFLES
Rich and delicious - a chocolate lover's delight!

Yields: 4 dozen

1/4 cup whipping cream
2 tablespoons kahlúa
6 ounces sweet baking chocolate

4 tablespoons butter, softened
cocoa powder

* Boil cream in heavy saucepan until reduced to 2 tablespoons.
* Remove from heat and stir in kahlúa and chocolate.
* Heat on low setting, stirring until chocolate melts.
* Whisk in butter and mix until smooth.
* Pour in shallow bowl and refrigerate until firm (40 minutes).
* Form into 1-inch balls and roll in unsweetened cocoa powder.
* Store in airtight container in refrigerator.
* Let stand 30 minutes before serving in tiny cupcake liners.

Georgia Draucker

CHOCOLATE FUDGE

Yields: 5 pounds

5 cups sugar
1 cup margarine, softened
1 (12-ounce) can evaporated milk

18 ounces chocolate chips
1 (7-ounce) jar marshmallow cream
1 cup chopped pecans (optional)

* Combine sugar, margarine and evaporated milk in large saucepan.
* Cook on medium high, stirring constantly.
* Bring to rapid boil; cook and stir for 7 minutes.
* Remove from heat; add chocolate chips. Stir until smooth.
* Add marshmallow cream. Stir until smooth.
* Add nuts, if desired.
* Pour into buttered pan and allow to cool before cutting. (Size of pan determines thickness of fudge.)

Melinda Mileham

COCOA CANDY CUPS

A favorite holiday treat - packs well to ship, too!

Yields: approximately 80 candies

2 pounds powdered sugar
2 cups sweetened coconut
1/4 cup cocoa
4 cups very finely chopped pecans
1 (14-ounce) can sweetened condensed milk

2 sticks margarine, melted
1 tablespoon vanilla
1 (12-ounce) package semi-sweet chocolate chips
1 (12-ounce) package milk chocolate chips

* Combine all ingredients except chocolate chips.
* Chill mixture well.
* Roll into balls and place into small paper candy cups.
* Indent top of each ball slightly.
* Melt chocolate chips in microwave or over double boiler.
* Spoon a small amount on top of each candy.
* Chill the candies.
* Pack in airtight container.

The Hawk

MOCHA FUDGE

Yummy rich chocolate - melts in your mouth!

Yields: 2 pounds

1 (5 ounce) can evaporated milk
1-2/3 cups sugar
2 tablespoons butter
1/2 teaspoon salt
1 tablespoon instant coffee granules,
  decaffeinated

2 cups miniature marshmallows
1 (6-ounce) package semi-sweet chocolate
  chips
1 teaspoon vanilla
1/2 cup chopped pecans (optional)

* Combine milk, sugar, butter, salt and coffee in top of double boiler.
* Cook over medium heat, stirring constantly until sugar dissolves.
* Bring to a boil, stirring constantly. This will take 15 to 20 minutes.
* Boil 3 minutes, or until temperature reaches 225° on a candy thermometer.
* Working quickly, remove from heat and add remaining ingredients, stirring until melted. Quickly pour in buttered 8x8-inch pan.
* Cool and slice. Store in refrigerator.

Brandon Chapman

RUM FUDGE

Make ahead

1/2 cup golden raisins
2 tablespoons rum
2 cups firmly packed light brown sugar
1 cup sugar
1 cup evaporated milk

1 stick margarine
1 (7-ounce) jar marshmallow creme
1 (12-ounce) package butterscotch chips
1 cup chopped pecans or walnuts
1 tablespoon vanilla

* Cut raisins in half. Pour rum over halves, let stand several hours.
* In heavy saucepan combine sugars, margarine and milk.
* Cook over medium heat, stirring to prevent sticking, until mixture reaches soft ball stage or 230° on candy thermometer.
* Remove from heat and stir in marshmallow creme and chips.
* When well blended, add raisins, rum, nuts and vanilla. Stir completely and quickly.
* Pour into buttered 9x13-inch pan. Cool; cut into squares.
* Store in airtight container and allow to mellow a day or two before serving.

Barbara Funderburk

ORANGE BALLS

Yields: 4-5 dozen

1 (12-ounce) package vanilla wafers, crushed
1 stick margarine, softened
1 box powdered sugar

1 (6-ounce) can frozen orange juice concentrate
1 cup chopped pecans
1 (6-ounce) package flaked coconut

* Mix all ingredients except coconut in large bowl.
* Shape into balls.
* Roll in coconut.
* Store in airtight container.

Gretchen Downer

PEANUT (OR CASHEW) BRITTLE
A no-fail recipe

Yields: 1-1/2 pounds

1 cup sugar
1/2 cup light corn syrup
1 cup salted peanuts or cashews

1 teaspoon butter or margarine
1 teaspoon vanilla
1 teaspoon baking soda

* Have ingredients measured and cookie sheet greased before you begin preparation. It is important to work quickly with this recipe.
* In a 2-quart pyrex measuring cup combine sugar and corn syrup; stir.
* Cook on high in microwave for 4 minutes.
* Add peanuts; stir well.
* Cook at high for an additional 3 to 3-1/2 minutes.
* Add butter and vanilla; stir well.
* Cook on high 1 minute.
* Add baking soda and stir gently until light and foamy.
* Immediately pour mixture onto well-greased cookie sheet, working quickly and spreading thinly.
* Cool completely. Break into small pieces.
* Store in airtight container.

Margaret Akers-Hardage

PEANUT BUTTER BON BONS

These freeze nicely.

Yields: 100-150 balls

1 pound butter or margarine, softened
12 ounces peanut butter
2-1/2 pounds powdered sugar
2 tablespoons vanilla

2 (12-ounce) packages plus 1 (6-ounce)
package semi-sweet chocolate chips
1 (4-ounce) bar paraffin wax

* Cream butter and peanut butter - works best if done with your hands.
* Add sugar and vanilla.
* Mold into balls and freeze.
* Melt chocolate and paraffin in top of double boiler.
* Insert a toothpick into each bon bon and dip into chocolate.
* Cool on wax paper.
* Keep refrigerated.

Beth Love
Gail Latham

CHARLESTON ROASTED PECANS

Yields: 1 cup

1 cup pecans
2 tablespoons sherry
1 tablespoon butter, melted

1 tablespoon sugar
1/4 teaspoon salt

* In pan large enough to hold pecans in single layer, combine sherry and melted butter.
* Stir in pecans and roast in 400° oven just until they sizzle and no longer; they will darken as they cool.
* Drain on paper towels.
* While still warm, toss in mixture of sugar and salt to coat.
* Store in tightly closed container in refrigerator, but serve at room temperature.

Marty Viser

PECAN BITS

Yields: 4 cups

2 cups sugar
2 teaspoons ground cinnamon
1-1/4 teaspoons salt
1 teaspoon ground nutmeg

1/2 teaspoon ground cloves
1/2 cup water
4 cups pecan halves

* Combine all ingredients except nuts in a deep 3-quart casserole.
* Mix well and cover with wax paper.
* Microwave on high 5 minutes; stir well.
* Microwave 4 minutes longer.
* Add pecans and stir until well coated.
* Spread on wax paper and separate quickly.
* Cool.

Sandy Hibberd

MISSISSIPPI PRALINES

Yields: 25-30

1 cup whipping cream
1 pound light brown sugar

2 tablespoons butter, softened
2 cups pecan halves

* Mix cream and sugar in large microwave-safe bowl.
* Microwave on high 10 to 14 minutes.
* Remove from microwave. Test temperature with candy thermometer. Candy must reach 220° on candy thermometer. Do not stir.
* Allow mixture to sit for 2 minutes. Stir in butter and nuts.
* Drop by tablespoonfuls onto foil and cool.

Kathy Burris Jones

SHORT CHEFS

PINEAPPLE MILKSHAKE

Yields: 1 serving

1 cup pineapple juice
2 tablespoons orange juice
1 teaspoon lemon juice

3 tablespoons sugar
2 cups milk
1/3 cup finely crushed ice

* Blend first 4 ingredients in blender until sugar dissolves.
* Add milk and ice. Blend until smooth.
* Serve at once.

Lil' Hawk

BRAIDED YUMS

Yields: 10 braids

1 (12-ounce) package refrigerated
  biscuits
10 teaspoons butter, softened
1/3 cup sugar

1 teaspoon cinnamon
1/2 cup sifted powdered sugar
1 tablespoon water

* Separate biscuits and flatten each one.
* Spread each biscuit with a teaspoon of butter.
* Combine sugar and cinnamon and sprinkle over biscuits.
* Cut biscuits in half. Place buttered sides together and twist.
* Place on cookie sheet.
* Bake at 400° for 10 to 12 minutes.
* Mix powdered sugar and water to form glaze. Drizzle glaze over top.

Scott Whelchel

CINNAMON STICK PUFFS

Yields: 8 puffs

1 can refrigerated crescent rolls
8 large marshmallows
1/4 cup butter, melted

cinnamon and sugar mixed
1/3 cup powdered sugar
2 teaspoons milk

* Separate dough into 8 triangles.
* Dip each marshmallow into melted butter and roll in cinnamon sugar.
* Place marshmallow on narrow end of triangle and roll dough toward wide end. Cover marshmallow with dough. Seal ends.
* Dip in melted butter and place in muffin tins.
* Bake at 375° for 10 to 15 minutes.
* Remove from pan and cool.
* Mix powdered sugar and milk together to make glaze. Drizzle over each puff.

Anna Katherine Whelchel

RAISIN NO-BRAN MUFFINS

Yields: 12 muffins

2 cups biscuit baking mix
1/4 cup sugar
1/2 teaspoon cinnamon
Glaze:
2/3 cup powdered sugar
1/4 teaspoon vanilla

3/4 cup raisins
1 egg
3/4 cup milk

1 tablespoon warm water

* Combine first 4 ingredients.
* Mix egg and milk in a bowl.
* Add egg and milk mixture to the other ingredients and stir until moistened.
* Pour into greased muffin tins.
* Bake at 425° for 15 minutes.
* Remove and cover with glaze if desired.
* To prepare glaze, mix powdered sugar and warm water.
* Add vanilla and beat until smooth.
* Spoon over muffins while hot.

Scott Whelchel

GOOD LUCK BEAN SOUP MIX
A nice way to remember someone special with a homemade gift

Yields: about 26 pints bean mix

13 different 1-pound packages dried beans: (kidney beans, navy beans, black-eyed peas, great northern beans, lentils, cranberry beans, chili beans , adzuki beans, baby lima beans, green split peas, yellow split peas, pinto beans, garbanzo beans, field peas, black beans or anasazi beans)

* Fill pint jars with the dried beans, include recipe for Good Luck Bean Soup and give as gifts. (Children love to open the packages of beans, stir them together and fill the jars with their homemade gift!)

Good Luck Bean Soup Recipe:

2 tablespoons salt
1 large sliced onion
1 country ham hock or vegetable
  bouillon cubes
2 quarts water
1 (28-ounce) can tomatoes

1 garlic clove, minced
2 tablespoons fresh lemon juice
salt and pepper to taste
1 large pod red pepper or a sprinkle of red
  pepper flakes (optional)

* Wash 1 pint bean mixture. Cover with water; add 2 tablespoons salt. Soak overnight.
* Drain and put beans into 2 quarts water, adding 1 large sliced onion and sliced country ham hock or vegetable bouillon cubes for flavor. Cook mixture 2 to 2-1/2 hours.
* When cooked, add tomatoes, garlic, lemon juice, salt and pepper, and either red pepper pod or red pepper flakes, if desired. Remove ham and chop meat. Return to soup.

Laura Bethune

FIVE-CUP SALAD

Easy

Serves: 8-10

1 (11-ounce) can mandarin oranges
1 (15-ounce) can pineapple tidbits
1 cup shredded coconut

1 cup miniature marshmallows
1 cup nonfat yogurt

* Drain fruits well and place in bowl. Fold in coconut, marshmallows and yogurt.
* Cover and refrigerate.

Lil' Hawk

GUMDROP SALAD

Serves: 10-12

1/2 pound miniature marshmallows
1/2 pound miniature gumdrops (assorted
   flavors, no blacks)
1 (20-ounce) can pineapple chunks,
   drained (reserve juice)
Dressing:
1/2 cup sugar
4 tablespoons flour
1 tablespoon vinegar
juice of 2 lemons

1 pound seedless white or red grapes,
   halved
1 (8-ounce) bottle red or green maraschino
   cherries, drained

1/8 teaspoon salt
3/4 cup pineapple juice
1 pint heavy cream, whipped

* Blend sugar and flour. Add vinegar, lemon juice, salt and pineapple juice.
* Cook in double boiler until smooth and thick, stirring constantly.
* Cool mixture. Fold in whipped cream, then marshmallows, gumdrops and remaining fruits.
* Cover and refrigerate for 24 hours. Stir before serving.

Cynthia Barnes

CINNAMON SUGAR APPLES
Easy, easy, easy but delicious

Serves: 1-2

1 apple, cut into fourths, seeds removed
1/4 teaspoon cinnamon

1/4 teaspoon sugar

* Cut each fourth into thirds and place in microwave-safe dish.
* Combine cinnamon and sugar. Sprinkle over apple.
* Cover with wax paper. Place dish in microwave. Cook 1 to 2 minutes or until hot. Cook 1 minute for a crisp apple and 2 minutes for a softer apple.

Variation: Add 1 tablespoon raisins and 1 tablespoon chopped nuts before cooking.

Anne Highley

SPICY APPLESAUCE
Get your mom to help you peel and cut the apples.

Serves: 8

3 pounds Red Delicious apples
1/3 cup unsweetened apple juice
1/4 cup packed brown sugar

1/2 teaspoon ground cinnamon
1/8 teaspoon ground cloves

* Peel, core and cut each apple into 8 wedges.
* Combine all ingredients in a large heavy pot. Cover and cook over medium heat 15 minutes or until very tender.
* Spoon into a large bowl and mash, or pour into a food processor and pulse until desired consistency is reached.
* Serve warm or cold.

Lil' Hawk

CORN OYSTERS
Fun to make and eat!

Serves: 6-8

2 cups frozen corn kernels
1/4 cup milk
1/3 cup flour
1 egg

1/2 teaspoon salt
1/4 teaspoon pepper
2 tablespoons butter
2 tablespoons vegetable oil

* Rinse frozen corn with water until ice crystals disappear.
* Place corn in bowl. Add milk, flour, egg, salt and pepper. Stir to mix.
* In heated skillet, melt butter with oil.
* Drop corn mixture by rounded spoonfuls into skillet. Cook 2 to 3 minutes or until bottom is golden brown.
* Turn gently. Cook 2 to 3 more minutes.
* Place corn oysters on paper towels to drain. Serve warm.

Carroll Thompson

MACARONI AND CHEEZE PIZZA

Serves: 6-8

1 (7-1/4-ounce) box macaroni and
   cheese
2 eggs, beaten
1 (14-ounce) jar spaghetti or pizza sauce

1 cup shredded mozzarella cheese
favorite pizza toppings (pepperoni, onion,
   mushrooms, peppers, additional cheese,
   etc.)

* Prepare macaroni and cheese according to directions on package.
* Stir in eggs.
* Spread in bottom of 13x9-inch pan.
* Bake at 350° for 10 minutes.
* Remove from oven. Spread sauce over macaroni.
* Sprinkle with grated mozzarella cheese and toppings of choice.
* Bake an additional 10 minutes at 350°.

Beth Love

PIZZA SANDWICH

Yields: 3 (8-inch) sandwiches

1/2 pound ground beef
1 (8-ounce) jar pizza sauce

3 (8-inch) French rolls
1-1/2 cups shredded mozzarella cheese

* Brown meat in microwave. Drain fat.
* Add pizza sauce to meat.
* Cut rolls in half lengthwise, saving the top. Hollow out some of the bottom.
* Spoon 3 tablespoons cheese, then meat mixture, then 3 more tablespoons cheese into bottom of roll.
* Replace top of bread. Wrap in foil.
* Bake at 375° for 40 minutes.

Note: Can be frozen after sandwich is made. Bake right from freezer at 375° for 60 to 70 minutes.

Elaine Hoffmann

PIEROGIES
You can fix dinner for mom tonight.

Serves: 8

1 (16-ounce) package pierogies (potato   1 (14-ounce) jar meatless spaghetti sauce
and onion-filled pasta pockets)

* Break apart frozen pierogies. Arrange single layer in 13x9-inch glass baking dish.
* Pour spaghetti sauce evenly on top.
* Cover dish tightly with aluminum foil. Bake at 350° for 25 to 30 minutes or until bubbly.

Variation: Sprinkle mozzarella cheese on top if desired.

Reed Gaskin

CHOCOLATE CHIP POUND CAKE

Serves: 16

1 box yellow cake mix with pudding   1/2 cup oil
1 small box instant vanilla pudding mix   1-1/2 cups water
1 small box instant chocolate pudding   1 teaspoon vanilla flavoring
   mix   1 (12-ounce) package chocolate chips
4 eggs

* Stir all ingredients together except chocolate chips.
* Beat with mixer 2 minutes.
* Stir in chocolate chips.
* Pour into tube or Bundt pan that has been sprayed with cooking spray.
* Bake at 350° for 60 to 75 minutes.
* May substitute other flavors of pudding, and use butterscotch or peanut butter chips instead of chocolate chips.

Sessions Povall

FUNNEL CAKES

Serves: 8

2-1/2 cups self-rising flour
1/4 cup sugar
1-1/3 cups milk
2 eggs, slightly beaten

vegetable oil
sifted powdered sugar, fresh fruit or
   chocolate syrup for topping

* Combine flour, sugar, milk and eggs in a bowl. Beat until smooth.
* Heat 1/4-inch oil to 375° in a skillet.
* Pour 1/4 cup batter into funnel with a 3/8-inch wide stem, covering opening with finger.
* Hold funnel over skillet. Remove finger from opening and move funnel in a slow circular motion to form batter in a spiral.
* Fry each funnel cake 1 minute or until edges are golden brown.
* Turn and fry until golden. Drain on paper towels.
* Repeat with remaining batter.
* Serve warm; sprinkle with topping of powdered sugar, etc., if desired.

Lauren Bowman

STRAWBERRY SHORTCUT CAKE

It's fun to see the marshmallows rise to the top!

1 cup miniature marshmallows
2 cups frozen sliced strawberries
1 small package strawberry gelatin
2-1/4 cups flour
1-1/2 cups sugar
1/2 cup shortening

3 teaspoons baking powder
1/2 teaspoon salt
1 cup milk
1 teaspoon vanilla
3 eggs, beaten

* Grease 13x9-inch metal pan.
* Place marshmallows in bottom of pan.
* Combine strawberries and gelatin and pour over marshmallows.
* Combine remaining ingredients and pour over gelatin mixture.
* Bake at 350° for approximately 50 minutes.

Matthew Kelly

CARAMEL APPLE FONDUE
A fun dessert

Yields: 2-1/2 cups

1/4 cup butter
1 cup dark brown sugar
1/2 cup light corn syrup
1 tablespoon water

6 ounces sweetened condensed milk
1/2 teaspoon vanilla extract
Granny Smith apples, sliced

* Melt butter in double boiler.
* Add sugar, syrup, water and condensed milk. Stir until thickened.
* Add vanilla extract. Blend well.
* Serve in chafing dish or fondue pot with apple slices for dipping.
* Fondue will keep up to 6 weeks in refrigerator.

Note: Dip apple slices in lemon juice to prevent browning.

Lauren Bowman

QUICK APPLE DESSERT
Your mom can help slice the apples.

Serves: 5-6

4 cups sliced tart apples
1/4 cup sugar
1/2 teaspoon cinnamon
1/4 cup water

1/4 cup packed brown sugar
1/3 cup margarine or butter
2/3 cup graham cracker crumbs

* Put apples into a 9-inch pie or cake pan.
* Mix cinnamon with sugar. Sprinkle over apples. Spoon water over top.
* Mix brown sugar, margarine and cracker crumbs together in a small bowl.
* Sprinkle mixture over apples.
* Bake at 350° for 30 minutes, or microwave on high for 8 minutes or until apples are tender.

Matthew Frucella

CARAMEL DIP
Wonderful with fruit

Easy   Yields: 2 cups

3/4 stick margarine   1 cup sour cream
1/2 pound light brown sugar

* Melt margarine in saucepan and stir in sugar until melted.
* Add sour cream.
* Chill in refrigerator.
* Serve with fresh fruit as dip.
* Store in refrigerator.

Anna Katherine Whelchel

CHOCOLATE CHERRY DESSERT

Serves: 8-12

26 chocolate wafers   1 small box instant chocolate pudding mix
1/4 cup butter or margarine   1-1/4 cups milk
1 (8-ounce) carton sour cream   1 (21-ounce) can cherry pie filling

* Crush wafers and set aside 2 tablespoons. Put remaining wafers into 8x8-inch baking dish.
* Melt butter or margarine and pour over crushed wafers in dish.
* Using a fork, stir together wafers and margarine. Spread over bottom of dish and press to form crust.
* Put in freezer for 10 minutes.
* Spoon sour cream into small bowl and add dry pudding mix and milk. Beat at low speed for 1 minute. Scrape bowl and beat another 30 seconds.
* Spread pudding over crust. Spoon pie filling over pudding layer. Sprinkle remaining wafer crumbs over top.
* Cover and refrigerate for 3 hours or freeze for 1 hour.

Variation: May substitute 33 vanilla wafers, vanilla pudding and peach pie filling to make Vanilla Peach Dessert.

Carroll Thompson

COOKIE CRUMBLE BALLS

Serves: 8

1-1/2 cups chocolate sandwich cookie crumbs
hot fudge sauce (optional)

1-1/2 quarts vanilla ice cream, or frozen yogurt

* Using a medium ice cream scoop, make 8 ice cream balls. Roll ice cream balls immediately in crumbs; place in serving dishes. Top with hot fudge sauce if desired.
* Crumbed ice cream balls can be frozen on a cookie sheet and kept in the freezer until serving time. Serve individually or arrange, pyramid style, on a serving platter.

Lil' Hawk

ICE CREAM CRUNCH CAKE

Serves: 12-16

1 (12-ounce) package chocolate chips
2/3 cup smooth peanut butter

6 cups crispy rice cereal
1/2 gallon vanilla ice cream

* Melt chocolate chips and peanut butter in large saucepan, or in large bowl in microwave. Add cereal. Mix well. Spread on cookie sheet to cool.
* When cool, break into small pieces. Reserve 1 cup.
* Soften ice cream. Fold in all but 1 cup of the cereal pieces.
* Spread in 10-inch springform pan. Sprinkle reserved cup of cereal pieces over top.
* Freeze overnight. Remove from freezer a few minutes before serving.

Mary Moon Guerrant

NO-CHURN ICE CREAM

6 peaches, peeled and chopped plus 1/2 teaspoon almond extract or
1 (10-ounce) package frozen strawberries plus 1/2 teaspoon vanilla

1 can sweetened condensed milk
1 medium carton whipped topping, thawed

* Mix all ingredients and place in covered container. Freeze.

Joy Litaker

LOWELL'S BEST BROWNIES

Yields: 2 dozen

1 stick butter
1 cup sugar
4 eggs
1 teaspoon vanilla

1 cup flour
1 teaspoon baking powder
1 (16-ounce) can chocolate syrup

* Cream butter and sugar. Add eggs one at a time and beat well.
* Add vanilla, then flour and baking powder.
* Add chocolate syrup. Mix thoroughly.
* Pour into greased 13x9-inch pan. Bake at 350° for 20 minutes. Frost if desired.

Lowell Rayburn

CHOCOLATE-FILLED MARSHMALLOW BARS

Yields: 16 bars

1 (6-ounce) package semi-sweet chocolate
  chips
1/2 cup powdered sugar
2 tablespoons margarine
1 tablespoon water
1/4 teaspoon vanilla

1/4 cup margarine
5 cups miniature marshmallows
1/2 cup creamy peanut butter
1/4 cup light corn syrup
5 cups chocolate-flavored rice cereal

* Butter 11x7-inch baking pan.
* Combine first 4 ingredients in medium glass bowl. Microwave on high until chocolate chips melt, stirring once. Stir in vanilla.
* Place 1/4 cup margarine in large glass bowl. Microwave until melted, about 30 seconds.
* Add marshmallows and stir. Microwave until marshmallows puff, about 1 minute. Stir until smooth.
* Mix in peanut butter and corn syrup. Stir in cereal.
* Spread half the cereal mixture in pan. Spoon chocolate filling over cereal mixture.
* Top with remaining cereal mixture.
* Cover and refrigerate at least 20 minutes. Cut into bars.

Carroll Thompson

OATMEAL TOFFEE BARS

Yields: 2-3 dozen bars

4-1/2 cups uncooked oatmeal
1 cup packed brown sugar
3/4 cup margarine, melted
1/2 cup dark corn syrup
1 tablespoon vanilla

1 (12-ounce) package semi-sweet chocolate
  chips
2 tablespoons shortening
2/3 cup chopped nuts

* Combine oats, sugar, margarine, syrup and vanilla. Mix well.
* Firmly press mixture into 13x9-inch pan. Bake 12 minutes or until mixture is brown and bubbly. Cool completely.
* Melt chocolate and shortening in a saucepan over low heat, stirring constantly until smooth. Spread evenly over oat crust. Sprinkle with nuts.
* Chill until set. Cut into bars.

Jewel Freeman

AUNT ADA'S CRUNCHY CANDY

Great by itself or served as a topping for ice cream

40 low-salt soda crackers
2 sticks margarine
1 cup firmly packed brown sugar

1 (12-ounce) package semi-sweet chocolate
  chips
2 tablespoons finely chopped black walnuts

* Line jellyroll pan with aluminum foil. Spray with no-stick vegetable spray.
* Cover with soda crackers.
* Bring margarine and brown sugar to a boil in a saucepan. Boil 3 minutes.
* Pour over crackers making sure all crackers are covered.
* Bake for 5 minutes at 325°.
* Remove from oven. Sprinkle with chocolate chips.
* Bake for 3 minutes at 325°. Remove from oven. Spread chocolate chips evenly with back of spoon.
* Sprinkle with nuts.
* Refrigerate for 24 hours. Break into serving-sized pieces.

Scott Martin

BRYAN'S PEANUT CLUSTERS
Delicious Christmas gifts

Yields: 4 dozen

1 pound white chocolate
1 pound semi-sweet chocolate chips
1 milk chocolate bar

1 (6-ounce) package butterscotch chips
1/2 gallon Spanish peanuts or nuts of your
*   choice*

* Melt first 4 ingredients over low heat in a heavy pan.
* Stir often.
* Remove from heat. Add nuts.
* Drop on wax paper. Cool in refrigerator.
* Store in airtight container.

Mary Jane Bennett

CHOCOLATE SPIDERS
Great for Halloween

Yields: 3 dozen

1-1/2 cups chocolate chips
1 (5-ounce) can chow mein noodles

1 cup salted peanuts

* Melt chocolate chips in microwave or double boiler.
* Add peanuts and noodles, stirring well.
* Drop chocolate mixture by teaspoonfuls onto greased baking sheet or wax paper.
* Refrigerate 8 hours or overnight.
* Keep chilled until serving time.

Eric Pierce

Variation: Substitute 1 (12-ounce) package butterscotch chips for chocolate chips.

Abbey Rawald

PLAYDOUGH

1 cup water
1 cup flour
1 tablespoon oil
1/2 cup salt

1 teaspoon cream of tartar
food coloring drops
peppermint extract, a few drops to scent
(optional)

* Mix all ingredients in heavy saucepan, adding food coloring until desired color is reached.
* Cook mixture over medium heat until it pulls away from sides of pan and becomes playdough consistency.
* Knead until cool.
* Store in ziploc bags. Will keep 3 months unrefrigerated.

John Bethune

SPICE-SCENTED ORNAMENTS
Smell delicious - but don't eat!

3/4 cup ground cinnamon
1 tablespoon ground allspice
2 tablespoons ground cloves

1 tablespoon ground nutmeg
1 cup applesauce

* Mix dry ingredients. Add applesauce. Mix well until the texture is like stiff cookie dough.
* Roll to 1/4-inch thickness on wax paper.
* Cut in various shapes, using cookie cutters. Make a hole in the top of each with a nail, toothpick or small straw.
* Air dry for 4 to 5 days on a cookie sheet.
* Insert a ribbon or ornament hanger in each.

Laura Bethune

DAD DOES
DINNER

TEXAS CAVIAR

Easy - Prepare ahead

Yields: 2 cups

1 (23-ounce) can black-eyed peas
1 (4-ounce) can diced green chilies
1 medium onion, chopped

1/4 cup olive oil
1/4 cup white vinegar

* Drain and rinse peas.
* Combine peas with remaining ingredients.
* Cover and refrigerate for at least 24 hours.
* The olive oil may congeal when refrigerated, so let stand at room temperature for an hour or so and mix well before serving.
* May be served as a dip with crackers or warm flour tortillas or as a Mexican vegetable side dish.

Wes Baldwin

HIGGINS HERB ROLLS
Great with everything

Easy

Serves: 10

1 package brown and serve sour dough
   rolls
1 stick butter, softened

salt-free Mrs. Dash
Morton's Nature's Seasons
Parmesan cheese

* Brown rolls in oven.
* Cut in half and cool.
* Spread softened butter heavily on rolls and sprinkle with seasonings to taste.
* Cover with Parmesan cheese.
* Broil for 1 to 2 minutes, watching very carefully.

Bill Higgins

IRISH SCONE
Traditional St. Patrick's Day offering

Easy   Yields: 2 loaves

3 cups flour   *2 eggs*
1/2 cup sugar   *2 tablespoons oil*
2 tablespoons baking powder   *1-1/2 cups raisins*
1 teaspoon baking soda   *3/4 cup buttermilk*
1/2 teaspoon salt

* Sift together flour, sugar, baking powder, baking soda and salt.
* Combine eggs, oil and buttermilk.
* Mix raisins with dry ingredients and then add wet mixture. Mix well.
* Pour into 2 greased loaf pans.
* Bake at 350° for 45 to 50 minutes. Test for doneness.

Bob Kelly

DAD'S BLUEBERRY PANCAKES

Easy   Yields: 14 pancakes

1-1/2 cups sifted flour   *3 tablespoons butter, melted*
1 teaspoon salt   *1 cup milk*
3 tablespoons sugar   *1-1/2 cups fresh blueberries*
1-3/4 teaspoons baking powder   *vegetable oil, if necessary*
2 eggs

* Sift flour with salt, sugar and baking powder into a large mixing bowl.
* Separate eggs and add the yolks, butter and milk to the dry ingredients. Mix but do
  not overbeat; a few lumps are fine.
* Add blueberries and stir in gently.
* Beat the egg whites until stiff but not dry. Fold lightly into batter.
* Heat a few drops of oil in a large, heavy skillet or griddle to medium high temperature.
  Spoon batter onto surface and cook, turning once when bubbles appear on top of cakes
  but before they break.
* Serve immediately.

Steve Horsley

LIGHT-FLAVOR BUCKWHEAT CAKES

Easy   Yields: 20 medium pancakes

1 cup buckwheat flour   *3 tablespoons sugar*
1 cup flour   *2 eggs, well beaten*
3 teaspoons baking powder   *1-1/2 to 1-3/4 cups milk*
1/2 teaspoon salt   *3 tablespoons oil*

* Mix all ingredients.
* Spoon batter onto greased griddle and cook slowly, turning once.

Mark Starner

CLAM CHOWDER OKC
From Robert's, a Charleston restaurant

Serves: 6

1 stick butter   *1 teaspoon pepper*
1 cup chopped onions   *1/2 teaspoon dried thyme*
1/2 cup flour   *1 bay leaf*
3 cups clam juice   *1/4 teaspoon chopped garlic*
1 (15-ounce) can chopped clams in   *1/8 pound salt pork, diced and browned*
  juice   *(save rendered fat)*
2 cups cooked, diced potatoes   *1-1/2 cups half-and-half*

* In a heavy 4-quart pot, melt butter and sauté onions until transparent.
* Add flour and stir to make a roux. Cook slowly for 2 minutes over low heat or until bubbly.
* Whisk in clam juice and stir until smooth.
* Add all remaining ingredients except salt pork and half-and-half. Cook uncovered over medium heat for 5 minutes.
* Add salt pork with its rendered fat.
* Scald cream in a separate pan and stir into finished soup.
* Remove bay leaf and serve.

Variation: May substitute 1/8 pound bacon for salt pork.

Todd Chapman

DAD'S GLORIOUS GLOP

1-1/2 pounds cubed or ground beef or
   venison
2 large onions, chopped
2 (16-ounce) cans tomatoes
1 (8-ounce) can mushrooms
1 green pepper, chopped
2 handfuls uncooked rice
1/2 to 1 cup red wine

1 tablespoon minced garlic
1 teaspoon oregano
1 teaspoon thyme
1 teaspoon tarragon
1 bay leaf
hot pepper sauce to taste
salt and pepper to taste

* Brown meat in Dutch oven and pour off excess fat.
* Reduce heat to simmer and add other ingredients.
* Cook on top of stove for about 1 hour, or until the mixture is hot and the flavors have blended.
* Adjust seasoning to taste during the cooking process.
* Serve with rolls or garlic bread and a tossed salad.

Variation: Elbow macaroni can replace rice; celery can be added.

Peter Fenninger

OYSTER STEW

Outstanding when served the next day

oysters with their liquor (fresh-pack
   container)
half-and-half

salt and pepper to taste
celery seed or celery salt, to taste
M.S.G.

* Heat 1 part half-and-half in pot. (Always keep the ratio 1 part half-and-half to 1 part oysters.) Do not let boil.
* In a separate pot, heat 1 part oysters with their liquor on moderate heat until edges are just curled. Skim off any foam.
* Combine oysters and liquid with half-and-half. Immediately add 1/4 to 1/2 stick of butter.
* Season with salt, pepper, celery seasoning and at least 1/2 teaspoon M.S.G. per quart of stew.
* Remove from heat and let cool to room temperature. Refrigerate and let flavors blend.
* Tastes great when reheated within a few hours, even better the next day.

Dick Stafford

AUNT GLAD'S SPAGHETTI

Serves: 12

3 green peppers, chopped
2 onions, chopped
1-1/2 pounds ground beef
2 pints tomato juice
1 (12-ounce) can tomato paste

1 (7-ounce) bottle catsup
1 tablespoon hot pepper sauce
salt and pepper to taste
1 (2-pound) package spaghetti, cooked and
drained

* Sauté peppers and onions in vegetable oil in a large skillet.
* Add ground beef and brown. Drain excess oil from skillet.
* Stir in tomato juice, tomato paste, catsup, hot sauce, salt and pepper.
* Simmer on low heat for 1 to 1-1/2 hours.
* Serve over spaghetti.

Richard Herring

CRIPPLE CREEK RED CHILI

Very hot and spicy

Serves 12-15

1/2 pound bacon
1-1/2 pounds trimmed pork shoulder,
  cut into 1/4-inch cubes
1-1/2 pounds lean beef (round or sirloin)
  trimmed and cut into 1/4-inch cubes
3 tablespoons flour
2 medium onions, chopped
5 cloves garlic, minced
1 (28-ounce) can tomatoes
28 ounces diced green chilies

1 (28-ounce) can white hominy
1 tablespoon oregano
6 tablespoons chili powder, medium hot
3 tablespoons cumin
2 cups beef broth
12 ounces beer
3 dashes hot pepper sauce
4 splashes white wine vinegar
1 green pepper, seeded and chopped
salt and pepper to taste

* In a large skillet fry bacon until crisp. Crumble; set aside. Reserve 1 cup bacon grease.
* Dredge beef and pork in flour and brown in reserved grease.
* Add onions and garlic and cook until clear. Transfer to large stockpot.
* Add all other ingredients and crumbled bacon.
* Bring to boil. Simmer 1-1/2 to 2 hours.
* Serve with tortilla chips. Even better the second day.

Tom Henson

WES'S TEX-MEX CHILI
Award-winning 5-alarm chili

Serves: 12-16

6 pounds sirloin tip
4 (14-1/2-ounce) cans chicken broth
1 tablespoon Worcestershire sauce
1 tablespoon New Mexico or similar
   hot chili powder
8 small onions, pureed
2 teaspoons white pepper
2 teaspoons black pepper
Spice Paste:
1 tablespoon ground oregano
1 can beer
3 tablespoons California or similar
   mild chili powder
9 tablespoons New Mexico or similar
   mild chili powder

13 cloves garlic, pureed
1 (15-ounce) can tomato sauce
1-1/2 teaspoons ground cumin
1 tablespoon salt
1/4 teaspoon cayenne pepper
1 teaspoon garlic powder
1 teaspoon onion powder

1 tablespoon ground dried jalapeño pepper
3 tablespoons paprika
2 tablespoons ground cumin
2 tablespoons garlic powder
2 tablespoons onion powder

* Cut sirloin tip into 1/4 to 1/2-inch cubes. Cover with water and boil 15 minutes. Drain and return to pot.
* Add chicken broth, Worcestershire and hot chili powder. Boil 30 minutes.
* Add pureed onions and cook 15 minutes.
* Add white and black peppers and cook 30 minutes.
* Add pureed garlic and cook 20 minutes.
* Add tomato sauce and cook 10 minutes.
* To prepare Spice Paste, boil oregano in beer for 5 minutes.
* Remove from heat and add remaining ingredients. Blend thoroughly.
* Add the entire recipe of Spice Paste to chili and cook 45 minutes.
* Add the remaining ingredients and cook only 15 minutes more. Do not over cook.

Note: A variety of chili spices may be purchased at food specialty stores.

Wes Baldwin

DICK'S CAESAR SALAD

Serves: 4-6

3 tablespoons olive oil
4 slices bread, cut in cubes
1 clove garlic, chopped
1 clove garlic, halved
1 (2-ounce) tin rolled anchovy fillets
   with capers
1 tablespoon chopped garlic
juice of 1 lemon

4 tablespoons olive oil
1/4 teaspoon ground pepper
1/4 teaspoon salt
1 coddled egg
1 large head romaine lettuce, chilled and
   torn into pieces
Parmesan cheese

* To prepare croutons, heat olive oil and 1 clove garlic in iron skillet. Add bread cubes. Place in 400° oven until bread cubes brown. Set aside.
* Rub wooden salad bowl with garlic clove halves. Discard garlic. Place bowl in refrigerator to chill several hours before serving.
* Mix next 7 ingredients together in salad bowl.
* Add torn romaine and toss well. Sprinkle with Parmesan cheese and croutons.
* Serve immediately on chilled salad plates.

Dick Austin

TOMATO, MOZZARELLA AND BASIL SALAD

Easy - Prepare ahead

Serves: 6

6 large, very ripe tomatoes, peeled and
   cut into 1/3-inch slices
1 pound fresh mozzarella, cut into
   1/3-inch slices
1/3 cup chopped fresh basil leaves

1/3 cup olive oil
1/4 cup Niçoise olives
coarse salt and freshly ground black pepper
   to taste

* Arrange alternating slices of tomato and mozzarella on a platter.
* Sprinkle with basil, olive oil, salt and pepper. Garnish with olives.
* Cover and allow to stand at room temperature 30 minutes to 1 hour before serving.

Steve Horsley

SHRIMP AND PASTA WITH BASIL-LEMON DRESSING

Serves: 8-10

2 cups mayonnaise
1/4 cup lemon juice
1/2 cup fresh basil leaves, chopped
2 cloves garlic, chopped
1 pound medium pasta shells, cooked
  and cooled
2 pounds medium shrimp, cooked,
  shelled and deveined

1 cup frozen peas, thawed
1 (6-ounce) can sliced black olives
1 sweet red pepper, chopped
1/3 cup sliced scallions
salt and pepper to taste
1/3 cup Niçoise olives
1/2 sweet red pepper, cut in thin strips

* Combine first 4 ingredients. Mix thoroughly and reserve.
* Combine next 7 ingredients. Add reserved dressing.
* Refrigerate to allow flavors to blend.
* Serve chilled on a platter lined with lettuce. Garnish with olives and red pepper.

Steve Horsley

OPRAH WINFREY'S MASHED POTATOES

Easy   Serves: 6-8

instant mashed potatoes
1 (8-ounce) package cream cheese
1 egg

1/2 cup finely chopped onion
freshly ground pepper to taste

* Prepare mashed potatoes according to package directions for 8 servings.
* Add cream cheese, egg and onion. Mix well.
* Grind pepper over potatoes.
* Pour into a dish and bake at 375° for 30 to 40 minutes or until potatoes are brown.

John Leistler

FETTUCCINE WITH MUSHROOM MADEIRA CREAM SAUCE

Easy   Serves: 4

1/4 cup unsalted butter   *1/2 cup chicken broth*
1/2 cup minced shallots   *3/4 cup heavy cream*
1-1/2 pounds mushrooms, trimmed and   *1/4 cup chopped fresh dill*
*   sliced*   *salt and freshly ground pepper to taste*
1/2 cup Madeira wine   *1 pound fettuccine*

* In a large heavy skillet, melt the butter over moderately low heat.
* Add shallots and cook, stirring, until just softened.
* Add mushrooms and cook over moderate heat until tender, approximately 15 to 20 minutes.
* Add the Madeira and the broth. Boil until the liquid is reduced by half.
* Add cream and cook until thickened slightly.
* Stir in dill, salt and pepper. Keep warm while preparing the pasta.
* Prepare fettuccine according to package directions.
* Serve sauce over piping hot fettuccine.

Steve Horsley

BUFFY'S FAVORITE CHICKEN

Easy

1/2 cup oil   *2 teaspoons dry mustard*
1/2 cup soy sauce   *1 garlic clove (or equivalent powder)*
1/4 cup white wine   *up to 2 whole chickens cut into pieces*
2 teaspoons ginger

* Combine all ingredients except chicken and mix well.
* Place cleaned chicken pieces in shallow pan and pour marinade over chicken. Allow to sit for 30 minutes.
* Grill for 30 to 40 minutes over medium heat. Spoon marinade over chicken pieces when turning them. Turn several times throughout the cooking process.

David Love

CHICKEN WAIKIKI BEACH

Serves: 4

4 chicken breasts
1/2 cup flour
1/3 cup oil
1 teaspoon salt
1/2 teaspoon pepper
1 (20-ounce) can pineapple chunks
1 cup sugar

2 tablespoons cornstarch
3/4 cup vinegar
1 tablespoon soy sauce
1 teaspoon ginger
1 chicken bouillon cube
1 large green pepper cut crosswise in
    1/4-inch rounds

* Wash chicken breasts and pat dry with paper towels. Coat chicken with flour.
* Heat oil in skillet and add chicken. Brown and sprinkle with salt and pepper.
* Transfer chicken to a 9-inch square baking dish.
* Drain pineapple, pouring juice into a 2-cup measure. Add water to make 1-1/4 cups.
* Combine pineapple juice and next 6 ingredients in medium saucepan.
* Bring to boil, stirring constantly. Boil 2 minutes. Pour sauce over chicken.
* Bake uncovered at 350° for 30 minutes.
* Add pineapple chunks and green pepper; bake additional 30 minutes. Serve with rice.

John Leistler

MARINATED TURKEY BREAST

1 turkey breast (approximately 6 pounds)
1/2 cup dry white wine
1/4 cup sesame oil
1/4 cup soy sauce
3 tablespoons fresh lemon juice

4 teaspoons minced garlic (approximately
    3 cloves)
1 teaspoon thyme
1/2 teaspoon crushed red pepper flakes

* Remove skin from turkey and cut each breast half away from bone (can have butcher do this).
* Mix all ingredients of marinade in a large plastic bag. Place boneless breasts in the bag and marinate in refrigerator overnight or at room temperature for 2 hours.
* Remove turkey and reserve marinade.
* Place breasts in shallow baking dish and broil on one side 3 to 4 inches away from heat source for 10 minutes or until brown.
* Roast 30 to 45 minutes at 375°. Meat thermometer will read 175° to 180°.
* While baking, baste often with marinade. Cut across the grain and serve.

August Guida

HUNTER'S RECIPE FOR SMALL GAME BIRDS

quail or dove
flour
salt and pepper to taste

vegetable oil, butter, bacon drippings or a
combination of these

* Heat oil in skillet.
* Dredge whole birds in flour, salt and pepper mixture.
* Brown birds quickly in hot oil.
* Place birds in baking dish. Bake covered at 325° until done - but do not over cook.
* Use drippings for gravy if desired.

Howard Phillips

GRILLED DOLPHIN WITH THYME BUTTER

Easy

Serves: 4

1/2 cup olive oil
1/4 cup lemon juice
1/2 cup chopped fresh scallions
2 tablespoons chopped fresh thyme
4 cloves garlic, chopped
2 teaspoons salt

2 teaspoons fennel seeds
freshly ground black pepper
4 (8-ounce) dolphin (mahi-mahi) fillets
5 tablespoons sweet butter
2 teaspoons chopped fresh thyme
vegetable cooking spray

* Combine first 8 ingredients to make marinade.
* Place dolphin in a glass bowl just large enough to hold it.
* Pour marinade over dolphin.
* Cover and refrigerate at least 2 hours, turning occasionally.
* Cream butter and 2 teaspoons thyme in a small bowl. Form into cylinder.
* Cover with plastic wrap and refrigerate.
* When firm, slice butter into 4 pats.
* Prepare medium-hot fire and coat cooking surface with cooking spray.
* Cook fillets for a total of 10 minutes per inch of thickness, turning once.
* Top with pats of thyme butter.
* Serve immediately.

Steve Horsley

LOW COUNTRY STEW

12 ears fresh corn
4 pounds smoked sausage
1/2 gallon cleaned blue crabs and claws

4 pounds fresh, unshelled shrimp
1/4 cup Old Bay seasoning

* Shuck fresh corn and break each ear in half. Put aside.
* Cut smoked sausages into 1 to 2-inch pieces. Place in a large skillet and sauté until lightly browned on all sides. Remove sausage from pan and reserve both the sausage and the drippings.
* Put large steamer basket in sink. Load with crabs, shrimp, corn and cooked sausage pieces. Sprinkle with Old Bay seasoning. Toss contents to distribute evenly. Place basket over about 1 inch of rapidly boiling water in a large steamer pot. Pour sausage drippings over mixture. Cover and steam, tossing occasionally, until crab is bright red and shrimp are all pink.
* Remove basket from steamer pot; pour contents onto large platters. Place on a newspaper-covered table. Paper towels, cracking tools and bowls for shells will be needed. Serve with favorite seafood sauce and butter.

Serving Suggestion: Warm cornbread, fresh tomato and cucumber slices and ice cold watermelon complete the dinner.

Harold Fletcher, Ellen Bickett, Jane Coley

HONEY BUN CAKE

Easy

Serves: 12-15

1 box yellow cake mix
2/3 cup vegetable oil
1/3 cup water
4 eggs

1 cup sour cream
1 teaspoon cinnamon
1 cup light brown sugar
1 cup chopped pecans

* Grease and flour a 13x9-inch cake pan.
* Mix cake mix, oil, water, eggs and sour cream. Beat until well blended.
* Mix together cinnamon, brown sugar and pecans.
* Pour 1/2 of cake batter into pan and spread 1/2 of sugar, cinnamon and nut mixture over the batter. Top with remaining batter and sprinkle remaining sugar mixture on top. Swirl with knife blade.
* Bake at 350° for 35 to 40 minutes or until cake tests done.

Ken Smith

CARAMEL CORN

Easy   Yields: 6 quarts

6 quarts popped popcorn   *1 teaspoon salt*
1 cup butter or margarine   *1/2 teaspoon baking soda*
2 cups firmly packed brown sugar *1 teaspoon vanilla*
1/2 cup corn syrup

* Preheat oven to 250°.
* Coat bottom and sides of a large roasting pan with vegetable spray.
* Place popped corn in the pan.
* In a separate pan, slowly melt butter and stir in brown sugar, corn syrup and salt. Bring to a boil, stirring constantly. Boil without stirring for 5 minutes.
* Remove from heat and stir in baking soda and vanilla.
* Gradually pour over popped corn, mixing well. Bake 1 hour, stirring every 15 minutes.
* Break apart and store in a tightly covered container.

Ken Smith

Variation: Add 2 cups pecans and 2 cups almonds to popcorn mixture.

Marvin Bethune

MICROWAVE DIVINITY

Easy   Yields: 2-3 dozen

2 egg whites   *1/4 teaspoon salt*
2-1/4 cups sugar   *1-1/2 teaspoons vanilla*
1/2 cup water   *1/2 cup chopped nuts*
1/2 cup light corn syrup

* Beat egg whites until stiff; set aside.
* Mix together sugar, water, corn syrup and salt in 2-quart microwave-safe casserole.
* Loosely cover casserole with plastic wrap; microwave on high for 5 minutes. Uncover and microwave on high for 8 additional minutes.
* Slowly pour hot syrup over stiff egg whites while beating at high speed.
* Add vanilla and continue to beat 4 to 5 minutes until candy holds shape.
* Fold in nuts and drop by teapoonfuls onto wax paper.

Richard Herring

INDEX

INDEX

INDEX

INDEX

INDEX

INDEX

INDEX

INDEX

NOTES

COOKING WITH CLASS - A SECOND HELPING
P.O. Box 6143
Charlotte, N.C. 28207

Please send _____ copies of **COOKING WITH CLASS - A SECOND HELPING** at $19. 70 per copy ($16.95 plus $2.75 for postage and handling). Add $1.00 (packaging charge) for each additional book. Enclosed is my check for $_____.
(North Carolina residents add $.96 sales tax for each book.)

If this is a gift, card should read: _____

_____

Name _____

Address _____

City _____ State _____ Zip _____

Make checks payable to: **CLS Parents' Council.**
Proceeds from the sale of this book are returned to *Charlotte Latin School* througprojects of The Parents' Council.

COOKING WITH CLASS - A SECOND HELPING
P.O. Box 6143
Charlotte, N.C. 28207

Please send _____ copies of **COOKING WITH CLASS - A SECOND HELPING** at $19. 70 per copy ($16.95 plus $2.75 for postage and handling). Add $1.00 (packaging charge) for each additional book. Enclosed is my check for $_____.
(North Carolina residents add $.96 sales tax for each book.)

If this is a gift, card should read: _____

_____

Name _____

Address _____

City _____ State _____ Zip _____

Make checks payable to: **CLS Parents' Council.**
Proceeds from the sale of this book are returned to *Charlotte Latin School* through projects of The Parents' Council.

I would like to see this marvelous cookbook in the following stores:

Store Name _____

Address _____

City _____ State _____ Zip _____

Store Name _____

Address _____

City _____ State _____ Zip _____

I would like to see this marvelous cookbook in the following stores:

Store Name _____

Address _____

City _____ State _____ Zip _____

Store Name _____

Address _____

City _____ State _____ Zip _____

COOKING WITH CLASS - A SECOND HELPING
P.O. Box 6143
Charlotte, N.C. 28207

Please send _____ copies of **COOKING WITH CLASS - A SECOND HELPING** at $19. 70 per copy ($16.95 plus $2.75 for postage and handling). Add $1.00 (packaging charge) for each additional book. Enclosed is my check for $_____.
(North Carolina residents add $.96 sales tax for each book.)

If this is a gift, card should read: _____

_____

Name _____

Address _____

City _____ State _____Zip _____

Make checks payable to: **CLS Parents' Council.**
Proceeds from the sale of this book are returned to *Charlotte Latin School* through projects of The Parents' Council.

COOKING WITH CLASS - A SECOND HELPING
P.O. Box 6143
Charlotte, N.C. 28207

Please send _____ copies of **COOKING WITH CLASS - A SECOND HELPING** at $19. 70 per copy ($16.95 plus $2.75 for postage and handling). Add $1.00 (packaging charge) for each additional book. Enclosed is my check for $_____.
(North Carolina residents add $.96 sales tax for each book.)

If this is a gift, card should read: _____

_____

Name _____

Address _____

City _____ State _____Zip _____

Make checks payable to: **CLS Parents' Council.**
Proceeds from the sale of this book are returned to *Charlotte Latin School* through projects of The Parents' Council.

I would like to see this marvelous cookbook in the following stores:

Store Name _____

Address _____

City _____ State _____ Zip _____

Store Name _____

Address _____

City _____ State _____ Zip _____

I would like to see this marvelous cookbook in the following stores:

Store Name _____

Address _____

City _____ State _____ Zip _____

Store Name _____

Address _____

City _____ State _____ Zip _____